Human Resource Management

Studies in Global Business

Edited by

D.S. Chundawat
Shurveer S. Bhanawat

ATLANTIC
PUBLISHERS & DISTRIBUTORS (P) LTD

Published by
ATLANTIC
PUBLISHERS & DISTRIBUTORS (P) LTD
7/22, Ansari Road, Darya Ganj,
New Delhi-110002
Phones : +91-11-40775252, 23273880, 23275880, 23280451
Fax : +91-11-23285873
Web : www.atlanticbooks.com
E-mail : orders@atlanticbooks.com

Branch Office
5, Nallathambi Street, Wallajah Road,
Chennai-600002
Phones : +91-44-64611085, 32413319
E-mail : chennai@atlanticbooks.com

ISBN 978-81-269-1898-0

Printed in India at Nice Printing Press, A-33/3A, Site-IV,
Industrial Area, Sahibabad, Ghaziabad, U.P.

PREFACE

It gives us great pleasure to publish and present the edited book entitled *Human Resource Management: Studies in Global Business*. It is the outcome of International Conference on Global Business Research (special Reference to Human Resource, Banking and Accounting), September 20-22, 2012, under the joint auspices of Master of Human Resource Management and Master of Banking and Insurance programme of Mohanlal Sukhadia University, Udaipur, Rajasthan, India.

Every conference is a mirror of academic activities and events bringing out many avenues of learning research problems and deliberations. The major objective of this conference was to develop a consensus about basic parameters of Human Resources Management in special reference to global business. Today's economic progress is idea centric and talent driven. Good ideas give birth to good products. Innovative ideas are driving Indian economy, creating wealth and making people rich. What business entities should do or avoid, coping with radical changes in technological, environmental, and global economy, has remained a question yet to be answered. However, most paper presenters agreed that the intellectual capital is critical to the success of an organization. The conference concluded that a proper Human Resource Management can help to solve the basic problems of business crisis. It helps the organization to align the limited resource in the optimum way. The future challenges of managing human resource in virtual organization, the effectiveness of performance management and the rising demand of emotional intelligence that is need to understand others' behaviour and taking care of their feelings, managing the knowledge pool and developing talent management were the key issues discussed. Hectic work life has led to stress and that's why many papers were also presented on how to manage stress and keep a balance between personal and professional life. This way it provided holistic view on contemporary issues.

Shri Gajendra Singh Shaktawat, Parliamentary Secretary, Govt. of Rajasthan was the Chief Guest at inaugural function and key note speakers were Prof. Som Deo, Dean, Faculty of Commerce, Rajasthan University, Jaipur and Prof. B.P. Singh, former Dean, Delhi School of

Economics, New Delhi. Honourable Vice Chancellor, Mohanlal Sukhadia and University Prof. I.V. Trivedi, presided over the function and delivered the inaugural address. We are highly obliged to these dignitaries for their valuable suggestions and comments.

We express our thanks to our learned contributors who have enriched the purpose and have satisfied the objective of conference. We also express our thanks to the persons who helped directly or indirectly and assisted in the work of editing the volume.

We also extend our thanks to Atlantic Publishers and Distributors (P) Ltd. New Delhi for the interest evinced in publishing this book.

Editors

CONTENTS

CHAPTER 1 MANAGERIAL SKILLS AND EFFECTIVENESS—A COMPARATIVE STUDY OF DEFENCE PERSONNEL VS CORPORATE EXECUTIVES

–D.S. Chundawat and *Flt. Lt. Manmeet Sardalia*

ABSTRACT

Globalisation and liberalisation have made the business world dynamic. Constantly changing customer needs and market environment have made effective management necessary for every organization. Effective management means thinking and acting in the right manner. The key element towards managerial effectiveness is to get people to do their jobs and get them to do it in the best of their abilities.

How does one really get the employees to do the job well? It is challenging to align people's delivery to the targets to be achieved from the organisation and from the managers' perspective. It is an ongoing exploratory journey and every manager figures out his own style and mantra to do that. Over a period of time, one realizes there is no magic mantra to get the best out of the employees as no employee is same as the other and it is an incredibly challenging task to deal with diverse people and make them work towards one goal.

This paper would highlight on various skills required by the mangers to perform various complex tasks or implement various policies in global environment, skills are essential to utilize the scare resource of organization. It is a comparative study of managerial skills of Defence personnel and corporate executives.

Selection and adoption of appropriate scientific methodological approach is the most important element of conducting a research investigation. It adds to the precision, reliability and validity of the research findings. The study was carried out on 120 officers of corporate and armed forces sector. The sample was chosen by Stratified Random Sampling. A well-constructed questionnaire was constructed and administrated on the sample to elicit their response. Pre-testing of the questionnaire was done and some questions were reframed after it. The data collected was statistically analysed using various tools. The primary data collected through survey method with the help of the questionnaire has been analysed by using MS Excel and SPSS (Statistical Package for Social Sciences) 19.0 version. Various tools and techniques were used to analyse the data gathered.

This research implies that executives who are from Non-Defence sector are equally developed when it comes to managerial skills which is a pre-requisite for being effective. However, the Defence personnel are more organized in the sense that they maintain a proper filing system and their work surroundings are mostly tidy and organized. They also do not delay uninteresting tasks and take frequent support of their colleagues in their work.

Introduction

Managerial skills are sets of qualities and attributes in the personality of managers that enable them to effectively manage the working of a firm. Good managerial skills can create a world of difference in the efficiency and performance of the organization.

Researchers have found that traditional manager skills wouldn't bring favorable change at workplace. So manager has to learn some special skills which bear on employee's behavior and attitudes. So that organization can benefit by their labour. It is fact that managers cause productivity and non-productivity of employees and organization.

Managers may directly influence the worker's attitude, interest, and aptitude or change their behavior toward commitment to work and objectives. Organization can stand to bear the challenges of change through only right managerial style and behavior.

For effective execution of work or policies, managers should focus to develop such skills which make them effective. In the era of globalization, it has become difficult to handle expectations from customers, employees and external factors. So to handle these issues managers should enhance his managerial skills for organizational effectiveness. This was all about some of the important managerial skills that every manager should try to inculcate in their personality so that they can guide organizations towards success.

Managerial functions refer to the different roles and responsibilities of managers, who need certain skills to execute these functions. Small businesses, especially startup companies, may not have the resources to hire managers for each of their functional and product areas. This means that small-business managers have to be flexible enough to learn a range of skills and perform different roles.

The basic managerial functions are controlling, directing, organizing, planning and staffing. The controlling function involves setting strategic and operational goals, measuring the performance of subordinates against these goals, and taking corrective action when performance does not live up to expectations. In the directing role, managers communicate operational goals, motivate employees to achieve these goals, and provide regular feedback. The organizing function includes preparing schedules and budgets, delegating authority, and coordinating research and development activities. The planning function relates to strategic activities such as formulating long-term plans, looking for acquisition opportunities and planning overseas expansions. The staffing function refers to human resource functions such as recruiting, selecting, hiring and training new staff.

Managers need technical, resource allocation, communication, political and intellectual skills. Managers also need multitasking skills to manage multiple projects in large businesses or to juggle multiple roles in small businesses. Small-business owners also need entrepreneurial skills, which involve dealing with constant change, managing with limited financial resources, and imagining new ways of looking at problems. Managers require networking skills because establishing relationships with suppliers, investors and board members is important for sustaining and growing businesses. Successful managers need emotional intelligence, which involves the ability to empathize with others and understanding your own strengths and weaknesses. Managing a business with a diverse employee base requires an appreciation of different cultural norms.

Managerial effectiveness depends partly on the fit between managerial functions and skills. For example, a service center manager needs resource allocation skills to organize and train the center's representatives. He also needs conflict-resolution skills to deal with unhappy customers and employees. A manager's effectiveness also depends on his core values and personality. For example, an optimistic and honest manager is usually an effective manager.

Management is a learned skill, which is why companies invest in training and mentoring programs to nurture the next generation of managers and leaders. Successful and experienced managers know how to bring out the best in their employees.

Business owners will be entrepreneurs until they become managers. When they become managers, they will feel real managerial problems. Management is a not simple task, because it needs knowledge and experience. Therefore, there is hierarchy, and possibilities to go through it. There is no existing individual who after receiving educational skill has become a top without having developed managerial skills.

Managerial skills represent knowledge to fulfill some activities or tasks. This knowledge can be learned. But it also can be acquired through practical fulfillment of these activities. Therefore, skills can be acquired through learning and experience of individuals.

There are many definitions about skills that define it as some type of talent. Talent is something personal in an individual and represents a native gift from nature, about something in that individual. All individuals cannot be artists. Usually, artists are born with the gift of art and after that they develop their talent in quality art skills through educational systems.

When we talk about managerial skills those are skills used from managers that enable them maintaining efficiency in the way how employers performing working tasks. Because of that managers must have a skill with which they will manage people and technology with the purpose of effective and efficient fulfillment of their working tasks.

A manager has a combination of technical, human and conceptual skills that can make him an effective leader. In fulfilling their duties, managers use managerial skills. These skills directly affect the results of the manager, but they can be learned and gained by training. Areas of skills and practices are categorized according to the four major functions of management, including planning, organizing, leading and controlling. As managers, people carry out the managerial functions of planning, organizing, staffing, leading and controlling.

However, the four functions are actually highly integrated when carried out in the day-to-day realities of running an organization.

Besides the three managerial skills, other skills are required, which enable a manager to perform basic activities (functional skills) of planning, organizing, leading and controlling. Other skills such as interpersonal skills, time management skills, administrative skills, conflict resolution skills, emotional intelligence, team building skills, etc. can also be considered to be the part of human skills.

A study was conducted to examine the managerial skills of Defence personnel and corporate executives.

Research Methodology

Selection and adoption of appropriate scientific methodological approach is the most important element of conducting a research investigation. It adds to the precision, reliability and validity of the research findings. The study was carried out on 120 officers of corporate and armed forces sector. The sample was chosen by Stratified Random Sampling. A well-constructed questionnaire was constructed and administrated on the sample to elicit their response. The questionnaire contained both open-ended and close-ended questions. The questionnaire was designed in such a manner so as to elicit maximum information from the respondents. The questions were simple, clear, undisguised, well organised and to the point. Pre-testing of the questionnaire was done and some questions were reframed after it. The data collected was statistically analysed using various tools. Data analysis was done in order to search out meaningfully the trend and establish relationships that exist among various data groups. The primary data collected through survey method with the help of the questionnaire has been analysed by using MS Excel and SPSS (Statistical Package for Social Sciences) 19.0 version. Various tools and techniques were used to analyse the data gathered.

The questionnaire dealt with information relating to these four basic skills. The information gathered helps us to analyse the managerial skills of armed forces personnel and corporate executives. The data follows a bi-variate distribution as we are given a set of pairs of observations (armed forces personnel and corporate executives), thus, here we try to find if there is a relationship between two variables under study. To comprehend the respondent's opinions regarding managerial skills, the following hypothesis was framed:

"There is a significant variance in managerial skills developed in the corporate sector and Indian armed forces."

Opinions of Respondents Regarding the Four Basic Managerial Skills

The researcher measured the importance of ten managerial skills which are essential for effective management, i.e. organizing, planning, directing, controlling, decision making, problem solving, communication, time-management, inter-personal and administrative. The relative importance attributed to these skills in day-to-day working, by armed forces personnel and corporate executives are assessed.

The perusal of Table 1 reveals that in case of armed forces the maximum mean score of 4.7 was obtained for leading and organizing skills (near to 5 maximum score that could be obtained), which shows that, score is very high meaning first preference is given to Leading and Organizing skills. Then comes Communication, with a mean score of 4.72 which is also at high level, thereafter comes Planning and Decision Making at third position.

On the basis of Table 1, we can say that almost similar views were expressed by corporate executives regarding the significance of managerial skills. Leading, Decision Making and Communication skills were given very much importance hence, occupied the first three positions. An important observation was that only 46.7% respondents gave very much importance to interpersonal skills, compared to 63.3% of armed forces executives.

Table 1: Significance of Managerial Skills

Managerial Skills	*Armed Forces*		*Corporate*	
	Mean Score	*Rank*	*Mean Score*	*Rank*
Organizing	4.77	1	4.58	6
Planning	4.68	3	4.65	4
Leading	4.77	1	4.75	1
Controlling	4.00	8	3.95	8
Decision Making	4.68	3	4.72	2
Problem Solving	4.52	5	4.52	7
Communication	4.72	2	4.70	3
Time Management	4.58	4	4.60	6
Interpersonal	4.47	6	4.62	5
Administrative	4.25	7	3.78	9

None of the respondents of corporate sector found any of the ten skills insignificant. Only controlling skills were given very little importance by 1.7% of executives. Communications skills were also given little importance by 1.7% of corporate executives. A similar percentage of respondents, i.e. 3.3% found little importance of Problem Solving and Decision Making skills, which are essential for managing the job effectively.

The basic managerial skills of planning, organizing, directing and controlling were examined/tested. The Kolmogorov-Smirnov test of normality showed that the distribution was not normal, hence, non-parametric test was chosen. Mann-Whitney U test was opted in this case. The data was ranked to carry out further analysis. The analysis of these four functional skills essential for managerial effectiveness are entailed as follows:

Planning Skills

Table 2: Analysis of Planning Skills by Mann-Whitney U Test

Test Statistics	*Planning*
Mann-Whitney U	1612.000
Z	–.995
Asymp. Sig. (2-tailed)	.320
Exact Sig. (2-tailed)	.322
R	–0.09

a. Grouping Variable: Category
b. The significance level is .05
c. Effect size r is –0.09

An independent sample Mann-Whitney U test was conducted to compare the planning skills of armed forces and corporate executives (Table 2). The planning skills of armed forces personnel was same as the corporate executives (Mdn = 58.00). U = 1612.00, Z = –.995.

Asymptotic significance is 0.320, non-significant ($p > .05$) hence the null hypothesis is retained. There is no variance in the planning skills of armed forces executives and corporate executives.

Organizing Skills

Table 3: Analysis of Organizing Skills by Mann-Whitney U Test

Test Statistics	*Organizing*
Mann-Whitney U	1180.500
Z	–3.270
Asymp. Sig. (2-tailed)	.001
Exact Sig. (2-tailed)	.001
R	–0.34

a. Grouping Variable: Category
b. The significance level is .05
c. The effect size is –0.34

In case of organizing skills also an independents sample Mann-Whitney U test was conducted to compare both category of executives (Table 3). The organizing skills of armed forces personnel (Mdn = 30.00) did not differ from Corporate executives, (Mdn = 27.42) although not significantly. U = 1180.50, Z = –3.27. Asymptotic significance is 0.001, significant ($p < .05$) hence the null hypothesis is rejected and alternative hypothesis is accepted. There is significant variance in the organizing skills of armed forces executives and corporate executives.

Directing Skills

Table 4: Analysis of Directing Skills by Mann-Whitney U Test

Test Statistics	*Directing*
Mann-Whitney U	1558.500
Z	–1.280
Asymp. Sig. (2-tailed)	.200
Exact Sig. (2-tailed)	.202
R	–0.12

a. Grouping Variable: Category
b. The significance level is .05
c. Effect size R is –0.12

The results of Mann-Whitney U test conducted to compare the Directing skills of both category of executives, revealed that there was a difference in the median (Table 3). For armed forces executives Mdn = 65.00 and corporate executives Mdn = 56.00. U = 1558.50, Z = –.1.28. Asymptotic significance is 0.200, non-significant ($p > .05$) hence the null hypothesis is accepted. There is no significant variance in the directing skills of armed forces executives and corporate executives.

Controlling Skills

Table 5: Analysis of Controlling Skills by Mann-Whitney U Test

Test Statistics	*Controlling*
Mann-Whitney U	1493.000
Z	–1.627
Asymp. Sig. (2-tailed)	.104
Exact Sig. (2-tailed)	.104
R	–0.15

a. Grouping Variable: Category
b. The significance level is .05
c. Effect size is –0.05

As regards the controlling skills, the Mann-Whitney U test indicated that median did not differ significantly in both categories of executives (Table 4). U = 1493.00 and Z = –1.62. Asymptotic significance is 0.10 non-significant, ($p > .05$), hence the null hypothesis is accepted. There is no significant variance in the controlling skills of armed forces executives and corporate executives.

Hypothesis Testing

Null Hypothesis

"There is no variance in managerial skills developed in the corporate sector and Indian armed forces."

Alternative Hypothesis

"There is a significant variance in managerial skills developed in the corporate sector and Indian armed forces."

As seen above in the Mann-Whitney U test on factors, i.e. Planning, Directing and Controlling Skills that $p > 0.05$ (except in case of organising skills where $p < 0\ .05$), hence difference is non-significant, therefore on an overall basis we can say that—

Null hypothesis is accepted and alternative hypothesis is rejected. Thus, the analysis reveals that there is no significant variance between managerial skills developed in the corporate sector and Indian armed forces.

The Research Implications

Research implications have been categorised on important differentiating factors—

- As we know that managerial skills of individuals differ from person to person, this research suggests that these ten skills, namely organizing, planning, leading, controlling, decision-making, problem-solving, communication, time management, interpersonal and administrative are vital for effective management.
- The respondents from both armed forces and corporate sector exhibit similar view regarding their significance. The mean scores of respondents helped to infer that leading, decision-making and communication skills rank at the top three positions.

Regarding the significance of the functional skills, i.e. planning, organizing, directing and controlling, both armed forces personnel and corporate executives possessed the same skills, except of course the organizing skills which showed variance among the two categories of executives.

- Though the planning skills of armed forces executives and corporate executives showed no variance, time management skill was more prominent in armed forces executives. A majority of corporate executives agreed that they were mostly late to work than the specified time of reporting. This could be attributed to the difference in the nature of work and late working schedules of corporate executives.
- Majority of corporate executives had to stay back beyond working time to complete unfinished task. Meeting of deadlines is a significant reason for this and often upsets the work life balance.
- Both category of executives were of the opinion that meetings took more time than required. All respondents agreed that time management should be given serious consideration, and thus planning is essential for effectiveness.
- This implies that executives who are from non-Defence sector are equally developed when it comes to managerial skills which is a pre-requisite for being effective. However, the Defence personnel are more organized in the sense that they maintain a proper filing system and their work surroundings are mostly tidy and organized. They also do not delay uninteresting tasks and take frequent support of their colleagues in their work. Before delegating their task they consider the capability of employees and also can balance their work and family.
- Organizing your activities go a long way to accomplish the objectives of the organisation, it involves bringing together human and material resources. Developing this skill would go a long way in being managerially effective.

REFERENCES

Bartlett, Christopher and Sumantara Ghoshal (1992), "What is a global manager?" *Harvard Business Review.*

Bartol, K. and Martin, D. (1991). *Management.* New York: McGraw-Hill.

Bennis, Warren and Burt Nanus. "Leaders, Strategies for taking Charge. 2nd ed. Harper Business, 1997.

Behindenemylines Vol. I, http://www.bridgehead.in

Beth, J. Asch – "Military support for youth Development". An exploratory analysis—Arroyo center US army.

Brig, S.K. Wadhawan, from National Defence College (NDC), Delhi., "Transforming India's Defence Forces: Need for a Paradigm Shift".

Carol Page, Marie Wilson and Denny Meyer, Paper at ABAS Conference, Barcelona, Spain (1999).

CCL, Report, Greensboro, North Carolina (2002).

Colonel Prasad, V.R.K. (2003) "Managerial Effectiveness: The Winners Edge"—ICFAI University Press.

Field, Andy 2009, "Discovering Statistics Using SPSS", Third edition, Sage Publications.

Kumar, Sunil, "Managerial Effectiveness: Indian Insights", Excel Books, New Delhi.

Lieblich, Amia "Transition to adulthood during Military service". The Israeli case – 1989 State University of NewYork Press.

Mendock, Alexander and Carol N. Scutt, "Personal Effectiveness" (second edition).

Miller, Bill, *A Textbook on Evaluation, Statistics, and Measurement.*

CHAPTER 2

EMOTIONAL INTELLIGENCE: IMPLICATIONS ON WORKFORCE

–Shilpi Kothari, Khushboo Ameta and *Shurveer S. Bhanawat*

ABSTRACT

Emotional intelligence is one of the most important human factors which is responsible for high service quality. Emotional intelligence is defined as a person's self-awareness, self-confidence, self-control, commitment and integrity, and a person's ability to communicate, influence, initiate change and accept change (Goleman, 1998). It is all managing the human emotions. An individual's emotional intelligence is an indicator of how he or she perceives, understands and regulates emotions.

Emotional intelligence is as important as intellectual quotient at the time of hiring workers in contemporary organization. Since deficiencies in interpersonal skills abound in the work environment, high levels of emotional intelligence are needed to perform adequately. Leaders need to inculcate emotional intelligence skills into their leadership repertoire in order to lead effectively and successfully.

Viewing employees as the most valuable assets, the impetus of the study was to determine whether a correlation exists in use of emotional intelligence between the gender and the age of employees. The literature underscores the importance of emotional intelligence in cultivating successful leaders and workers in the workplace. This research project also finds out the differences in implementation of the emotional intelligence in various segments.

Introduction

Emotions are highly powerful. They can construct and may even destroy the total world. The art of managing these emotions is emotional intelligence. Goleman and Gottman view that EQ predicts higher work performance better than IQ. Still some other argue emotional intelligence to be the priority to get employment. EQ is found to be twice as important as IQ. In today's fast forward world, when people are ready to take the opportunity to prove themselves a better leader, EQ management is found to be the most important to bring the success.

Emotional intelligence is one of the most important human factors which is responsible for high service quality. Emotional intelligence is defined as a person's ability to communicate, influence, initiate change and accept change. It is all managing the human emotions. An individual's emotional intelligence is an indicator of how he or she perceives, understands and regulate emotions.

Emotional Intelligence

Emotional intelligence attracts the employer and any candidate who reflects the same in a right proportion has a higher chance of getting selected. Emotional skills with the combination of the intelligence skills in the right proportion are always desired. With emotional intelligence, traits such as optimism, effective productivity, self-esteem, motivation, empathy, personal interaction skills are developed. High emotional intelligence, combined with efficient work skills, make achievement faster, more productive and more innovative. With enhanced EQ, people think more clearly under pressure, are calmer and less stressed as they spend less energy on internal emotional turmoil.

Emotional intelligence requires a person to know one's emotions, manage them, constantly recognize, understand and acknowledge emotions of others, which means effective management of relationships at work.

Emotional intelligence has been found to be an acquired skill, as against the popular belief that intelligence is inborn. It is quite easy to acquire a better EQ, what is actually required at work. One needs to be able to assess the requirements of the company, self-introspect, enhance learning, self-motivate, rationalize thinking, set goals, work on effective communication, manage change, effective communication, etc.

The Emotional Quotient-Inventory—There are five factors of EI, which contributes to success in life that are intrapersonal functioning (self-awareness and self-expression), interpersonal skills (social awareness and interpersonal relationships), adaptability (change management), stress management (emotional management and regulation) and general mood (self-motivation).

Within each dimensions are several items measured on a five point scale from strongly agree to strongly disagree, for a total of 15 items. For survey respondents, instructions are also included, and each statement is accompanied by a five point scale ranging from "Strongly Agree = 5" to "Strongly Disagree = 1". The 5 composite scale and 15 subscales of EQ-i are following:

1. *Intrapersonal (Self-Awareness and Self-Expression)*

Intrapersonal is the ability to manage our feelings. When a person is extremely angry, and yet can exercise self-control and conquer his anger, is the example of good self-management. The person is able to know why he feels this way, and can see whether he is being reasonable or not. It includes five more dimensions in it which are self-regard, self-awareness, assertiveness, independence and self-actualization

2. *Interpersonal (Social Awareness and Interpersonal Relationship)*

Establish and maintain mutually satisfying relationships that are characterized by intimacy and giving and receiving affection. It includes the following dimensions, namely empathy, social responsibility and interpersonal relationship.

3. *Stress Management (Emotional Management and Regulation)*

The term stress management includes managing reasonable workloads, establishing clear priorities, and meeting realistic deadlines. It includes the two parameters: stress tolerance and impulse control.

4. *Adaptability (Change Management)*

Empathy is the ability to aware of the feelings of others and the ability to understand why they feel this way. Empathy allows us to leverage diversity and see things from different perspectives. It focuses on practicality and not on unrealistic expectations. Create viable alternative solutions, including a cost/benefit analysis/long-term implications. Perform better in positions where tasks are dynamic and changing. It includes the following dimensions reality-testing, flexibility, problem-solving

5. *General Mood (Self-Motivation)*

Self-motivation refers to the ability to motivate ourselves. A person with strong drive to succeed, able to sustain the motivation throughout the years, and maintain a positive attitude has strong self-motivation. Many successful persons share this characteristic. It includes optimism and happiness.

Objective of the Study

- To identify level of emotional intelligence with reference to the age and gender of respondents.
- To analyze the variation in EQ level of employees in the varied sectors named MNC's, private and public sector.

Hypotheses

Hypothesis taken for the study are as follows:

- There is no significant correlation between the age and EQ level of respondents.
- There is no significant difference between the EQ level of respondents on the basis of gender.
- There is no significant difference in the EQ level in relation with MNC's, public and private sector employees.

Data Collection

The entire present study is concentrated on primary data. The primary data are collected through questionnaire. The questionnaire were distributed and collected from four cities of India, viz. Gurgaon, Pune, New Delhi, Udaipur and Byawar.

Sample Size

Convenience sampling was administered in the study. Questionnaires were distributed to the employees of MNC's, private and public sector. Out of 150 only 105 respondents were returned the questionnaire.

Techniques

The questionnaire was constructed based on the Bar On EQ-i technique to record various factors relating to Emotional Quotient. It consists of 15 questions relating to the emotional Intelligence. The responses were measured on a five point scale.

Statistical Tools

Under the present research paper ANOVA, and T-test has been used.

Analysis and Discussions

The EQ-i comprises 15 items in the form of short sentences and employs a 5-point response format ranging from "Disagree or Strongly Agree" (1) to (5). It takes approximately 30 minutes to complete and can be done online as well as in the paper-and-pencil format. This measure is used to assess individuals over 20 years of age and belongs from MNC, private and public sector. The respondents were selected from Wipro, Shree Cement, Symantech, HCL, J.K. Tyre, Government schools, Hitachi, Pyrotech, SBI, Bank of Baroda.

The EQ-i is based on the Bar-On model of emotional-social intelligence. The raters' responses are averaged to create a total EQ score and the following 5 composite scale scores and 15 subscale scores: companies whose employee.

1. *Sector-wise Analysis of Various Dimensions of EQ*

Table 1: Sector-wise EQ Scores

Sectors/Dimensions	*Intrapersonal*	*Interpersonal*	*Stress Management*	*Adaptability*	*General Mood*	*Total*
Private	115.821	123.55	95.25	115	111.75	112.27
Public	102	114.75	121.2	128.6	114.9	116.29
MNCs	100.41	116.85	78	100.85	81.375	95.49
Average	106.07	118.38	98.15	114.81	102.67	108.02

By examining Table 1, it clearly indicates that the first dimension of emotional intelligence, i.e. intrapersonal skill clearly reveals that private sector employees are better in recognizing and understanding their own feelings and emotions in comparison to the public and MNC sector employees.

The next dimension interpersonal does not vary much in three of the sectors and signifies that private, public and MNC sector are equally efficient in establishing and maintaining mutually satisfying relationships that are characterized by intimacy and giving and receiving affection.

The third dimension states that MNC employees have the lowest EQ score in the stress management dimension which indicates that MNC employees are poor in managing reasonable workloads, establishing clear priorities, and meeting realistic deadlines where as the public sector employees are good enough in managing the same.

The scores of adaptability dimension denotes that the public sector perform better positions where tasks are dynamic and changing and MNC employees performs better at more defined tasks requiring reliability and consistency. The public sector employees have the highest dimension in the overall EQ scores.

The MNC employees scored least in the fifth dimension which shows that MNC employees are least satisfied with their life; they don't enjoy oneself and being with others.

2. *Age-wise Analysis of Various Dimensions of EQ*

Table 2: Age-wise EQ Scores

Age/Dimensions	*Intrapersonal*	*Interpersonal*	*Stress Management*	*Adaptability*	*General Mood*	*Total*
21-30	106.92	122.9	102.15	104.9	101.25	107.62
31-40	108.96	129.95	77.775	114.8	105	107.29
41-50	112.29	106.8	100.2	125	117	112.25
51-60	96.15	113.95	112.425	114.8	87.375	104.94
Average	106.08	118.4	98.13	114.87	102.65	108.03

Table 2 indicates the age-wise analysis of five dimensions of emotional quotient. It has been clearly identified that the employees who are more than the age of 50 are having less EQ on an average. There is almost the same frequency of EQ of the employees who are in the age span of 20 to 40 and the employees who are more than 50 having lowest emotional quotient.

The maximum EQ in the above table is found in the interpersonal dimension and in the age of 20-40. It signifies that the employees with less age can maintain good relationship with their peers in comparison to the senior employees there in the organization whereas in the age of 31-40 it is found that they are poorest in managing stress in their worklife.

The table also signifies that the employees with the age of 51-60 are less motivated and not having positive attitude towards their work. The fourth dimension specifies the employees between 41-50 years are willing to accept challenging tasks, to see things from different angles. That enables them to find a win-win solution to benefit all stakeholders.

3. *Gender-wise Analysis of Various Dimensions of EQ*

Table 3: Gender-wise EQ Scores

Sectors/Dimensions	*Intrapersonal*	*Interpersonal*	*Stress Management*	*Adaptability*	*General Mood*	*Total*
Female	100.53	112	80.4	114.2	95.475	100.52
Male	111.66	124.85	115.875	115.43	109.875	115.53
Average	106.095	118.425	98.1375	114.815	102.675	108.03

In Table 3 the gender-wise dimensions of emotional quotient was analysed. On observing the above table, it signifies that the males are having high EQ in comparison with the females.

The maximum gap was found in the stress management dimension which shows that the females are weak in managing stress at work whereby there is no considerable difference found in the adaptability criteria which signifies that both are having the similar ability to understand others feeling.

The males were having the best scores in the interpersonal dimension which reflects that they maintain satisfying relationship with the other employees and the best scores of females were found in the adaptability criteria which shows that they can easily adapt the situations at the workplace and can easily change themselves according to the circumstances.

Overall Scores

The average EQ score were 108.4 of the various employees of different sector and different age. The highest average score were found in the public sector employees. By analysing the data as per the age it reveals that the EQ is maximum in public sector employees after the age of 50 and a substantial amount of difference is found in the EQ scores of public and private. The another perceptible point found in the table is the score of MNC employees. The data found to be the lowest in comparison with the other two segments and in the age group of 20-30 the MNC employees are having the least scores.

Table 4: Average EQ Scores

Sector (Avg Scores)/Age	*20-30*	*30-40*	*40-50*	*50-60*	*Average*
Private	115.2	113.75	119.2	101	112.28
Public	115	103.66	121.44	125.33	116.36
MNCs	92.5	104.5	97	88	95.5
Average	107.56	107.31	112.5	104.77	108.04

11. Testing the Hypotheses

The first assumptions taken for the study is that there is no significant correlation between the age and EQ level of respondents and the another assumption was that there is no significant difference in the EQ level in relation with MNC's, public and private sector employees. To test the same ANOVA—two way is applied as under:

Table 5: Anova Table

Source	*SS*	*Df*	*MS*	*F*	$F_{critical}$	p-*value*	
Age	95.178	3	31.7258	0.3743	4.7571	0.7750	Accept
Sectors	977.89	2	488.947	5.7688	5.1433	0.0400	Reject
Error	508.54	6	84.7569				
Total	1581.6	11					

1. *Age and Level of EQ SCORES (Table 5)*

On examine Table 5 it reveals that the hypothesis with the table value of *F* (0.3743) at 5% level of significance, the hypothesis is accepted proving that there is no significant correlation between the age and EQ level of respondents.

The proven hypothesis indicates that there is no varied implication of EQ as per the age of the employees.

2. *Public, Private, MNCs and Level of EQ (Table 5)*

With the significant table value of *F* (5.7688) the hypothesis is rejected establishing that there is a significant difference in the EQ level in relation with MNCs, public and private sector employees. The hypothesis clearly verifies that the employees of different sectors are having different levels of EQ.

3. *Gender and Level of EQ (Table 6)*

Table 6: Gender and Level of EQ

Age	*Male*	*Female*	*Average*
21-30	116.54	98.77	107.6
31-40	126.3	88.327	107.31
41-50	116.74	107.62	112.18
51-60	102.5	107.49	104.99
Average	115.52	100.55	108.04

Table 6 states that the mean of female is significantly less in comparison with male respondents. The age span of 20-40 the mean of females was found to be the lowest which reveals after the age of 40 females have better emotional stability. The table also brings the fact into light that the males are having good EQ score in the age of 20-50 and later on it declines where as the results of females are in contrast which shows that females have better EQ in the later stage that is after 40.

This clearly denotes that the EQ scores of female are positively correlated with their age and there is inverse relationship found in the age and EQ scores of males.

Table 7: Basic Statistics

	Male	*Female*
Size	62	43
Mean	115.52	100.56
Std Deviation	9.8	9.14

Table 8: T-Test

Pooled Variance	90.9427
Test Statistics	7.9047
Df	103

Table 9: Results

Hypothesis	*At 5%level of significance*
$H_0 : \mu 1 — \mu 2 = 0$	Reject
$H_0 : \mu 1 — \mu 2 > = 0$	Accept
$H_0 : \mu 1 — \mu 2 < = 0$	Reject

With the significant value of t (7.9047) the hypothesis is rejected proving that there is a significant difference in EQ level of respondents on the basis of gender.

12. Concluding Remarks

To summarize—attitude, feelings, heart, all these direct our ability to perform better. Emotional intelligence attracts the employer and any candidate that reflect the same in right proportion has a brighter chance of getting selected.

The EQ-i will help organizations and individuals alike assess the potential they have for continuous learning in a very simple manner. If nothing more, the EI profiles that emerge can provide valuable input into the high-potential identification process as well as into individual's personal development plans. Many organizations do have competencies labeled independence or flexibility in their competency models. Another important implication for practice is the organizations must, very carefully, separate high potentials from high performers.

The study proves that there is a noticeable difference in the various sectors and the public sector employees are found to be more emotionally intelligent and adaptable as per the circumstances. The paper gives an input that the emotional intelligence does not vary as per the age factor which proves that EQ does not show any relationship with the age factor.

Furthermore, in light of retention management, paying sufficient attention to employee's emotional states (e.g. happiness, frustration) will benefit organizations more than focusing on compensation and benefits. The relevance of cultivating positive emotions at work is further supported by the finding that optimism and (a low score on) reality testing show a significant relationship with individual job performance with high potentiality.

So, a person should focus on emotional strengths to harness goals and vision in order to keep the success graph high and to achieve sustainable growth.

REFERENCES

Bar-On, R. (2004). The Bar-On Emotional Quotient Inventory (EQ-i): Rationale, description and psychometric properties. In G. Geher (Ed.), *Measuring Emotional Intelligence: Common Ground and Controversy.* Hauppauge, NY: Nova Science.

Bar-On, R. (2006). The Bar-On model of emotional-social intelligence (ESI). *Psicothema*, 18, 13-25.

Goleman, D. (1998). "Working with Emotional Intelligence", 1st ed. New York: Bantam Books.

Gottman, J. DeClaire, J. (1998). "Raising an emotionally intelligent child", 1st ed. New York: Simon and Schuster.

J.D., Salovey, P. (1993). "The intelligence of emotional Intelligence", 17:432-42.

Podsakoff, P.M., MacKenzie, S.B., Lee, J. and Podsakoff, N.P. (2003), "Common method biases in behavioral research: A critical review of the literature and recommended remedies", *Journal of Applied Psychology*, Vol. 88, No. 5, pp. 879-903.

Salovey, P. and Mayer, J.D. (1990), "Emotional intelligence", *Imagination, Cognition & Personality*, Vol. 9, No. 3, pp. 185-211.

Salovey, P. and Pizarro, D. (2003), "The value of emotional intelligence", in Sternberg, R.J., Lautrey, J. and Lubart, T.I. (Eds), *Models of Intelligence: International Perspectives*, American Psychological Association, Washington DC, pp. 263-78.

Schmidt, F.L. and Hunter, J.E. (2000), "Select on intelligence", in Locke, E.A. (Ed.), *The Blackwell Handbook of Organizational Principles*, Blackwell, Oxford, pp. 3-14.

Spector, P.E. (1994), "Using self-report questionnaires in OB research: A comment on the use of acontroversial method", *Journal of Organizational Behavior*, Vol. 12, No. 5, pp. 385-92.

Sternberg, R.J. (1986), "A framework for understanding conceptions of intelligence", in Sternberg, R.J. and Detterman, D.K. (Eds), *What is Intelligence? Contemporary Viewpoints on its Nature and Definition*, Ablex, Norwood, NJ, pp. 3-15.

Sternberg, R.J., Forsythe, G.B., Hedlund, J., Horvath, J.A., Wagner, R.K., Williams, W.M., Snook, S. and Grigorenko, E.L. (2000), *Practical Intelligence in Everyday Life*, Cambridge University Press, New York, NY.

Takeuchi, R., Yun, S. and Tesluk, P.E. (2002), "An examination of crossover and spillover effects of spouse and expatriate adjustment on expatriate outcomes", *Journal of Applied Psychology*, Vol. 87, pp. 655-66.

CHAPTER 3

AWARENESS OF HR SHARED SERVICES, ITS EFFECTIVE UTILIZATION

–*Manashvi I. Singh*

ABSTRACT

India is one of the fast growing economies, for the development and growth of the country different sectors contribute a lot. Major succession of any organization is lead on its human assets. These human assets are maintained by efficient Human Resource (HR). Ulrich (1997), suggested ways about how Human Resource could contribute in the search for competitive advantage by advocating new organizational structures and roles such as Human Resource Shared Service Center or the new role of Human Resource Business Partner. These new roles and structures can be seen as an extension of best fit and best practice thinking and provide with a tool to cope up with the challenges faced by today's organizations. The objectives of this paper are to come up with a reasonable understanding about these different changes in roles and structures of HR, to find the possibility to find Key Success Factors which would work across different business environments and come up with implications for today's organizations accordingly. This study is a primary research undertaken by targeting the respondents from HR industry of Rajkot region. Research suggests the following compelling reasons why companies should consider shared services in their HR organizations.

- Most companies report cost cutting by switching their HR delivery mechanism to shared services.
- It helps in delivering a consistent service experience to employees with huge reduction in errors.
- It allows sustaining a consistent set of HR practices across an enterprise which are derived and continuously improved on basis of industry benchmarking.

The research is based upon statistical data, interviews with business house, research article, and expert talk.

1. INTRODUCTION

India is one of the fast growing economies, for the development and growth of the country different—different sectors contribute majorly. Major succession of any organization is lead on its human assets. These human assets are maintained by efficient Human Resource Service. In HR services many activities are undertaken right from Employment Law and Relations, Performance Management and

Appraisal, Learning and Development, Recruitment & Selection, Rewards, etc. In today's rapidly changing global business world, companies are facing more complex and competitive environment. Companies are no longer able to see their fortune (Hosking, 2006). Executives and managers are increasingly in need to think and act with a sharper business-mind. HR departments must recruit, train, and retain the most talented people while at the same time should also focus on improving organizational competencies and capabilities. Being successful in Human Resource Management requires not only the capacity to observe a competitive fast changing environment, but also the ability to adapt and work in such conditions. Ulrich, the most famous management educator and the most influenced person in HR suggests that "to deal with these difficult challenges, organization should move away with HR and apply four new strategic HR roles: Strategic Partners, Administrative Experts, Employee Champions, and Change Agents". The model is the process of aligning HR strategy with corporate strategy. It is claimed that regular use of this model naturally increases the flexibility of the organization and manages organizational change more effectively. After studying about these changes rigorously in the literatures, the researcher came to the conclusion that most of the new organizational structures and roles in HR are a result of applying Ulrich (1997) model into strategic HR. The most common forms of organizational structures and roles are Human Resource Business Partner (HRBP) and Human Resource Shared Service Center (HRSSC).

The researcher conducts this study to determine the views of HR and information technology (IT) managers, on how a shared-services approach to human capital management (HCM) can reduce costs and optimize the value and impact of employees. For the purposes of this white paper, shared services is defined as a service delivery model that enables organizations to apply the economic principles of supply and demand and economies of scale to internal processes. This paper includes at large and midsize companies known to be implementing a shared-services approach to HCM.

LITERATURE REVEIWS

1. **Schuler and MacMillan, 1984:** They suggest that the changes in an organization and business environment of the last decade have attracted attention of company's top executive management on the need to search out, establish and utilize competitive advantage for business existence. The emerging trends of new information technology, the growth of global competition, and the increasing of knowledge workers have lead to broader perspectives and create number of new opportunities for organizations and for the employees too. As a result, organizations have to pay even more attention to customer services and to the need for overall quality improvement. They have concentrated on bringing new products into the market to stay one step beyond the competition and to maximize their efficiency. However, these traditional methods to competitive advantage are undoubtedly necessary but not sufficient to bring a sustained competitive advantage. Companies must recognize and build organizational capabilities through better deployment of human resources in order to gain sustained competitive advantage.
2. **Caldwell, 2003:** Caldwell asserts that role of the HR managers and HR functions have changed tremendously due to several significant reasons. The HR professional's role

has become more multifaceted and challenging than before. Human resource management practices are distinctly an essential part of the corporate business strategy in organization that not only deals but also develops the human assets of the organisation.

3. **Lawler and Mohrman, 2005:** The recent trends in HR is a combination of business strategy and people management together which generate a new set of role demands, a greater challenge for HR management and a raising expectations for HR services deliveries. Thus, HR must be able to recognize and implement changes required in order to support the new roles and capabilities that the business needs.

METHODOLOGY

Hypothesis

H_1: The respondents were not aware about the HR shared services.

H_1: The organization did not make any savings by adapting HR shared services.

H_1: There was no significant reduction in error occurrence during the task performance.

Population

A population of 200 managers and IT professionals were taken in order to undertake this research. As it is a primary research, the data collection had to be one to one basis.

Sample Size and Model

A sample size of 120 managers and IT professionals is taken in reference to the research. For this research purpose, the primary data has been collected. This data is collected through the filling up the questionnaire.

Study Period

A study period of 20 days was taken in order to the get the questionnaire filled up by the HR managers and the IT managers of different companies and educational institutes of the Rajkot region. This duration was taken as to get the questionnaire filled up by the respondents.

RESULTS/ANALYSIS

By conducting this study, the researcher has found that all the hypotheses that were constructed have been rejected.

Hypothesis – 1

✓ **Null Hypothesis**

H_0 = The respondents were not aware about the HR shared services.

✓ **Alternative Hypothesis**

H_1 = The organisation does make profit by adapting HR shared services.

μH_0 = 93.25% (from practiced data obtained)

Awareness obtained data was 373 out of the standardized figure kept in project, i.e. 400.

Therefore, the percentage comes out to be 93.25%.

$\bar{X}$ = 50% agreeable level kept in calculation.

$\sigma = X\sqrt{n}$

$$Z\ cal = \frac{93.25-50}{\frac{93.25}{\sqrt{120}}}$$

$= 5.08$

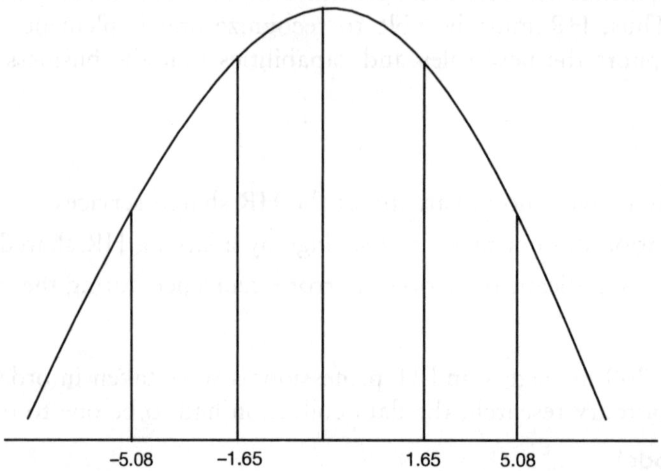

H_1 = The respondents were not aware about the HR shared services is REJECTED.

Reason: The calculated value of Z does not fall in the range of tabulated value of Z, i.e. 1.65, therefore our Null Hypothesis is REJECTED. Because the HR managers were aware about the concept of HR shared services, hence it can be proved from the survey.

Hypothesis – 2

✓ **Null Hypothesis**

H_0 = The organisation does not make profit by adapting HR shared services.

✓ **Alternative Hypothesis**

H_1 = The organisation does make profit by adapting HR shared services.

μH_0 = 56% (from practiced data obtained)

Result after adapting HR shared services obtained data was 224 out of the standardized figure kept in project, i.e. 400.

Therefore, the percentage comes out to be 56%.

$\bar{X}$ = 50% agreeable level kept in calculation.

$\sigma = X\sqrt{n}$

$$Z\ cal = \frac{56-50}{\frac{56}{\sqrt{120}}}$$

$= 1.74$

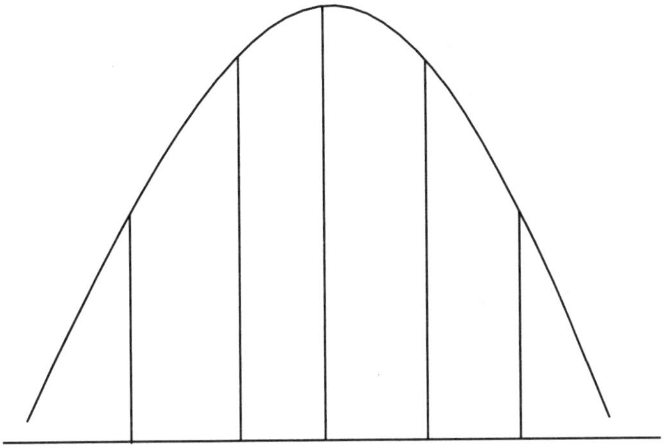

H_0 = The organisation does not make profit by adapting HR shared services is REJECTED.

Reason: The calculated value of Z does not fall in the range of tabulated value of Z, i.e. 1.65, therefore our Null Hypothesis is REJECTED. Because the organisation does make profit by adapting HR shared services hence it can be proved from the survey.

Hypothesis – 3

✓ **Null Hypothesis**

H_0 = There was no significant reduction in error occurrence during the task performance

✓ **Alternative Hypothesis**

H_1 = There was significant reduction in error occurrence during the task performance

Sr. No.	*Parameters*	*Outcomes*		*Total*
		Practiced	*Need*	
1	Pilot project and scale up	120	340	460
2	Centralized service centre	59	233	292
3	Clear governance structure	65	224	289
4	Alignment of shared services with ERP	120	329	449
5	Functional training	120	344	464
6	Integration of help desk services	120	315	435
7	Outsourcing additional services	82	265	347
8	Quality management	120	349	469
9	Team bonding activities	120	340	460
10	Soft skill training	120	373	493
	Total	1046	3113	4159

Source of Variation	*SS*	*df*	*MS*	*Fc*	*Ft*
Between	190.8375	7–1=6	190.8375/7 = 27.2625	27.2625/790.73 = 0.03	F(6,14) = 3.88
Within	11070.20	21–7=14	11070.20/14 = 790.73		
Total	11261.04	21–1=20			

H_0 = There was no significant reduction in error occurrence during the task performance is REJECTED.

Reason: The main reason behind the rejection of null hypothesis, i.e. there was no significant reduction in error occurrence during the task performance is because the employees skill does get enhanced after effective training programs implied through the organization.

Conclusion

- Firstly, with the help of data tabulation, data analysis has been done.
- On the basis of data analysis, the hypothesis testing has been performed, whereby the significant difference between the variables has been tested and the conclusions are derived.
- Hypotheses 1 and 2 suggest that most of the respondents believe that they were aware about the HR shared services and the organization makes significant profit after implementing HR shared service.
- They are satisfied with the concept of HR shared services. All employees are motivated as their error occurrence level is almost zero.
- Employees and organization both have beneficial training and development program and it's also reducing turnover ratio in the organization.

REFERENCES

Adler, P.S. (2003). Making the HR Outsourcing Decision. *Sloan Management Review*, 45, 53-60.

Aksin, O.Z., and Masini, A. (2008). Effective strategies for internal outsourcing and offshoring of business services: An empirical investigation. *Journal of Operations Management*, 239-56.

Amaratunga, D., Baldry, D., Sarshar, M., and Newton, R. (2002). Quantitative and qualitative research in built environment: Application of "mixed" research approach. Work Study, 51 (1), 17-31.

Baird, L., and Meshoulam, I. (1988). Managing two fits of strategic human resource management. *Academy of Management Review*, 13(1), 116-28.

Baldwin, L.P., Irani, Z., and Love, P. (2001). Outsourcing Information Systems: Drawing Lessons from a Banking Case Study. *European Journal of Information Systems*, 15-24.

Beatty, R.W., and Schneier, C.E. (1997). New HR roles to impact organizational performance: From—partners? to—players?. *Human Resource Management*, 36(1), 29-37.

Becker, B., and Gerhart, B. (1996). The impact of human resource management. *Academy of Management Journal*, 39(4), 779-801.

Beckett, G.H. (2005). Perfect Partners. *People Management Guide*, 16-23.

Beer, M., Spector, B., Lawrence, P.R., Mills, O.N., and Walton, R.E. (1984). *Managing Human Assets*. New York: Free Press.

Bergeron, B. (2003). *Essentials of Shared Services*. Hoboken, New Jersey, United States: Wiley.

Boroughs, A., and Saunders, J. (2007). Shared services that work for the business. *Strategic HR Review*, 28-31.

Boxall, P., & Purcell, J. (2000). Strategic human resource management: Where have we come from and where should we be going? *International Journal of Management Reviews*, 2(2), 183-203.

Gonzáles, B., Ellis, Y.M., Riffel, P.J., and Yager, D. (1999). Training at IBM's Human Resource Service Center: Linking People, Technology, and HR processes. *Human Resource Management*, 38(2), 135-42.

Herbert, I. (2008). The role of shared service. *Management Services*, 53(1), 43-47.

Mayo, A. (2005). Serious Behaviour. *People Management.*

Ulrich, D., and Brockbank, W. (2005). Role call. *People Management*, 11(12), 24-28.

Ulrich, D., and Brockbank, W. (2009). The HR Business-Partner Model: past Learnings and Future Challenges. *People and Strategy*, 32(2), 5-7.

Ulrich, D., Brockbank, W., and Johnson, D. (2009). The role of strategy architect in the strategic HR Organization. *People & Strategy*, 32(1), 24-31.

Ulrich, D., Yeung, A.K., Brockbank, W., and Lake, D.G. (1995). Human resource competencies: An empirical assessment. *Human Resource Management*, 34(4), 473-95.

CHAPTER 4

VISUALIZED CREATIVITY IN WEB-BASED ADVERTISEMENTS FOR HR PERSONNEL WHILE SURFING ON INTERNET

–*Bhagwan Singh* and *Sachin Kumar*

ABSTRACT

Nowadays, Internet has a wider scope for advertisements in HR for Creative Advertising. All this is possible because of Internet affordability worldwide. The organizations are totally equipped with sophisticated Internet facility today and they provide it to their stakeholders and HR personnel like ERP system, CRM system, etc.

The research is being carried on the idea that these stakeholders and HR personnel while working online must have been surfing sites and have been observing creativity of these sites. The period of study is July 2012 to August 2012 on a sample of 100 respondents. The study mainly focuses on "Does Creativity in Web-based Advertisements Make HR Personnel Expert in Creating the Awareness". The research is empirical study based on cluster and simple random sampling. Data was collected from questionnaire circulated to all respondents. The paper's literature review is based on various research reports pertaining to HR growth, promotion and control with add on to Web-based Advertisements papers published in various journals. It is blending of IT and HR with marketing tools of Internet usage for development of HR.

This paper also deals with the appeals in creativity with survey on aspects of creativity. A pilot study followed by main study which has been carried out on the various aspects of creativity.

Introduction

In today's world, the Internet has become one of the advertisement's hubs for all the businesses and customers. Everybody uses to spend his/her leisure time on Internet. All this is, because the technology has changed at such a rate that every human being possesses the electronic gadgets with him/her to have fun or for other purposes. Also most of HR personnel while working in the offices are always online either on social networking sites or on other sites through mobile phones or laptops/computers. While surfing, they always go through some advertisements.

Internet has a wider scope of advertisements nowadays. These advertisements are creative advertisements. So a large number of companies either national or international are spending a lot in this area. Besides stakeholder/consumer the HR personnel is also showing keen interest in the online advertising. They can have full access to online advertising. Creativity in WBA is the main factor that draws the attention of visitors towards the advertisement. If an advertisement is not creative, attention of visitors is not drawn. So in order to survive for a long time, advertisement companies either online or off-line have to continuously upgrade in terms of creativity.

So we can say that the web-based advertising is not the advertising only, but it's an advertising that is fully backed and powered by creativity. All this is possible because of multimedia and Internet availability. Today not only the big business houses but the educational organizations are also fully provided and equipped with Internet facility.

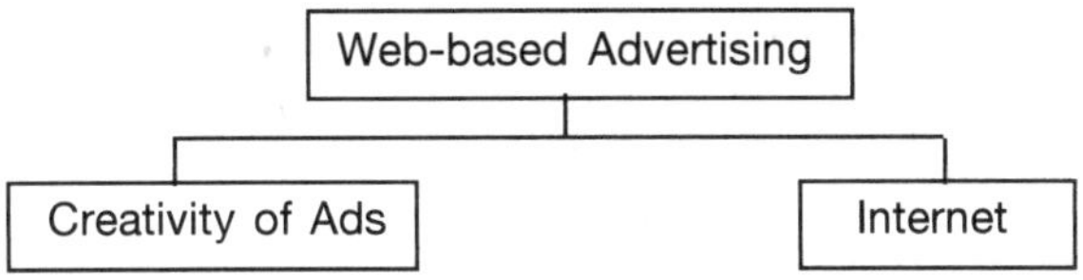

Fig. 1

What is Internet Adverting?

Internet Advertising (IA) includes many forms of commercial content—from electronic advertisements that are similar to traditional advertisements (e.g. billboards, banner ads, etc.) to formats that are different from traditional advertisements. IA can be delivered via any channel (e.g. video clip, print or audio), in any form (e.g. an e-mail message or an interactive game), and provide information at any degree of depth (e.g. a corporate logo or an official website).[1]

What is Web-based Advertising?

Advertising through Internet and on Internet is Web-based Advertising (Fig. 1). WBA or online advertising is a form of promotion that uses the Internet and World Wide Web for the expressed purpose of delivering marketing messages to attract customers. Examples of online advertising include contextual ads on search engine results pages, banner ads, rich media ads, social network advertising, interstitial ads, online classified advertising, advertising networks and e-mail marketing, including e-mail spam.

What is creativity? (Franken)

Creativity is defined as the tendency to generate or recognize ideas, alternatives, or possibilities that may be useful in solving problems, communicating with others, and entertaining ourselves and others.[2]

Creativity Defined as Per Surveyed Study

Creativity is an appeal in the form of animation, color combination, text style, graphics, etc. that makes the advertisement appealing to the users of Internet. All the things are arranged in well manner, so that people using it first time are really influenced. While visiting sites HR personnel are mostly influenced by the creative work of the websites. This is because they have to surf on Internet and while surfing they access the creative advertising sites. This can help the organization either to build more strong relationship with the users of Internet and of people visiting these sites.

Appeals in Creativity[3]

1. Rational 2. Emotional 3. Moral 4. Sex appeal

Survey on Aspects of Creativity

Creativity can be seen in following aspects like:

1. Animation 2. Colour combination 3. Text style and presence 4. Graphics
5. 3D 6. Sound effect 7. Balance or equilibrium
8. Uniformity 9. Movement 10. Content

The creativity makes HR personnel feel enjoyment and influence them to buy the products. In simple words, the web-based advertisements are successful only when they are powered by creativity in them. This not only helps the websites to be attractive for visitors of the sites but also they feel related with them.

Basis of Problem Defined

HR people feel that they can't be promoted unless until having exposure to the current media or technology.

Problem Defined

"Does Creativity in Web-based Advertisements Make HR Personnel Expert in Creating the Awareness".

Literature Review

It's the people, not the products, which are an innovative company's major assets. These companies carefully analyze personal needs and hire creative HR people to fulfill organizational goals. An award system is makes them to boost up the creativity (Gupta and Singhal, 1993).

Success in product and service innovation depends on creativity. He took strategic view of creativity as a key element of competitive advantage. Also creativity is not predominantly something that can be "forced" through creativity "techniques". It depends crucially on the setting of an appropriate context for ideas to emerge and their subsequent mobilization into innovative products and services. When the context is right techniques can play their part in raising the level and type of creativity within organizations (Peter Cook, 1998).

Leading business gurus have launched an online campaign to encourage creativity in the workplace. The Space for Ideas Campaign has a website where thinkers such as Charles Handy, Baroness Susan Greenfield, Robert Heller and Professor Richard Wiseman, and entrepreneurs John Timpson and *Teletubbies* creator Anne Wood, have all posted essays. They give companies and their employees an insight into the process of "ideas generation, capture and commercialization", including sources of inspiration, how to set up ideas processes, encouraging ideas from staff, and advice on winning support for your ideas (*Personnel Today*, 2005).

HR departments have had many of the same issues over the past decade as we have reduced staff sizes, expanded job responsibilities and tried to take advantage of technology to standardize delivery of services. When you are overworked, understaffed and dealing with implementing systems there is just not a lot of time or drive to be creative or innovative. An IT department works well for HR departments too. He said "...business-facing...staff must be able to 'challenge' their business partners, not just build relationships and seek consensus" (Michael Haberman, 2011).

The HR personnel being the backbone of any organization is more important asset than products. If creativity is added in their work, the organization goals can be attained. This creativity is in turn a part of advertising and can be viewed while surfing on Internet. The HR personnel develop the organization by recruitment and selection, problem solving for HR, office work, and while surfing on Internet they also creativity is visualized by them. So the study is conducted to find out following objectives.

Objectives of the Study

1. To know the awareness among genders about creativity in WBA.
2. To know whether the HR personnel are aware of web-based advertisement empowered with creativity.
3. To know what is the most attractive impression of creativity that influences the HR personnel surfing Internet.
4. To know which of the creativity appeals have maximum influence on HR personnel.
5. To know whether the creativity in web-based advertisements make HR personnel expert in creating the awareness

Research Methodology

Data

The primary data is collected by questionnaires (through mails and manually filling) with single and multiple options answering. The secondary data is collected is from thesis, journals, magazines and surfing websites.

Study Period: The period of study taken is July 2007 to August 2012.

Justification: To develop know-how of HR personnel while surfing on Internet and developing organization by recruitment and selection for period of five years.

Sample Size

100 respondents

Sampling Used

Multi Phase Sampling

Models Used

Cluster and convenience sampling model

Results and Analysis

Questions asked while interview was in two parts

Data Analysis

Respondents Personal and Survey Information RPI and RSI

Q.1 Age Group of the Respondents

Table 1

Age Group	*Responses*	**%age*
(a) 18 – 25	80	80%
(b) 25-30	12	12%
(c) 30-35	6	6%
(d) 35-40	1	1%
(e) 40 above	1	1%
Total	100	100%

*%tage = Percentage

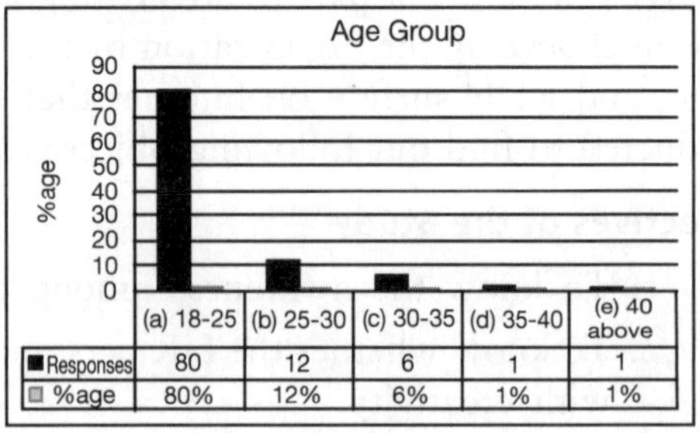

Fig. 1

Analysis

A major section under study belongs to age group between 18-30 years and very few in numbers from age group of more than 30 years.

Q.2 Gender-wise Distribution of the Respondents

Table 2

Gender	*Responses*	*%age*
(a) Male	56	56%
(b) Female	44	44%
Total	100	100%

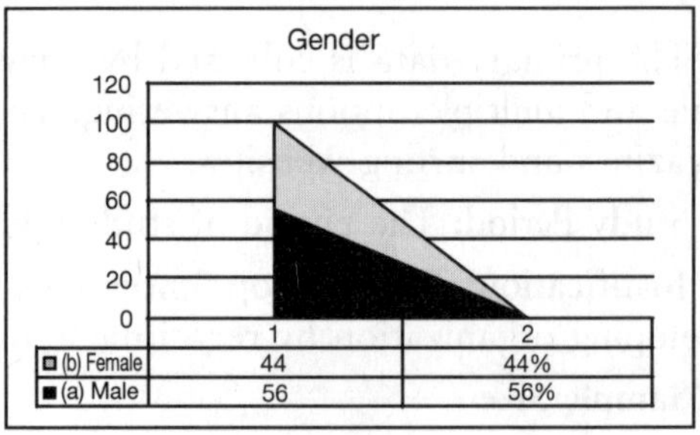

Fig. 2

Analysis

Majority sections of respondents are male but females are also in an approximate number.

Q.3 While Surfing on Internet, You were Mainly Focused For

Table 3

Options	*Responses*	*%age*
(a) Recruitment sites	21	15%
(b) Viewing competitor markets/strategies	6	4%
(c) Office work	22	16%
(d) New trends & innovations in technology	11	8%
(e) Problem solving for HR	79	56%
(f) Other	2	1%
Total	141	100%

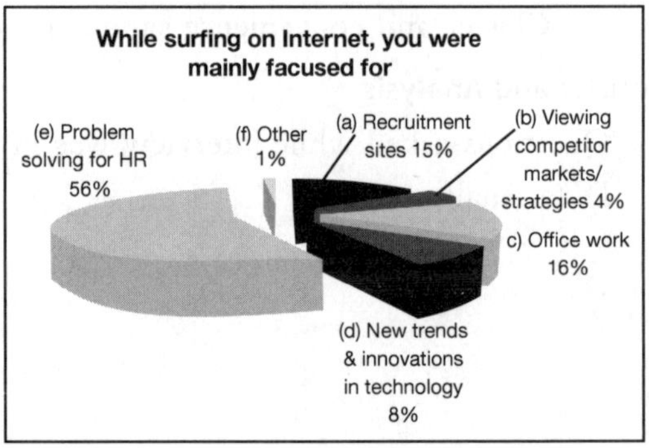

Fig. 3

Analysis

56% HR personnel while surfings were focused on problem solving for HR and 16% for office work.

Q.4 Number of Sites Observed for Creativity and HR Strategies

Table 4

Options	Responses	%age
(a) 1-3	46	46%
(b) 3-6	36	36%
(c) 6-9	10	10%
(d) 9-12	7	7%
(e) More than 12	1	1%
Total	100	100%

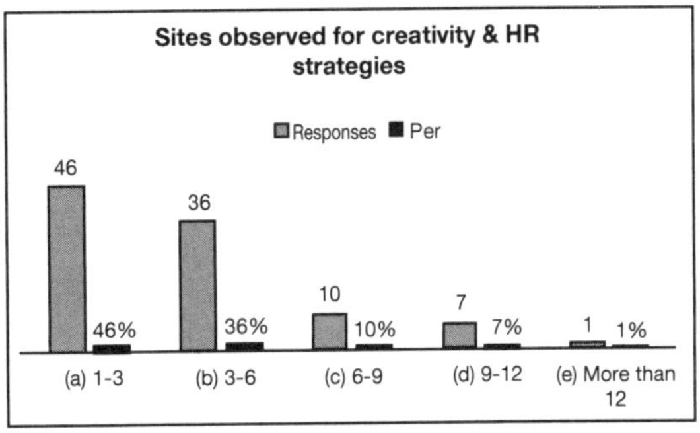

Fig. 4

Analysis

82% of HR personnel observed 1-6 sites for creativity. Only 18% favored for six and more than six sites for creativity.

Q.5 Most attractive impression while surfing sites?

Table 5

Options	Responses	%age
(a) Animation	29	19%
(b) Colour combination	18	12%
(c) Text style & presence	23	15%
(d) Graphics style	8	5%
(e) 3-D	20	13%
(f) Sound effect	15	10%
(g) Balance or equilibrium	7	5%
(h) Uniformity	8	5%
(i) Movement	4	3%
(j) Content	22	14%
Total	154	100%

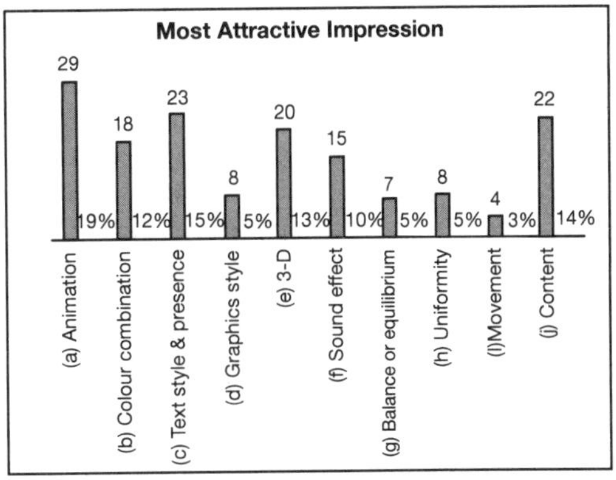

Fig. 5

Analysis

Majority of HR personnel said that animation, colour, 3-D, text style, content and sound are the most attractive impression for them while surfing sites. Very few said about graphics, uniformity and movement.

Q.6 Which Appeal of Creativity Influences?

Table 6

Options	*Responses*	*%age*
(a) Rational	35	38%
(b) Emotional	18	19%
(c) Moral	35	38%
(d) Sex appeal	4	4%
(e) Others	1	1%
Total	93	100%

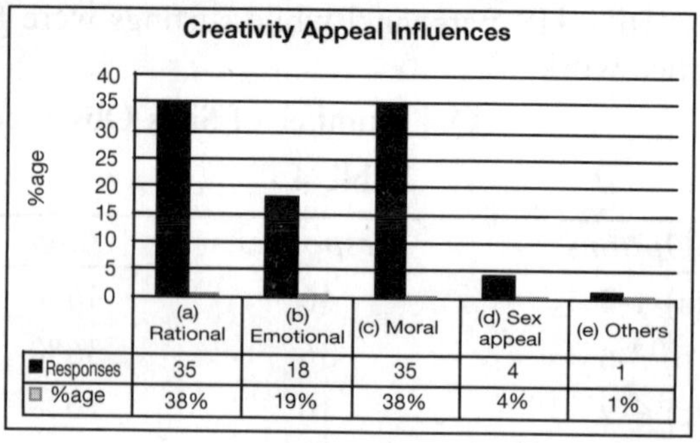

Fig. 6

Analysis

Majority of 76% HR personnel are influenced by rational and moral appeal of creativity and rest all are influenced by emotions, sex and others.

Q.7 Does Creativity in Web-based Advertisements Make HR Personnel Expert in Creating the Awareness?

Table 7

Options	*Responses*	*%age*
(a) Yes	58	58%
(b) No	39	39%
(c) Can't say	3	3%
Total	100	100%

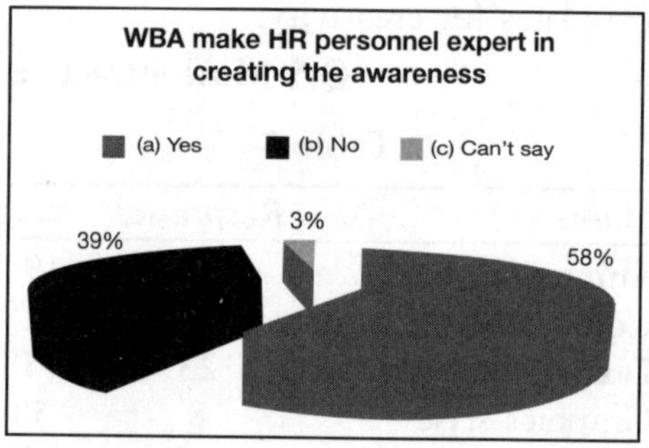

Fig. 7

Analysis

Creativity in Web-based Advertisements makes 58% HR personnel expert in creating the awareness.

List of Analysis

1. Maximum users of Internet are HR personnel from age group between 18-30 years. From this it may be concluded that creativity is observed between groups of HR personnel who are till 30 years.
2. Most of the HR personnel are male but female HR personnel are also approximately equal in number. This shows that female HR personnel are also equally interested in Internet assessing and also aware of creativity in WBA.
3. HR personnel surf Internet to problem solving for HR.
4. The Web-based Advertisements have creativity but it is less observed by larger number of HR personnel.

5. HR personnel are influenced by a large number of attractive impressions on the sites, rather than by a single impression.
6. HR personnel are influenced by only two creativity appeals, i.e. rational and moral.
7. Creativity in Web-based Advertisements make HR personnel expert in creating the awareness.

Conclusion

In conclusion, empirical result shows that maximum of Internet users (HR personnel) are from age group of 18-30 years including both males and females. Along with male HR personnel, female HR personnel too are interested in Internet assessing and aware of creativity in WBA. HR personnel always surf Internet to gain knowledge and while surfing they always visit the creative sites. The analysis results that these people know about the creativity and creative sites.

The analysis of the problem is that creativity in Web-based Advertisements makes 58% HR personnel expert in creating the awareness of HR policies. The results are found to be true. Talking about the influence of creative sites, it's found that there is not only a single attractive impression on sites but a large number of impressions that influence the HR personnel and attract them. These are animation, colour combination, text style and presence, graphics, 3D, sound effect, balance or equilibrium, uniformity, movement, content. People are mostly influenced by rational and moral appeals in creativity. Emotional appeals too have influence on HR personnel and mostly sex appeal is avoided in the advertisement. Similarly, creativity in Web-based Advertisements make HR personnel expert in creating the awareness. Because an awareness to what creativity is, in advertising makes HR personnel equipped with loads of knowledge about creative advertising.

With this vast knowledge about what creativity is, in advertising, the HR personnel can use this in regards of recruitment and selection, in developing the organisation websites, for doing various offices works, making their company leading the competitors in terms of profit and goodwill. Also this helps HR personnel to build a healthy relation with the creative sites.

REFERENCES

Ann, E. Schlosser, Sharon Shavitt, Alaina Kanferf (1999). A survey of Internet users' attitudes toward internet advertising. *Journal of Interactive Marketing*. 13 (3). CCC 1094-9968/99/030034-21.

CREATIVESTRATEGYLECTURE.doc Retrieved on 18 June 2012 from /http:// www.jou.ufl.edu/faculty/.../

Franken, Robert E. (1994). *Human Motivation*: Thomson/Wadsworth, 3rd ed.

Other References

- Chunawala, S.A. (2011). *Advertising, Sales and Promotion Management*: Himalaya Publishing House, pp. 88-92.
- Chunawala S.A., K.J. Kumar, Sethia K.C. (2011). *Advertising Theory and Practices*: Himalaya Publishing House. pp. 244-65.
- Cook, Peter (1998). The creativity advantage—is your organization the leader of the pack? *Industrial and Commercial Training*: MCB University Press. 30(5) · pp. 179-84. Retrieved on 8 August 2012 from www.emeraldinsight.com/.../journals.htm?issn=0019-7858...30...5...

- Creativity campaign launched online (2005 January 17). *Personnel Today*.
- Creativity-in-Advertising. Retrieved on 18 June 2012, from http:// www.docstoc.com/docs/12163025
- Gupta, K. Ashok and Arvind Singhal (1993). Managing Human Resources for innovation & Creativity. Research. *Technology Management.*
- Haberman, Michael (2011). Human Resources, Creativity and Innovation. Retrieved on 8 August 2012 from Omega HR Solutions, Inc Website:http://omegahrsolutions.com/2011/05/human-resources-creativity-and-innovation.html
- Sontakki, C.N. (2010). *Advertising and Sales Management:* Kalyani Publishers, 2003, pp. 55-59.
- Wells, D. William, John Burnett, Sandra Moriarty (2011). *Advertising Principles and Practice 2006*: Pearson Prentice Hall, pp. 327-35.

CHAPTER 5

IMPACT OF GLOBAL FINANCIAL CRISIS ON IT AND OUTSOURCING INDUSTRY

–*O.P. Roonwal* and *Shipra Chainani*

ABSTRACT

With the US economy slowing down Indian IT and outsourcing industry has come into focus. In USA, Merrill Lynch has emerged with Bank of America, Washington Mutual Operations was being apprehended by FDIC and Wachovia was auctioned by Citigroup. And the rest of American financial landscape was altered by Lehman Brothers Holdings Inc. (LBHI), the 158-year-old U.S. investment bank. This was all due to the failure of the government regulators to keep watch on the stock markets and financial firms or banks. The global financial crisis has put many negative effects upon different businesses and industries. In Wall Street, all the investment banks converted themselves to commercial banks, mergers and acquisitions of financial institutions took place. Several banks and financial institutions merged with other institutions or were simply bought out. Few were lucky enough to receive a government bailout and are still functioning.

The negative attention towards outsourcing took place at the time of global financial crisis. As the global economy slows down and due to currency fluctuations, companies reduced their business i.e., IT and BPO outsourcing. For the past several years due to global outsource demand, the Employee Attrition Rate has increased in the Indian IT and BPO market. As the global demand for outsourcing decreased companies laid-off bottom performers. The slowdown in US economy is making it necessary for Indian companies to look for business opportunities outside US in countries of Asia Pacific, Europe, Africa and Middle East.

Introduction

Outsourcing involves the transfer of the management or day-to-day execution of an entire business function to an external service provider. Business segments typically outsourced include information technology, human resources, facilities and real estate management, and accounting. Global outsourcing mitigates risks for the customer as it is not country-specific or geography-dependent. It allows businesses to learn, adapt, grow and provides more freedom and flexibility in decision-making and operations during the outsourcing process. To get competitive advantage and to save cost some of the key industries used global outsourcing like the banking and financial services industry, the insurance industry, the IT industry, the telecom industry, the retail industry, the healthcare industry, the travel industry, the real estate industry, the engineering industry.

The IT and outsourcing industry is one of fastest growing businesses in India and it is not only generating billions of revenue but also providing employment opportunities to millions of people. India is one of the leading service providers and service sector contributed 62.5% to the GDP and employ 34% of the workforce. With large base of English speaking educated people, India has become a preferred destination for business services. The Information Technology and outsourcing services have been the biggest contributor to India's growth.

The US economy has been bad since summer 2008 and its turbulence has been felt world over which was started with the housing sub-prime mortgage has spread out lavishly to the financial markets and taken the whole economy for a downfall. Almost 60% of the total business of Indian IT and outsourcing industry comes from the US and 20% from UK, the rest comes from other European countries, Australia, etc. With US economy slowing down and edging towards recession, Indian IT and outsourcing industry has come into focus and affected the global economy.

Methodology

The present study focuses on

- The origin and root causes of global financial crisis.
- The impact of the crisis on the Indian Economy and IT and outsourcing industry.
- Strategies adopted by big five companies.
- Measures.
- The data for the study has been collected from secondary sources.

Reasons for Global Financial Crisis

Credit policy acts as a major reason for this financial turmoil, as the whole American economy is built on credit. But credit is a great tool if used wisely. There are many other reasons of this financial crisis include increased demand in housing sector, sub-prime mortgage, failure of Lehman Brothers and other big financial institutions, poor regulation by government and globalization.

1. Increased demand for housing—Sub-prime borrowing and easy credit policy was a major contributor to an increase in demand of housing ownership. Excess supply of houses placed significant downward pressure on prices. As prices declined, more house owners were at risk of default and foreclosure. The reality is housing prices are increasingly significant. People invested in this risky area, hoping to get a lot of profit.

2. Sub-prime mortgage—It all started with the housing sub-prime mortgage and now it trickled into the entire financial market. They are more risky and harmful than standard loans because they are given to people with lower and unpredictable incomes. Thousands of people took out loans larger than they could afford in the hopes that they could either flip the house for profit or refinance later at a lower rate and with more equity in their home—which they would then leverage to purchase another "investment" house. This caused heavy losses in mortgage backed securities and many banks and investment firms crashed.

3. Failure of Lehman Brothers and other big financial institutions—In USA, Merrill Lynch has emerged with Bank of America, Washington Mutual Operations are being apprehended by

FDIC and Wachovia is being auctioned by Citigroup. And the rest of American financial landscape was altered by Lehman Brothers Holdings Inc. (LBHI), the 158-year-old U.S. investment bank. It has filed for bankruptcy. This is the largest bankruptcy in the history of the United States with $638 billion in assets listed and the largest failure of an investment bank. The collapse of Lehman Brothers in September 2008 has been the outcome of the reduction in net capital inflows and the significant correction in the domestic stock markets on the back of sell-off in the equity market by FIIs.

4. Poor regulation by government—In the last decade, credit went unchecked and it got out of control. This was due to the failure of the government regulators to keep watch on the stock markets and financial firms or banks. These heavy losses caused many banks to tighten their lending requirements, but it was already too late for many of them, the damage had already been done. Several banks and financial institutions merged with other institutions or were simply bought out. Few were lucky enough to receive a government bailout and are still functioning. The worst of the lot or the unlucky ones crashed.

5. Globalization—Globalization is a process of interaction and integration among the people, companies, and governments of different nations, a process driven by international trade and investment and aided by information technology. This process has effects on the environment, on culture, on political systems, on economic development and prosperity, and on human physical well-being in societies around the world. It helps in creating new markets and wealth, at the same time it is responsible for extensive suffering, disorder, and unrest. The great financial crisis that just happened was the biggest example of how negative globalization can turn. A failure of one bank can have a strong contagion on the rest of the banks, even if they are healthy. It clearly revealed the dangers of an unstable, deregulated, global economy.

Impact of Global Financial Crisis

The collapse of Lehman Brothers in September 2008, and the subsequent breakdown of Merrill Lynch caused downturn in the global banking and financial services industry. Markets tanked, companies went bankrupt and the global economy plunged into recession. As the impact of global financial crisis, industrial production declined, unemployment rates had shot up in the United States and it had continued to affect the Indian industries as well. The global financial crisis has put negative effects upon different businesses and industries. This bubble of financial crises burst into several consequences. As November 2008, the IT industry was under pressure, particularly from the downturn in the US Banking, Financial Service and Insurance (BFSI) sector which accounted for almost 40% of the Indian IT sector's revenues.

According to the latest assessment by the NASSCOM, the software trade impact on other sectors of the US economy and worldwide markets. About 15 association, the current developments with respect to the US financial markets are very eventful, and may have a direct impact on the IT industry and likely to create a downstream per cent to 18 per cent of the business coming to Indian outsourcers includes projects from banking, insurance, and the financial services sector which is now uncertain.

Effect on IT and Outsourcing Industry

1. Negative outlook towards outsourcing deals—With the global financial crisis, the elections were also heating up in the US. The companies in US didn't favor off shoring jobs in such a scenario. The negative attention towards outsourcing took place. As the global economy slows down, companies reduced their IT and BPO outsourcing.

With that economic situation, it is said that there were lesser and lesser outsourcing deals made, but this doesn't mean that the outsourcing world went down to a downward spiral. Ultimately, deals are still being made, with the occasional high-stakes and risk but the fact is that business is still going on. While in that scenario, most outsourcing deals were decided on the basis of cost rather than value. Outsourcing can never be separated from business goals because to achieve the desired results, outsourcing relationships must constantly evolve.

2. Employment and attrition—For the past several years due to global outsource demand, the Employee Attrition Rate has increased in the Indian IT and BPO market. As the global demand for outsourcing decreased, companies laid-off bottom performers and Pink slips and rightsizing became the norm for them. The growth in salary hike also came down from 13.5 per cent to 9 per cent that time.

Three years ago in Bangalore, financial and health-care Software Company Misys had employee turnover rates of around 30% and higher at the offshore center it runs there. By the most recent quarter, the rate had plummeted to zero. "I've been doing business as a software professional in India for 20 years and I've never seen attrition levels at zero," says Cory Eaves, CIO and CTO for Misys. Eaves said that for the past few years, wage inflation in India has been about 15% to 17%, and for 2009 he estimated that will go down to 7%. "2009 will be a challenging year for India," he said.

3. Stress at workplace—Most companies believed that an increase in working hours would increase productivity and this would reduce the ill-effects of the global economic slowdown on their revenues by increasing the per employee utilization levels. But long working hours and erratic work timings resulted in high level of stress at the workplace for employees.

4. Mergers and acquisition—In Wall Street, all the investment banks converted themselves to commercial banks, mergers and acquisitions of financial institutions took place. This means no more lavish IT and BPO budgets for them to spend and this will significantly reduce the profit margin for the Indian IT companies.

"We expect a sharper contraction of merger volume in 2009, versus 2008, whereas the number of mergers and acquisitions will rise. Reasons are obvious, all being linked to global financial downturn and its negative impact in domestic economy," Ciprian Paltineanu, head of UniCredit CA IB Romania told Wall-Street.

5. Improvement in productivity and quality—With that lucrative growth rate of salary structure, IT professionals were changing jobs frequently. Frequent change of jobs affected the job culture and overall productivity of the industry. But after this crisis, the scene was totally reversed. As a result of this financial crisis, professionals were not only in favor of changing the job but also ready to work more with the same salary with the objective to keep their job secure. Definitely, it would help in the improvement of this sector as well as the productivity of the IT industry. Indian outsourcing industry was making a progressive advance towards more quality-oriented business operations. The BPO sector was making a shift in terms of value addition towards KPO.

6. Stock market—The downturn of economy in the global market has also affected the Indian stock market. It witnessed its steepest ever fall. The Sensex of the Indian share market fell by 1,070 points on October 24, 2008.

7. Obama's judgment—With the US economy slowing down, Indian companies received a bad news from US President Barrack Obama. He said, "I will stop giving tax breaks to companies that ship jobs overseas, and I will start giving them to companies that create good jobs right in America". America was in a very precarious situation with respect to their economy. The economy was battered and millions of US citizens were losing jobs. At this juncture. Obama was right in curtailing outsourcing when his own people were suffering and it was the only way to overcome that situation. Americans are highly skilled and also might work for lesser pay like Indians till the situation revives.

Other Effects

1. Balance of payment—By the middle of 2008, even before the global crisis really hit India, this process too was reaching its limits. The crisis made matters much worse by causing sharp declines in exports of manufactures and reversal of capital flows such that both current and capital accounts of the balance of payments have worsened.

2. Employment—Official sources suggest that there has already been a sharp fall in employment in the export-oriented sectors like textiles and garments and gems and jewellery, and even in industries catering more to the domestic market like metal products, automobiles and construction.

3. Lower income segment—The effects of the economic crisis were amplified for the lower income segments of population due to reduction in wage employment opportunities; and increase in cost of food.

4. Finance of government—Another serious consequence of the financial crunch was the impact on the finances of State Governments, who are responsible for human development such as basic infrastructure, health, sanitation and education.

Strategies Adopted by Big Five Companies

Big companies were employing various strategies to beat the U.S Economy slowdown. India's top five IT companies—TCS, Infosys, Wipro, Satyam and HCL Tech—collectively lost over ₹ 2,50,000 crore in market value in 2007-08. They all imposed hiring freezes on hiring experienced professionals and deferred joining dates on newcomers. TCS had cut new hiring from 35,000 to 30,000. Infosys also followed suit and announced reduced hiring from 35,000 last year (2007) to 25,000 this year (2008). All companies were looking at decreases and the mood in the industry currently favors slower expansion and outright cuts in certain sectors. Operating profits were also down, with margins for the companies decreasing by 6 to 15 per cent that year. The banking, financial services and insurance (BFSI) vertical, which had been the stronghold of the many IT firms had been the worst hit by the sub-prime crisis.

Measures

Some of the measures being taken by the industry are:

1. Bailouts—These are act by governments to allocated funds to purchase the bad debts held by banking companies, it is a "Rescue Plan". Bailouts program from governments is the best way to overcome this financial crisis because they are a regulator who issued the money and control velocity of money. They can and have the money to rebuild and help companies and make this crisis end.

2. Proper regulation—We must think of the longer term implications for monetary policy and financial regulatory mechanisms to avoid this problem in future.

3. Efficiency and cost competitiveness—In turbulent times, clients expect greater flexibility and business value from service providers. We must focus on operational efficiency and enhance cost-competitiveness.

4. New policies—More creative and imaginative policy responses are required, in terms of changing directions of investment and consumption in the home market to emphasize wage-led growth, diversifying exports and generally making moves designed to turn economic adversity to advantage.

Conclusion

To summarize, the impact of the global economic downturn is beginning to be pervasive.

The global market bottomed in the first half of the year and turned in the second half. It now shows signs of recovering slowly and steadily. Enterprises are finding their business feet after being in freefall with the downturn and are now shifting more of their work to outsourcers to cut costs and streamline operations both short- and long-term. There have been observations that it is most likely that the outsourcing community will get out of this worldwide financial crisis virtually unscathed. This is not to say that it has not been affected by the financial crisis. There have been less of the major deals struck before crisis hit, but deals are still being made and outsourcing companies continue to hire people because of the great demand, particularly in call centers.

However, India, with its strong fundamentals and a favorable environment, is in a relatively strong position amongst all global sourcing destinations to cater to client requirements in volatile and uncertain market. Despite of economy downturn, India continues to be the best place or top destination for outsourcing because of salary costs in which India is extremely competitive. In the long-term when the dust of financial crisis settles down in the US financial market, Indian IT and outsourcing companies will be in good position to attract more outsource work from the US businesses. It just needs to focus on increased productivity and value creation on the output side.

At last by keeping positive attitude and outlook, we can say that if there is any industry to come out stronger from this crisis, it is most probably the IT and outsourcing.

REFERENCES

Alex, Blumberg (2008) "How Credit Default Swaps Spread Financial Rot". National Public Radio Planet Money, October 30, 2008.

Atreya, Manohar M. (2008) "The U.S. Financial Crisis: Impact on the Indian IT Sector". From <http://www.vcircle.com> (Retrieved December 29, 2008)

Chandrasekhar, C.P. and Ghosh Jayanthi (2008) "India and the Global Financial Crisis". From <http://www.macroscan.org> (Retrieved October 8, 2008).

Ghosal, S.N. (2009) "Global Financial Crisis—Cause and Impact" Icfai Reader. Mar. 2009.

ILO (2008) "Economic meltdown to result in wage cuts". *The Hindu*, November 26, 2008, p. 14.

Larry, Elliott (2008) Credit crisis—How it all began". *The Guardian*.

Rakesh Mohan, RBI (2008) "Global Financial Crisis and Key Crisis: A Report".

Sengupta, Jayashree (2008) "The financial crisis and its impact on India". From <http://www.observerindia.com> (Retrieved December 6, 2008).

Venkitaramanan, S. (2008) "Global financial crisis: Reflections on its impact on India". *The Hindu*, October 10, 2008, p. 11.

Vardhani, D. and Sridevi, J. (2009) "Downturns and Impact of Global Meltdown" Icfai Reader. Mar. 2009.

CHAPTER 6

WEB-BASED ADVERTISING—AN INCREASING DEMAND IN HRD AND AGRICULTURE

–*G.S. Rathore, Bhagwan Singh* and *Sunita Yadav*

ABSTRACT

Emergence of Internet and other new media such as ATM, WAP devices and interactive TV are new ventures for advertising. HRD is spreading itself in the world of Internet to capture the company access in easy mode. Companies who are selling agricultural products are very nicely using this e-world for advertising their products and services.

The significance of the paper is expected to be an immense use to the society and the various companies who are giving the ad on the net for HRD and agribusiness. These companies may know that if they are expanding on the Internet advertising in smaller towns, is fruitful? This study supplies the information related to bulge of HRD and agribusiness via web-based advertising. The study promotes the differentiation theory for Web-based Advertising [WBA] over traditional advertising. As in this paper the survey predicts the usage and importance of Internet advertising of HRD and agribusiness.

Introduction

HRD is all about training and developing human beings for proper work in the company. The HRD people believe in good media planning and media buying. This is becoming highly specialized and thanks to the emergence of Internet as new media relating its characteristics with brand and consumer profile, there is a possibility that these two activities will move out of the range of services provided by a traditional advertising agency, implying splitting of the commission presently being earned. The major points for which web-based advertising is going popular are:

Online and offline media-buying companies are fully integrated and automated. In general, technology will drive initiatives in devising better ways to reach consumers. Web-based advertising is not the solution but is now a demand. Faced with increasing media cost and intense competition, many agencies are now trying to scale up quickly to become one-stop solution providers and reduce cost. The industry has already started witnessing a number of web advertising and strategic alliances.

The Globe is on Internet and Marketing is at the Click

Internet marketing ties together creative and technical aspects of the Internet, including: design, development, advertising, and sales. Internet marketing is sometimes considered to have a broader scope because it not only refers to the Internet, e-mail, and wireless media, but it includes management of digital customer data and Electronic Customer Relationship Management (ECRM) systems. The Internet has brought media to a global audience. The interactive nature of Internet marketing in terms of providing instant response and eliciting responses is a unique quality of the medium.

Internet marketing also refers to the placement of media along many different stages of the customer engagement cycle through Search Engine Marketing (SEM), Search Engine Optimization (SEO), banner ads on specific websites, e-mail marketing, and Web 2.0 strategies.

Study for Web-based Advertising Contribution in HRD and Agriculture

Web-based Advertising is part of Internet Marketing. Whenever Internet portal is opened the advertisements on Internet may be viewed on the sides of the portal. These portals have ads for agri-products and of HR also. The Web-based advertising is fruitful and it has good prospects. The problems are there but they are such that can be solved through further research. Web-based advertising/online advertising is a form of promotion that uses the Internet for the expressed purpose of delivering marketing messages to attract customers.

Research Methodology

Type of Research: Empirical

Data Collection: Primary Data

Sample Location: Eastern U.P.

Duration of Study: Three Years

Sample Size: Potential 300 respondents annually

Sampling Technique: Non-probability

Questionnaire with Data Analysis

Q. 1. Do you know that Internet advertising is contributing in HRD and Agriculture?

Table 1: Internet Advertising is Contributing in HRD and Agriculture

	Options	*2007*	*2008*	*2009*	*Total*	*Percentage*
(a)	Yes	187	219	274	680	75.56%
(b)	No	42	34	12	88	9.78%
(c)	Can't Say	71	47	14	132	14.67%
	Grand Total	300	300	300	900	100.00%

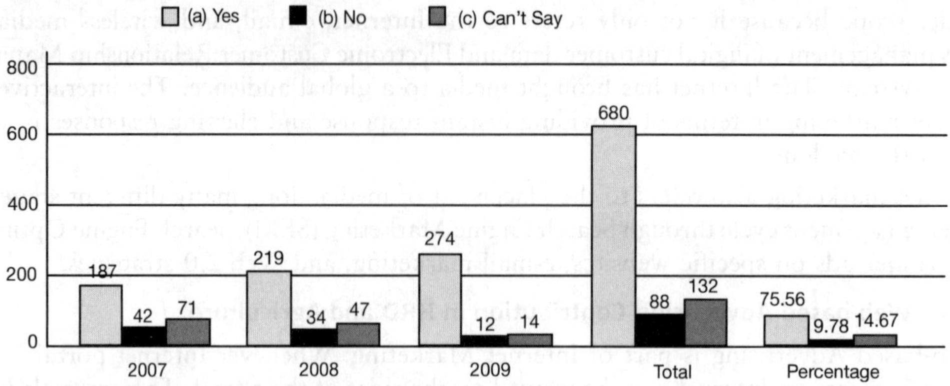

Fig. 1: Internet Advertising is Contributing in HRD and Agriculture

Q. 2. Do you know about web-based advertising?

Table 2: Awareness about Web-based Advertising

	Options	*2007*	*2008*	*2009*	*Total*	*Percentage*
(a)	Yes	179	207	221	607	67.44%
(b)	No	34	27	22	83	9.22%
(c)	Can't Say	87	66	57	210	23.33%
	Grand Total	300	300	300	900	100.00%

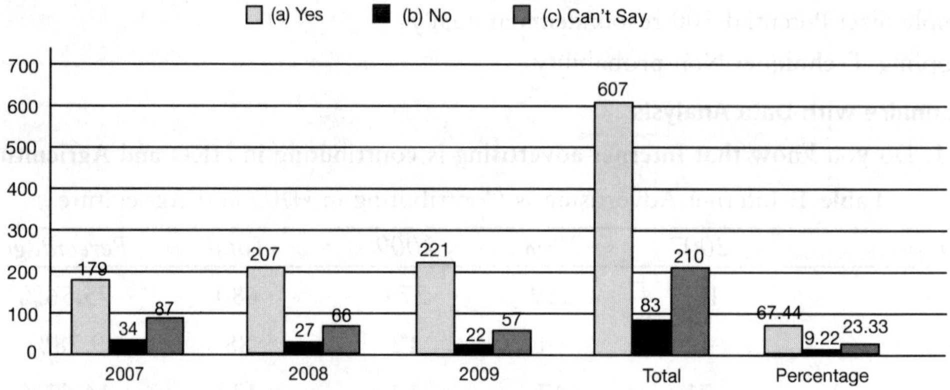

Fig. 2: Awareness about Web-based Advertising

Findings: In Eastern U.P. sample predicts that people know about the usage of Internet in advertising. 75.56% respondents said Yes they know about usage of Internet in advertising (Ref. Q1, Table 1, Fig. 1) and 14.67% said that they can't say how much Internet is used in advertising. Rest 9.78% denied about the know how of Internet usage in advertising.

As per awareness of Web-based advertising is concerned almost 76.44% respondents said that they know about it. 23.33% respondents cannot say about the experience of web-based advertising and 9.22% responded negatively for it (Ref. Q2, Table 2, Fig. 2).

Conclusion

The web-based advertising is giving more information regarding the product and services and helping HR people a lot to improve. The agricultural companies are also inflating this aspect. If right information is provided to the customers through proper awareness than definitely scenario will change the upcoming future. The e-business is becoming larger segment for business houses and hence leading the growth rate of net advertising. The most visited sites like naukari.com; eBay.in, gmail.com and the like have fascinating ads on Internet to attract the web user fast. A day will come when these multimedia web-based advertisements will be used higher than any other media advertisements.

The above discussion percolates the important factor of advertising awareness on global preview. Using animations is a step ahead for web-based advertisements and it is giving new avenues to HRD and agriculture. This signifies that web-based advertising is increasing its demand in HRD and agriculture.

REFERENCES

Chunawala, S.A. (2011). *Advertising, Sales and Promotion Management*: Himalaya Publishing House.

Consumer Experience Probe (1996), "Web Advertising Report", Jupiter Communications/The Westport Company.

DeCenzo, David A. and Stephen P. Robbins, *Personnel/Human Resource Management*, Third edition, PHI/Pearson.

Delaney, Kevin (2007). "Microsoft Fires Volley At Google in Ad Battle". *The Wall Street Journal.*

Dessler, Gary, *Human Resource Management*, Seventh edition, Prentice-Hall of India P. Ltd., Pearson.

International Journal of Economics and Managerial Thoughts [IJEMT], Vol 1, No 1.

Knight, Christopher, Email Advertising Media Terminology List.

Simon, Broadbent, Advertising Effects: More than Short Term, Vol. 35, No. 1, 1993.

Sontakki CN (2010). *Advertising and Sales Management.* Kalyani Publishers, 2003.

Spike, Cramphorn, How to use advertising to build brands: In search of the philosopher's stone, Vol. 48, No. 3, 2006, pp. 255-75.

CHAPTER 7

EFFECTIVE STRATEGIES FOR VIRTUAL ORGANIZATIONS AND VIRTUAL TEAMS

–Kasturi Sahay and Utpal Baul

ABSTRACT

In accordance with the globalization of trade and business, a new paradigm of work pattern known as Virtual Organization (VO) emerged in 1990s. VO particularly removes time and location barriers but links companies via ICTs (Information Communication Technologies) which enable them to collaborate on a worldwide scale. While at same time being engaged in collaboration, VO partners have been increasingly relying on Virtual Team (VT) to fulfill designated tasks or projects, in which interaction and collaboration take place among geographically distributed and often culturally disparate individuals.

This study focuses on e-leadership strategies, which basically refers to how to effectively and strategically lead VT members that are geographically dispersed. Clearly, leadership and relationship in VOs or VTs can prove challenging to build or sustain in virtual context where trust is difficult to build, influence is hard to articulate, and communication is often ambiguous. Among a range of e-leadership challenges inherent to the dispersed and often impersonal nature, technology, communication, cultural differences, trust, and logistics are the typical issues, thus will be addressed in this study.

The present study shows that E-leaders should be aware that VTs require supplementary relational links between team members because of the lack of physical proximity. A set of specific efforts should be targeted towards high degree of trust and cohesion within VTs.

1. INTRODUCTION

Throughout the last two decades, a remarkable revolution has been taking shape in organizations across the globe. This revolution involves the wiring of corporations so that various aspects of human interactions are now mediated by diverse ICTs (Information and Communication Technologies). As a result, a large number of traditional vertically-aligned organizations have been shifting to a more flexible and versatile structure to meet the demands of the rapidly changing marketplaces.

This new organizational structure is introduced as VO (Virtual Organization), which particularly removes time and location barriers but links corporations via ICTs that enable them to collaborate on a worldwide scale. While being engaged in collaboration, VO partners have been increasingly relying on VTs (Virtual Teams) to fulfill designated tasks or projects, in which interaction and collaboration take place among geographically distributed and often culturally disparate individuals. These teams are able to perform their work without concern of space or time constraints since they adopt the technology richness to coordinate their activities and share all the resources needed.

However, the implementation of VOs and VTs poses significant challenges for organizations that wish to deploy them. Although many of these challenges are present in traditional teams, they may become even more critical in virtual settings. One such challenge is e-leadership, which basically refers to how to effectively lead VT members that are geographically dispersed through a set of leadership strategies.

Although there is an abundance of studies and researches to explain leadership theory in traditional team settings, little empirical work examined e-leadership or posited relevant strategies in virtual context. The objective of this study thus is to address this gap through investigating e-leadership effectiveness and strategies. The following research questions summarize this effort:

What are the key concepts of VOs?

How does e-leadership differ from traditional leadership?

What factors contribute to effective leadership in virtual environment?

What major challenges have e-leadership been embracing?

How to strategically address these challenges?

Objective

This study aims to investigate the transition from traditional management to e-leadership in VOs or VTs; additionally, in order to establish a theoretical framework of leadership in VOs, this study will synthesize the leadership theories and models on the basis of literature reviews. The experimental study focuses on NRC (Nokia Research Center) and IBM (IBM India Pvt. Ltd.), which is representative in mobile and IT fields respectively. By conducting interview and survey as the methodologies, this study will explore how VOs and VTs are operated as well as how to improve the effectiveness of e-leadership.

2. RESEARCH METHODOLOGY

This experimental study aims to investigate VT formation, address the challenges associated with virtual environment, and improve the effectiveness of e-leadership. Focusing on NRC and IBM we conducted the experimental research by using interview and survey methodology to examine the current leadership conditions and elicit relevant implications and propositions.

2.1 Case Study: NRC and IBM

The two firms involved in this case study are NRC and IBM, which are representative in mobile and information technology fields respectively. This section briefly introduces each firm's background information and virtual collaboration status under consents by NRC and IBM.

2.1.1 NRC

NRC, founded in 1986, is Nokia's corporate research unit of about 700 employees. Its mission is to renew Nokia through strategic and long-term research, while its vision is to become the global leader of open innovation for human mobility systems of the fused physical and digital world, giving birth to the growth of businesses for Nokia. Today, NRC is very much a living organization, always ready to renew itself and blaze new trails. The organization reflects dual approach to innovation to seek core technology breakthroughs and identify new business opportunities through exploratory systems research.

NRC cooperates with many leading academic institutions and other technology companies in many research projects. NRC works in open innovation mode and has built network of leading universities including MIT in USA, Stanford University in USA, Tsinghua University in China, Cambridge University in UK, Tampere University in Finland, Helsinki University in Finland, and EPFL and ETHZ in Switzerland.

Furthermore, NRC has built worldwide networks with R&D (Research and Development) centers in 10 countries to facilitate global collaborations. Morph and 100 cars project are the recent examples of NRC's cooperation projects. The Morph concept was conceived out of a scientific partnership between NRC and the Cambridge Nanoscience centre for the Museum of Modern Art in New York; 100 cars project was under the collaboration of NRC and UC Berkeley, aiming to provide real-time traffic information based on speed and location data from GPS-enabled mobile devices carried by motorists.

2.1.2 IBM

IBM is the only IT company in the world and also in India that offers end-to-end solutions to customers from hardware to software, services and consulting. IBM has been present in India since 1992 (re-entry, after an exit in the 1970s). Since inception, IBM in India has expanded its operations considerably with regional headquarters in Bangalore and offices in 14 cities including regional offices in New Delhi, Mumbai, Kolkata and Chennai. Today, the company has established itself as one of the leaders in the Indian Information Technology (IT) Industry.

IBM Global Services (IGS) is the world's and also India's largest information technology services and consulting provider. IGS provides the entire spectrum of customers' e-business needs—from the business transformation and industry expertise of IBM Business Consulting Services to hosting, infrastructure, technology design and training services. IGS delivers integrated, flexible and resilient processes—across companies and through business partners—that enable customers to maximize the opportunities of an on-demand business environment.

2.2 Methodology

The experimental study was conducted using interview as the main methodology and survey as the minor. The leadership framework in theory part was used as a basis for interview and survey question constructions. All the interview questions and questionnaires were pre-tested with a small group of participants who were not used in the final analysis. After some basic analysis of the reliability of each preliminary scale, all instruments were correspondingly modified and then used to elicit opinion or capture data in experimental study.

2.2.1 Participants

Those individuals who participated in experimental study were both male and female employees, and ranged in age from their 20s to late 40s. Different educational and socio-economic background was represented, from workers with bachelor's degree to those with Ph.D. diploma. In addition, these participants came from a variety of professional settings including research, product development, sales, marketing, recruiting, and management consulting with different levels in organizations from the workers up to a company president. These participants were anonymous in the sense that records of their identities were not kept and identifying information was removed from their data.

2.2.2 Procedure

Interview participants were scheduled for an interview time, and met the interviewer in a private office or small meeting room. Each participant received a written copy of the interview questions as well as a verbal explanation of the objectives of this study prior to the interview session. The interview lasted approximately 30 minutes on average. The interview questions were designed to focus participants on e-leadership challenges, strategies, and effectiveness. The interview format consisted of four basic sections, which were: technology, communication, trust and leadership style, and closure. Grounded on these aspects, interview participants were requested to describe their observations and perceptions of e-leadership challenges and strategies associated with the virtual context.

In order to complementarily examine the current situation of e-leadership, two questionnaires were also designed, one of which is designed for e-leaders whereas the other is for followers. Questionnaire participants were asked to complete either of these two questionnaires conforming to their role in the company. The ensuing sections will synthesize the research data (including interview and survey) elicited from NRC and IBM. Furthermore, grounded on these data, the current leadership conditions will be analyzed and assessed.

3. E-LEADERSHIP PERFORMANCE AND STRATEGIES

The constant parade of ICT development has unfolded a new context for leadership, referring to e-leadership or virtual leadership. E-leadership is considered extremely crucial to organizational performance, while e-leaders play pivotal roles in modeling effective teamwork and setting ground rules for team members to engage in successful team processes.

As much as we have learned about leadership in general, we start to consider particularly how to build and sustain e-leadership in virtual context where trust is difficult to build, influence is hard to articulate, and communication is often ambiguous. Among a range of e-leadership challenges inherent to the dispersed and often impersonal nature, technology, communication, cultural differences, trust, and logistics are the typical issues. Without addressing these challenges before moving forward, e-leadership and VOs can be problematic and fragile.

This field-based study was undertaken to assess the current e-leadership performance in NRC and IBM from four perspectives: technology, communication, trust, and leadership style. Grounded on the e-leaders' descriptions of their VT experiences, each area is discussed in details and followed by a set of implications and related strategies that outline specific critical success factors for effective e-leadership.

3.1 Technology

The innovative technology allows transmission of any information across vast distances in little time and at little expense, thus leading traditional collaboration into the virtual context. However, the technology tools at the disposal of VTs hamper leaders from addressing the difficulties of coordination, thus in turn posing new requirements on e-leaders who aim at creating a cohesive and consistent teamwork environment.

3.1.1 Research Analysis

This sub-section aims to practically explore the current conditions of technology utilizations drawing from the interview and survey results in NRC and IBM.

➤ **Monotonous Use of Technology**

In order to examine the current situation of technology utilization, the research participants were requested to rank the first three technology tools they used most frequently and commonly in virtual environment. Our findings reflected that e-mail was so prominent for these VTs that all participants marked it as the most frequently and commonly used technology tool in VT settings. Figure 4 illustrates the first three frequently used technology tools in NRC and IBM. Figure 4. the first three frequently used technology tools in VTs.

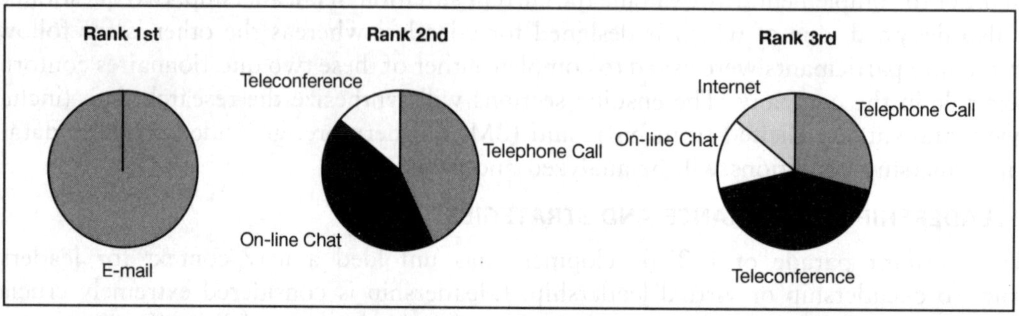

Fig. 4: The first three frequently used technology tools in VTs

According to Figure 4, an overwhelming majority of research participants communicated with their peers by monotonously relying on common information technologies, most of which were e-mail, telephone call, and on-line chat. These lean technology tools were used by e-leaders and team members everyday to exchange routine business information.

On the other hand, team-based communication technologies including group telephone conferences, groupware applications, and video conferences were not often used. Significantly, video conferencing, the very tool that could possibly mitigate the teams' difficulties related to infrequent face-to-face interaction by electronically bringing team members together was used merely once a month by majority of research participants, and even less in some cases.

3.2 Communication

Although effective communication is essential to team performance in both traditional and virtual environments, VTs comparatively are facing a much greater strain on communications as team members endeavor to achieve interaction, mutual understanding, and consensus in the absence of rich face-to-face interaction. The ability to implement effective communication patterns is pivotal to the success of VO and VT functioning.

3.2.1 Research Analysis

This sub-section analyzes the current communication patterns and manners in NRC and IBM from aspects of vision, feedbacks, face-to-face meeting, and time zone diversity.

Vision

One of e-leader's main roles is to articulate the vision of the team's or organizational goals. The creation of a shared vision is an essential manifestation of leadership in knowledge-oriented groups. While there is a significant direct effect of vision on team performance, the indirect effects through vision communication are equally important.

In other words, while a vision affects performance directly, it is more likely to upgrade performance if the vision is thoroughly understood and comprehended by employees. Nevertheless, simply articulating and communicating a well-formulated vision is scarcely.

Feedbacks

From e-leader's perspective, one critical aspect of effective communication is to provide regular and continuous feedbacks to followers throughout the life of the project. Our study observed effective leaders put a high priority on maintaining regular communication and providing valuable advices, while at the same time soliciting opinions from individual team members.

In contrast, it was evident that the absence of continual feedback was considered intolerable by team members and had adverse effects on leadership effectiveness and team performance. Focusing on strategy for providing continual feedbacks, majority of leaders participated in our research had a high degree of awareness of distinguishing negative feedbacks from positive ones by accordingly adopting different communication media. Nevertheless, when e-leaders intended to provide feedbacks in a swift manner particularly in time-driven projects, telephone call became the resort.

Face-to-face Meeting

The previous sections support the notion that ICTs have limitations and may fail to convey the same rich social, emotional, and non-verbal information present in face-to-face settings. Consequently, even those VTs that utilize rich web-based collaboration technologies are inevitably suffering from the lack of face-to-face contact. Obviously, face-to-face interaction is far more effective and efficient than communication through technology platforms. It enables VT members to see facial and body expressions, to hear voice emphasis and inflection, as well as to sense approval and misunderstanding.

According to our research data analysis, 85.7% of the overall participants necessitated the face-to-face meeting in developing virtual relationship. Concretely, among this cluster of participants, about three-fifths claimed face-to-face meetings ought to be arranged as often as possible during the collaboration if budget permits. On the other hand, the rest two-fifths considered physical proximity is only necessary in two particular scenarios: when a VT is at initial set-up phase, or when VT leader and members are not acquainted with one another.

3.2.2 Strategies and Recommendations

Our analysis of VT comments identifies several leadership strategies useful for facilitating effective communications in virtual environments.

(a) Effective team leaders should set clear visions to individual team members.

(b) E-leaders are suggested to provide feedbacks in a frequent and ongoing manner.

(c) E-leaders should seek to establish specific rules of engagement that govern exactly how and when team members should communicate with each other.
(d) The importance of getting to know VT peers is vitally important to subsequent VT communication effectiveness.
(e) E-leaders are suggested to conduct periodic face-to-face meetings either through video conferencing or in actual face-to-face settings, especially during the set-up phase of VT or when they are not acquainted with each other.
(f) In order to schedule a session via synchronous technologies, e-leaders should elaborately negotiate time and availabilities with dispersed members.

3.3 Trust

Ultimately, leadership involves engaging people and directing them toward fulfilling a specific task or achieving a particular goal. At its core, leadership is about the development of relationships (Avolio and Kahai, 2003), wherein trust is the framework upon which any relationship can be built (Moustafa-Leonard, 2007). Without a high degree of trust, the virtual relationship will be extremely fragile and e-leadership is doomed to be eroded.

3.3.1 Research Analysis

Our experimental study mainly focused on trust in VT settings. We divide trust in VTs into three sub-constructs: trust from team members in leader, trust from leader in his/her team members, and trust among team members. The interview participants were requested to identify which trust of the three categories is the most important for team performance. In addition, the interviewees were also asked to describe which leadership style (i.e. transformational or transactional leadership style) they were conducting as well as which one they consider more appropriate and effective for trust building in virtual context.

3.3.2 Strategies and Propositions

(a) Clearly, communication builds trust.
(b) Commitments are necessary and important in sustaining trust.
(c) E-leaders should be constantly aware of trust inside the team, especially trust among team members.
(d) Circumstance dictates which leadership style should be encouraged in VT environment.
(e) E-leaders may consider circumstantially adopting "swift trust" with precaution.

4. CONCLUSION AND PROPOSITIONS

Although certain limitations may impact the ability to generalize the findings of this study, several conclusions are still warranted. First of all, the research was successful not only in determining a number of critical success factors for e-leadership effectiveness but also addressing the relevant strategies. Since the participants came from different departments, companies, and geographic settings, the results were fairly generalized for an exploratory study.

According to the research analyses, e-leader ought to prompt followers connected with his/her vision and value, achieve efficient interaction, establish positive team processes, develop supportive team member relations, and select only those team members who are qualified to do the work. These aspects exhibit strong associations with e-leadership strategy and clearly constitute a comprehensive set of best practices for designing and leading VTs.

E-leaders should be aware that VTs require supplementary relational links between team members because of the lack of physical proximity. A set of specific efforts should be targeted towards high degree of trust and cohesion within VTs. Specifically, e-leader should carefully pre-screen all the conditions such as task complexity and team formation, boundary crossing, organizational policies and resources, and technology at the initiation phase of VT, but also target the appropriate level of relationship ground on his/her personal experience of what degree of proximity with team members would be optimal in order to achieve the objective.

Based on the results of this study, organizations choosing to implement VTs should recognize that VTs differ substantially from traditional co-located teams, such as how a team is formed, how to effectively communicate via ICTs, and how to lead team members towards cohesive collaboration. Evidently, these differences along with e-leadership strategy and working capability in VT settings can be illuminated through diverse training programs. However, most of organizations only concentrate on training managers to improve leadership qualities but despise the significance of improving employees' capabilities of working in the virtual environment. Grounded upon participants' narrative responses from NRC and IBM, only training programs catering for managers were currently explicitly performed ("Inspiring Leader" in NRC; "Academy & Simulation" in IBM). In fact, the followers' capabilities of working under virtual environment were not as simple as being able to use e-mail or on-line chat but covering a wide range of VT aspects such as circumstantially adopting different communication patterns, realizing the culture differences in working styles and manners, and maintaining high degree of trust among team members. Hence, these organizations should focus much more of their efforts on training not only leaders but also followers to improve capability of working in the virtual environment so that VTs' efficiency and effectiveness can be reinforced as a whole.

REFERENCES

Ahuja, M.K. and Carley, K.M., 1998. Network Structure in Virtual Organizations. *JCMC*. [Online]. Available at: http://jcmc.indiana.edu/vol3/issue4/ahuja.html [accessed 30 March 2008].

Aimee, A.C., 2002. Trust and technology in the virtual organization. *SAM Advanced Management Journal*. [Online]. Available at: http://www.allbusiness.com/human-resources/employee-development-employee-ethics/345829-1.html [accessed 1 April 2008].

Asman, M.F. and Essex, P.A., 2001. Electronic monitoring of employees. *The Ohio CPA Journal*. [Online]. 60(1), pp. 25-28. Available at: http://www.accessmylibrary.com/coms2/summary_0286-9174548_ITM [accessed 1 April 2008].

Avolio, B.J. & Kahai, S.S., 2003. Adding the "E" to E-Leadership: How it May Impact Your Leadership. *Organizational Dynamics*. [Online]. 3(4), pp. 325-38. Available at: http://www.sciencedirect.com [accessed 1 April 2008].

Berners-Lee, T., Hendler, J. and Lassila, O., 2001. The Semantic Web. *Scientific American*. [Online]. Available at: http://www-personal.si.umich.edu/~rfrost/courses/SI110/readings/In_Out_and_Beyo nd/Semantic_Web.pdf [accessed 31 March 2008].

Clark, D., 1997. Leadership-Character and Traits. s.n. [Online]. Available at: http://www.nwlink.com/~donclark/leader/leadchr.html [accessed 5 April 2008].

Fiedler, F.E., 1976. *Theory of Leadership Effectiveness*. New York: McGraw-Hill Education.

Gupta, B., Iyer, L.S. and Aronson, J.E., 2000. Knowledge management: practices and challenges. *Industrial Management & Data Systems*. [Online]. 100(1), pp. 17-21. Available at: http://www.emeraldinsight.com [accessed 31 March 2008].

Howell, J.P. and Costley, D.L., 2001. *Understanding Behaviors for Effective Leadership*. Upper Saddle River: Prentice-Hall.

Kotter, J.P., 1990. *A Force for Change How Leadership Differs from Management*. New York: Free Press.

Lau, F., Sarker, S. and Sahay, S., 2000. On managing virtual teams. *Healthcare Information Management Communications* Canada. 14(2), pp. 46-53.

Robbins, S., 1974. *Managing Organizational Conflict*. Englewood Cliffs, NJ: Prentice Hall.

CHAPTER 8

EFFECT OF ORGANIZATIONS OBTAINED HR SHARED SERVICES—A SELECTIVE STUDY

–Akondi Srikanth

ABSTRACT

This paper helps in fulfilling the objective of understanding the effect of HR shared services in the selective four organizations specifically Kellogg, Air France, Rolls Royce and Renault Nissan under selective three industries, namely cereals, transport and automobiles using case study approach under exploratory research design. Along with this, major critical success factors for shared services and HR shared services were identified by several studies as clear vision and governance, strong leadership, identification of clear-cut processes, sufficient investment, technology, management support, stakeholders concern and key performance indicators. The findings of the study resulted in reduction of employee inquiries, productivity raised by 30%, 60-70% fall in first call resolution, increased efficiency and 20% staff productivity, 80% increase in customer satisfaction and better provision of administrative tasks. This paper provides an understanding about shared services for private organizations, thinking about the pros and cons in implementing shared services concept. The study has uncovered the governments' implementation of shared services concept and it is confined to the private organizations under above-mentioned industries along with its results and also to the single function in-house form of shared service implementations, i.e Human Resources (HR), acts as a major limitation provides a path for the future scope of research.

INTRODUCTION

In the recent global shared services survey conducted by Delloite (2011 Global Shared Services Survey Results 2011), the responses from 270 include majorly 54% of manufacturing and 47% of consumer product segments. The maximum of 29% of shared service centres are in USA/Canada and only 6% of shared service centres are covered in India as observed from the collected data of 718 shared service centres under the survey. From the survey, it was also revealed that the 93% of organizations were obtaining shared services in finance and 60% in HR shared services. This paper is confined to the study of four organizations undergone HR shared service centres implementation, namely Kellogg, Air France, Rolls Royce and Renault Nissan covering three industries including cereals, transport and automobiles respectively. The study has uncovered the government's implementation of shared services concept and it is confined to the private organizations under above-mentioned industries and the results are confined to those industries only and also to the single function in-house form of shared service implementations, i.e Human Resources (HR), acts as a major limitation of the study. The scope of this paper had excluded the other four forms of five shared services, namely multi-function in-house, co-opt model, joint venture model and outsourcing model, left for future research (Goodman and Haigh, 2009). This paper also discusses certain most important critical success factors for the successful implementation of HR shared service centres in the organizations. The objectives of the study are

(i) To examine the effect of HR shared services implemented by chosen organizations.
(ii) To explore the most important critical success factors for the successful implementation of shared services and HR shared services by the organizations.

The next section deals with the literature helps in strengthening the basics of the shared services and HR shared services. The third and fourth sections deal with the research methodology and results respectively followed by discussion and conclusion in the fifth section. Let's move to the next section, literature review.

LITERATURE REVIEW

(i) Shared Services Concept

One of the reports has discussed that the division of business processes as core business processes, non-core key business processes and non-core non-key business processes (Shared service centres—Enabling you business for success, 2011). The non-core key business process, i.e shared services includes finance, customer services, human resources, procurement/supply chain and information technology.

(a) *Definition*

The concept of shared service(s) is an operational philosophy that fundamentally involves centralizing functions those are usually performed in separate divisions or locations. The shared services are naturally back office functions including finance, purchasing, inventory, payroll, Human Resources (HR) and Information Technology (Goodman and Haigh, 2009). Simply, the shared services can be referred as a consolidation and sharing of services by different units or locations within an organization. Shared services are typically driven in the aspiration of achieving economies of scale, enhancing consistency or standardization across the organization, to improve quality, leverage technology investments, and manage labour costs within certain functions to provide greater value to the business (Kroll and Carpenter, 2008). Shared service is a service that provides corporate change through the convergence and streamlining of processes within multiple organizations or group companies (Kimura, 2007).

(b) *Operating Models of Shared Services*

There are five forms of shared services as mentioned above from which joint venture model or outsourcing model can further be classified into four target operating models, namely captive, shared captive, outsourced and hybrid. In captive model, the organization owns facility and employees whereas third party assists and advice them. Under shared captive model, the facilities, employees and management activities are shared among the organization and third party. In the third model of outsourcing, third party fully owns facility, employees and manages all. The last model hybrid is a mixed composition of any of the other three models.

(c) *Location Variations*

When the discussion of location variations comes to the picture, four variations are usually studied. They are onsite, on-shore, near-shore and off-shore. In onsite, work is carried out on the organizations' premises whereas in on-shore work is carried out in any location within the country. Under the near-shore, the work is carried out of the country but nearer to it while in off-shore, work is carried out of the country in any part of the world (Goodman and Haigh, 2009). There are so many multinational shared service providers, namely Accenture, Unisys, IBM, EDS and others help organizations for leveraging benefits of the concept. From the studies, it was also identified that nine out of ten organizations have applied shared services concept (Fershet et al., 2011).

In one of the surveys conducted by A Beam Consulting, only 65 companies responded out of 600 companies surveyed. Out of these, 71% of companies already implemented shared services and about 12% are planning for implementation. Only 17% of organization decided not to implement shared services considering the unsatisfactory know-how and their firm's size (45% of overall 17%), implementation risk and external outsourcing (55%) as the identified reasons behind by them. Overall 93%, 67% and 54% of 65 companies have adopted shared services for their cost reduction, improving product quality and for aggregation of process know-how. The survey resulted that 57%, 64% and 66% of companies were almost satisfied with their implementations respectively, towards achieving their objectives. Overall results showed that 57% of the companies informed that they are satisfactory by implementing shared service centers. In 2003, Shared services Business Process Outsourcing Association (SBPOA) conducted worldwide survey on shared services including 188 companies, where it was found that 41% were American's, 36% were Europeans, 10% were Asian's and the rest were others implemented shared services (Kimura, 2007). Some of the early implementers of shared services were Electronic Data systems (EDS), Essar (Implemented by Capgemini), Shell (6 SSCs), Royal Philips Electronics (3 SSCs), American Express, British Airways, HP, Citigroup, Dell, JP Morgan, AT&T, Sykes, ITEL, Convergys, GE, HBSC and so on.

(ii) HR Shared Services-concept

When it comes to the discussion of the second most important function in shared services, it was observed as Human Resources as per the Deloitte consulting survey, 2011. Human Resources Shared Services (HRSS) can be regarded as internal outsourcing providing well defined services for internal customers that consist of more than one unit (Cooke, 2006). The basic classification of HR shared services in to administrative, operational and strategic segments (HR Shared Services, 2006).

The major activities of HR shared services function includes payroll changes, employee records administration, relocation services, recruitment administration, benefits administration, company car provision, pension administration, employee welfare support, training administration, absence monitoring and management information (Reilly, 2010). Some other studies also relieved that learning, staffing and global services are also major activities of HRSS (HR Shared Services, 2006).

There are four reasons identified by the studies in setting up HR shared services. The first reason is to become a part of wider business change, second is to achieve a greater structural facility, third and fourth are to improve organizational learning across organizational boundaries and to be more strategic. The increasing advanced call center technologies enabled HR shared services adoption by large number of firms like Barclyas, Motorola, Shell, Compaq, Deutsche Bank, Alied signal Inc. etc. The most common delivery models include e-HR and HR shared service centers (Cooke, 2006).

The studies had recommended a multi-tier approach for organizations in implementing HR shared services including three tiers, namely Tier 0, Tier 1 and Tier 2, where Tier 0 meant for employees self-service, Tier 1 sends tickets to shared services help desk and Tier 2 helps in solving those queries unanswered by Tier 1 by the experts support. The Senior Vice-president of Enwisen, a HRSS provider, intimated that the multi-tier approach resulted very well by stating two examples, one company had 33,000 portal hits per month with 80% calls resolved on first call saved USD 2,75,000 and in the other company 10,000-14,000 hits per month on portal where 93% of calls resolved on first call (Abbatiello, 2009). The famous service delivery model was given by US academic, Dave Ulrich that includes three elements, namely shared services those deal with administrative tasks, centers of expertise and business partners called Ulrich model (Reilly, 2010).

There are several advantages and disadvantages obtained by organizations in implementing HR shared services. The major advantages are lower costs, more efficient resourcing, better quality of service, customer satisfaction ratings increased, greater transparency of costs, improves match between customer expectations and service delivery, ease of access, career development, cross-group learning and better management of information where neglecting the significance of the knowledge of users, boundary management issues, absence of effective accountability, communication difficulties, project misconceptualization and allocation of resources are some of the major disadvantages (Reilly, 2000). There are several organizations those got benefited by implementing HR shared services. Naming a few are Bayer AG, Henkel of America Inc., Monsanto Co., Swisscom Group, Unilever, Airfrance, Kellogg, Rolls Royce, Renault-Nissan, Thales UK, RATP, Cuna Mutual Group, BP and Whirlpool. This paper will discuss in detail four cases among these organizations as mentioned in the introduction. Let us understand the research methodology involved in this paper.

RESEARCH METHODOLOGY

In this paper, the methodology applied is exploratory research method, i.e case study. Researchers can use case study methodology for many purposes such as to *explore* new areas and issues, to *describe* a process or the effects of an event, especially when such events influence many different parties and to *explain* a complex phenomenon (Kohn, 1997). Four organizations are considered for the study those went for HR shared service centres implementation, namely Kellogg, Air France, Rolls Royce and Renault Nissan covering three industries including cereals, transport and automobiles respectively. Let us know the effect of HR shared services implemented by chosen organizations in the next section.

RESULTS

A. Cases Analysis

The four cases are in detail discussed below.

Case I

Name of the Company	: Kellogg
Year of Establishment	: 1906
Present Location	: Battle Creek, Michigan
Industry	: Cereals and convenience foods; convenience foods include cookies, crackers, toaster pastries, cereal bars, fruit flavoured snacks, frozen wafers and vegetarian foods.
Spread	: Production facilities in 18 countries and marketing facilities in 180 countries.
Employee Workforce	: 31,000
Challenges Before	: To harmonize HR policies and processes across the company. Overcome the problem of decentralization and inefficient data entries by employees. Self-service portal creation for better employee support for reducing their access time.
Solution Provided	: Self-service portal, call center operated in four languages—English, Spanish, Portuguese and French Canadian.
Delivery Model	: Enwisen's Saas solution—online HR knowledge base using multi-tier approach
Duration of Implementation	: 13 months
Critical Success Factors (CSF)	: Change Management, Stakeholder's communication, Auditing Information availability.
Outcome (Effect)	: Attended 12000 calls, 3000 Manager Self-Service (MSS) transactions, 1700 Employee Self-Service (ESS) transactions per month, less than 30 seconds to answer, more than 60%-70% first call resolution, 13% reduction in staff time on first call resolution, 80% of customers were satisfied.

Case II

Name of the Company	: Air France
Year of Establishment	: 1933
Present Location	: Paris, France
Industry	: Transport airline
Spread	: 272 destinations (as on mid-2012)
Employee Workforce	: 1,32,000
Challenges Before	: To manage increased volume of inquiries due to merger with Dutch airline. To establish global shared service centers for

		managing its Roissy and Orly airports in France to manage request load of 34,000 employees.
Solution Provided	:	Neocase HR, provided two identical HRSS at Roissy and Orly.
Delivery Model	:	Highly secured Saas (Software as a service)
Period of Implementation	:	Few weeks
Outcome (Effect)	:	30% reduction in inbound employee requests, increased efficiency and staff productivity up to 20%, 40% increase in employee satisfaction.

Case III

Name of the Company	:	Rolls Royce
Year of Establishment	:	1904
Present Location	:	United Kingdom
Industry	:	Automobile manufacturer
Spread	:	50 countries
Employee Workforce	:	39,000
Challenges Before	:	Volatile oil prices, currency exchange challenges and then a global economic crisis created a challenging backdrop for the Rolls-Royce HR Function. To manage all HR processes like benefits, rewards, learning, pension and employee data administration (named a few).
Solution Provided	:	HR Shared Service in support for SAP ERP
Delivery Model	:	Ulrich HR model (Three elements—Shared services, Centers of Excellence Business Partners)
Critical Success Factors (CSF)	:	Change management
Year of Implementation	:	2007
Outcome (Effect)	:	Providing services to 22000 employees at UK (first HRSSC). In total five HRSSC supporting around 38700 personnel. Supporting 1,20,000 personnel under pension administration dealing with 1500 internal and external vacancies/year. Reduced to six recruitment agencies from 280 agencies. Supporting the corporate circulars and learning management HRIS—Human Resources Information Systems Support. Supporting all benefits, rewards, employee data administration along with global mobile services.

Case IV

Name of the Company	:	Renault-Nissan Alliance
Year of Establishment	:	1999
Present Location	:	Paris, France
Industry	:	Automobile manufacturer.

Spread	:	118 countries
Employee Workforce	:	1,30,000
Challenges Before	:	To establish an HRSSC for increasing HR operational efficiency and employee satisfaction and to provide a manager-employee rapidly adaptive solution. To increase productivity at least up to 30%, reports of daily performance, queue management and meeting strategic objectives.
Solution Provided	:	Neocase Self service portal Neocase Knowledge base and Neocase HR
Delivery Model	:	Saas (Software as a service) Delivery model
Period of Implementation	:	50 days
Outcome (Effect)	:	Productivity raised over 30% and Reduction of inbound inquiries, employee and manager satisfaction by 40%

B. Critical Success Factors (CSFs)

(i) *Critical Success Factors for Shared Services*

The past studies have found several CSFs for shared services. Findings from the 2010 conference sponsored by MIDAS gave seven factors. They are

1. Ensure the content for the shared services journey
2. Get the right sponsor and shared service center director.
3. Developing a compelling vision
4. Build a staged TOM and have clarity about how it will be achieved.
5. Drive a positive culture and equilibrium between customer service, quality and efficiency.
6. Manage stakeholders well.
7. Apply governance appropriately.

Some other studies reveal six factors and seven factors combinely identified as follows (Rethore, 2009; shared services in social housing 2006).

1. Clear, strong leadership and right decisions
2. Shared understanding
3. End-to-end processes management
4. Clear governance
5. Early identification of barriers
6. Sufficient investment
7. Tangible benefits
8. Complexity reduction.

The other critical success factors identified are strong project management skills, senior-level support, effective communication, strong change management and a phased approach to implementation (Burns and Yeaton, 2008).

(ii) *Critical Success Factors for HR Shared Services*

The critical success factors are the one required for the successful implementation of HR shared services. Dovetail software has provided five areas that are often overlooked but critical to your HR SSC success. They are processes, roles, technology, improvement and measures.

1. Standardizing common HR processes.
2. Redefining roles, responsibilities and performance goals for professionals.
3. Right technology to manage employees effectively.
4. Measuring Key Performance Indicators (KPIs) such as HR Service Level Agreement first call resolution rates, response times, time to resolution and the number of incoming requests being resolved by HR SSC advisors.
5. Took the support of KPIs to improve your service delivery model.

For the successful implementation of HR shared services, the above-mentioned factors are critical.

DISCUSSION AND CONCLUSION

From the results, it is revealed that the maximum number of companies had applied shared services and achieved successful results in reducing cost and better managing administrative tasks. But certain studies revealed that for further better management of shared services implementation, critical success factors should be considered whether it may come under private or public sector. The clear-cut vision, strong leadership, clear governance, management support, processes identification, KPI, technology are major CSFs to be considered. Finally, it can be concluded that organizations can implement shared services happily under the preview of CSFs.

REFERENCES

2011 Global Shared Services Survey Results. Survey, Deloitte consulting LLP, 2011.

7 critical success factors to setting up shared services. MIDAS, 2010.

Abbatiello, Christine. *HR Shared services: Best practices, Business model and technology*. Human capital Institute, 2009.

Burns, Trimothy J., and Karthryn G. Yeaton. *Success factors for implementing shared services in Government*. IBM center for Business of government, 2008.

Cooke, F.L. "Modeling an HR Shared Services Center: Experience of an MNC in the United Kingdom." *Human Resource Management*, 2006: 211-27.

Fershet, Phil, Tony Filippone, Charles Aird, and Derek Sappenfield. *THE EVOLUTION OF GLOBAL BUSINESS SERVICES: Enhancing the benefits of shared services and outsourcing*. HFS Research, 2011.

Goodman, Hannah, and Michael Haigh. *Stick or Twist? Is shared services right for my buisness?* Tata Consulting Services Limited, 2009.

HR Shared Services. Corporate Leadership Board, 2006.

Judd, Mark. *Changing the wheels while the wagon is rolling*. Shared services and outsourcing network, 2010.

Kimura, Kimiaki. *Success factors in Japanese shared service*. A Beam Consulting, 2007.

Kroll, Mercer Marsh, and Guy Carpenter. *Finding place on the HR shared services continuum*. MERCER, 2008.

Neocase software. http://www.neocasesoftware.com/images/files/Air%20France%20Success%20Story.pdf (accessed August 15.08.2012).

Neocase software. http://www.neocasesoftware.com/images/files/success_stories/Renault_Casestudy.pdf (accessed August 16, 2012).

Reilly, P. *HR shared services and the Realignment of HR*. The Institute for the Employement Studies, 2000.

Reilly, Peter. *Setting up HR Shared services in Local government*. Improvement and Development Agency, 2010.

Rethore, Tara J. *Implementing shared services: Lessons learned*. M. Beacon Enterprises, 2009.

Saba, Jayson. *Building the case for HR shared services*. Aberdeen Group, 2011.

Shared service centres—Enabling you business for success. Ernst and Young, 2011.

Shared services in social housing. Northern Housing Consortium, 2006.

CHAPTER 9 MIGRATION, SETTLEMENT AND HUMAN RESOURCE MANAGEMENT: A STUDY OF INDIAN DIASPORA IN INDONESIA

–*Badruddin*

ABSTRACT

In South East Asia, Indonesia has been the among the most popular destination for overseas Indians with small minority ethnic group only 0.10% of local population, roughly twenty times less than that of Chinese and Thai Diaspora. Despite small size, Indians played a leading role in the reformation of Indonesia's social economy into an organized segment. Indians in corporate and social sectors increasingly reflect their ability and intelligence. Special database networks pertain to Indian community has been established to provide ready-made information about NGOs, educational and technical institutions, research centers, individual and professional bodies and their demographic representation. India, a generic supplier of brains and skills to Indonesia, is intensifying greater prominence to promote bilateral dialogues. Indians are mushrooming with the help of study centers, cultural associations, co-religious sentiments, social affinity, innovation, key business strategy and philanthropic activities. Contemporary, Indonesian Indians encompasses different ecological, social, economic and educational issues to see local economy at the international levels, thanks to large number of brains from Indians who have initiated number of project with support of corporate sectors and social networking. Key objective of this paper is to analysis role of MNCs with direct activities, supply investments and identification of new potential bottlenecks in the implementation of human resource data as crucial determinants. Bollywood films, festivals, multi channel TV programmes, cuisine, archival and modern photographs enjoy considerable popularity in corporate as well as social fields in Indonesian economy. Several studies and observations do indicate that Indians comparatively feel more secure in due to cohabitation and long cultural relations and cooperative entrepreneurship. Hence, there are demands and expectations from Indian Diaspora for dual citizenship, liberalization of venture capital, flexibility on the execution of philanthropic project, simplification of corporate tax clearance, transparency at immigration counters and assistance in legal and property matters. Indians have made sacrifices both to their host countries and internationally in areas as diverse in literature, popular culture, economy, sports and political life. Key findings: values-based social economy, higher growth and return, management quality and prospective opportunities have immense potentiality between India and Indonesia to promote an organized corporate social responsibility within the transnational frameworks.

Background: History and Geo Economic Settings

Migration is a dynamic phenomenon that has been taking place for thousands of years. When individuals can no longer acquire adequate resources to sustain the livings with their locals, they must migrate to the destination where resources are available for sustainability. India, the largest and second most populated country in the world, next to China, is undergoing with serious domestic problems. It is well-known fact that the Indians, throughout the ages, have been migrating to several parts of the world and forming the means of their own settlements. But the dawn of 21st century entered into a new phase of Information Communication Technology (ICT) which made extensive networking to maintain strong relations with the homeland *Hindustan* besides their Diaspora counterparts worldwide. Indians Diaspora offers a unique example probably nowhere in the world. It is truly said that the sun never set as Indians are found all over the world with beautiful combinations. South East Asia (Indonesia, Malaysia, Thailand, Myanmar and Singapore) always remains the favorite destination of Indians.[1]

Indonesia, officially Republic of Indonesia, formerly Netherlands Indies Archipelago countries, located off the coast of mainland of South East Asia. With highest number of 13670 islands in the world and more than 7,000 uninhabited and natural, it offers a wonderful satellite image. Among the South East Asian region, it is rare but interesting example with 300 different ethnic group reminds parallel to Indian culture. The official language is *Bhasha Indonesia* while 250 languages and dialects from different groups are also spoken in Indonesia. More than 80% are followers of Islam while Buddhism, Jainism, Christianity and Hinduism are also observed by Chinese, Indians and other non-identified groups.[2]

Historically, Indians in Indonesia are living for over two millennia who made the journey to Indonesia—a name derived from the Latin Indus, meaning "India". Greek *Nesos* (island), in search of economic opportunities find sources of livelihood and success for themselves and their families. For Indians, it has been like home coming because after all, Indonesia is a cultural Godchild of India where Bali island has existence of dozens of historical Hindu Temples. The Hindu literary works known as *Vedas*, the *Mahabharata* and *Ramayana* epics gained popularity and continue to be an integral part of present-day Indonesia. The underlying philosophical concepts introduced since the 5th century by the Brahman priests have had a profound effect in shaping every facet of Indonesian society now and then.[3] The historical traces of Indian culture in Indonesia probably goes back to 4th and 5th centuries when Sanskrit language was used on inscriptions. Dravidians who first arrived in India also made an influenced on the Indonesian islands. Since the 7th century onwards, the Indian scripts were used more and more to write down indigenous languages which by now already contained many loans not only from Sanskrit, but also various Prakrit and Tamil.[4] In addition to that, indigenous Indonesians began to embrace Indian religions, history and culture in particular way of professing Buddhism. But some were followers of Vishnuism and Tantrism—the symbol of Hindu God and Goddess. It is believed that various Indian people also settled in Indonesia, intermixed and assimilated with the local population. The traces of Indian people are also seen in Kalinga, Aryans, Dravidians, Chams and Khmer during 9th century. Many of these groups are also found in Thailand and Malaysia.[5] Later on with the rise of the Islam, the Islamic culture was brought to Indonesia by the Gujarati people from the 11th century onwards that changed the social contours of Indonesia.

Historically, the traces about the arrival of Indians in Indonesia began at the end of 19th century when number of unskilled and semi-skilled labourers of Tamil origin joined Dutch and English plantation in East Sumatra. During sixties and seventies, large number of undocumented Indians entered in Indonesia to work with textile industries and rubber plantation. During eighties, the economic boom brought many changes when Jakarta officials recruited thousands of IT professionals from India. Soon number of related professions like medical science, management, engineering, accounts and law added priorities.

Today, migrations of people from India still occur. In Medan, North Sumatra, there is a large number of Tamil community estimated at 4,000 people. Besides, large number of North Indians from Punjab, Haryana, Uttar Pradesh and West Bengal are also inhibited. Indian Diaspora also includes several thousand Sindhi families who constitute the second wave of Indian immigrants who made Indonesia their home in the first half of the 20th century. The Sindhi community is mainly engaged in trading, commerce and miscellaneous category of local business. Though there are no official figures, it is estimated that there are around 25,000 PIOs/NRIs living in Indonesia, of whom the Indian expatriate community registered with the Embassy and the Consulate in Medan numbers around 5,000. Demographically, another figure of Indian Indonesians stand 1,09,000 by the end of January 2012.[6] The modern aspect of the relationship between the two countries grew out of their respective struggles for independence and through personal friendship between the leaders of the new nations—Sukarno, Mohammad Hatta, Sutan Sjahrir and Jawaharlal Nehru. There is no doubt that large number of leader in power often visited Indonesia to promote better understudying between the two countries. During her 10-day visit to Southeast Asia on 24 November 2008, the then India's President Pratibha Patil said "Today, India and Indonesia share a common commitment to democracy, pluralism and unity in diversity and at the same time face similar challenges and opportunities".[7] For no reason, Indonesia continues to be a popular human resource centre for large number of migrants from India who contribute sizeable growth to Indonesian economy.

India-Indonesia: Contemporary Trade and Economic Relations

The inflow of major Indian investments opportunities in Indonesia started in 1970s. It drew a fresh communication of Indian investors and management consultants. The group of entrepreneurs and business professionals further expanded over the past two and half decades, that include engineers, consultants, chartered accountants, bankers, catering technology, English teachers, taxi drivers, hotel owners, and large number of miscellaneous professionals. During eighties just at the initial phase of globalization, the economic boom brought many changes when Jakarta officials recruited thousands of IT professionals, nurses, civil contractors, media personnel and teachers from India. Soon number of diverse professions like medical science, biotechnology, management, engineering, accounts and catering business added priorities. The economic crisis in 1997 resulted into a severe blow to Indian expatriates in Indonesia. Now there is a constant competition of entrepreneurs and Indian companies setting up plants and offices in Indonesian cities. India's 'Look East' Policy and expansion of financial deregulation in recent years have led to a significant upsurge in the economic dimension of the relationship leading to mutually beneficial bilateral trade agreements and a high level of cooperation. The recent global financial crisis has further put a spotlight on the tremendous inherent potential between India and Indonesia. These growing economic powerhouses are being variously clubbed together. New areas of cooperation are being added and there is a continued renewed entrepreneurial effort by businessmen of both countries to capitalize on human resource developments. The new Indian migrant to Indonesia is no longer ethno-centric but opportunistic and individualistic, investing in the shared bilateral dream. The sense of the local ethnic Indian Indonesian too has changed from a rigid network to a more flexible and social community due to increased acceptance and points of interaction. There is also a focus on community development and philanthropy, with a genuine feeling of oneness.[8]

In order to spur growth and attract investment, the Republic of Indonesia organized the Indonesia Infrastructure 2006 from 1-3 November 2006 at Jakarta with the agenda titled "A World Forum—A National Priority". This was a second conference and exhibition of its kind. The first one titled "Indonesia Infrastructure Summit 2005" was held in January of that year. India was conspicuous by its absence in the first Summit. However, in the second event, Indian participation was quite encouraging. Four companies, namely BHEL, TCS, Punj Lloyd and ESSAR exhibited in Indonesia Infrastructure 2006 and many more such as ICICI, IDFC, NTPC, etc. were present in the conference with support of India. There have been continuous efforts to promote entrepreneurial abilities through exhibitions, contact programme, conferences and workshops for prospective human resource management practice between India and Indonesia.

Broad Framework of Economic Agreements

Trade relations between India and Indonesia were formalized under a Trade Agreement signed in June 1978 committing both countries to take all appropriate measures to facilitate, strengthen and diversify bilateral trade. Periodic discussions have taken place at the Ministerial and official levels to strengthen economic and commercial ties within the framework of this agreement. JBC/business level meetings have also been convened periodically, particularly in conjunction with high level visits. However, no forum for regular talks over a range of cooperative issues with Indonesia existed during the Soeharto years and only a bilateral Agreement on Avoidance of Double Taxation between the two countries was concluded in January 1986.

An Agreement for the Promotion and Protection of Investments, which was signed in February 1999, came into force in January 2004. The first ever India-Indonesia Joint Commission Meeting (JCM) was held in Yogyakarta in September 2003. Apart from taking major decisions to promote bilateral economic and commercial relations in various fields, the JCM decided to constitute an "India-Indonesia Expert Working Group" with the specific mandate of reporting to the JCM with concrete recommendations for enhancing and diversifying bilateral trade, economic and investment relations. This Expert Working Group held its first meeting in New Delhi on 24 February 2005. The Second Meeting of JCM was held in New Delhi on 1 March 2005. Specific areas for enhancement of bilateral trade and economic relations were identified. The Third JCM was held in Jakarta from 16-19 June 2007 in which a comprehensive "Plan of Action" in all areas including cooperation in economic, trade, industrial and infrastructure, financial and investment sectors was agreed upon. Opening remarks by External Affairs Minister at the Joint Media Interaction during the visit of Foreign Minister of Indonesia to India on 27 July 2012 are the long-lasting agreed principles between the two countries. India and Indonesia enjoy an excellent relationship which rests on the solid foundation of historical and cultural linkages.[9]

Bilateral Relations

Indonesia is our second largest export market in ASEAN (after Singapore) and one of India's major trading partners in the region. The recovery of the Indonesian economy after the Asian financial crisis coupled with political change gave a fresh lease of life to our economic relations. Dr. Manmohan's visit to Indonesia in April 2005 for Asian-African Summit soon followed by Indonesian President Megawati Sukarnoputri to India in November 2005 acted as a catalyst in enhancing our bilateral trade. During 2004, the bilateral trade expanded by 36% to reach US$ 3.27 billion and got a further boost of 20.90% in 2005 to reach US$ 3.93 billion. The growth rate has been sustained in the year 2006 by a quantum jump of 22.08% which has brought the two-way trade to US$ 4.798 billion. In 2007, bilateral trade reached US$ 6.55 billion or an increase 36.6% from the previous year. However, there remains vast untapped potential for future growth. The net balance of trade is in favour of Indonesia, as India is Indonesia's largest buyer of Crude Palm Oil (CPO) and an importer of its mining (particularly coal and copper ore), petroleum, rubber, pulp and paper and textile products. India exports refined petroleum products, hydrocarbons and its derivatives, animal feeds, iron and steel products, cotton, copper and dyes and chemicals to Indonesia.

Bilateral trade during from January to December 2008 rose by 53.5% to reach US$ 10 billion as compared to the same period in 2007. India's overall exports registered an increase of 80% to reach US$ 2.9 billion. India's leading exports include petroleum products (refined), hydrocarbons and derivatives, animal feed and Telecommunication equipment and parts. India's imports have registered phenomenal increase of 45% that has touched to US$ 7.1 billion. India's leading imports include vegetable oils and coal. Bilateral trade was down by 12.8% during Jan-Mar 2009 as compared to the same period in 2008 due to some economic upheavals. There has been a steady increase in the number of persons traveling to India from Indonesia and also from India to Indonesia. Regarding travel from Indonesia to India, Indian Embassy issued 8,038 visas to Indonesians in 2004, 8227 in 2005 and 8797 in 2006, which reflects a steady increase of 2.35% and 6.92% respectively. Likewise, the total number of business travelers from Indonesia to India in the last five years has been 2,672 in 2004, 3,409 in 2005, 4103 in 2006, 4889 in 2007 and 5345 in 2008. This reflects an increasing trend of people-to-people contact between the two countries with many more Indonesians visiting India than in the past. The 'visa-on-arrival' facility extended by the Indonesian Government to India in August 2005 has also given a fillip to easier travel from India to Indonesia. In December 2010, another agreement was signed to promote 'Tourism Industry' between both partners. In short, Indo-Indonesia relations have been based on cordial agreements for peace, prosperity and mutual agreement based on *'Panchasheel'* doctrine of Nehru.

Philanthropic Activities

Philanthropic activities may often be referred as social welfare service rendered by the philanthropist in the form of donations, establishment of trusts, charities and social services. India has been a leading case in several streams. Presently, 55,000 Indian origin, most of them concentrated at North Sumatra (Medan) and in the Javanese cities of Jakarta, Surabaya and

Bandung have entered in various professions. Soon the socio-cultural and economic links were maintained with India. Bollywoood films, theatres, yoga, dance and Tabla promoted by Indians are liked by the Indonesians. The Economic Association of Indonesia and India is the step forward to promote bilateral relations. While Sindhi association so-called Gandhi Seva Lok and Gandhi Memorial International School and Jawaharlal Nehru Indian Cultural Centre at Jakarta are actively coordinating with locals. Jakarta is also famous for Indians bazaar so-called Pasar Bharu. There are number of gurudwaras, churches, temples, and other religious places in different parts of Indonesia. There have also been notable examples of Indians for their philanthropic activities that broadly included in Table 1.

Table 1: Indian Philanthropy in Indonesia (Selected Ones only)

Sl. No.	*Philanthropist*	*Contributions/Biography*
1.	Michelle Alicia Saram	Actress and model, born to a Chinese Indonesian mother and Indian Indonesian father.
2.	The Punjabi Brothers H.S. Dillon, and Gurnam Singh	Indonesian cineaste and media tycoons.
3.	The Azhari sisters (Ayu Azhari and Sara Azhari)	Media Personnel and Theatre Actress
4.	Gurnam Singh	Indonesian athlete who won three gold medals in the 1962 Asian Games in Athletics.
5.	H.S. Dillon	Prominent figure in Indonesian politics
6.	Prakash Lohia	Prominent Billionaire

Source: http://en.wikipedia.org/wiki/Indian_Indonesians

Cultural and Political Status: A Door to Corporate Social Responsibility

Indian community in Indonesia have maintained a vibrant and dynamic socio-cultural life within the framework of its numerous organizations and association. There are a number of social, cultural and political organizations. The prominent ones are Indonesian Association of Indian University Graduates (IAIUG), Global Organization of People of Indian Origin (GOPIO), Society of Medical Graduates of India and Indonesia (SOMGRII). University of Jakarta, has maintained a Department of South Asian Studies which focus extensive on Indian language, culture, dance, music.

There are dozens of school and independent NGOs maintained by Indians, mainly Tamilians. Prominent ones are Temple of Fine Arts, Sutra Dance Theatre, Shektra Dance Group, and Tanji Kamla Dance Group. Besides, two Indian expertise associations: Bharat Club and Expatriate Tooling Family of Indonesia are working successfully. Obviously, close to two million Indians in Indonesia plays a significant role in vote banking that extremely important for various political decisions. Most of these leaders remained on the forefront whenever there ethnic violence erupted in Indonesia against Indians due to racial feelings, nationalist attitude or otherwise and are working with support of diverse organizations as mentioned in Table 2.

Table 2: Indian Organizations in Indonesia (Selected Ones Only)

Organizations	*Names and Alignments*
Religious Based	1. Geeta Ashram 2. Hindu Samaj 3. Indian Muslim Association 4. Gurudwar Committees 5. Arya Samaj 6. Sri Guru Singh Sabha 7. Namdhari Sangat 8. Indonesia Hindu Sangat
Social and Cultural	1. Indonesia-Bharat Cultural Sanstha 2. Namdhari Sangat of Indonesia 3. Indian Women's Club
Educational/Academic	1. Mahatma Gandhi Memorial School, Jakarta 2. Indian Council for Cultural Relations, Jakarta
Ethnic Based	1. Tamil Cultural Association, Indonesia Tamil Manram, 2. Malayalee Samaj, 3. Thai KannadaBalaga, 4. Bharati Bengali Association 5. Indonesia-Sindhi Association 6. Gujarati Marwari Society 7. South Indian Association (Tamil Based)
Business and Corporate	1. India Trade Promotion Organization (ITPO) 2. India-Indonesia Business Association (IMBA) 3. Asian Network Quality (ANQ) 4. Indonesia Baroda Industries Limited 5. Indo Rama Group 6. Aditya Birla Group 7. Indonesia Board of Investment 8. Bombay Merchant Association 9. Gandhi Seva Loka formerly Economic Association of Indonesia and India (ECAII) 7. Indonesian Chapter of the Institute of Chartered Accountants of India (ICAI).

Note: Information has been collected from diverse sources

Indian Consulate at Jakarta continues to work as channel of communication between the two countries and promote multilateral dialogues. Besides, Indians are also popularizing their talents and profession through Tamil dailies, namely *Tamil Nasiol*. Some TV channels Astro and Mega also play significant role in Indian programmes. Indonesia also welcomes the religious activities of Indians that help the community to cope with the stresses of adjustment in foreign land. Indian community organizes numerous cultural and religious festivals that assist in establishing links with India. Tamil Colander Year is celebrated on 13 and 14 April with great pomp and show. While Christian faith practiced by the Indians is Easter as All Souls Day. There are also mushrooming of temples, gurudwaras and churches. Besides, Hindus festivals like Ugadhi, Thaipusam, Deepavali, Durga Puja, Laxmi Puja, and Sikh festivals like Guru Gobind Singh Jayanti, etc. are celebrated with great pomp and show.

Demands and Expectations from Indians

Indian's relations with Indonesia has to be viewed in the context of overall foreign policy and nature of relations with big powers of the West. However, no relation is complete without understating the corporate social set up of Indians who settled in the region. The level of expectation from Indians on the issues concerning the Indian community particularly in Indonesia is crucially important. There are several overlapping issues that need to be tackled delicately. People of Indian Origin (PIO) in Indonesia strongly feel that Indians should not have any visa requirements like inter-state European community. The choice of dual nationality, renunciation, resumption of cooperation media, health and education have earned credible support, though it is still not in practice. But PIOs who return to India after retirement or completion of projects, should be made aware of their rights. The issue of illegal immigration need to be tacked democratically and the matters related to Protectors of Immigrants (POE) and

Emigration Clearance Not Required (ECNR) should support single window clearance system from PIOs to avoid red tapism. Foreign Mission Abroad should give proper guidance in this regard. Renewal and grant of new passport should not involve time consuming reference. It is widely felt that there should be direct and regular flight from major cities of India with respective major cities of Indonesia.

Proper safety and security during stay with no racial or ethnic discrimination must also be guaranteed. It would facilitate greater interaction between human resource organizations within the member of South East Asian Region. Greater need of promotional linkages of the youth with India—exchange of cultural troupes and regular interaction with Consulates Officials to access the aspiration. The recent move to promote technical as well as professional education has earned credible support. In this direction, Indonesian officials have shown willingness to establish and manage institutions of higher learning in India vis-à-vis their homelands to facilitate inter-academic exchange programmes. Suggestions to establish NRI Welfare Fund has been strongly urged by Indian community to assist in legal, banking and property matters and redressal of problems faced by NRIs in the matters of investment, trade, industry, etc. The Government of India should frame special Economic Assistance Policy for the development of PIOs requirements. PIOs in projects offers, entrepreneurial support and programme are important imperative. Indonesian Indians have been ever ready willingness in this direction.

Conclusions

Migration studies encompass the great scholarly debate during the age of globalization which is highly illusive yet a fashionable concept. Unfortunately, the inadequate literature about Indians in Indonesia still remains the fundamental problems in various policy agenda. Thanks to globalization of transnational culture, IT revolution and changing strategic position in South East Asia that have necessitated to promote the arguments of human rights and national security for creating knowledge based new world order. The political bargainers, empty promise for economic security and the lack of social confidence; the spell of ethnicity and population movements have become more relevant to explore new possibilities in the direction of human development.

True knowledge about the social cultural set up and balanced understandings about the South East Region during the age of globalization can help Diaspora community to design more effective bargaining strategies to construct rational polices. Number organizations established by Indians in the regions like Indonesia Association and the role played by their promoters are significant in identifying the talent and leadership qualities with local communities. Hence, there is greater need to establish Migration Study Programme with study centers and Overseas Employment Agencies for proper guidance in collaboration between India and Indonesia to promote bilateral security. This will also facilitate interesting information to evaluate the quality of living, cultural intermixing, and acceptable social migration with no fear of race, colour and creed. There is a greater need to establish database software networks to provide readymade information about important NGOs, educational and technical institutions, research centers, broad spectrum of agencies, individuals, professional bodies and their demographics representation between India and Indonesia. It is now that Indians in Indonesia, people who belong to many different regional and linguistic groups, castes, religions, and traditions are developing, with greater confidence, a sense of Indian identity, unity and sense of pride. They are indeed living up to their host country's official national motto *Bhinneka Tunggal Ika*—a unity that draws strength from diversity. The Indian Government, and the foreign policy establishment in particular, can do more to leverage the vast collective experience of Indians in Indonesia and channel it towards the larger ends of bilateral cooperation. Until that happens, the profound sense of affinity which Indians have towards Indonesians through shared history, culture and aesthetics, language and civilization will remain dormant.[10]

NOTES

1. Ravindra Kumar (2004), "Indian Diaspora, Old and New: Culture, Class and Mobility", *Indian Anthropologists* (Delhi), Vol. 34, No. 1, pp. 2-3.
2. *Britannica Ready Reference Encyclopedia* (2006), Encyclopedia Britannica (India), Pvt. Ltd, New Delhi, p. 120.
3. htpp://en.wikipedia.org/wiki/Indian_indonesia.Data Accessed on 20 August 2012.
4. http://www.poonamsagar.com/a-touch-of-magic-indians-in-indonesia/
5. *Ibid.*
6. Note 3.
7. http://www.newstrackindia.com/information/locations/India/1025855-city-chichondi-patil.htm
8. http://indianembassyjakarta.com/Business%20Guide.pdf
9. http://www.mea.gov.in/mystart.php?id=190019809.
10. "Why Indonesia is important to India" visit at http://www.idsa.in/system/files/IB_Indonesia_ Navrakha.pdf, accessed on 19 August 2012.

CHAPTER 10

INNOVATIONS IN HR PRACTICES

–*Asha Ganjsinghani, Neetu Baid* and *Nitesh Asani*

ABSTRACT

This research is important for the HR profession because it defines what it means to be an effective HR professional. Being an effective HR professional is not just knowing the body of knowledge that defines the profession, but being able to apply that knowledge to business challenges. HR effectiveness matters more than ever because leaders of business and not-for-profit leaders have increasingly recognized the importance of individual abilities (talent), organization capabilities (culture), and leadership as key to the success of their organizations. HR professionals should become insightful advisors and architects on these issues. In an increasingly world of change, there has never been a greater need to identify what HR professionals must be, know, do, and deliver to contribute more fully to their organizations.

Collaboration and co-operation within the value chain have become a new concept of work organization, based on individual skills as well as teamwork; even between competitors. Collaborative commerce is emerging characterized by more fluid, dynamic and complex relationships. Such multidimensional relationships are often described as "value constellations".

Organizational change, creativity, and innovation schemes have been installed with individual 'champions'. The vision is that these changes to the organizational culture will lead to greater organizational effectiveness and consequently, change agents are used to guide and facilitate the change process. Employees who are innovative in their workplace are, in essence, satisfied with their jobs and this triggers them to come up with new ways to improve current conditions. One of the ways of how innovative employees express themselves is through performance of Organizational Citizenship Behaviour (OCB). Individual innovativeness contributes to an organization's renewal, survival and growth in today's turbulent and competitive business environment through the performance of OCB. Computer use and knowledge management will become key innovation and competition factors for all types of businesses, notably the manufacturing and related service industries.

Introduction

Innovative HR practices build competencies and capabilities for superior and winning performances today and simultaneously create long-term fertility for innovation of business ideas and strategies for future.

Employees by performing spontaneous behaviours go beyond their role prescriptions and are especially valued by the management. This phenomenon is critical for organizational effectiveness because managers cannot for see all contingencies or fully anticipates the activities that they may desire or need employees to perform. Work behaviour that goes beyond the reach of organizational measures of job performance holds promise for long-term organizational success because these types of action are purported to improve organizational efficiency, effectiveness and adaptability. Doing jobs beyond what is required without expecting to be rewarded is what is referred to in this study as Organizational Citizenship Behaviour (OCB).

Enhancing an organization's competitive ability is increasingly critical and behaviours, which may improve individual and organizational efficiency, become more valuable.

Objective of the Study

All HR managers heard and read countless time how to build teams, empower workforce and develop trust. The common place human resource practices prevalent across the entire business world are just as relevant to this business as any other. The HR policies must be integrated with business policies. The HR professionals must have balance in terms of centralization or decentralization of HR practices are ethnocentric while others management be geocentric or regiocentric.

Enhancing an organization's competitive ability is increasingly critical and behaviours, which may improve individual and organizational efficiency, become more valuable. Although there have been many studies of OCB in organizations, this study has examined the linkage of individual innovativeness with OCB where the effect of superior-subordinate as a mediator.

HR Competencies Research Methodology

To define competencies for HR professionals, we have relied on focus groups, theory and research, and experience to identify what HR professionals should know and do. In 2012, this work resulted in 139 specific behavioural competencies (secondary data). To determine if HR professionals possessed these competencies, we used a 360 methodology where HR professionals filled out a self-report survey and then invited both HR and non-HR professionals to assess their ability to deliver these competencies. In addition, the survey had two outcome variables: personal effectiveness (compared to other HR professionals) and business performance on an index of seven dimensions of business success.

Findings

Across the HR field, companies are finding creative ways to "do more with less". Following are four simple ideas one can use to help and reengineer his HR:

- Analysis of HR Practices
- Develop a Strategic HR Plan
- Embrace Technology
- Leverage the Resources

Analyze Your HR Practices

One of the most valuable tools to help is an HR audit. An HR expert can review and evaluate company's HR operations, top to bottom to uncover those compliance risks that can derail an organization. Company's practices can be compared to industry leaders and new ideas to improve can be determined.

Develop a Strategic HR Plan

A strategic HR plan aligns the department's goals with those of the organization. For example, when a regional service firm creats a five-year strategic plan to expand its single-state presence to the entire Midwest through a series of acquisitions, the HR executive will create a plan to support those goals. He or she will focus on learning the employment laws in the new states, securing regional benefit brokers and will create step by step processes to integrate the acquired staff members.

Embrace Technology

Technology can streamline HR workflow, provide communication and accessibility to a non-centralized workforce and allow staff greater flexibility. Some great technological time-savers are: web-based payroll and HR management system applications, employee intranets and electronic applicant tracking systems.

Leverage the Resources

This concept is about accomplishing HR objectives, especially those strategic goals, more efficiently. Break free of traditional practices. Rather than hiring a new staff member, consider alternate forms of employment such as payrolling. Payrolling is the practice of referring a contingent worker to a staffing vendor or payroll provider. The vendor acts as the employer of record, responsible for employer taxes, payroll and all legal matters pertaining to employing workers, thereby reducing contingent workforce costs.

The Challenges Before HR Managers

Issues coming on the radar of an HR manager today are diverse; from micro level issues where an individual employee needs hand holding to the macro issues pertaining to a global workforce and virtual teams. HR managers are expected to offer instant solutions for these issues and strategies. For an HR manager there are a number of areas where he might want to bring in an external consultant.

A strong team needs individuals who are dedicated to giving their best at work. Highly self-motivated, committed, ambitious employees give the most to their company and get the most from their work. But if there is lack of employee motivation in the workplace, the effects can be dramatic. Low team morale, lack of initiative, lack of energy, mistakes and high staff turnover are just some of the clues that motivation is an issue.

By following this simple three-step process one can create an action plan that will get him and his employees motivated.

STEP 1: Clarify the Goal

The first step of Self-Motivation Action Plan is to be clear about the end-result. Identify a project that you lack motivation about. The goals should be SMART, viz. Specific, Measurable, Agreed, Realistic and with a Timescale.

STEP 2: Identify the Obstacle

The second step of your Self-Motivation Action Plan is to be clear about what is standing in the way. There are two types of obstacles—practical and emotional. Examples of practical obstacles are lack of time, resources or information. Examples of emotional obstacles are lack of confidence or fear of failure or rejection.

Enlist all the obstacles standing in the way of achieving the goal.

STEP 3: Handle Each Obstacle

The third step of your Self-Motivation Action Plan is the most challenging that is to go through each obstacle and handle it.

The findings begin to capture what HR professionals need to know and do to be effective. They are further refined in tables which show the specific factors within each of these six domains and how they affect both perceived effectiveness of HR professionals and business success.

Respondents in the HRCS 2012 Data Set

Respondent Role	*Definition*	*N* *% Female* *% Male*
All Respondents	All Respondents who completed a majority of the 139 competency items	20,013
HR Associates	All Respondents, participants and associates, who work in HR	**9,897** F 65% M 35%
Non HR Associates	All Respondents, associate raters, who are not part of the HR organization	**7,488** F 31% M 69%
Participants	HR participants who elected to participate. Each participant has associate raters as well	**2,638** F 62% M 38%

Exclusive: The Six Competencies to Inspire HR Professionals for 2012

Our research found that by upgrading their competencies in six domains, HR professionals can respond to these business themes and create sustainable value. These six HR competence domains come from assessment by HR professionals and their line associates (over 20,000 global respondents) to 139 specific competency stated survey items (secondary data).

- *Strategic Positioner.* High performing HR professionals think and act from the outside/in. They are deeply knowledgeable of and able to translate external business trends into internal decisions and actions. They understand the general business conditions (e.g. social, technological, economic, political, environmental, and demographic trends) that affect their industry and geography. They target and serve key customers of their organization by identifying customer segments, knowing customer expectations, and aligning organization actions to meet customer needs.
- *Credible Activist.* Effective HR professionals are credible activists because they build their personal trust through business acumen. Credibility comes with HR professionals do what they promise, build personal relationships of trust, and can be relied on. Being a trust advisor helps HR professionals have positive personal relationships. It means to communicate clear and consistent messages with integrity. As an activist,

HR professionals have a point of view, not only about HR activities, but about business demands.

- *Capability Builder.* An effective HR professional melds individual abilities into an effective and strong organization by helping to define and build its organization capabilities. Organization is not structure or process; it is a distinct set of capabilities. Capability represents what the organization is good at and known for.
- *Change Champion.* As change champions, HR professionals make sure that isolated and independent organization actions are integrated and sustained through disciplined change processes. HR professionals make an organization's internal capacity for change match or lead the external pace of change. As change champions, HR professionals help make change happen at institutional (changing patterns), initiative (making things happen), and individual (enabling personal change) levels. To make change happen at these three levels, HR professionals play two critical roles in the change process.
- *Human Resource Innovator and Integrator.* Effective HR professionals know the historical research on HR so that they can innovative and integrate HR practices into unified solutions to solve future business problems. They must know latest insights on key HR practice areas related to human capital (talent sourcing, talent development), performance accountability (appraisal, rewards), organization design (teamwork, organization development), and communication.
- *Technology Proponent.* In recent years, technology has changed the way in which HR people think and do their administrative and strategic work. At a basic level, HR professionals need to use technology to more efficiently deliver HR administrative systems like benefits, payroll processing, healthcare costs, and other administrative services. In addition, HR professionals need to use technology to help people stay connected with each other. This means that technology plays an increasingly important role in improving communications, do administrative work more efficiently, and connecting inside employees to outside customers.

Because these six domains of HR competence respond to the external trends we identified, they have an impact on both the perception of the effectiveness of the HR professional and the business performance where the HR professional works.

Impact of HR Competences on Perception of HR Effectiveness and Business Performance

	Mean score on this competence domain (1 to 5)	*Impact on perception of HR effectiveness (Beta weights scaled to 100%*	*Impact on business performance (Beta weights scaled to 100%)*
Strategic Positioner	3.89	17%	15%
Credible Activist	4.23	22%	14%
Capability Builder	3.97	16%	18%
Change Champion	3.93	16%	16%
Human Resource Innovator and Integrator	3.90	17%	19%
Technology Proponent	3.74	12%	18%
		Multiple R^2 42.5%	8.4%

These data show that to be seen as personally effective, HR professionals need to be credible activists who build relationships of trust and have a strong business and HR point of view. They also have to have a mix of competencies in positioning the firm to its external environment (strategic positioner), doing organization capability and culture audits (capability builder), making change happen (change champion), aligning and innovating HR practices (HR integrator), and understanding and using technology (technology proponent). These competencies explain 42.5% of the effectiveness of an HR professional.

These HR competencies also explain 8.4% of a businesses' success. But it is interesting that the competencies that predict personal effectiveness are slightly different that those that predict business success, with insights on technology, HR integration, and capability building having more impact on business results. Again, the key issue is for HR professional and department to work together and to mutually reinforce their efforts so that they collectively reach the tipping point of high performance.

Sub-factors for HR Competence on Individual Effectiveness and Business Success

Sub-factor for the Six HR competency domains	*Mean (1 to 5)*	*Individual Effectiveness 100%*	*Business Success 100%*
Strategic Positioner			
Interpreting global business context	3.83	4.4	4.2
Decoding customer expectations	3.83	4.4	5.2
Co-crafting a strategic agenda	3.96	6.3	4.6
Credible Activist			
Earning trust through results	4.36	6.9	4.0
Influencing and relating to others	4.24	7.0	4.1
Improving through self-awareness	4.08	6.5	4.7
Shaping the HR profession	4.13	4.4	2.9
Capability Builder			
Capitalizing organizational capability	4.03	5.4	5.3
Aligning strategy, culture, practices, and behavior	3.94	5.3	6.1
Creating a meaningful work environment	3.94	4.1	5.2
Change Champion			
Initiating Change	3.94	5.4	4.8
Sustaining Change	3.91	4.7	5.7
HR Innovator & Integrator			
Optimizing human capital through workforce planning and analytics	3.95	5.5	5.6
Developing Talent	3.83	4.0	5.3
Shaping organization and communication practices	3.94	5.8	5.6
Driving performance	3.87	4.7	5.2
Building leadership brand	3.87	4.9	5.4
Technology Proponent			
Improving utility of HR operations	3.72	2.9	5.0
Connecting people through technology	3.77	4.6	6.3
Leveraging social media tools	3.68	2.7	4.7
Overall R^2		.431	.108

We also found that an effective HR department has more impact on a business' performance (31%) than the skills of individual HR professionals (8%). HR professionals need to work together as a unified team to fully create business value. The specific requirements of an effective HR department and their impact on business success are shown in the table below.

The impact of characteristics of an HR Department and business success

To what extent are the following true of your HR Department?	*Mean (1 to 5)*	*Relative Weighting on Business Success (100 points)*
Interacts effectively with the Board of Directors	3.67	7.7%
Has clear roles and responsibilities for each of the groups within HR (e.g., service centers, centers of expertise, embedded HR)	3.65	7.6%
Matches the structure of the HR department with how the business is organized	3.64	7.8%
Ensures that HR initiatives enable the business to achieve strategic priorities	3.62	9.7%
Develops an HR strategy that clearly links HR practices to business strategy	3.61	9.2%
Ensures that the different groups within HR work effectively with each other to provide integrated HR solutions	3.50	8.2%
Effectively manages external vendors of outsourced HR activities	3.49	8.3%
Invests in training and development of HR professionals	3.46	7.3%
Ensures that HR is a cultural role model for the rest of the organization	3.42	8.4%
Holds line managers accountable for HR	3.38	8.2%
Connects HR activities to external stakeholder expectations (e.g., customers, investors)	3.25	8.9%
Tracks and measures the impact of HR	3.22	8.8%
Multiple Regression R<sup2< sup=""></sup2<>		.317

Conclusion and Suggestions

Finally, we conclude that in the competitive world the organization should have the innovative ideas then only it can lead the organization very successful. Human resource leader/ manager should follow creative practices that practices should help to develop the employer as well as employee. Then only the organization can run successful.

Here is a collaboration of top ten HR practices that can help to achieve organizational goals every year.

1. Safe, Healthy and Happy Workplace

Creating a safe, healthy and happy workplace will ensure that employees feel homely and stay with organization for a very long time.

2. Open Book Management Style

Sharing information about contracts, sales, new clients, management objectives, company policies, employee personal data, etc. ensures that the employees are as enthusiastic about the business as the management. Through this open book process one can gradually create a culture of participative management and ignite the creative endeavour of your workforce.

3. Performance-linked Bonuses

Paying out bonuses or having any kind of variable compensation plan can be both an incentive and disillusionment. Bonus must be designed in such a way that people understand that there is no payout unless the company hits a certain level of profitability. Never payout bonus without measuring performance, unless it is a statutory obligation.

4. 360 Degree Performance Management Feedback System

This system, which solicits feedback from seniors (including the boss), peers and subordinates, has been increasingly embraced as the best of all available methods for collecting performance feedback. Every person in the team is responsible for giving relevant, positive and constructive feedback. Senior managers could use this feedback for self-development.

5. Fair Evaluation System for Employees

Each employee should have well-defined reporting relationships. Self-rating as a part of evaluation process empowers employees. Evaluation becomes fairer if it is based on the records of periodic counselling and achievements of the employee, tracked over the year. For higher objectivity, besides the immediate boss, each employee should be screened by the next higher level (often called a reviewer). Cross-functional feedback and relative ratings of all subordinates will add to the fairness of the system.

6. Knowledge Sharing

When an employee returns after attending any competencies or skills development program, sharing essential knowledge with others could be made mandatory. Innovative ideas (implemented at the workplace) are good to be posted on these knowledge sharing platforms. However, what to store and how to maintain a knowledge base requires deep thinking to avoid clutter.

7. Highlight Performers

Create profiles of top performers and make these visible through company intranet, display boards, etc. It will encourage others to put in their best, thereby creating a competitive environment within the company.

8. Open House Discussions and Feedback Mechanism

Employees are the biggest source of ideas. The only thing that can stop great ideas flooding organization is the lack of an appropriate mechanism to capture ideas. Open house discussions, employee-management meets, suggestion boxes and ideas capture tools such as critical incidents diaries are the building blocks that can help the managers to identify and develop talent.

9. Reward Ceremonies

Merely recognizing talent does not work, there is need to couple it with ceremonies where recognition is broadcast. Looking at the Dollar Check is often less significant than listening to the thunderous applause by colleagues in a public forum.

10. Delight Employees with the Unexpected

The last but not least way is to occasionally delight the employees with unexpected things that may come in the form of a reward, a gift or a well-done certificate. Reward not only the top performers but also a few others who are in need of motivation to exhibit their potential.

HR Practices for Tomorrow

In turn trends like these are changing the way firms are managed organizations today must grapple with revolutionary trends accelerating product and technological change, globalizes competition, deregulation, demographic changes and trends towards a service society and the information. These trends have dramatically increased the degree of competition in virtually all industries, while forcing firms to cope with unprecedented product innovation and technological change. Companies in such an environment either become competitive high performers or they die.

We are optimistic about the present and the future of the HR profession. And we have empirical reasons for our optimism. We now have specific insights on what HR professionals need to know and do to become better and more effective deliver value to employees, organizations, customers, investors, and communities. And, we know what the HR department should excel at to help business be successful.

It becomes important for this relatively new profession to define what it means to be effective. HR effectiveness matters more than ever, because leaders of businesses and non-profit organisations increasingly recognise the importance of individual abilities (talent), organisation capabilities (culture) and leadership as key to their success. HR professionals should become insightful advisers and architects on these matters. In a constantly changing world, there has never been a greater need to identify what HR professionals must be, know, do and deliver to contribute more fully to their organisations.

In this round of research, we have identified six domains of competencies HR professionals must demonstrate to be personally effective and to have an impact on business performance. These competencies respond to a number of themes facing global business today:

- *outside/in:* HR must turn outside business trends and stakeholder expectations into internal actions
- *business/people:* HR should focus on both business results and human capital improvement
- *individual/organisational:* HR should target both individual ability and organisation capabilities
- *event/sustainability:* HR is not about an isolated activity (a training, communication, staffing, or compensation programme) but sustainable and integrated solutions
- *past/future:* Respect HR's heritage, but shape a future
- *administrative/strategic:* HR must attend to both day-to-day administrative processes and long-term strategic practices.

REFERENCES

A.K. Nayak, H.R.D. *Management—A Strategic Approach*, Commonwealth Publishers Edition, 1986.

Arun Monappa, Mahrukh Engineer, *Liberalisation and Human resources Management*, Eage Publication First Edition, 1999.

Arun Msnappa, Mirza and Saiyasain, *Personnel Management*, IInd edition Tata McGraw Hill Publishing Company, 1996.

B.L. Mathur, *H.R.M. and Development*, Arihant Publication House, First Edition, 1994.

C.B. Mamoria, *Personnel Management*, Himalaya Publishing House, 2001.

Das Gupta N., *Human Resource Accounting*, 1988.

Davis Keith, *Human Behaviour at Work*, 1972.

Ginzberg Eli, *Human Resource: The Wealth of Nation*, 1978.

Joshi, N.C. and Banerjee, S. (Eds.), *Readings in Public Sector*, 1986.

Katiyar, R.C., *Accounting for Human Resource: Standards and Practices in Anglo-Saxon Countries and India*, 1992.

MC. Heshwami. B.L. and Sinha. D.P., *Management Change Through HRD*. Tata McGraw Hill New Delhi 1991.

Prasad, Lallan and Banerjee, A.M., *Management of Human Resources*, 1985.

R.S. Davar, *Personnel Management and Industrial Relations*. 10th Edition, Vikas Publication.

Sharma, R.K., *Performance Appraisals of Public Enterprises in India*, 1989.

Magazines, Journals and Newspapers

Business India

Business Today

Business World

Journal of Accounting and Finance (Jaipur)

Public Enterprises Survey

The Charted Accountant (New Delhi)

The Indian Journal of Commerce

Internet Websites

http://www.bbcworld.com

http://www.businessindia.com

http://www.cnbcindiya.com

http://www.google.com

http://www.indiya.com

http://www.ndtv.com

http://www.rajasthanpatrika.com

http://www.bhaskar.com

http://www.yahoo.com

http://www.yahoo.com.in

CHAPTER 11 MIGRATION AND ITS IMPACTS (A CASE STUDY OF HRM OF MINERS IN TSP REGION OF RAJASTHAN)

–S.S. Choudhary and Ali Asgar Joon

ABSTRACT

The Tribal Sub Plan (TSP) region of Rajasthan State occupies southern part of Rajasthan comprising districts of Banswara, Dungarpur, Pratapgadh, nine tehsils of Udaipur and Abu road tehsil of Sihrohi district. It spreads over to 19180 sq. km. 23 blocks of these five districts are declared as Tribal Sub Plan (TSP) area by the State Government for speedy development of tribes of the region. Tribal Area Development Department (TADA) is responsible for the development of the TSP area having headquartered at Udaipur. This area of Rajasthan is prone to various economic and social problems. The State is endowed with rich mineral wealth. The tribes of this region are mainly dependent on agriculture which is the game of monsoon so the poverty is the main problem in their way for development. Besides poverty, low literacy, social drawbacks, death feast, bride price, intoxication, blind faith, fatalism, untouchability, communalism, unemployment, dependency on moneylenders and local traders, etc. are the other evils and problems prevailing among the tribe.

The Bhils and the Minas are regarded as the original inhabitants of Rajasthan, but they are believed to be push into the Aravalli Range because of the powerful Aryan invasions. One of the oldest inhabitants in India, Bhils form the largest tribal group in Rajasthan, constituting about 40% of total tribal population. Famous for their exceptional archery skills, they are mainly residing in the districts of Bhilwara, Chittaurgarh, Dungarpur, Banswara, Udaipur, and Sirohi. The Minas are the second largest tribal group in Rajasthan after the Bhils and live in the regions of Shekhawati and eastern Rajasthan. The Gaduliya Lohars, the nomadic blacksmiths, were originally a martial Rajput tribe. These tribes derive the name Gaduliya from their beautiful bullock carts "gadis". The Garasias of southern Rajasthan is known for their interesting custom of marriage through elopement, in which a bride price is paid to the bride's father. The Sahariyas are jungle dwellers and are the most backward tribe in Rajasthan.

Located in the districts of Kota, Dungarpur and Sawai Madhopur, Sahariyas are shifting cultivators. The Rabaris of the Marwar region are nomadic cattle breeders.

The motives of migration are difficult to ascertain because they are at times so mixed up that the individual himself is unaware of the factors responsible for migration. Combination of attractive as well as repulsive forces always work simultaneously and migrants may not be able to identify clearly responsible for their migration.

In fact, a number of factors are taken into consideration. A satisfied worker may not think in terms of migration even if the economic opportunities at the place of migration are considered better. Of course, this has a direct relationship with the aspiration of an individual.

Introduction

Since ages, people have been shifting from place to place as families, tribes and as social groups for food, shelter, security and other reasons. The movement of people from one place to another for the purpose of setting down has been commonly known as migration, and become universal phenomena. In other words, migration means the settlement or shifting of an individual from one cultural area or place of habitation to another, either temporarily or permanently.

Migration is not merely physical movement of people from one place to another; it has its social, economic and cultural dimensions also.

One of the important features of migration is that an individual who moves from one place to another continues (in the initial stages) to maintain contact with his family, caste and other social group which he has left behind. This tendency often leads to absenteeism and turnover.

Rajasthan, commonly known for the heroic deeds of the Rajput Kings and the Jauhar of ladies had a rich tradition of mining and metallurgical industries. "The Tribal Sub Plan (TSP) region of Rajasthan State occupies southern part of Rajasthan comprising districts of Banswara, Dungarpur, Pratapgadh, nine tehsils of Udaipur and Abu road tehsil of Sihrohi district. It spreads over to 19180 sq. km. 23 blocks of these five districts are declared as Tribal Sub Plan (TSP) area by the State Government for speedy development of Tribes of the region. Tribal Area Development Department (TADA) is responsible for the development of the TSP area having headquartered at Udaipur".[1] This area of Rajasthan is prone to various economic and social problems. The State is endowed with rich mineral wealth. The tribes of this region are mainly dependent on agriculture which is the game of monsoon so the poverty is the main problem in their way for development. Besides poverty, low literacy, social drawbacks, death feast, bride price, intoxication, blind faith, fatalism, untouchability, communalism, unemployment, dependency on moneylenders and local traders, etc. are the other evils and problems prevailing among the tribe.

The Bhils and the Minas are regarded as the original inhabitants of Rajasthan, but they are believed to be push into the Aravalli Range because of the powerful Aryan invasions. One of the oldest inhabitants in India, Bhils form the largest tribal group in Rajasthan, constituting about 40% of total tribal population. Famous for their exceptional archery skills, they are mainly residing in the districts of Bhilwara, Chittaurgarh, Dungarpur, Banswara, Udaipur, and Sirohi. The Minas are the second largest tribal group in Rajasthan after the Bhils and live in the regions of Shekhawati and eastern Rajasthan. The Gaduliya Lohars, the nomadic blacksmiths, were originally a martial Rajput tribe. These tribes derive the name Gaduliya from their beautiful bullock carts "gadis". The Garasias of southern Rajasthan is known for their interesting custom of marriage through elopement, in which a bride price is paid to the bride's father. The Sahariyas are jungle dwellers and are the most backward tribe in Rajasthan. Located in the districts of Kota, Dungarpur and Sawai Madhopur, Sahariyas are shifting cultivators. The Rabaris of the Marwar region are nomadic cattle breeders.

Objectives of the Study

(1) To find out the reasons which compel for migration.

(2) To find out the good and bad impact of migration.

(3) To compare the stability of migrated labour of government sector mine and private sector mine.

Research Methodology

Sources of Data Collection

To study the migrating nature of the tribal labor working in mines and quarries purposely four minerals, namely marble, soapstone, rock phosphate and lead-zinc of southern Rajasthan were taken. For this purpose, in-depth field work was conducted in the areas of Udaipur (Jhamar kotdha), Kesriyaji, Dungarpur, Banswada, Dharyawad and Sirohi.

Field data were collected from the sample units through the administration of schedules. The filling up of schedules were followed by long interviews. The aggregate data were collected though secondary source, namely annual reports, published works such as Census Reports, Hand-outs, etc. released by the State Directorate of Mines and Geology, MMTC, Statistics of Rajasthan, Indian Year Book, Five Year Plans, Gazette, IBM, companies record, etc.

Sample Design

While drawing samples of study it was our earnest effort to give a representative coverage to the different types of minerals and labourers in the universe under study. We used purposive sampling while drawing the sample units. The southern Rajasthan being home of mineral deposits and the minerals of relative importance, it was our objective to study the minerals of diverse importance. For instance, strategic mineral, i.e. those which have a crucial importance in industrial development, lead-zinc mine was selected and for agriculture growth rock phosphate was taken. For cosmetic and ornamental value soap stone and marble quarries were taken. Out of the universe of 70 minerals we drew a purposive sample of four minerals, namely lead-zinc, rock phosphate, soap stone and marble.

In the region of southern Rajasthan, the lead-zinc mines and Jhamarkotda Rock Phosphate Mine (controlled by State Government) are the biggest installations where about 4000 labourers work.

The labourers interviewed were drawn on the basis of purposive sampling for the study. Thus, a sample of two hundred labourers was taken for interview in depth (50 labourers from each type of mines/queries).

Table 1: Size of Sample

Mines/Quarries	*No. of mines/quarries*	*Size of Sample (No. of labourers interviewed)*
Government Controlled Mines		
(1) Lead-Zinc	1	50
(2) Rock Phosphate	1	50
Private Controlled Mines		
(1) Marble	5	50
(2) Soap Stone	5	50
Total		200

Findings

The study reveals that in lead-zinc mines and phosphate quarries, a number of skilled workers have permanently migrated from distant places like Bihar, Bengal, Tamil Nadu, etc. but in case of private sector quarries, most of the workers come from within a radius of 15 km, in case of private sector mine 74% to 78% workers are either local or from the state itself. Similarly, in private sector the percentage varies between 92 to 96. Gujarat being an adjoining satet some workers (4-6%) have permanently migrated to the TSP region.

So far migration is concerned, there is pretty great variation among the workers of government sector mines and private sector mines.

Table 2: Native Places of Migrants

Native Places	*Mines*					
	Public Sector			*Private Sector*		
	Lead Zinc	*Rock Phosphate*	*Total*	*Soap Stone*	*Marble*	*Total*
State itself	37	39	76	46	48	94
Gujarat	5	2	7	3	2	5
Tamil Nadu	1	—	1	—	—	—
West Bengal	2	2	4	—	—	—
Bihar	5	7	12	1	—	1
Total	50	50	100	50	50	100

From Table 2, it indicates that in public sector mines 76% and in private sector mines 94% workers are from the state itself in which majority come from within a radius of 10 to 15 kms. Bihar is on the top from where 12% workers working in public sector mines are, while Gujarat ranks at second position having contributed 7% workforce. On the other hand, in private sector mines only 5% workers have been reported from Gujarat and the two in soap stone quarries at Dungarpur.

Table 3: Causes of Visit to Native Places (in %)

Sr. No.	*Mines*	*No. of Repondent*	*Local Residents Including Updown Persons*	*Visitors To Native Places*	*Meeting Spouses*	*Marriage & Social Ceremonies*	*Religiuos Ceremonies*	*Sowing and Harvasting of Crops*	*Metting Spouses*
1	Lead zinc	92	17	75	39	9	10	2	40
2	Rock phosphate	40	8	32	32	7	9	—	52
3	Soap stone	30	22	8	38	11	13	4	34
4	Marble	25	12	8	27	17	18	3	35

Table 3 reveals that the causes the tempt workers to visits there home villages. From the table, it is clear that meeting spouses and sowing and harvesting of crop constitute 39% and 40% of the reasons respectively. In the same way, Table 3 reveals that economic condition is the root cause of migration of workers in both types of ownership. The first preference is given to economic reasons, followed by prospects for better employment inadequate cultivable land, family differences and social disparities.

Table 4: Motives of Migration (Level of Preference)

Sr.No.	*Motives*	*Mine Group*			
		Government Controlled Mines		*Private Controlled Mines*	
		Lead Zinc	*Rock Phosphate*	*Soap Stone*	*Marble*
1.	Economic Reason	I	L	I	I
2.	Inadequate Cultivable Land	III	III	II	II
3.	Prospects for Better Employment	II	II	III	III
4.	Family Deference	IV	IV	IV	IV
5.	Social Disparities	V	V	V	V

Thus, the migration of workers to mining areas for economic and social upliftment proves our hypothesis that "socio-economic conditions are the main cause of migration".

Model of migration given depicts that a number of reasons are responsible for migration which may lead to either positive or negative impacts. Due to a satisfied and committed workforce, productivity increases. But frequent visits to native places may lead to absenteeism or labour turnover.

The percentage of workers from nearby and distant state proves that there is a dearth of skilled workers in the state. But at the same time it has been proved that semi-skilled and unskilled workers are largely local and most of them come from within a radius of 10 to 15 km from mines. As no housing facility is provided by the employers in the private sector mines, so, workers either make a daily up and down trip for the work or live in juggies in nearby mines. But most of the workers in Zawar mines and Jhamar Kotda mines (public sectors) enjoy labour quarter facilities provided by the employers.

Table 5: Migrants With/Without Families

Family	*Mines*					
	Public Sector			*Private Sector*		
	Lead Zinc	*Rock Phosphate*	*Total*	*Soap Stone*	*Marble*	*Total*
With family	35	27	62	42	43	85
	70%	54%	62%	84%	86%	85%
Without Family	15	23	38	8	7	15
	30%	46%	38%	16%	14%	15%
Total	50	50	100	50	50	100

As in most of the cases particularly in private sector mine workers are not provided shelter by their employers, a majority of them does not live with their families (Table 5). It is also clear from the table it is clear that even in public sector mines 38% stay away from their families, while it is 15% only in case of private sector mines. The reason behind has already been made clear that in the absence of housing facility, workers are forced to live in juggies in the nearby areas of mines.

The motives of migration are difficult to ascertain because they are at times so mixed up that the individual himself is unaware of the factors responsible for migration. Combination of attractive as well as repulsive forces always work simultaneously and migrants may not be able to identify clearly responsible for their migration.

In fact, a number of factors are taken into consideration. A satisfied worker may not think in terms of migration even if the economic opportunities at the place of migration are considered better. Of course, this has a direct relationship with the aspiration of an individual. D.J. Bouge,[2] believes that migration is caused by economic, social, political, medical and physiological reasons. Davis[3] has the view that in India some conditions have favored migration. According to him, religious festivals, dire famine, general war and ruthless taxation in past accelerated the movement of population. Certain other conditions during the British rule in India also favored migration. These are the development of means of transportation and communication, educational facilities, the decline of cast and family soldiery, the growth of large-scale industries, development of cities and expansion of cities. The Royal Commission of Labour observed, "The driving force in migration comes almost entirely from one end of the channel, that is the village and the industrial is not prompted by the lure of the city life or by any great ambition. The city as such has no attraction for him and when he leaves the village he has seldom and ambition beyond that of securing the necessities of life. Few industrial workers would remain in industry if they could secure sufficient food and clothing in the village; they are pushed, not pulled to the city".[4]

NOTES

1. I.V. Trivedi and Pallavi Mehta, Tribal Indebtedness: A study of TSP region of southern Rajasthan, International Seminar on Tribal Development organized by PAHER, June 2012, p. 87.
2. D.J. Bouge, Internal Migration, Inhauser Vs. Dancan.
3. K. Davis, *The Population of India and Pakistan*, Princesston, New Jersey 1951, p. 108.
4. The Royal Commission on Labour, p. 16.

CHAPTER 12

ROLE OF HR IN MERGERS AND ACQUISITIONS

–Rajesh Sharma and *Brijesh Awasthi*

ABSTRACT

People issues can make or break a deal. The priority areas for HR are effective communications, cultural alignment, and change management plan, securing the top performing team, prioritizing activities, developing a staff model, and developing a reward strategy for the new organization. However, the common role for HR mainly revolves around ad hoc advice for senior management, retention of key talent, and due diligence on compensation and benefit plans of the merging firms. If not handled well, M&As can lead to failures and wastage of valuable resources. Bungling the management of a merger can result in losing people, who are a valuable asset. The management team has to anticipate and prepare for the emotional responses of the employees at the earliest. Some of the reasons for M&A failures are: cultural incompatibility, non-existent or over-rated synergies, inability to manage change in the organization. So the report throws a deep insight by the analyzing the M&A issues in three companies, viz. NTPC, Bank of Baroda and P&G. By the valuable insights provided by the authorities at the three places and with the help of the available sources of information we concluded that HR needs at least three-fourth of the weightage in various M&A issues, neglecting it would lead to losses of unimaginable volume.

Introduction/Conceptual Framework

Merger has been defined as an arrangement whereby the assets of two or more companies become vested in, or under the control of one company, which has, as its shareholders, all or substantially all the shareholders of the two companies. It may also include fusion of two or more companies into another.

One of the two existing companies merges its identity into another existing company, or one or more of existing companies may form a new company and merge their identities into the new company by transferring their businesses and undertaking including all other assets and liabilities to the new company. The shareholders of companies whose identities have been merged gets substantial shareholding in the merged company based on the share exchange ratio incorporated in the scheme of merger as approved by majority of shareholders of both merged and merging companies.

It is, thus, one of the various forms of corporate restructuring modes. It is the combination of two or more companies in which one company survives in its own name and the other cease to exist as a legal entity. The survival company acquires assets and liabilities of the merged companies. Generally, the company which survives is the buyer which retains its identity and the seller company is extinguished. Consolidation is a combination of two or more companies in which all companies cease to exist as legal entity and a new company is created. In finance literature, thus, merger and consolidation are technically differentiated. Merger and consolidation are also differentiated in accounting texts wherein former is called absorption and the latter is called amalgamation. However, as per Companies Act, 1956, consolidation and merger are both treated as amalgamation. On the other hand, an acquisition involves acquiring ownership in a property (tangible and/or intangible). In the context of business combination, an acquisition is the purchase by one company, of controlling interest in the share capital of an existing company. An acquisition may be effected by either of the following:

- An agreement with the person holding majority interest in the company management
- Purchase of new shares by private agreement
- Purchase of share in the open market (open offer)
- Acquisition of share capital of a company by means of cash, issuance of share capital, etc.
- Making a buyout offer to general body of shareholders when a company is acquired by another company, the acquiring company has two options:
  - Merge both the companies into one and operate as single entity
  - To operate the taken over company as an independent company, probably with changed management and changed policies.

The first option is known as merger and the second option is known as takeover.

M&A: Trends in India

The present business environment has altered radically with the changes in economic policies and introduction of new institutional mechanism. It is now characterized by globalization, opening up of the economy, worldwide competition, expanding markets, fast changing technologies, never ending need for finance and necessity for diversification. The Indian corporate world, while benefiting from decontrol and deregulation has begun to feel the effect of these changes. To meet the challenges of global economy and to face the increased global competition, Indian companies are changing their strategic focus and re-orienting their operations through restructuring processes to achieve the efficiencies required to survive and integrate into global economy. This restructuring process is leading to an unprecedented rise in the business strategies like mergers, acquisitions and strategic alliances. Mergers and acquisitions are accepted as effective routes to enhance corporate efficiency and shareholder wealth.

Despite being tied up within the shackles of tight regulatory system wherein prior government approval for M&A was required in the pre-liberalized regime, mergers and acquisitions were not uncommon in the decade of 80s. During 1980-89, 80 amalgamations and 52 takeovers were approved by the government. Table 1 gives the distribution of amalgamations and takeovers during 1980-89 under the MRTP Act, 1969.

Table 1: M&A Announcements in India: 1988-1998

Year	*Number of M&A*	*Percent Change*
1988	15	——
1989	18	20.0
1990	5	38.9
1991	71	184.0
1992	135	90.1
1993	88	113.3
1994	363	26.0
1995	430	18.5
1996	541	25.8
1997	636	17.6
1998	730	14.8

Source: IIM Calcutta, Data Base on M&A

Table 2: List of Mergers and Takeovers Since 1999

Deal Type	*Deal Date*	*Target/Seller Co.*	*Merged/Acquirer Co.*
Takeover	13 Apr 2009	Lotte India Corpn. Ltd.	Lotte Confectionery Co. Ltd.
Takeover	06 Oct 2008	Lotte India Corpn. Ltd.	Lotte Confectionery Co. Ltd.
Takeover	10 Jul 2008	Lotus Chocolate Co. Ltd.	Shri Peraje Prakash Pai and Shri Peraje Anantha Pai
Takeover	13 Jun 2006	Nutrine Confectionery Co. Ltd.	Wadala Commodities Ltd.
Merger	01 Feb 2006	BVR Expellers Pvt. Ltd. [merged]	Nutrine Confectionery Co. Ltd.
Takeover	26 Nov 2004	Lotus Chocolate Co. Ltd.	D Durga Prasad
Takeover	16 Jan 2004	Lotte India Corpn. Ltd.	Lotte Confectionery Company, Korea
Takeover	27 Aug 2003	Lotus Chocolate Co. Ltd.	Mr. Alapati Ramakrishna & Mr. Devabhuktuni Durga Prasad
Merger	11 Apr 2003	Confectionery Specialities Ltd. [merged]	Lotte India Corpn. Ltd.
Merger	14 Nov 2002	Van Melle Confectionery India Pvt. Ltd. [merged]	Perfetti Van Melle India Pvt. Ltd.
Merger	12 Aug 2002	BVR Packers Pvt. Ltd. [merged]	Nutrine Sweets Pvt. Ltd.
Merger	12 Aug 2002	BVR Confectionery Pvt. Ltd. [merged]	Nutrine Sweets Pvt. Ltd.
Merger	12 Aug 2002	Nutrine Chewing-gum Pvt. Ltd. [merged]	Nutrine Sweets Pvt. Ltd.
Takeover	17 May 2002	Cadbury India Ltd.	Cadbury Schweppes Plc & Cadbury Mauritius Ltd.
Sale of Asset	09 May 2002	Cadbury India Ltd.	Kalpataru Properties Pvt. Ltd.
Sale of Asset	23 Apr 2002	Candico (i) Ltd.	I.T.C. Ltd.
Takeover	11 Apr 2002	Lotte India Corpn. Ltd.	Santhanalakshmi Investments Pvt. Ltd. [merged]
Takeover	11 Dec 2001	Cadbury India Ltd.	Cadbury Schweppes Plc & Cadbury Schweppes Mauritius Ltd.
Takeover	29 Jun 2001	Confectionery Specialities Ltd. [merged]	Lotte India Corpn. Ltd.
Sale of Asset	31 Aug 2000	Cadbury India Ltd.	Fc Allana
Takeover	17 Jun 1999	Joyco India Pvt. Ltd.	Agrolimen Group
Merger	27 May 1999	Cocoa Products & Beverages Ltd. [merged]	Lotte India Corpn. Ltd.

Source: CMIE

Since mid-nineties, the concept of M&A has caught fire. Courts have also favored mergers, as is evident from the following remarks of Supreme Court of India in the Hindustan Lever Ltd. (HLL) TOMCO merger case.

"In this era of hyper competitive capitalism and technological change, industrialists have realized that mergers/acquisitions are perhaps the best route to reach a size comparable to global companies so as to effectively compete with them. The harsh reality of globalization has dawned that companies which cannot compete globally must sell out as an inevitable alternative."

M&A Wave in India

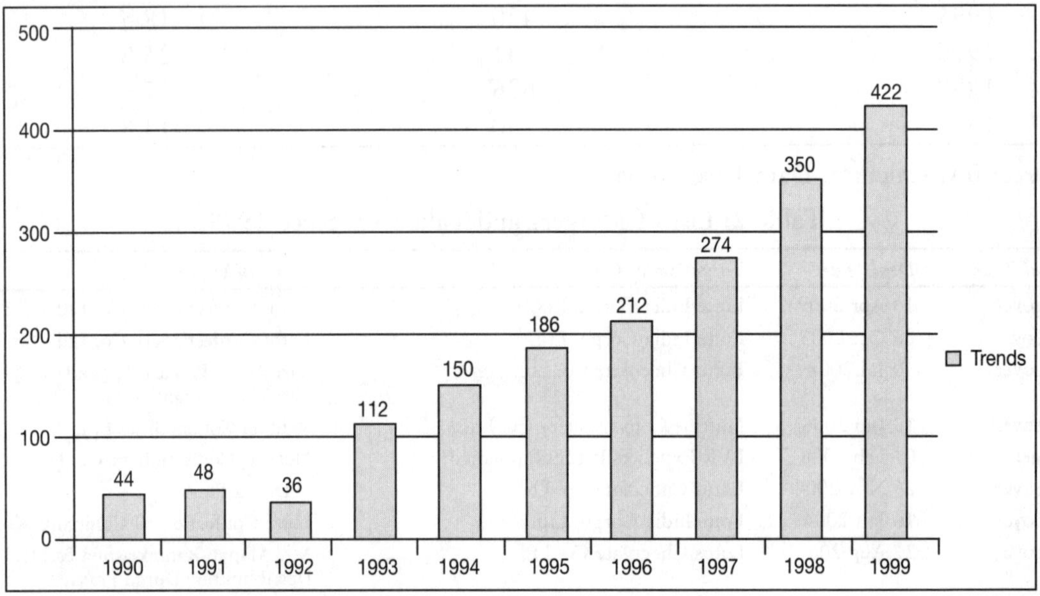

Source: Sushil Khanna, "Financial Reforms and Industrial Sectors in India", Article 9, *Economic and Political Weekly*, November 1999, pp. 32-33.

However, out of total mergers and acquisitions which have taken place in India, during the last decade (especially between 1991-97) more than 50% of mergers and 74% of acquisitions were horizontal. About 16% of mergers and 41% of acquisitions were vertical and the rest were all conglomerate in nature.

M&A Trend: International Scenario

Weston (1953) has identified three merger waves while studying U.S. business behavior and environment after these waves. The first wave occurred during the turn of the century (1898-1903) when companies such as U.S. Steel and Standard Oil were created by acquiring firms within an industry. During this period, market gave way to partial monopoly. Corporate laws were relaxed and effective mergers took place.

The second wave coincided with the bull market of 1920s (1926-29) when firms embarked upon acquisitions as a way of expanding new markets and increasing market share. Stigler

(19500 described the second wave as being "mergers for oligopoly" in contrast with the first as "mergers for monopoly" wave.

The third merger wave (1940-47) occurred when firms such as Gulf and Western focused on acquiring firms in other lines of business with the intention of diversifying and forming conglomerates. This period saw the disappearance of 2500 firms and growth of eight largest steel corporations in US.

Fourth wave of mergers occurred in mid-80s, when firms were acquired primarily for restructuring the assets and recapitalization.

In 1980s-1990s, companies in US responded to similar set of environmental factors by opting for restructuring due to macro-level trends of globalization of markets, deregulation of financial and real estate sectors and increasing credit of takeover bids.

According to World Investment Report 2000 (UN 2000), M&A worldwide have grown over past two decades (1980-99) at an average annual rate of 42% and reached $2.3 trillion in 1999 in relation to GDP. Total M&A in the world were hardly 0.3% in 1980 rose to 2% in 1990 and further 8% in 1999.

The trends have, however, reversed recently in 2000. Number of deals in US slipped from 12,300 to 10,800. Banking business activity also fell by 20%.

Objective

The objective of the study is to find out the role of HR in mergers and acquisitions in various stages.

Research Methodology

Met	Methodology Used	Explorative research
Data	Source	Secondary, includes data from various sources like Internet, books, journals, etc.

Scope of Study

The study only deals with three companies and an in-depth study and analysis has been done for these companies only. As the study includes a sample of three companies, the study was based on mergers/acquisitions by these companies. To know the role of HR in them, discussions published and reported by the concerned authorities and the HR were involved. All the results were analyzed in the light of the above and are presented in the study.

Mergers and Acquisitions: The Strategic Role of Human Resource Management

Mergers and acquisitions are a common feature of the global business landscape. There has been a marked increase in merger activity since the 1990s. The main drivers of such deals are the changing market conditions which require businesses to regroup their activities and deregulation which lead to consolidation. Furthermore, mergers take place for various reasons. Some of these reasons are: entering new markets, developing new products and services, and achieving economies of scale.

Several studies conducted across the globe aimed at analyzing the true benefits of such strategies reveal that more than 50% of mergers and acquisitions (M&As) are financial failures.

Some studies put this figure at 60-70%. These failures are due to financial, market, and HR-related reasons. In the aftermath of these failures, critics, management writers, consultants, and analysts put the blame on inadequate assessment of the human costs of M&As. HR has a crucial role to play in steering the M&A strategy in the right direction. The involvement of HR from the pre-merger stage itself can help in avoiding substantial human costs related to the merger and also maintain the momentum at the right pace.

The US has witnessed a lot of M&A activity during the 1990s. Europe and Asia are currently very active in this area. While the experiences in different regions vary, there are some common aspects of managing M&As, which need close attention. The involvement of HR through all the different phases of the M&A is one such.

The merging entities give a great deal of importance to financial matters and the outcomes; HR issues are the most neglected ones. Ironically, studies show that most of the mergers fail to bring out the desired outcomes due to people related issues. The uncertainty brought out by poorly managed HR issues in mergers and acquisitions have been the major reason for these failures.

HR Best Practices in Mergers and Acquisitions: Respondents to the SHRM Foundation/ Towers Perrin Mergers and Acquisitions survey recommended the following human resource best practices, based on their M&A experience.

Pre-deal: The number one recommendation was identifying the people-related issues and planning for due diligence. Second was assessing people and working out the organizational/ cultural fit. And the third recommendation was educating the deal team on the HR implications of a deal.

Due Diligence: During this stage, estimate the people-related transactional costs, the people-related ongoing costs and the people-related savings. Identify and assess all cultural issues.

Integration Planning: There were six major recommendations: develop employee communication strategies; design key talent retention programs; plan and lead integration efforts; develop a new strategy for the new entity; help the organization cope with change; and define an organizational blueprint and staffing plan.

Implementation: During this phase, HR professionals should focus on managing ongoing change and employee communications; advising management on dealing with people issues; aligning total rewards and other HR policies; monitoring the process of organizational and people-related integration activities; and ensuring the capture of synergies via incentives.

The merging entities give a great deal of importance to financial matters and the outcomes; HR issues are the most neglected ones. Ironically, studies show that most of the mergers fail to bring out the desired outcomes due to people related issues. The uncertainty brought out by poorly managed HR issues in mergers and acquisitions have been the major reason for these failures.

Findings

The human resource issues in the mergers and acquisitions (M&A) can be classified in three phases: the pre-merger phase, integration phase and the post-merger phase.

The three cases studied reveal quite a bit about the success or failure of mergers and acquisitions, and from these we can pinpoint specific reasons why a merger or acquisition might fail or succeed and how it should be managed in order to make it a successful deal. It should be noted that these findings are by no means exhaustive, nor should the substitute for a full-blown study of the causes of success or failure in mergers and acquisition. Rather, they are meant to paint a broad picture of the variety of issues that companies generally face, and serve as a leaping point from which we can dive into recommendations for companies considering a merger or acquisition.

Pre-Merger Phase

NTPC

Being known for its HR department and the initiatives, which the department takes for giving quality of work life to its employees, NTPC took all HR aspects very well into consideration to avoid all those problems which they faced in earlier plant takeovers.

On a higher, more strategic level, HR due diligence dealt with issues related to corporate culture, talent retention, training and development integration, employee communication strategies, compensation issues in transition, stay pay, quality of work life, workforce composition, past change management initiatives, and finally the interface of technology and people issues.

Bank of Baroda

The issues that needed to be addressed during the pre-implementation stage were mainly concerning issues like

- Overstaffing
- Demographic factors
- Disparities occurring due to varied working styles
- Compensation packages disparities

So the role of HR was pretty challenging, though it could not do anything about it as the deal was done on the specific guidelines as laid by RBI. So HR personnel formulated an excellent questionnaire and the agendas discussed and successfully managed included

- Retention to avoid havoc and dissent amongst the employees
- Change management issues so as to target the merger and the deal in the minds so that when it actually takes place the delivery is pretty smooth
- Striking an accurate trade-off between the working styles of both the companies so that none of the employees feel the pressure of the change. In other words, deriving a so-called *Common*.

Procter and Gamble

Both the companies being brands in their own respective fields had the added pressure of keeping up to their existing rapport in their fields. So The role of HR

- Formulation of a team of experts belonging to various departments and having a varied range of experience so that all issues could be dealt with.

- The main function of this team was to indulge in ice breaking sessions so as to put into effect the concept of "delivering change with ease".
- Meetings interviews and management games were some of the techniques that were made use of to make people accustomed to the new environment.

Integration Phase

The role of HR during this stage is of utmost importance because this the time when actually the deal which was thought of in the minds of the strategic heads, materializes.

NTPC

Here the role of HR mainly focused on the following parameters:

Compliance with the specified and predetermined laws so that no loopholes are left.

- Ensuring that the confidentiality of the information is maintained and there is no leakage of any sorts so as to avoid any mental stampede.
- Formulation of a core team which consisted of approximately 15 members belonging to cross functional departments from across plant boundaries.
- Proper use of HR interventions.
- Communication is the backbone in all such coalitions so keeping a clear-cut communication pattern in mind so as to answer questions like who reports to whom, when, what and how?
- Issues that needed to be answered included
    1. Continuous and visible improvement
    2. Quantity v/s quality
    3. Risk taking ability
    4. Transparency and non-discrimination
    5. Simplification of procedures.

Bank of Baroda

Here the role of HR mainly focused on the following parameters:

- Chalking out specific training programs based on the demographic segmentation to address specific needs.
- Orientation programs were properly arranged and the HR team ensured that they were properly followed.
- Ensuring that the amalgamation laws and rights were properly addressed.
- Arranging various ice breaking sessions so as to reduce the cultural shock.
- Dealing properly with the customers who were confused about their plight amidst all the chaos.
- Dealing with the day long strike which added to the tensions.

Procter and Gamble

The role of HR here revolved around:

- A core team was formed, which comprised of all the personnel of different departments.
- Bifurcation of employees and dividing them into various strata depending upon their ability and competency.
- Gap analysis so as to deal with issues that popped up because some of the key personnel left their duties at P&G, confused about their future.
- Dealing consciously with the retention, training, and compensation issues so as to avoid any further losses.

Post-Merger Stage

NTPC

Here the role of HR is very significant because after two entities have been added to each other it's very important to gel them into one so that whatever the overlapping boundaries are evacuated. Some initiatives taken by HR here include

- Managing well the change in organization design
- Developing quality of work life groups
- Holding appreciative enquiry sessions
- Designing training programs, etc.

Bank of Baroda

Here the HR initiatives were as under:

- Dealing with issues related to change in organizational size and structure
- Making the climate friendly and conducive for easy enablement of retrenchments strategies
- Putting into place an effective grievance management system, etc.

Procter and Gamble

Some HR initiatives are as under:

- Organization of job fairs to provide equally good employment to the retrenched employees
- Development of an open-ended communication system to deal with grievance of any sort.
- Organizing training programs to deal with any sort of disparities.

REFERENCES

S.V.V.S.V. Prasad, Swarnika Dixit, "HR in Mergers and Acquisitions: A Ringside View", *Journal HRM Review*, The Icfai University Press, January 2007.

Ministry of Manpower, "The role of HR in Mergers and Acquisitions", Case study series 1/2003.

Amit Pande, Sandeep K. Krishnan, "Knotted forever...", Paper, IIMA fellow Programme in Management.

Cairnes, Margot "Surviving Super Mergers", *Human Resources*, Asia Pacific, October 2001.

Fitz-enz, Jac, *The ROI of Human Capital*, Jac Fitz-Enz, AMACOM, 2000.

Gaplin and Henron, *The Complete Guide to Mergers and Acquisitions* (1999).

Kay, Ira and Shelton, Mike "The People Problem in Mergers", *Human Resources*, Singapore Volume 4:3.

Neiger, David "Merging Interests", *HR Monthly*, Australia, October 2001.

Powell, Mark "Managing the Asian M&A wave", *Economic Bulletin*, Singapore, January 2002.

Rubis, Leon "Merger Mania Means Much Work for HR", editorial director of SHIRM

Schmidt, Jeffery, Making Mergers Work, The Society for Human Resource Management, October 2001.

Shea, Thomas H. "Employee Retention Through Mergers and Acquisitions", Workforce Website.

Sidel, Robin "Volatile U.S. Markets Cool Desire for Mergers" *The Asian Wall Street Journal*. January 6, 2002 p. 56.

Weatherseed, Stephen "What makes a successful merger", *Insight Newsletter*, May 2001.

"After the Deal", *The Economist*, January 1999.

"Big gains vindicate DBS-POSB merger: poll", *The Business Times*, October 30, 2002.

"Mergers and Acquisitions", Andersen Website, May 2001.

"Mergers and acquisitions down 53%:KPMG", Bloomberg, *The Business Times*, December 11, 2001.

CHAPTER 13

EMPLOYEE TURNOVER: A POSITIVE PERSPECTIVE

–*P.K. Khicha* and *Netra Pal Singh*

ABSTRACT

Employee turnover is a natural process for any organization, still, it is giving sleepless nights to HR managers in many countries. Various factors work at different levels, which result in turnover. Turnover may be voluntary or involuntary resulting in loss of either good or bad employees. Whatever may be the case, it results in a vacant post and increased work pressure in the organization. Zero turnover is neither desirable nor feasible for several reasons. Therefore, it is often informative to look at turnover from more than one perspective at a time. It provides the organization an opportunity to introspect and make necessary changes within and in the recruitment procedure, enabling to create a fresh and more enthusiastic workforce. Dealing with the turnover in right spirit can rejuvenate the entire working environment of an organization. Production may be automated, but the driving force of any organization is its people.

Introduction

World has become a small place with the advent of globalization, efficient means of communication, fast and better means of transportation. As the new era brings in new advancement and new knowledge, it brings new challenges and new problems too. In India also, the growth and job opportunities have increased with the fast economic growth. Many MNCs have entered the market giving rise to better employment opportunities for all.

Coupled with the expansion of knowledge and service-oriented economy has resulted in a growing demand for skilled personnel. This has resulted in an increase in the mobility of skilled employees, which is a natural response to this increasing inter-connection and inter-dependency between our societies and economies. Fundamentally, there is no problem with this phenomenon, but when skilled intellectuals and technical employees are lost and cannot be readily replaced, this can pose complex challenges and have adverse implications for a source organization, especially if these are budding up organizations. Broadly, this unwanted loss of desirable employees is called Employee Turnover.

When an employee resigns our minds immediately turn to recruitment, training, cost and time delays involved in getting a replacement.

It is easy to focus strictly on the negative aspects of employee turnover and overlook the positive elements. Employee turnover can cost companies a huge amount in recruitment and training, but it also opens up opportunities for improvement worth many times this cost. Planning for a healthy level of turnover can improve business and reduce the costs associated with finding and retaining new staff.

Understanding Employee Turnover

"Employee Turnover" as a term is widely used in business circles. Many researchers and management experts have defined employee turnover in different ways:

Abassi et al. (2000) defined "Employee turnover is the rotation of workers around the labor market; between firms, jobs and occupations; and between the states of employment and unemployment".

Woods (2001): Managers refer to turnover as the entire process associated with filling a vacancy. Each time a position is vacated, either voluntarily or involuntarily, a new employee must be hired and trained. This replacement cycle is known as turnover.

Price (1977) defined the term "turnover" as the ratio of the number of organizational members who have left during the period being considered divided by the average number of people in that organization during the period.

There are three types of employee turnover and each has its positive side and unfortunately there is also a negative side.

- First, we have the employee who decides to retire or through some other life event decides that the time has come to leave the workforce. It may be voluntary, like marriage one has to shift or involuntary, like after certain age one has to retire. But the fact is that organization cannot avoid this turnover. It is bound to happen. In most of the cases, employees leave on good note. Therefore, even though the organization feels a loss, there is no bad feeling.
- Then, there are employees who leave to seek a better position elsewhere because of money, opportunity, location or some other reason. It is a voluntary and avoidable turnover, if required. Normally, employees leave for advancement in career, higher income, dissatisfaction in present job, etc. Most of these issues can be addressed properly and sorted out for real good employees. By working on these issues optimally, company can retain a good workforce. If good employees leave, the company surely feels the loss.
- Finally, there are those employees who need to be moved out of the organization by a prompt management decision. It is generally an involuntary turnover and the organization does not feel the loss either. There might be some employees in company who are not worth keeping. If such employees leave on their own, its in the benefit of the organization, else the company management has to think of ways to say them good-bye. Though the vacant post need to be filled, yet company does not feel any loss.

Benefits of Employee Turnover

Understanding why employees are leaving voluntarily and involuntarily, by reviewing termination records and exit interviews, one can expose a weak supervisor or find a recurring reason why employees might be leaving—poor benefits, low pay. Armed with this information, employers are better equipped to deal with any issues and make positive changes.

- While employee turnover may signal that an organization has issues that have not been fully addressed, employee turnover can also provide employers with an opportunity to refresh the talent pool or make needed changes to infrastructure.
- Provides scope for analyzing and improvement in selection procedures, which may be faulty at times resulting in attrition rate. Company can review the job profile and hire a more suitable employee, avoiding over-qualified or under-qualified staff.
- Unproductive employees are considerable liability that can cost more in the long run in terms of poor client service, poor organization and poor time management. In such cases, it is better to do away with employees who do not work towards promoting the company goals.
- When an employee leaves an organization, one can often replace that employee with someone who will accept less money. One of the main financial benefits of turnover is that it provides an opportunity to reset salaries. As employees at the high end of the pay structure leave, cost savings are typically seen when a company brings in a replacement at a lower rate, or promotes from within and lowers the rate for that employee's replacement.
- Maintaining the same workforce year in year out threading through the same work culture and norms can restrain much needed organizational change that can be made possible through newly recruits with fresh ideas.
- Keeps other employees on their toes. Long-term employees tend to resent newcomers, simply because they are set in their ways and don't want anyone else to show them up. However, in the long run, it can be a good thing, because it reminds older members of staff that they can't afford to slack off. There is also the possibility that relations between staff members will improve as the result of new members of staff.
- Gets rid of troublesome employees. Most organizations have at least one or two members of staff that cause trouble, perhaps because they gossip or are moody. Their behaviour may be detrimental to the office as a whole. Once they have left, the office environment may become a much better place, unless the trouble-makers are replaced by other trouble-makers of course.
- From employees' point of view, it gives the remaining employees an opportunity to receive promotion and take up new responsibilities which in turn would be a great morale boost for them.

Conclusion

Employee turnover is a natural process for any organization which brings in some change that may be desirable or undesirable. Still every business needs change in order to survive and thrive. Change is a function of keeping the organization alive, allowing it to grow or to recover from setbacks in the market and in the economy. Production may be automated, but the driving force of any organization is its people.

Staff turn-over is a healthy and necessary part of any organization. It offers new opportunities and helps to prevent an organization from becoming stale. In fact, less than five per cent turnover is actually considered unhealthy.

The fact is that employee turnover creates a great opportunity to make changes to how things are currently run. Though an excessive level of employee turnover can indicate serious problems within an organization, yet a moderate level of employee turnover can be both healthy and desirable.

It's important to remember that the strengths in turnover outweigh the weaknesses in turnover, if one simply creates "purposeful, directed turnover".

REFERENCES

Abassi, S.M., Hollman, K.W. (2000). "Turnover: The real bottom line", *Public Personnel Management*, 2(3): 333-42.

Batt, R. (2002). "Managing Customer Services: Human Resource Practices, Quit Rates, and Sales Growth." *Academy of Management Journal*, 45: 587-97.

Dess, Gregory G. and Jason D. Shaw (2001). "Voluntary Turnover, Social Capital, and Organizational Performance". *Academy of Management Review*, 26(3): 446-56.

Harris, Mark, Tang, Kam-Ki and Yi-Ping Tseng (2002) Optimal employee turnover rate:theory and evidence. Melbourne Institute Working Paper No. 19/02.

http://www.helium.com/knowledge/69087-the-positive-side-of-employee-turnover, April 2012.

http://www.ere.net/2009/04/06/not-all-employee-turnover-is-bad-celebrate-losing-the-losers/, April 2012.

http://www.braunconsulting.com/bcg/newsletters/summer2005/summer20055.html, May 2012.

Jovanovic, Boyan (1979). "Job Matching and the Theory of Turnover". *The Journal of Political Economy*, 87(5): 972-90.

McElroy, James C., Morrow, Paula C. and Scott N. Rude (2001). "Turnover and Organizational Performance: A Comparative Analysis of the Effects of Voluntary, Involuntary and Reduction-in-force Turnover". *Journal of Applied Psychology*, 86(6): 1294-99.

Price, J.L. (1977). The study of turnover, 1st edition, Iowa State University Press, IA pp. 10-25.

Shaw, Jason D., Gupta, Nina and John E. Delery (2005). "Alternative Conceptualizations of the Relationship between Voluntary Turnover and Organizational Performance". *Academy of Management Journal*, 48(1): 50-68.

Wendy, S. Harman, Thomas W. Lee, Terence R. Mitchell, William Felps, Bradley P. Owens (2007). "The Psychology of Voluntary Employee Turnover". *Current Directions in Psychological Science*, 16(1), 51-54.

CHAPTER 14 AWARENESS TOWARDS THE PERFORMANCE APPRAISAL SYSTEMS IN HRH GROUP OF HOTELS—A CASE STUDY

–*Dhiraj Jain* and *Shweta Garg*

ABSTRACT

Performance appraisal systems help the organizations to accomplish their mission and vision by judging effectiveness of the employees, i.e. recruitment, selection, training and development. The purpose of the study is to understand the awareness among the employees regarding the performance appraisal system adopted in HRH groups of hotels.

The performance appraisal system in HRH group of hotels, which is a leading chain of heritage and hotels preserving royal palaces, hotels and resorts in Rajasthan and India, does a proper assessment of the employee contribution. The performance appraisal system is very important for the efficient functioning of the organization.

The research design adopted was descriptive in nature where a structured questionnaire are administered and 30 respondents were selected of the employees of the HRH groups of hotels by using stratified random sampling method. The study concluded that the employees were very well aware of the performance appraisal methods adopted within the organization and proper training were conducted before employee induction.

Introduction

Performance appraisal means the systematic evaluation of performance of the employee in the organization and for the purpose of evaluation, the criteria selected should be in quantifiable or in measurable terms. It helps the employee to know where he stands in the organization and also to identify the problems in their work and to overcome them. It diagnoses the employee's strong and weak points, so that the organizations can direct their efforts to upgrade their performance by providing them training, which would help them in getting promotion, transfer, financial rewards, and good placements in the organization. The significance of an appraisal system is that an individual get a feedback of their present performance in the job which gives them a clear sense of their responsibilities and the expectations which are to be fulfilled by them. It also helps the organizations to accomplish their mission and vision by judging truly the effectiveness of the employees, i.e. recruitment, selection, training and development.

The nature of performance appraisal and its effectiveness depends a great deal on how human resource are viewed and treated in the organization. The performance appraisal also gives a proper assessment of the employee's contribution and promotes a good and positive working environment, which contributes to the productivity in the organization. By this performance appraisal, the management finds out that how effective it has been at hiring and placing employees in their organization and the information received from the appraisal system help in counseling of the employees.

There are several methods which are adopted in the performance appraisal—human resource accounting, behaviorally anchored rating scales, paired comparisons, forced distribution, appraisal through MBO, graphic rating scales. The performance appraisal system adopted in HRH group of hotels is a very simple system both different for above manager and below manager.

Review of Literature

Robert D. Bretz Jr. (1992) examined the performance appraisal literature published in both academic and practitioner outlets between 1985 and 1990, briefly discussing the current state of performance appraisal practice, highlighting the juxtaposition of research and practice, and suggested directions for further research. Paul E. Levy (2004) broadened the traditional conceptualization of performance appraisal effectiveness to include and emphasize rate reactions. The influence that the feedback environment or feedback culture had on performance appraisal outcomes was a focus that seemed to have both theoretical and applied implications. Annan-Prah (2007) examined employees' perceptions of the performance appraisal system of a Ghanaian tertiary institution in terms of satisfaction and fairness to the system, utilizing a hypothesized four-factor justice model of organizational justice as the theoretical basis. Prawitowati (2011) attempted to design competence-based performance appraisal system for higher education institutions. It was found that there were three competencies, namely core competency, managerial competency, and technical competency. Rakesh Kumar (2011) defined appraisal as "the process of periodically reviewing one's performance against the various elements of one's job". His study described the purpose and developmental criteria of an appraisal program that regularly assessed the performance of hospital employees. Azman Ismail (2011) examined the effect of performance appraisal politics on job satisfaction. The results confirmed that performance appraisal politics acted as important predictors of job satisfaction in the studied organization. Sanjeet Singh Sharma (2011) examined the effect of performance appraisal on individual as well as on the organizations. The findings of the research showed that there was a noticeable effect of the performance appraisal on the organizations as well as on the individuals. Choon Jin Teha (2012) explored the relationship of organizational culture (OC) and the performance appraisal (PA) process and their impact on the organizational citizenship behavior (OCB) of academic staff. Khan (2011) investigated most of the Omani companies are still had reactive HR strategies with little emphasis on a proactive performance management system. For them, Omanisation of the workforce and adhering to the Omanisation target set by the government appeared to be high on the agenda. Gone (2010) paid attention to job analyses centered on job-related work behaviors and results by communicating these and providing training in their use to employees and supervisors, and by documenting and monitoring the process for accuracy and fairness they found that an organization could achieve a valid appraisal system. Shu-qing (2008) probed into the complete process of performance appraisal for cooperative manufacturing project and combined this with the practice of performance appraisal of power products of cooperative manufacturing projects in virtual enterprises. Harvey (1997) developed an evaluation process for home, host, and third country nationals working in a variety of international environments. Kumbhar (2011) examined the role of HR in performance appraisal processes. It included the importance of the appraisal process, the different types of appraisals and their effectiveness. Performance appraisal was an important basis for corporate personnel decisions. Omboi Bernard Messah (2011) investigated the effectiveness of performance appraisal systems in Kenya Tea Development Agency with special focus on, Githongo, Imenti Tea Factory, Kiegoi and Miciimikuru Tea factories in Meru County in Kenya. Richard Bitange Nyaoga (2010) evaluated the effectiveness of performance appraisal system at private universities in Kenya. Their study evaluated the purpose of performance appraisal in private universities and identified relevant factors for achieving an effective performance appraisal. Sutheparaks (2011) presented the generic model for not only human resource performance appraisal system, but also other business domains. The model could be extended and adapted to constant changes of appraisal policies. A.A. Adekunle (2010) examined the relationship between open reporting system of performance evaluation and teachers' perceived productivity in Lagos State, and suggested that teachers performance appraisal system should be based on objectivity and be devoid of prejudices and biases. Jaisheela (2010) examined the employee satisfaction regarding the performance appraisal, which had a large bearing on the overall performance of the employees in South Central Railways. B. Sripirabaa (2009) investigated the influence of partnering and financial support on the functions of performance management system. The capacity of the system to align its functions to help achieve an organization's strategic goals was also examined.

Objective of the Study

- To study the appraisal system existent in HRH group of hotels.
- To study the awareness among the employees towards the performance appraisal system.
- To examine the satisfaction level of the performance appraisal system among the employees in the organization.
- To study the association between the demographic determinants and their perception towards performance appraisal existent in HRH group of hotels.

Hypothesis Framed for the Study

Null Hypothesis

H_0: There is no significant association between the demographic profile of the employees and their awareness towards the performance appraisal systems adopted in HRH group of hotels.

Research Methodology

- The study is based on primary data collection among 30 respondents from HRH groups of hotels, Udaipur.
- Research design was descriptive in nature.
- Stratified random sampling technique was used.
- A well-structured questionnaire was used to collect primary data for analysis. A survey was carried out on the randomly selected employees of HRH group of hotels.
- Chi square test was used to test the association or non-association between the variables.
- Data has been presented in the forms of tables in order to make the analysis easy.
- Statistical softwares along with MS-Excel had been extensive used for the study.

Data Analysis and Interpretation

H_1: There is no significant association between the demographic factors and the perception that a proper assessment of the employee contribution to the organization was done for performance appraisal.

Table 1

		Proper assessment of employee contribution to the organization					Total
		Strongly Agree	Agree	Neutral	Disagree	Strongly Disagree	
Age	20-30 years	0	2	1	1	0	4
	30-40 years	5	6	4	0	2	17
	40-50 years	3	3	1	1	1	9
	Total	8	11	6	2	3	30
Department	Front office	2	1	2	0	0	5
	Food & beverages	2	7	3	2	3	17
	Finance	2	2	1	0	0	5
	Repair & maintenance	2	1	0	0	0	3
	Total	8	11	6	2	3	30
			Age			Department	
	Calculated value		5.887			9.85	
	df		8			12	
	Tabulated value		15.507			21.026	
	Accepted/rejected		Accepted			Accepted	

Interpretation: As null hypothesis is accepted in both the cases, we can conclude that there is no significant association between the demographic determinants and the perception that a proper assessment of the employees' contribution is done before performance appraisal.

H_2: There is no significant association between the demographic determinants and the awareness of the performance appraisal model used in the organization during induction.

Table 2

		Awareness of the performance appraisal model used in the organization					Total
		Strongly Agree	Agree	Neutral	Disagree	Strongly Disagree	
Age	20-30 years	2	1	1	0	0	4
	30-40 years	6	7	3	1	0	17
	40-50 years	3	5	0	0	1	9
	Total	11	13	4	1	1	30
Department	Front office	2	1	2	0	0	5
	Food & beverages	6	8	1	1	1	17
	Finance	2	3	0	0	0	5
	Repair & maintenance	1	1	1	0	0	3
	Total	11	13	4	1	1	30
			Age			Department	
	Calculated value		5.182			7.591	
	df		8			12	
	Tabulated value		15.507			21.026	
	Accepted/rejected		Accepted			Accepted	

Interpretation: As null hypothesis is accepted in both the cases, we can conclude that there is no significant association between the demographic determinants and the awareness of the performance appraisal model used in the organization during induction.

H_3: There is no significant association between the demographic determinants and the awareness towards the continuous review of performance of the employee.

Table 3

		Continuous review of performance of employee				*Total*
		Strongly Agree	*Agree*	*Neutral*	*Strongly Disagree*	
Age	20-30 years	1	2	1	0	4
	30-40 years	7	4	2	4	17
	40-50 years	2	3	4	0	9
	Total	10	9	7	4	30
Department	Front office	3	1	1	0	5
	Food & Beverages	3	6	4	4	17
	Finance	2	2	1	0	5
	Repair & maintenance	2	0	1	0	3
	Total	10	9	7	4	30
			Age		Department	
	Calculated value		7.292		8.016	
	df		6		9	
	Tabulated value		12.592		16.919	
	Accepted/rejected		Accepted		Accepted	

Interpretation: As null hypothesis is accepted in both the cases, we can conclude that there is no significant association between demographic determinants and the awareness towards the continuous review of performance of the employee.

H_4: There is no significant association between the demographic determinants and the perception that performance appraisal is important for employee performance.

Table 4

		Performance appraisal is important in employee performance				*Total*
		Strongly Agree	*Agree*	*Neutral*	*Disagree*	
Age	20-30 years	3	1	0	0	4
	30-40 years	6	7	3	1	17
	40-50 years	4	4	1	0	9
	Total	13	12	4	1	30
Department	Front office	4	0	0	1	5
	Food & beverages	5	9	3	0	17
	Finance	3	2	0	0	5
	Repair & maintenance	1	1	1	0	3
	Total	13	12	4	1	30
			Age		Department	
	Calculated value		3.016		12.917	
	df		6		9	
	Tabulated value		12.592		16.919	
	Accepted/rejected		Accepted		Accepted	

Interpretation: As null hypothesis is accepted in both the cases, we can conclude that there is no significant association between demographic determinants and the importance of performance appraisal in the employee performance.

H_5: There is no significant association between the demographic determinants and the awareness of the fact that a simple model of performance appraisal is used in the organization.

Table 5

		Performance appraisal model is simple in organization					Total
		Strongly Agree	*Agree*	*Neutral*	*Disagree*	*Strongly Disagree*	
Age	20-30 years	0	3	1	0	0	4
	30-40 years	10	4	1	1	1	17
	40-50 years	2	5	2	0	0	9
	Total	12	12	4	1	1	30
Department	Front office	2	2	1	0	0	5
	Food & beverages	8	5	2	1	1	17
	Finance	1	4	0	0	0	5
	Repair & maintenance	1	1	1	0	0	3
	Total	12	12	4	1	1	30
		Age				Department	
	Calculated value	9.918				6.549	
	df	8				12	
	Tabulated value	15.507				21.026	
	Accepted/rejected	Accepted				Accepted	

Interpretation: As the null hypothesis is accepted in both the cases, we can conclude that there is no significant association between demographic determinants and the awareness of the fact that a simple model of performance appraisal is used in the organization.

H_6: There is no significant association between the demographic determinants and the awareness towards the identification of training need in the organization.

Table 6

		Identification of training need in the organization					Total
		Strongly Agree	*Agree*	*Neutral*	*Disagree*	*Strongly Disagree*	
Age	20-30 years	2	1	0	1	0	4
	30-40 years	8	5	2	0	2	17
	40-50 years	4	3	0	2	0	9
	Total	14	9	2	3	2	30
Department	Front office	3	0	0	1	1	5
	Food & beverages	7	6	2	1	1	17
	Finance	3	2	0	0	0	5
	Repair & maintenance	1	1	0	1	0	3
	Total	14	9	2	3	2	30
		Age				Department	
	Calculated value	7.092				8.775	
	df	8				12	
	Tabulated value	15.507				21.026	
	Accepted/rejected	Accepted				Accepted	

Interpretation: As null hypothesis is accepted in both the cases, we can conclude that there is no significant association between demographic determinants and the awareness towards the identification of training need in the organization.

H_7: There is no significant association between the demographic determinants and the perception whether the assessment of performance matches employee expectations.

Table 7

		Performance appraisal matches to employee expectation					*Total*
		Strongly Agree	*Agree*	*Neutral*	*Disagree*	*Strongly Disagree*	
Age	20-30 years	3	0	0	1	0	4
	30-40 years	11	4	0	1	1	17
	40-50 years	3	5	1	0	0	9
	Total	17	9	1	2	1	30
Department	Front office	4	0	0	1	0	5
	Food & beverages	8	7	0	1	1	17
	Finance	3	1	1	0	0	5
	Repair & maintenance	2	1	0	0	0	3
	Total	17	9	1	2	1	30
			Age			Department	
	Calculated value		10.423			10.853	
	df		8			12	
	Tabulated value		15.507			21.026	
	Accepted/rejected		Accepted			Accepted	

Interpretation: As the null hypothesis is accepted in both the cases, we can conclude that there is no significant association between demographic determinants and the perception whether the assessment of performance matches employee expectations.

H_8: There is no significant association between the demographic determinants and the perception that the appraisal system adopted adequately appraises the potential of the employees.

Table 8

		Appraisal system adequately appraises the employee potential					*Total*
		Strongly Agree	*Agree*	*Neutral*	*Disagree*	*Strongly Disagree*	
Age	20-30 years	1	2	1	0	0	4
	30-40 years	9	4	1	2	1	17
	40-50 years	1	7	0	1	0	9
	Total	11	13	2	3	1	30
Department	Front office	3	1	1	0	0	5
	Food & beverages	7	6	1	2	1	17
	Finance	1	4	0	0	0	5
	Repair & maintenance	0	2	0	1	0	3
	Total	11	13	2	3	1	30
			Age			Department	
	Calculated value		10.884			10.549	
	df		8			12	
	Tabulated value		15.507			21.026	
	Accepted/rejected		Accepted			Accepted	

Interpretation: As null hypothesis is accepted in both the cases, we can conclude that there is no significant association between demographic determinants and the appraisal system which adequately appraises the potential of the employees.

H_9: There is no significant association between the demographic determinants and the perception as to whether proper feedback is given for employee performance appraisal.

Table 9

		Getting proper feedback					Total
		Strongly Agree	Agree	Neutral	Disagree	Strongly Disagree	
Age	20-30 years	1	2	0	1	0	4
	30-40 years	4	5	5	1	2	17
	40-50 years	2	3	1	3	0	9
	Total	7	10	6	5	2	30
Department	Front office	0	3	1	1	0	5
	Food & beverages	5	5	3	2	2	17
	Finance	1	2	1	1	0	5
	Repair & maintenance	1	0	1	1	0	3
	Total	7	10	6	5	2	30
			Age			Department	
	Calculated value		6.712			6.455	
	df		8			12	
	Tabulated value		15.507			21.026	
	Accepted/rejected		Accepted			Accepted	

Interpretation: As null hypothesis is accepted in both the cases, we can conclude that there is no significant association between demographic determinants and the perception that a proper feedback of employee performance appraisal is given.

H_{10}: There is no significant association between the demographic determinants and the perception that promotion, transfer, demotion and suspension is purely based on the performance appraisal.

Table 10

		Promotion, transfer, demotion & suspension is purely based on performance appraisal				Total
		Strongly Agree	Agree	Neutral	Disagree	
Age	20-30 years	1	1	2	0	4
	30-40 years	4	9	3	1	17
	40-50 years	2	3	4	0	9
	Total	7	13	9	1	30
Department	Front office	1	2	1	1	5
	Food & beverages	6	6	5	0	17
	Finance	0	3	2	0	5
	Repair & maintenance	0	2	1	0	3
	Total	7	13	9	1	30
			Age		Department	
	Calculated value		3.679		9.243	
	df		6		9	
	Tabulated value		12.592		16.919	
	Accepted/rejected		Accepted		Accepted	

Interpretation: As null hypothesis is accepted, we can conclude that there is no significant association between demographic determinants and the perception that promotion, transfer, demotion and suspension are purely based on the performance appraisal.

H_{11}: There is no significant association between the demographic determinants and the perception that employees are satisfied with the existent performance appraisal system.

Table 11

		Employee are satisfied with existent performance appraisal system					*Total*
		Strongly Agree	*Agree*	*Neutral*	*Disagree*	*Strongly Disagree*	
Age	20-30 years	1	1	1	1	0	4
	30-40 years	4	8	1	3	1	17
	40-50 years	1	5	0	3	0	9
	Total	6	14	2	7	1	30
Department	Front office	2	1	2	0	0	5
	Food & beverages	3	9	0	4	1	17
	Finance	1	2	0	2	0	5
	Repair & maintenance	0	2	0	1	0	3
	Total	6	14	2	7	1	30
			Age			Department	
	Calculated value		5.09			15.513	
	df		8			12	
	Tabulated value		15.507			21.026	
	Accepted/rejected		Accepted			Accepted	

Interpretation: As the null hypothesis is accepted in both the cases, we can conclude that there is no significant association between demographic determinants and the perception that employees are satisfied with the existent performance appraisal system.

H_{12}: There is no significant association between the demographic determinants and the perception that the performance appraisal system is acceptable.

Table 12

		Performance appraisal system adopted is acceptable				*Total*
		Strongly Agree	*Agree*	*Neutral*	*Disagree*	
Age	20-30 years	0	2	2	0	4
	30-40 years	9	6	2	0	17
	40-50 years	2	4	2	1	9
	Total	11	12	6	1	30
Department	Front office	1	2	2	0	5
	Food & beverages	6	8	2	1	17
	Finance	2	2	1	0	5
	Repair & maintenance	2	0	1	0	3
	Total	11	12	6	1	30
			Age		Department	
	Calculated value		8.177		5.159	
	df		6		9	
	Tabulated value		12.592		16.919	
	Accepted/rejected		Accepted		Accepted	

Interpretation: As null hypothesis is accepted, we can conclude that there is no significant association between demographic determinants and the acceptability of the performance appraisal system adopted.

H_{13}: There is no significant association between the demographic determinants and the perception that past performance appraisals are considered during performance appraisals.

Table 13

		Past performance consider during performance appraisal				*Total*
		Strongly Agree	*Agree*	*Neutral*	*Disagree*	
Age	20-30 years	1	1	1	1	4
	30-40 years	5	7	4	1	17
	40-50 years	1	7	0	1	9
	Total	7	15	5	3	30
Department	Front office	1	2	1	1	5
	Food & beverages	3	8	4	2	17
	Finance	1	4	0	0	5
	Repair & maintenance	2	1	0	0	3
	Total	7	15	5	3	30
			Age		Department	
	Calculated value		6.35		7.094	
	df		6		9	
	Tabulated value		12.592		16.919	
	Accepted/rejected		Accepted		Accepted	

Interpretation: As null hypothesis is accepted in both the cases, we can conclude that there is no significant association between demographic determinants and the perception that past performance appraisals are considered during the performance appraisals.

H_{14}: There is no significant association between the demographic determinants and the perception that the employee performance appraisal program is beneficial.

Table 14

		Employees get the benefit of the performance appraisal programs				*Total*
		Strongly Agree	*Agree*	*Neutral*	*Disagree*	
Age	20-30 years	2	0	2	0	4
	30-40 years	6	8	2	1	17
	40-50 years	7	1	0	1	9
	Total	15	9	4	2	30
Department	Front office	1	2	2	0	5
	Food & beverages	8	5	2	2	17
	Finance	5	0	0	0	5
	Repair & maintenance	1	2	0	0	3
	Total	15	9	4	2	30
			Age		Department	
	Calculated value		11.857		11.903	
	df		6		9	
	Tabulated value		12.592		16.919	
	Accepted/rejected		Accepted		Accepted	

Interpretation: As the null hypothesis is accepted in both the cases, we can conclude that there is no significant association between demographic determinants and the fact that the employee are benefited by the performance appraisal program.

H_{15}: There is no significant association between the demographic determinants and the perception that the performance appraisal is important for efficient functioning of the organization.

Table 15

		Performance appraisal is important for effective function of organization					*Total*
		Strongly Agree	*Agree*	*Neutral*	*Disagree*	*Strongly Disagree*	
Age	20-30 years	0	2	1	1	0	4
	30-40 years	8	5	2	0	2	17
	40-50 years	3	3	1	2	0	9
	Total	11	10	4	3	2	30
Department	Front office	1	1	2	0	1	5
	Food & beverages	5	7	2	2	1	17
	Finance	3	2	0	0	0	5
	Repair & maintenance	2	0	0	1	0	3
	Total	11	10	4	3	2	30
			Age			Department	
	Calculated value		8.353			12.082	
	df		8			12	
	Tabulated value		15.507			21.026	
	Accepted/rejected		Accepted			Accepted	

Interpretation: As null hypothesis is accepted in both the cases, we can conclude that there is no significant association between demographic determinants and the perception that the performance appraisal is important for efficient functioning of the organization.

H_{16}: There is no significant association between the demographic determinants and the perception that the employees are given increment or are awarded by the employee performance appraisal program.

Table 16

		Employees are awarded, incremented by the performance appraisal program					*Total*
		Strongly Agree	*Agree*	*Neutral*	*Disagree*	*Strongly Disagree*	
Age	20-30 years	1	2	0	0	1	4
	30-40 years	5	6	2	1	3	17
	40-50 years	5	3	1	0	0	9
	Total	11	11	3	1	4	30
Department	Front office	1	2	1	0	1	5
	Food & beverages	5	7	1	1	3	17
	Finance	4	1	0	0	0	5
	Repair & maintenance	1	1	1	0	0	3
	Total	11	11	3	1	4	30
			Age			Department	
	Calculated value		4.573			8.847	
	df		8			12	
	Tabulated value		15.507			21.026	
	Accepted/rejected		Accepted			Accepted	

Interpretation: As the null hypothesis is accepted, we can conclude that there is no significant association between demographic determinants and the perception that the employees are given increment or are awarded by the performance appraisal program.

Conclusion

We can conclude that there is no significant association between the demographic determinants and the variables identified for performance appraisal. The employees get the feedback and the training during the induction which adequately appraises their potential. This shows the satisfaction level and the awareness among of the employees towards the performance appraisal system adopted in the HRH group of hotels. The performance appraisal system is very important for the efficient functioning of the organization.

REFERENCES

A.A. Adekunle, A.R. (2010). Correlation between Open Reporting System of Performance Evaluation and Teachers Perceived Productivity In Lagos State. An International Journal of Agriculture Sciences, Sciences, Environment & Technology, 5 (2).

Annan-Prah, E.C. (2007). Organisational Justice Theory Perceptions in Performance Appraisal System in a Ghanaian Tertiary Institution. *Journal of Business Research.*

Azman Ismail, N.A. (2011). An Empirical Study of the Relationship between Performance Appraisal Politics and Job Satisfaction. Acta Universitatis Danubius. *Œconomica*, 7(1).

B. Sripirabaa, R.K. (2009). Performance management systems in an Indian manufacturing sector: Partnering, monetary incentives and the alignment of organizational goal. *Management Research News*, 32(10), 942-52.

Choon Jin Teha, A.B. (2012). Organizational culture and performance appraisal process: Effect on organizational citizenship behavior. *Asian Business & Management.*

Gone, D.I. (2010). Performance appraisal systems in public institutions. *Econ Papers*, 3(38), 10.

Harvey, M. (1997). Focusing the international personnel performance appraisal process. *Human Resource Development Quarterly*, 8(1), 41-62.

Jaisheela, B. (2010). Employee Performance Appraisal System in South Central Railway. *Journal of Commerce & Management Thought*, 1(4), 363-72.

Khan, S.A. (2011). Managing Performance: The Case of an Omani Oil Company. Vision: *The Journal of Business*, 14(4), 285-93.

Kumbhar, P.S. (2011). Impact of performance appraisal on corporate profitability. *Indian System Research Journal*, 1(4).

Omboi Bernard Messah, S.M. (2011). The Effect of Performance Appraisal Systems on Employees in Kenya Tea Development Agency: A Survey of Selected Tea Factories in Meru County-Kenya. *Research Journal of Finance and Accounting*, 2(3).

Paul E. Levy, J.R. (2004). The Social Context of Performance Appraisal: A Review and Framework for the Future. *Journal of Management*, 30(6), 881-905.

Prawitowati, T. (2011). Designing CBA model of performance appraisal system as a merit rating for higher education institution. *Journal of Economics, Bussiness, and Accountancy*, 14.

Rakesh Kumar, P. (2011). Employee performance appraisal in health care. *International Journal of Management and Strategy*, 11(3).

Richard Bitange Nyaoga, K.S. (2010). The effectiveness of performance. *African Journal of Business & Management (AJBUMA)*, 1, 16.

Robert D. Bretz Jr., G.T. (1992). The Current State of Performance Appraisal Research and Practice: Concerns, Directions, and Implications. *The Current State of Performance Appraisal Research and Practice: Concerns, Directions, and Implications*, 18 (2), 321-52.

Sanjeet Singh Sharma, G.D. (2011). A Study of Effect of Performance Appraisal on the Organization and the Employee. *Social Science Research Network*, 19.

Schneier, C.E. (1986). Creating a Performance Management System. *Training and Development Journal*, 40(5), 74-79.

Shu-qing, L. (2008). Research on Performance Appraisal Model for Cooperative Manufacturing Project in Virtual Enterprise and its Application. *IEEE Xplore*, 2, 195-204.

Sutheparaks, U.P. (2011). Defining global schema for ETL of human resource performance appraisal system using REA ontology. *IEEE Xplore*, 275-80.

CHAPTER 15 STUDY OF AN EFFECTIVE LEADERSHIP ENVIRONMENT—A MOST WANTED NEED IN INDIAN BPOs

–Dhiraj Jain and *Yukti Sharma*

ABSTRACT

BPO stands for "business process outsourcing", which is simply another term for outsourcing. This is when a company contracts an outside provider for services or business processes. This might include manufacturing or back-office functions such as accounting and human resources. But BPO might also includes front-end services such as customer care and technical support. With increasing global competition, Indian BPOs need to constantly identify their weaknesses and make measures to ensure their survival in this competitive market. Managing employees with effective leadership is one of the biggest challenges of Indian BPOs. The following study aims to understand the leadership environment and the perception of the employees towards their leader. In this study, Chi-square test has been studied to find the association/non-association between variables.

Introduction

In India, Business Process Outsourcing (BPO) is the fastest growing segment of the ITES (Information Technology Enabled Services) industry. Factors such as economy of scale, business risk mitigation, cost advantage; utilization improvement and superior competency have all lead to the growth of the Indian BPO industry. Business process outsourcing in India, which started around the mid-90s, has now grown by leaps and bounds. The term business process Outsourcing or BPO as it is popularly known, refers to outsourcing in all fields. A BPO service provider usually administers and manages a particular business process for another company. BPOs either use new technology or apply an existing technology in a new way to improve a particular business process. India is currently the number one destination for business process outsourcing, as most companies in the US and UK outsource IT-related business processes to Indian service providers.

Today, India is the hottest destination for any company that wants to outsource its business processes. From a negligible size in early 2000 to a gigantic size today, the BPO sector has been growing at an unprecedented rate. In 2003, India accounted for 75 per cent of the total BPO offshore delivery value that was expected to increase by 55 per cent annually over the next five years (Neale 2004). The growth of BPO industry is the direct result of growth in retail marketing and the operation lying within it. The continuous growth of BPO sector in India is the new call for young generation who are the verge of making their careers. The BPO industry boom in India is bringing along numerous job opportunities for youngsters with different background. There is no doubt that the outsourcing business has come to stay in India. The advantage that India provides the foreign clients is the availability of a good English speaking population, who are well educated and ambitious, coupled with the savings that foreign clients make with respect to salaries and infrastructure.

In spite of tough competition, India has emerged as a global leader in the business process outsourcing (BPO) industry. India has the advantage of having a large English speaking and computer literate workforce, which are considered as important perquisites for the success of the BPO sector. It explores the factors that have contributed to the success of BPO industry in India. Sound infrastructure is crucial for the success of any industry including BPO. The improvements achieved in the telecom, aviation, power, offices, hotels and road facilities that have facilitated the growth of the BPO industry. Also the initiatives taken by the government including policy concessions, tax exemptions and removal of procedural hurdles have enabled the growth of this sector. Another unmatched advantage is the average age of the workforce in India, which is just 30 years, as compared to any other country in the world, where the average age varies between 45 and 50 years. Since the BPO industry requires a young crowd, this huge demographic advantage cannot be matched by any country in the world. Earlier only routine jobs were outsourced to India. This scenario has totally changed. Apart from routine jobs, high end jobs are also outsourced, which has paved the way for functions like KPO, RPO, technical writing and so on. The industry is by and large un-regulated compared to other industries and has grown rapidly unchecked over the past few years.

Major Challenges to the BPO Industry in India

The biggest challenge to the BPO industry in India has been the high attrition rates with a lack of proper leadership environment. Attrition means not only loss of talent, but also includes the cost of training the new recruits. The attrition rate in the industry has been hovering around 35%, which is quite high for any industry. An average Indian call center employee works with a company for 11 months, whereas an average call center employee in UK stays in a company for three years. It is expected that the attrition rates would come down once the growth stabilizes. Steep growth is one of the reasons for the high attrition rates, according to many in the industry.

Lack of proper leadership in BPOs has terrible effects on the organization. It increases the costs to the organization considerably. They have to combat the amount of disruption due to unplanned exits. The more the people leave an organization, the more it is a drain on the company's resources like recruitment expenses, training and orientation resources and the time. Lack of leadership environment accompanied with high attrition rate also affects the productivity of the organization. Therefore, it is extremely important to curb attrition and ensure a proper leadership environment not only for an individual firm but also for the industry as a whole. Dearth of motivation among the BPO employees is one of the bitter truths that is responsible for the lack of motivation in this sector, and it is time it be considered. The basic solution to the burning issue is laying stress on the leadership environment of the Indian BPOs and analyzing it to understand the problems and challenges.

Employees in the BPO industry are increasingly managing complex pieces of work and are expected to not only deliver outcomes but also offer continuous improvement with a keen eye on the client's profitability and success. They are also expected to continuously invest in their own skills and industry knowledge to be able to conceptualize and implement large-scale changes in their processes. The new generation of BPO employees needs to have good communication skills, professional and cultural ethos to be able to collaborate with similar professionals across the globe, deep industry knowledge and a desire to learn and invest more towards building their careers in the industry. Over the next few years, the industry will continue to build a voracious appetite for professionals with deep industry skills and service line knowledge.

To sum up, the key action themes for the IT-BPO industry to remain competitive and profitable in the future are:

- **Visionary Leadership**—means to develop visionary leaders with operational efficiencies, who have the discipline to work toward his or her vision single-mindedly, as well as to direct his or her actions and those of the team toward the goal.
- **Openness in Leadership**—means to have team leaders with the openness, which means being able to listen to new ideas, even if they do not conform to the usual way of thinking. Good leaders are able to suspend judgment while listening to others' ideas, as well as accept new ways of doing things that someone else thought of. Openness builds mutual respect and trust between leaders and followers, and it also keeps the team well supplied with new ideas that can further its vision.
- **Fairness in Leadership**—means dealing with other team members consistently and justly. A leader must check all the facts and hear everyone out before passing judgment. He or she must avoid leaping to conclusions based on incomplete evidence. When people feel they that are being treated fairly, they reward a leader with loyalty and dedication.
- **Magnanimity in Leadership**—means giving credit where it is due. A magnanimous leader in BPO scenario ensures that credit for successes and customer satisfaction is spread as widely as possible throughout the company. Conversely, a good leader takes personal responsibility for failures. This sort of reverse magnanimity helps other people feel good about themselves and draws the team closer together. To spread the fame and take the blame is a hallmark of effective leadership.

Due to the increasing gap between the supply and demand of the talent for BPOs, and the already saturated talent market, the companies are luring and attracting youngsters with attractive pay packages and other benefits as soon as they get out of college. But the youngsters have to face the realities of the industry as they fail to cope up with the stress and responsibilities of their work life. It is clearly a case of hyper-growth with an immediate fall-down as soon as the reality strikes. All these problems have triggered the problems of attrition and retention for the BPO industry itself. The industry has had systematic issues, especially related to coping with human resource management in times of rapid growth. Indeed most BPO human resource personnel are either recruiting or trying to control attrition. The increasing problems of lack of employee satisfaction and high turnover in the BPOs can be reduced only by assuring effective team leaders with aforementioned good leadership qualities who can handle the young team members and motivate them in the right direction which can be useful both for the individual and the company.

Review of Literature

The research in hand focuses on leadership environment. The main focus of the study is look into the part played by leadership environment with special reference to the Indian BPOs organization. The literature review section includes various key topics and issues like leadership values, organization culture and association with demographics.

On Leadership Environment

Crystal and Jim (2003) studied transformational and transactional leadership in both physical (i.e. face-to-face) and virtual settings were examined in a laboratory experiment. Leadership style (transformational or transactional) and group setting (face-to-face, immersive virtual environment, or intercom) were manipulated experimentally for three-person ad hoc work groups. Results indicated that, compared to transactional leadership, transformational leadership was associated with decreases in quantitative performance but increases in qualitative performance, leadership satisfaction, and group cohesiveness. Contrary to expectations, neither self- nor collective-efficacy mediated the performance effects of leadership style; trust, however, appeared to play an important meditational role. Group performance and cohesiveness were similar across group settings; however, group members were most satisfied with their leader when interacting face-to-face.

Clark, Kenneth (1990) found that "Measures of Leadership" promises to be a vital and effective tool to improve business productivity and efficiency. Part I provided an historical overview of the successes and failures of leadership education in the past and a guide to the meaning and significance of the twenty-nine studies reported in Part II. Part II contained twenty-nine papers authored by some of the field's most prominent scientists, delving into the many unanswered questions regarding the most effective way to evaluate and to enhance leadership success.

House (1997) proposed a theory of charismatic leadership that focused on how a leader can create an impression among subordinates that the leader has the competence and vision to achieve success. The result is an enthusiasm and commitment by subordinates to the group objectives.

Yukl (1994) has shown in his study that transformational leader gains a greater commitment from subordinates and induces them to transcend personal self-interest for the betterment of the group or organization not only with charisma but also by serving as a coach, teacher, or mentor.

Lowe, Kroeck, and Sivasubramaniam (1996) in their study proved that there are evidences present that transformational leaders enhance follower effort, satisfaction, commitment, and performance.

Staples (1997) further reported that organizational commitment of the employees was one of the most important abiding concerns of managers of virtual workers. Research has also shown that the dispersion and dislocation characterizing virtual organizations may reduce communication among employees, increase their feelings of isolation, and consequently reduce their commitment to the organization.

Challenges for Indian BPOs

P.S. Mishra (2007) in his study identified managerial challenges and opportunities faced by business process outsourcing (BPO) firms in India. Content analysis of the responses revealed human resources- and organization-related challenges as the most critical issues. The lack of proper handling of human resources was discovered as the biggest challenge of BPO units. In the current scenario, BPO has become a mantra of employment.

Mobley (1977) in his research mentioned that despite the momentous growth and bright future, the BPO industry continues to suffer from very high attrition rates. New employees come with a lot of enthusiasm but their motivation gets depleted as job realities unfold with the passage of time. It identified the main causal agents responsible for high attrition in the BPO industry and argues that there is a vicious circle of attrition because 'Low Perceived Value' drives the employees to quit which further lowers the perceived value. The rapid growth of the outsourcing industry has resulted in both high turnover and labor shortages and at the same time provided employment opportunities to a new group of employees: young upwardly mobile college graduates.

Santoshi Sen Gupta (2008) further mentioned in his work that particular demographic profile of young employees is prone to high turnover and presents new managerial challenges. The variety of recruitment and retention strategies that companies in the business process outsourcing industry are experimenting with and show that many novel HR strategies are being crafted to address the needs of this young middle-class workforce.

Sarosh Kuruvilla (2010) in his study mentioned that in the global business scenario, BPO is on top of the list today. The new age workforce comprises mostly of knowledge workers, who are techno savvy, aware of market realities, materially focused and who have higher propensity to switch jobs. The challenge of acquiring new talent and retaining the existing talent is only going to intensify with the coming times.

Pawan (2006) using a mixed method approach involving both in-depth interviews and self-completing questionnaires, analyzed the nature of HRM systems in BPO organizations operating in India. The analysis is based on a sample of 51 BPO companies, a majority of which are located near the capital of New Delhi. The results focus on the nature and structure of work and organization of Indian BPOs, as well as the strategic role played by HRM in such organizations. Furthermore, the findings highlight the way specific HRM practices such as recruitment, performance appraisal, training and development, and compensations are implemented. The study suggests the existence of formal, structured, and rationalized HRM systems in Indian BPOs. The key people management challenges that these organizations face like attracting and retaining talent. The case company adopts formal, structured, transparent and innovative human resource practices. The study also highlights that such enlightened human resource practices stand on the foundations laid by an open work environment and facilitative leadership.

Objectives of the Study

- To study the leadership environment existent in the Indian BPO industry.
- To study the association between various demographic variables and the perception towards the existent leadership environment in this industry.

Hypothesis Framed for the Study

H_0: There is no significant association between the demographic determinants (gender, age, time spent and the educational qualifications) and the perception towards the existent leadership environment in Indian BPOs.

Research Methodology

- The study is based on primary data collection among 50 respondents from leading BPO of Udaipur city.
- Research design was descriptive in nature.
- A well-structured questionnaire was used to collect primary data for the analysis purpose.
- Data has been presented in the form of tables in order to make the analysis easy.
- Statistical software along with Ms-Excel has been extensively used for the study.

Chi-square

The Chi-square statistics is used to test the statistical significance of the observed association in a cross-tabulation. It assists us in determining whether a systematic association exists between two variables. The null hypothesis H_0 is that there is no association between the variables. The test is conducted by computing the cell frequencies. These expected cell frequencies, denoted f_e, are then compared to the actual observed frequencies f_o, found in the cross-tabulation to calculate the Chi-square statistics. The greater the discrepancies between the expected and actual frequencies, the larger the value of the statistic. Assume the cross-tabulation has *r* rows and *c* columns and a random sample of *n* observation. Then the expected frequency for each cell can be calculated by using a simple formula shown below in equation (1):

$$f_e = \frac{nrnc}{n} \quad \text{... (1)}$$

Where *nr* = total number in the row, *nc* = total number in the column, *n* = total sample size Then the value of Chi-square is calculated by using the formula shown in equation (2):

$$\chi^2 = \Sigma \frac{(f_o - f_e)}{f_e} \quad \text{... (2)}$$

An important characteristic of the Chi-square statistics is the number of degrees of freedom (*df*) associated with it. In general, the number of degree of freedom is equal to the number of observations less than number of constraints needed to calculate a statistical term. In the case of Chi-square statistic associated with a cross-tabulation, the number of degree of freedom is equal to the product of number of rows (r) less one and the number of columns (*c*) less one, i.e. $df = (r - 1) \times (c - 1)$. The null hypothesis H_0 of number of association between the two variables will be rejected only when the calculated value of the test statistics is greater than the critical value of Chi-square distribution with the appropriate degree of freedom (Source: Malhotra, 2007).

Data Analysis and Interpretation

Table 1: Demographic Profile of the Respondents

		Frequency	*Per cent*
Gender	Male	35	70.0
	Female	15	30.0
	Total	50	100.0
Educational Qualification	Undergraduate	38	76.0
	Masters	12	24.0
	Total	50	100.0
TIME SPENT	< 1 year	45	90.0
	1-2 years	3	6.0
	2-5 years	2	4.0
	Total	50	100.0
Age	< 21 years	26	52.0
	21-25 years	21	42.0
	26-30 years	3	6.0
	Total	50	100.0

Most of the respondents were male (70%), majority of them undergraduates (76%), most of them had spent a time of less than one year within the organization and most of them were below the age of 21 years.

Null Hypothesis-H_1: There is no significant association between the demographic variables and the perception of the team members that the supervisor treats them fairly.

Table 2

		Supervisor treats team members fairly					*Total*	*Calculated value (Chi-Square)*	*Df*	*Tabulated Value*	*Accepted/ Rejected*
		Disagree	*Somewhat disagree*	*Neither Agree nor Disagree*	*Somewhat agree*	*Agree*					
Gender	Male	2	13	6	12	2	35	11.742	4	9.49	Rejected
	Female	6	5	3	1	0	15				
Total		8	18	9	13	2	50				
Educational	Undergraduate	3	15	7	11	2	38	8.208	4	9.49	Accepted
Qualification	Masters	5	3	2	2	0	12				
Total		8	18	9	13	2	50				
TIME SPENT	< 1 year	6	17	8	12	2	45	5.002	8	15.51	Accepted
	1-2 years	1	0	1	1	0	3				
	2-5 years	1	1	0	0	0	2				
Total		8	18	9	13	2	50				
Age	< 21 years	2	8	6	9	1	26	6.101	8	15.51	Accepted
	21-25 years	5	9	3	3	1	21				
	26-30 years	1	1	0	1	0	3				
Total		8		9	13	2	50				

From the above study we can conclude that only in the case of gender there is significant association with the perception of the team members that the supervisor treats them fairly. Whereas in the case of other demographic variables there is no significant association between the demographic variables and the perception of the team members that their selected supervisor treats them fairly. This implies that the gender of the respondents affects their perception that their supervisor treats them fairly.

Null Hypothesis-H_2: There is no significant association between the demographic variables and the perception of the team members that the supervisor handles their personal and work related issues satisfactorily.

Table 3

		Supervisor handles work related & personal issues properly									
		Disagree	*Somewhat disagree*	*Neither Agree nor Disagree*	*Somewhat agree*	*Agree*	*Total*	*Calculated value (Chi-Square)*	*Df*	*Tabulated Value*	*Accepted/ Rejected*
Gender	Male	5	8	12	9	1	35	5.578	4	9.49	Accepted
	Female	2	8	4	1	0	15				
Total		7	16	16	10	1	50				
Educational	Undergraduate	7	9	13	8	1	38	6.277	4	9.49	Accepted
Qualification	Masters	0	7	3	2	0	12				
Total		7	16	16	10	1	50				
TIME SPENT	< 1 year	7	13	15	9	1	45	5.25	8	15.51	Accepted
	1-2 years	0	1	1	1	0	3				
	2-5 years	0	2	0	0	0	2				
Total		7	16	16	10	1	50				
Age	< 21 years	5	4	10	7	0	26	10.999	8	15.51	Accepted
	21-25 years	2	10	6	2	1	21				
	26-30 years	0	2	0	1	0	3				
Total		7	16	16	10	1	50				

As the null hypothesis is accepted in all the cases, we conclude that there is no significant association between the demographic variables and the perception of the team members that the supervisor handles their personal and work related issues satisfactorily.

Null Hypothesis-H_3: There is no significant association between the demographic variables and the perception of the team members that the supervisor acknowledges their work.

Table 4

		Acknowledgement of work								
		Disagree	*Somewhat disagree*	*Neither Agree nor Disagree*	*Somewhat agree*	*Total*	*Calculated value (Chi Square)*	*Df*	*Tabulated Value*	*Accepted/ Rejected*
Gender	Male	2	12	10	11	35	15.794	3	7.82	Rejected
	Female	8	4	2	1	15				
Total		10	16	12	12	50				
Educational Qualification	Undergraduate	4	13	11	10	38	9.316	3	7.82	Rejected
	Masters	6	3	1	2	12				
Total		10	16	12	12	50				
Time Spent	< 1 year	8	15	11	11	45	3.65	6	12.59	Accepted
	1-2 years	1	0	1	1	3				
	2-5 years	1	1	0	0	2				
Total		10	16	12	12	50				
Age	< 21 years	3	6	8	9	26	7.985	6	12.59	Accepted
	21-25 years	6	9	4	2	21				
	26-30 years	1	1	0	1	3				
Total		10	16	12	12	50				

From the above table it can be concluded that in the case of the demographic variable time spent with the organization and age the null hypothesis has been accepted which clearly shows that there is no significant association between these variables and the perception of the team members that the supervisor acknowledges their work. In case of gender and education qualification, there is significant association which reflects that the perception of team members that their supervisor acknowledges their work is affected by these variables.

Null Hypothesis-H_4: There is no significant association between the demographic variables and the perception of the employees that the supervisor is open to feedback.

Table 5

		Supervisor is open to feedback									
		Strongly disagree	*Disagree*	*Somewhat disagree*	*Neither Agree nor Disagree*	*Somewhat agree*	*Total*	*Calculated value (Chi-Square)*	*Df*	*Tabulated Value*	*Accepted/ Rejected*
Gender	Male	8	4	7	10	6	35	9.423	4	9.49	Accepted
	Female	4	6	4	1	0	15				
Total		12	10	11	11	6	50				
Educational Qualification	Undergraduate	9	5	9	9	6	38	6.016	4	9.49	Accepted
	Masters	3	5	2	2	0	12				
Total		12	10	11	11	6	50				
Time Spent	< 1 year	12	8	9	10	6	45	4.864	8	15.51	Accepted
	1-2 years	0	1	1	1	0	3				
	2-5 years	0	1	1	0	0	2				
Total		12	10	11	11	6	50				
Age	< 21 years	5	2	6	8	5	26	11.083	8	15.51	Accepted
	21-25 years	7	7	4	2	1	21				
	26-30 years	0	1	1	1	0	3				
Total		12	10	11	11	6	50				

As the null hypothesis is accepted in all the cases, we conclude that there is no significant association between the demographic variables and the perception of the employees that the supervisor is open to feedback, which implies the various demographic determinants do not affect the perception that supervisor are open to feedback.

Null Hypothesis-H_5: There is no significant association between the demographic variables and the perception of the team members that the supervisor helps in the development of their potential.

Table 6

		Development of potential										
		Strongly disagree	*Disagree*	*Somewhat disagree*	*Neither Agree nor Disagree*	*Somewhat agree*	*Agree*	*Total*	*Calculated value (Chi-Square)*	*Df*	*Tabulated Value*	*Accepted/ Rejected*
Educational	Undergraduate	3	13	10	5	4	3	38	3.876	5	11.07	Accepted
Qualification	Masters	2	6	3	0	1	0	12				
Total		5	19	13	5	5	3	50				
Time Spent	< 1 year	2	18	13	5	4	3	45	19.708	10	18.31	Rejected
	1-2 years	2	0	0	0	1	0	3				
	2-5 years	1	1	0	0	0	0	2				
Total		5	19	13	5	5	3	50				
Age	< 21 years	3	6	7	4	4	2	26	13.154	10	18.31	Accepted
	21-25 years	1	12	6	1	0	1	21				
	26-30 years	1	1	0	0	1	0	3				
Total		5	19	13	5	5	3	50				
Gender	Male	0	12	10	5	5	3	35	17.958	5	11.07	Rejected
	Female	5	7	3	0	0	0	15				
Total		5	19	13	5	5	3	50				

From the above analysis, we can conclude that in the case of two demographic variables, i.e. gender and time spent with the organization the null hypothesis is being rejected which clearly demonstrates that there is significant association of these demographic variables and the perception of the team members that the supervisor helps in the development of their potential.

Conclusion

From the above study on the leadership environment in the existing Indian BPO industry, the basic findings that were highlighted were as follows. Gender had a significant association with the perception of the employees about their leadership environment. The gender difference could be significantly noted with reference to the supervisors' fair treatment towards them, the development of their potential as well as the acknowledgement of their work. Also the level of education of the employee significantly affected their perception towards acknowledgement of their work by the supervisor. It was also noticed that the time that an employee spends with the organization also had a significant association with the perception towards the leadership environment.

REFERENCES

Adrian, Furnham and Leonard, Goodstein (1997). The Organisational Climate Questionnaire, The 1997 Annual, Consulting, Pfeiffer and Company.

Annunzio, S. (2001). *E-Leadership: Proven Techniques for Creating an Environment of Speed and Flexibility in the Digital Economy*, Simon and Schuster NY.

Avolio, B.J. (1999). *Full Leadership Development: Building the Vital Forces in Organisations*, Thousand Oaks, CA: Sage.

Avolio, B.J. and Kahai, S. (2003). Adding the E to E-Leadership: How it may impact your leadership, *Organisational Dynamics*, Vol. 31, No. 4.

Bass, B.M. (1985). *Leadership and Performance Beyond Expectations*, New York: Free Press.

Buchanan, B. (1974). Building Organisational Commitment: The Socialization of Managers in Work Organisations, *Administrative Science Quarterly*, Vol. 19.

Clark, K.E. and Clark, M.B. (1990). *Measures of Leadership* (Vol. 17).

Crystal L. Hoyt, J.B. (2003). *Transformational and Transactional Leadership in Virtual and Physical Environments* (Vol. 34).

Gibb, J.R. Tori (1972). Theory and Practice, In Pfeiffer, J.W. and Jones, J.E. (Eds.), *The 1972 Annual Handbook for Group Facilitators*, La Jolla, Calif.: University Associates.

Gupta Santoshi, A.G. (2008). Vicious Circle of Attrition in the BPO Industry. *ICFAI Journal of Organizational Behavior*, Vol. 7 (2), 57-66.

House, R.J. and Aditya, R.N. (1997). The Social Scientific Study of Leadership: Quo Vadis?. *Journal of Management*, Vol. 23.

Malhotra, N.K. (2007). *Marketing Research: An Applied Orientation*, 5th Edition, Pearson Publication, New Delhi.

Mishra, P.S. (2007). Increasing Rate of Attrition in BPO. *Management and Labour Studies-Quaterly Journal, 32*, 17-21.

Mobley, W.H. (1977). Intermediate linkages in the relationship between job satisfaction and employee turnover. *Journal of Applied Psychology*, Vol. 62(2), 237-40.

Neale, Helan (2004). "*Offshore BPO Delivery*", Nelson-Hall BPO and outsourcing Subscription service, Nelson-Hall, www.nelson-hall.com.

Pawan, H. (2006). The dynamics of HRM systems in Indian BPO Firms. *Journal of Labour Research*, 27, 339-60.

Staples, D.S. (1997), *The Management of Remote Workers—An Information Technology Perspective*, Unpublished Doctoral Thesis, University of Western Ontario, London, Canada, S. Raghu Raman, Pawan Budhwar, G. Balasubramanian, (2007). People management issues in Indian KPOs, *Employee Relations*, Vol. 29, Iss: 6, pp. 696-710.

CHAPTER 16

HYBRID MATHEMATICAL MODEL FOR MANAGERIAL DECISIONS

–*Anil Kumar Menaria*

ABSTRACT

Problem-solving and decision-making are important skills for business and life. Problem-solving often involves decision-making, and decision-making is especially important for management and leadership. There are processes and techniques to improve decision-making and the quality of decisions. As a result of the rapid increasing and sustainable needs of organizations, relationship between organizations and suppliers has become essential to any business. In addition to all obstacles that will face the organization when poor decision is made. Decision makers and managers face challenges when they are about to select suppliers, for procurement of raw material and components for their manufacturing process. This paper presents a new hybrid model which combines linear weightage and analytic hierarchy process (AHP) models for supplier selection process. The final decision from this new approach will guarantee better decisions and provide a robust tool for assisting decision makers and managers to make the right decision and select the most suitable supplier. The proposed model has been applied in a real life example and finally ranking the supplier based on their scores obtained from this new approach.

Introduction

Decision-making is one of the crucial activities ever conducted in organizations by managers. It involves multiple participants and required conflicting resolution as well as multiple information sources. The outcomes of decision-making process absolutely affect business performance within companies. Therefore, supporting those decision makers is highly recommended and desirable. Quantitative-based decisions will always support the managers in their decision-making process.

In today's business context, maintaining supplier relationship is very important to reduce inventory, by introducing new concepts of just-in-time inventory and continuous replenishment of materials in the form of raw material, components or finished products. Organizations have been more concerned about suppliers regarding the rapid increase of purchasing materials and services which have been playing an important role in business process.

Moynihan et al.[1] state that on the average, about 60 purchased materials. For example, automobile manufacturers spend about 60 farm-implement manufacturers spend about 65 has been estimated that the labour costs represent only about 10 to 15 industries today. From these percentages mentioned above, the importance of purchasing processes can clearly be observed which comes to show that more attention should be given by decision makers towards this critical purchase process as well as selection of suppliers.

Suppliers are necessary entity to any business, however, wrong selection may affect the whole business processes; therefore the process of selecting suppliers is extremely important. According to Wei-kang Wang and others,[2] supplier selection or evaluation is the process of finding the supplier being able to provide customer with the products or services that have the right quality, right price, right quantity, and at the right time. Although purchasing function encompasses various numbers of processes, supplier selection was considered as the most important and critical, and it has been one of the vital research areas. Supplier selection is a multi-criteria problem which includes both qualitative and quantitative factors.[3] Thus, attention should be given to supplier selection problem by decision makers in order to make the right decisions. There are a variety of steps that often decision makers follow in order to make the right decisions and finally be capable of selecting the most appropriate supplier. It is agreed in the literature that supplier selection decision is so complicated and difficult to cope with. There are various reasons which make supplier selection problem a complex process and the authors used different mathematical model in supplier selection like linear programming, integer programming, mixed integer programming, non-linear the role of mathematical model in managerial decisions with special reference to supplier selection programming, total cost based approach, goal programming and data envelopment analysis, etc.[4-10]

Linear Weightage Model for Supplier Selection Process

Supplier selection is the most critical and complicated step in the business processes. Procurement department often responsible for providing materials and services needed to companies by evaluating and selecting suppliers. This paper proposes linear weightage model to assist in the decision-making activity and helps to select the best supplier among a number of potential suppliers. This model is mostly depended upon decision maker's judgment by assigning weights to the various criteria for the products as well as the suppliers which is the beginning process in decision making. In most cases, there are some criteria considered as more important than others such as product quality, product price, and delivery time. Decision makers should assign weight to each individual criterion in order to determine the relative importance of each one. These weights play a vital role in decision-making process and extremely affect the final decision. First of all, decision maker has to identify all criteria that are involved in the certain process before performing any other steps. After identifying all the criteria related to supplier selection decision, decision maker has to determine threshold for each criterion. Generally, threshold can be divided into two types, i.e. maximum and minimum. To establish a threshold to criterion, decision maker should classify all criteria into two groups. The first group known as "larger is better" while the other known as "smaller is better". For example, the delivery time, the distance between manufacturer and supplier location, and product cost can be categories as "smaller is better" where the threshold for this type of criteria must be maximum. On the other hand, most of the qualitative criteria can be considered as "larger is better" such as warranty, qualities, experience of suppliers, supplier flexibility and technical capability where thresholds must be minimum. Based on these two conflicting threshold, the decision maker cannot take this directly. The decision maker must do the normalization process to overcome this conflict. The normalization process is explained as follows. Once the attribute is considered as a maximum type of thresholds, formula 1 should be used

$$V_{\text{Max.}} = \frac{\text{Max.} - \text{Vender}}{\text{Max.} - \text{Min.}}$$

where $V_{\text{Max.}}$ = vendor value that has maximum type of threshold with respect to a particular attribute/criterion.

Vendor = specific vendor that is considered at the time.

Max = maximum value of particular attribute/criteria among all suppliers.

Min = minimum value of the same attribute among the whole suppliers.

In the other case, when the attribute is classified under the minimum type of threshold, formula 2 is the only option for calculating the vendor's value.

$$V_{\text{Min.}} = \frac{\text{Vender} - \text{Min}}{\text{Max.} - \text{Min.}}$$

where $V_{\text{Min.}}$ = vendor value that has minimum type of threshold with respect to a particular attribute/criterion.

Vendor = specific vendor that is considered at the time.

Max = maximum value of particular attribute/criteria among all suppliers.

Min = minimum value of the same attribute among the whole suppliers.

The use of these two formulae is explained in the numerical illustration. The idea of using formula 1 and formula 2 is extremely valuable because they provide a method that enables the comparisons among decision criteria. Usually, decision criteria have different units of measure so any comparisons among those criteria are not logically acceptable. By using the data normalization concept which was represented in formula 1 and formula 2, all the criteria will be having weights instead of a variety of measurement units and then the comparisons can simply be made. When all values of the criteria matrix are calculated, series of calculations should be achieved by multiplying weights W_i of criteria by the whole values X_i within the matrix. The total score should also be calculated using formula 3 for each vendor which represents the vendors' scores. The final decision table includes a total score for each supplier and the one who gains the highest score is recommended as the best supplier over all. The limitation of this model is assigning weights to various criteria.

$$\text{Total Score} = \Sigma \frac{W_i X_i}{W_i}$$

Analytic Hierarchy Process

Decisions involve many intangibles that need to be traded off. To do that, they have to be measured along side tangibles whose measurements must also be evaluated as to, how well, they serve the objectives of the decision maker. The Analytic Hierarchy Process (AHP) is a theory of measurement through pairwise comparisons and relies on the judgements of experts to derive priority scales. It is these scales that measure intangibles in relative terms. The comparisons are made using a scale of absolute judgements that represents, how much more, one element dominates another with respect to a given attribute. The judgements may be inconsistent, and how to measure inconsistency and improve the judgements, when possible to obtain better consistency is a concern of the AHP. The derived priority scales are synthesised by multiplying them by the priority of their parent nodes and adding for all such nodes.

Analytic Hierarchy Process (AHP) was originally designed by Saaty[11] to solve complicated multi-criteria decision problem, beside that AHP is appropriate whenever a target is obviously declared and a set of relevant criteria and alternatives are offered[12]. AHP has been proposed for supplier selection problem to support managers through the decision-making activity, which aims to select the right supplier among a pool of potential suppliers. AHP is a popular model to aggregate multiple criteria for decision making.[13] In AHP, the problems are usually presented in a hierarchical structure and the decision maker is guided throughout a subsequent series of pairwise comparisons to express the relative strength of the elements in the hierarchy. In general, the hierarchy structure encompasses of three levels, where the top level represents the goal, and the lowest level has the supplier under consideration. The intermediate level contains the criteria under which each supplier is evaluated. There are many ways to obtain the preferences from the decision makers, but the measurement scale proposed by Saaty[11] is most commonly used. Based on the pairwise comparison between criteria, the measurement scale enables the decision maker determines which degree of any single criteria is important to other. This measurement scale includes 1-9 scale point, each point represents different degree of preference. By assigning 1 for equal preferences, assigning 3 for moderate importance, 5 for strong importance, 7 for very strong importance and 9 for extreme importance during pairwise comparison. The values 2, 4, 6, and 8 may be assigned-based comparison between the above values. The final score obtain for each supplier across each criterion is calculated by multiplying the weight of each criterion with the weight of each supplier. The supplier who obtained the highest score is suggested as the best supplier and decision maker may consider that one as the best decision choice. Although AHP provides good solution to any problem, the computation and understanding to the decision maker view is difficult.

A New Hybrid Model Based on Decision Support System (DSS)

Decision-making process is a huge and crucial activity that must be given high attention by decision makers and managers as it affects all business strategies in organizations. Computer-based Decision Support System (DSS) is built and developed to assist decision makers in the activity of decision-making process. DSS includes different components that integrate together out of which the most important part is the model-based system. As a result of the rapidly increasing and sustainable needs of organizations, suppliers have become essential to any business. On the other hand, decision makers and managers face challenges when they are about to select suppliers due to the strong competitiveness among suppliers, obstacles that they will face when poor decisions are made, and many other reasons. Evaluating and selecting suppliers has been considered as the most critical and important process among the whole purchasing processes. This research intends to develop a new hybrid model base DSS for supplier selection process that can guarantee better decision making. The new proposed model provides a suitable tool for assisting decision makers and managers to make the right decisions and select the most suitable supplier. The proposed model depends upon linear weightage model and Analytic Hierarchy Process (AHP) approach. The proposed hybrid model will be applied using a real life case study to assess its effectiveness. In addition, What-if analysis technique will be used for model validation purpose. Finally, DSS software will be developed to utilize the proposed model to assist supplier selection decisions.

Based on the previous discussion about both models, there is an urgent need for new model that can support the supplier selection decision and offer a powerful tool which can ultimately produce satisfactory results. This paper intends to achieve this objective by proposing a new hybrid model. This new model concentrates on avoiding all the shortcomings mentioned above. It combines two different aspects from both AHP and linear weightage model. The new model uses the measurement scale of AHP model to determine to which degree each single criterion is preferred in comparison with others. Once the pairwise comparisons have been made, decision maker can obtain the weights of the whole criteria when the relative preference of criteria is specified. The next step in the proposed model is to assign thresholds to all criteria considering "larger is better" or "smaller is better". First stage is to obtain preference criteria matrix, by means of identifying various criteria against each other. Make pairwise comparison between the criteria by assigning weights in 1-9 scale. By performing three steps like sum the elements in each column, divide each value by its column total and calculate row averages. Finally, by doing all the three steps we can obtain weigtages of each criterion. The second stage is to apply linear weightage model by finding the thresholds from the original supplier data and after normalization process by multiplying the weights obtain from the above process, we can get the final decision table matrix. Calculation of the whole values in the decision table matrix has to be produced by considering the two formulae. If the threshold is maximum then formula 1 should be used, otherwise formula 2 is applied for minimum threshold. When the whole cells that represent each supplier across only criteria will be filled with a certain value in the decision table matrix, then each column will multiply by the column of criteria weights and obtain the new values of these cells. Now each column represents one of the competitive suppliers, the last step in the proposed model is to compute the sum of each column to get the final scores of all suppliers. The highest score indicates to the best supplier and that supplier will be recommended as the most appropriate supplier among the competitive suppliers.

Numerical Illustration

The data for this case study have been collected from the procurement department which is accountable for the whole purchasing processes at one of the top university in Malaysia. Interview has been conducted for the purpose of data collection. Eleven suppliers have responded with a quotation representing the prescribe product with their attributes, almost all the supplier got the similar experience with this university and they got interest to be involved in the purchasing process. First column in Table 1 shows the criteria of the purchased products which are server devices. These criteria which are involved in the supplier selection process are eight different criteria which describes each product that has been proposed by each supplier. The eight criteria for the server devices are processor, memory, power supply consumption, cache memory, internal storage, warranty, price, and delivery time. The rest of the columns represent the eleven competitive suppliers. S1 in the third column refers to supplier 1 and S2 in the next column refers to supplier 2 and so on till S11 which refers to supplier 11. Applying the proposed model to supplier selection decision implies that all the steps above have to be followed. Accordingly, the preference criteria matrix was obtained which compare each criterion to the others and Table 2 depicts the preference criteria matrix and gives a glimpse of decision maker's judgment and preference of criteria in a form of pairwise comparisons.

Table 1: Criteria and Supplier Information

Attributes	*Measurement Unit*	*S1*	*S2*	*S3*	*S4*	*S5*	*S6*	*S7*	*S8*	*S9*	*S10*	*S11*
Processor	Giga Hertz	1.86	3.66	1.86	1.6	1.65	1.75	1.86	1.68	1.6	1.57	1.58
Memory	Mega Byte	1024	2000	1024	1024	2000	1024	2000	1024	1024	1024	1024
Power Supply	Watt	835	1300	835	835	1300	1300	835	835	1300	835	1300
Cache Memory	Mega Byte	4	1	4	4	1	2	2	1	2	2	4
Int-Storage	Giga Hertz	146.8	440.4	146	146	146	73	73.4	146	73.4	146	146
Warranty	Month	36	36	36	36	24	36	24	36	36	24	24
Price	Rs	20352	48200	25530	23405	45250	32250	24250	26400	31100	23304	32450
Delivery	Week	4	3	6	6	4	6	4	6	4	7	4

Table 2: Pairwise Comparison Preference Criteria Matrix

Attributes	*Processor*	*Memory*	*Power Supply*	*Cache Memory*	*Int-Storage*	*Warranty*	*Price*	*Delivery*
Processor	1	1	7	5	2	7	1	7
Memory	1	1	7	5	2	7	1	7
Power Supply	1/7	1/7	1	1/2	1/3	1	1/7	1
Cache Memory	1/5	1/5	2	1	1/2	2	1/5	2
Int-Storage	1/2	1/2	3	2	1	3	1/2	3
Warranty	1/7	1/7	1	1/2	1/3	1	1/7	1
Price	1	1	7	5	2	7	1	7
Delivery	1/7	1/7	1	1/2	1/3	1	1/7	1
Total	**4.12**	**4.12**	**29**	**19.5**	**8.49**	**29**	**4.12**	**29**

Processor, memory and price have an equal preference of criteria that is why the cell across each two of them is filled with ones. On other hand, processor speed is more important than the power supply in the first row and four columns is filled with 7 according the AHP measure scale, and thus when compare power to processor it should be 1/7 = 0.14 because it is the opposite comparison. The same concept is followed to fulfill all the pairwise comparisons. The next step is to obtain the weight for each criterion by normalized the data in Table 2. Three procedures applied to preference criteria matrix and immediately the weights will be calculated.

1. Sum the elements in each column.
2. Divide each value by its column total.
3. Calculate row averages.

Performing the previous mathematical calculation yields the normalized matrix of criteria as illustrated in Table 3. The average weights of rows are computed in the last column to indicate the weights of the criteria.

Table 3: Weights of Each Criterion

Attributes	*Processor*	*Memory*	*Power Supply*	*Cache Memory*	*Int-Storage*	*Warranty*	*Price*	*Delivery*	*Weights*
Processor	0.242718	0.242718	0.241379	0.25641	0.235571	0.241379	0.242718	0.241379	0.243034
Memory	0.242718	0.242718	0.241379	0.25641	0.235571	0.241379	0.242718	0.241379	0.243034
Power Supply	0.033981	0.033981	0.034483	0.025641	0.038869	0.034483	0.033981	0.034483	0.033738
Cache Memory	0.048544	0.048544	0.068966	0.051282	0.058893	0.068966	0.048544	0.068966	0.057838
Int-Storage	0.121359	0.121359	0.103448	0.102564	0.117786	0.103448	0.121359	0.103448	0.111847
Warranty	0.033981	0.033981	0.034483	0.025641	0.038869	0.034483	0.033981	0.034483	0.033738
Price	0.242718	0.242718	0.241379	0.25641	0.235571	0.241379	0.242718	0.241379	0.243034
Delivery	0.033981	0.033981	0.034483	0.025641	0.038869	0.034483	0.033981	0.034483	0.033738
Total	1	1	1	1	1	1	1	1	1

From Table 3, the weight for the processor criterion is 0.243034 as well as memory criteria. The weight of internal storage criterion is 0.111847 and so on. The next step in the proposed model is to compute the criteria value matrix using the previous formulae relying upon the thresholds which have already been determined earlier. Once the threshold of a certain criterion is maximum type, thus formula 1 should be applied to compute the value of that criterion with respect to all suppliers.

Table 4: Normalized Criteria Values Matrix

	Threshold	*S1*	*S2*	*S3*	*S4*	*S5*	*S6*	*S7*	*S8*	*S9*	*S10*	*S11*
Processor	Min	0.14	1.00	0.14	0.01	0.04	0.09	0.10	0.05	0.01	0.00	0.00
Memory	Min	0.00	1.00	0.00	0.00	1.00	0.00	1.00	0.00	0.00	0.00	0.00
Power Supply	Max	1.00	0.00	1.00	1.00	0.00	0.00	1.00	1.00	0.00	1.00	0.00
Cache Memory	Min	1.00	0.00	1.00	1.00	0.00	0.33	0.33	0.00	0.33	0.33	1.00
Int-Storage	Min	0.20	1.00	0.00	0.20	0.00	0.00	0.00	0.20	0.20	0.20	0.20
Warranty	Min	1.00	1.00	1.00	1.00	0.00	1.00	0.00	1.00	0.00	0.00	0.00
Price	Max	1.00	0.00	0.82	0.89	0.11	0.57	0.86	0.78	0.89	0.89	0.57
Delivery	Max	0.75	1.00	0.25	0.25	0.75	0.25	0.75	0.25	0.00	0.00	0.75

The arrival of figure 0.14 in Table 4 in the first row and first column under processor speed of supplier 1 is explained as follows. From Table 1, the processor speed is in GHz, the figures are 1.86, 3.66, 1.86, ..., 1.58 of the suppliers s1, s2, s3,..., sll respectively. This criteria falls under larger is better, therefore use formula 2. For s1 we have 1.86 – 1.57 / 3.66 – 1.57 = 0.14. Repeating this process for supplier 2 up to supplier 11 gives normalized processor speed for s1 to s11, which will be 1.4, to 0.00. Let us take price is another criteria which is in RM, from Table 1, 20352, 48200, ..., 32450 of the suppliers s1, s2, ..., s1 respectively. Price criteria falls under smaller is better therefore use formula 1. For s1 we have 48200 – 20352 / 48200 – 20352 = 1.00. Repeating this process for supplier 2 up to supplier 11 gives normalized price for s1 to s11 will be 1.00 to 0.57. The next step in the proposed model is to use the weights column of Table 3 with the whole of Table 4 as shown in Table 5. The last step is to multiply each row of eleven supplier value by the row weight, giving Table 6. Table 6 depicts the final scores of suppliers. The most important thing is regarding the final results, the supplier who has the highest score is suggested as the best supplier for the proposed hybrid model.

Table 5: Weight and Criteria Values Matrix

	Weights	*S1*	*S2*	*S3*	*S4*	*S5*	*S6*	*S7*	*S8*	*S9*	*S10*	*S11*
Processor	0.243034	0.14	1	0.14	0.01	0.04	0.09	0.14	0.05	0.01	0	0
Memory	0.243034	0	1	0	0	1	0	1	0	0	0	0
Power Supply	0.033738	1	0	1	1	0	0	1	1	0	1	0
Cache Memory	0.057838	1	0	1	1	0	0.33	0.33	0	0.33	0.33	1
Int-Storage	0.111847	0.2	1	0.2	0.2	0.2	0	0	0.2	0	0.2	0.2
Warranty	0.033738	1	1	1	1	0	1	0	1	1	0	0
Price	0.243034	1	0	0.82	0.89	0.11	0.57	0.86	0.78	0.61	0.89	0.57
Delivery	0.033738	0.75	1	0.25	0.25	0.75	0.25	0.75	0.25	0.75	0	0.75

In accordance with the results generated by the proposed hybrid model, S2 has the highest score of 0.67 in comparison with the rest of potential suppliers. As a result, the proposed hybrid model would recommend S2 as the best supplier among all suppliers. With the help of Table 6, we can rank the supplier based on the final score. S7 is second in position.

Table 6: Final Decision Matrix

	S1	*S2*	*S3*	*S4*	*S5*	*S6*	*S7*	*S8*	*S9*	*S10*	*S11*
Processor	0.034025	0.243034	0.034025	0.00243	0.009721	0.021873	0.034025	0.012152	0.00243	0	0
Memory	0	0.243034	0	0	0.243034	0	0.243034	0	0	0	0
Power Supply	0.033738	0	0.033738	0.033738	0	0	0.033738	0.033738	0	0.033738	0
Cache Memory	0.057838	0	0.033738	0.033738	0	0.019087	0.019087	0	0.019087	0.019087	0.057838
Int-Storage	0.022369	0.111847	0.022369	0.022369	0.022369	0	0	0.022369	0	0.3022369	0.022369
Warranty	0.033738	0.033738	0.033738	0.033738	0	0.033738	0	0.033738	0.033738	0	0
Price	0.243034	0	0.199288	0.2163	0.026734	0.138529	0.209009	0.189567	0.148251	0.2163	0.138529
Delivery	0.025304	0.033738	0.008435	0.008435	0.025304	0.008435	0.025304	0.008435	0.025304	0	0.025304
Score	**0.45**	**0.67**	**0.39**	**0.37**	**0.33**	**0.22**	**0.56**	**0.3**	**0.23**	**0.29**	**0.24**

Conclusion

The proposed hybrid model is considered as a robust tool that can assist decision maker in the process of supplier selection. In addition, the proposed model saves time because there are only a few computations to be done. This model is easy to understand and easy to use. Also it saves effort due to its simplicity, and that will strongly accelerate the supplier selection decision as well as improve the whole business processes within organizations in turn. Other advantage of the proposed model is avoiding the limitation in the linear weightage model which assigns the weights of criteria directly by decision maker based on their experience and gut feeling. The proposed model uses the AHP pairwise comparisons and the measurement 1-9 scale to generate the weights for the criteria. This method provides good solution when compared to human judgment. Thus, the proposed model overcomes the absolute dependency on human judgment as in the case of linear weightage model.

In conclusion, the proposed model can be considered as a powerful model for supplier selection problem. It fully integrates the advantages of both linear weightage model and AHP approach. From the above supplier selection example, we can conclude that mathematical models are contributing more in managerial decisions.

NOTES

1. G.P. Moynihan, Saxena, P. and Fonseca, D.J. 2006, "Development of a decision support system for procurement operations", *International Journal of Logistics Systems and Management*, Vol. 2, No. 1, pp. 1-18.
2. Wei-Kang Wang, Wu Wen, Chang, W.B. and Hao-Chen Huang 2006, "A knowledge-based decision support system for government vendor selection and bidding, JCIS-2006 proceeding, pp. 170-76.
3. E.G. Marvin, Gioconda Quesada and Carlo 2004, "Determining the importance of supplier selection process in manufacturing: A case study", *International Journal of Physical Distribution and Logistic Management*, Vol. 34, No. 6, pp. 492-504.
4. Dongjoo Lee, Tachee Lee, Sue-Kyung, Ok-Ran Jeong, Hyenosang Eom, and Sang-Goo Lee 2006, "Best Choice: A decision support system for supplier selection e-marketplaces", The 2nd international workshop on data engineering issues in e-commerce and services DEECS2006, pp. 198-208.
5. Shi J., Weihong Huang, Zhang L, Huang G.Q. and Mark K.L. 2000, "Collaborative supplier selection on the web", *IEEE*, *International Conference on Management of Innovation and Technology*, Volume 2, pp. 827-31.
6. Hongwei Ding, Lyes Benyoucef, and Xiaollan Xie 2003, "A simulation optimization approach using genetic search for supplier selection", Proceeding of the winter simulation conference, pp. 1260-67.
7. Shuo-Yan Chou, and Yao Hui Chang 2008, "A decision support system for supplier selection based on a strategy-aligned fuzzy SMART approach", *Expert System with Application—An International Journal*, Vol. 34, Issue 4, pp. 2241-53.
8. Reza Mohammady Garfamy 2006, "A data development analysis approach based on total cost of ownership for supplier selection", *Journal of Enterprise Information Management*, Vol. 19, No. 6, pp. 662-78.
9. Ding-Zhong, Lei-Lei Chen, and Mei-Xian Jiang 2005, "Vendor selection in supply chain system: An approach using fuzzy decision and AHP", *IEEE*, *International Conference on Service Systems and Services Management*, Volume 1, pp. 721-25.
10. Masood A. Badri, and Mohammed H. Abdulla 2004, "Awards of excellence in institutions of higher education: An AHP approach", *International Journal of Educational Management*, Vol. 18, No. 4, pp. 224-42.
11. T.L. Saaty, 1980, *The Analytic Hierarchy Process: Planning, Priority Setting, Resources Allocation.* London: McGraw-Hill.
12. Ozden Bayazit, and Birsen Karpak 2005, "An AHP application in vendor selection", *ISAHP*, pp. 1-21.
13. K.F.Y. Kevin, and Henry C.W.L. 2008, "Software vendor selection using fuzzy analytic hierarchy process with ISO/IEC9126", *IAENG International Journal of Computer Science*,Vol. 35, No. 3, pp. 267-74.

CHAPTER 17 A STUDY OF EMPLOYEE SATISFACTION WITH SPECIAL REFERENCE TO "NATIONAL ENGINEERING INDUSTRIES LTD.", JAIPUR

–*Brijesh Awasthi*, *Yamini Bhojak* and *Monika Soni*

ABSTRACT

Employee satisfaction is essential to face the dynamic and ever-changing challenges of maintaining productivity of the manufacturing industry by keeping their workforce constantly engaged and motivated. In the present era of globalization, the varied and changing demands of consumers are putting consistent pressure on the employers to satisfy their needs and to be competitive in the manufacturing industry. Environmental pressures, rising health costs and various needs of the workforce also pose a challenge for the management. This could be overcome by creating a work environment that maintains employee satisfaction as well as motivates people towards exceptional performance at the workplace achieving work-life balance. This study explains the importance of employee satisfaction and the possible ways to enhance their performance on a sustainable basis in the manufacturing industry.

Today employees no longer are eager to join any new organization where their knowledge and skills do not get upgraded. Providing opportunities for learning is being used as a retention tool by large number of organization. Providing proper training have become the strategies of the best companies to magnetize, retain and get highest quality output from the employees.

Introduction

Employee satisfaction is essential to the success of any business. A high rate of employee contentedness is directly related to a lower turnover rate. Thus, keeping employees satisfied with their careers should be a major priority for every employer. While this is a well-known fact in management practices, economic downturns like the current one seem to cause employers to ignore it. There are numerous reasons why employees can become discouraged with their jobs and resign, including high stress, lack of communication within the company, lack of recognition, or limited opportunity for growth. Management should actively seek to improve these factors if they hope to lower their turnover rate. Even in an economic downturn, turnover is an expense best avoided.

Employee satisfaction refers to a person's feeling of satisfaction on the job, which acts as a motivation to work. It is not the self-satisfaction, happiness or self-contentment but the satisfaction on the job. The term relates to the total relationship between an individual and the employer for which he is paid. Satisfaction does mean the simple feeling-state accompanying the attainment of any goal; the end-state is feeling accompanying the attainment by an impulse of its objectives. Job satisfaction does mean absence of motivation at work. Research workers differently described the factors contributing to employee satisfaction and employee dissatisfaction. Employee satisfaction in these terms:

- Work Environment
- Communication
- Compensation and Welfare
- Training and Development
- Motivation
- Career Development
- Work Safety

Review of Literature

Although it has been more common to investigate employee attitude data at the individual employee level, researchers have begun to explore similar relationships at the business-unit level and the organizational level. Research conducted under the rubric of organizational climate has had success in aggregating individual employees' perceptions and investigating their relationship to both organizational-level and individual-level outcomes (Schneider, White, and Paul, 1998; Zohar and Luria, 2005). In addition, there are a handful of studies that have explored the relationship between aggregated employee job satisfaction attitudes and organizational (or unit-level) performance. Ostroff (1992) studying a sample of 364 schools, investigated the relationship between employees' attitudes and organizational performance. Ostroff found that aggregated teacher attitudes such as job satisfaction and organizational commitment were concurrently related to school performance, as measured by several performance outcomes such as student academic achievement and teacher turnover rates. Across 12 organizational performance indexes, the magnitudes of the correlations between teacher satisfaction and performance ranged from .11 to .54, with a mean of .28. When the unique characteristics of the schools were statistically controlled for, teacher satisfaction and other job-related attitudes continued to predict many of the organizational performance outcomes. Results were strongest for teacher satisfaction; thus, organizations with more satisfied employees tended to be more effective than organizations with dissatisfied employees. This study indicates that satisfaction is an important social process factor that fosters organizational effectiveness. The major limitation of this study pertains to the nature of the study sample; all organizations were secondary schools. The extent to which similar relationships would hold for organizations in other types of industries (manufacturing, service, etc.) and occupations cannot be determined. Ryan, Schmitt, and Johnson (1996) investigated similar relationships between aggregated employee attitudes, firm productivity, and customer satisfaction. The authors measured these relationships at two points in time from 142 branches of an auto-finance company. Results indicated employee morale was related to subsequent business performance indicators, customer satisfaction sentiments, and turnover ratios. These researchers attempted to study the causal relations among the variables; however, their attempts lead to mostly inconclusive findings. Interestingly, they did find evidence suggestive of customer satisfaction as a causal influence on morale (a finding that is opposite of the directionality assumed by the literature). Although a tentative finding, Ryan et al. (1996) discussed several possible explanations for it. For instance, the customer satisfaction index was monitored closely by unit managers and success or failure likely translated into management practices that influenced employees' job attitudes. Moreover, the researchers speculated that the particular setting may be unusual in that customer satisfaction might be inversely related to the amount of contact with the organization (e.g. customers without problems with the processing of their payments are likely to have less interaction with company representatives than customers with such problems). Similar to Ostroff's (1992) study, the major concern with Ryan et al.'s (1996) research is that the data were all from one organization which limits the generalizability of the findings. In a unique study conducted by Harter et al. (2002), the authors conducted a met analysis of studies previously conducted by The Gallup Organization. The study examined aggregated employee job satisfaction sentiments and employee engagement, with the latter variable referring to individual's involvement with as well as enthusiasm for work. Based on 7,939 business units in 36 organizations, the researchers found positive and substantive correlations between employee satisfaction-engagement and the business unit outcomes of productivity, profit, employee turnover, employee accidents, and customer satisfaction. More importantly, these researchers explored the practical utility of the observed relationships. For example, business units in the top quartile on the employee engagement measure yielded 1 to 4 percentage points higher profitability. Similar findings were found for productivity. Specifically, business units in the top quartile on employee engagement had, on average, from $80,000 to $120,000 higher monthly revenue or sales. Based on these data, it seems clear that aggregated measures of employee satisfaction and employee engagement are meaningfully related to business outcomes at a magnitude that is important to many (if not all) organizations. In comparison to prior studies, the strength of Harter and his colleagues' research is the large number of participants (n = 198,514), business units (n = 7,939), and firms (n = 36) included, thereby providing a level of precision and statistical power rarely found in scholarly (i.e. non-proprietary) research. Schneider et al. (2003) report analyses of employee attitude survey data aggregated to the organizational level of analysis. These authors explored the relationships between several facets of employee satisfaction and organizational financial (return on assets; ROA) and market performance (earnings per share; EPS) using data from 35 organizations over a period of eight years. Thus, in contrast to previous studies, Schneider and his colleagues' study was able to make some inferences about directional causality (i.e. are employee attitudes a stronger cause of organizational performance than the reverse). Their results showed consistent and statistically significant positive relationships (over varied time lags) between attitudes concerning satisfaction with security, satisfaction with pay, and overall job satisfaction with financial (ROA) and market performance (EPS). Although these findings are consistent with applied researchers' and managers' implicit beliefs, their study was not without some surprises. One of the more surprising findings was related to overall job satisfaction and the performance criteria. Results demonstrated that the causal directionality flows from financial and market performance to overall job satisfaction. This latter result does not deny the fact that there were significant relations going from overall job satisfaction to ROA and EPS; nevertheless, the reverse direction relationships tended to be stronger in magnitude. Moreover, the relationship between satisfaction with pay and the performance indicators appeared to be reciprocal in nature. The obvious strength of this research study is the longitudinal nature of both the aggregated employee data and the financial and market performance data. By collecting longitudinal data on both sets of variables, these researchers were able to examine and begin to disentangle a set of very important but complex relationships.

Are Companies with Happy Workers More Productive Companies?

One major issue regarding many of the reviewed studies relates to the causal nature of the relationship between aggregated employee satisfaction and organizational (or unit-level) performance. The implicit belief both in academy and practice is that the relationship runs from employee satisfaction sentiments to organizational effectiveness and efficiency outcomes. Moreover, this implicit assumption is apparent in the research studies reviewed here. That is, the attitude data were typically collected at one time period and performance outcomes were concurrently collected or at multiple time periods following the collection of the employee attitude data. The study conducted by Schneider et al. (2003) suggests that collecting data in this fashion may lead researchers to draw erroneous conclusions because their data prevent them from discovering significantly stronger relationships for performance causing satisfaction. It could be argued, for example, that employees who are in higher performing organizations are more likely to be satisfied than those in lower performing organizations simply because their organizations are doing well. Indeed, this causal pattern was found in the study conducted by Schneider and his colleagues (2003). Specifically, their data supported causal relationships between financial and market performance outcomes and employees' overall job satisfaction and satisfaction for security. Although more research is needed before concrete conclusions are drawn, Schneider et al.'s (2003) research demonstrates that employees can derive satisfaction from the knowledge or feedback that their organization is performing well and is accomplishing its goals—a finding that is in stark contrast to the presumption found in the academic literature (Likert, 1961). When we consider the studies collectively, directional causality may work in both directions; employee satisfaction causes organizational performance and vice versa. Therefore, it seems most likely that reciprocal relationships exist and that, as noted by Gross and Etzioni (1985), "organizational reality and human happiness go hand and hand" (p. 4). Thus, although directions of causality remain unresolved, initial evidence suggests that aggregate employee attitudes have connections with organizational performance outcomes.

What can We Do to Create Happy Employees, Then?

Given the fact that significant and practically important relationships exist between aggregated employee attitudes and organizational performance, it is important to question what factors contribute to satisfaction. The predominant view has focused on the situational context (e.g. supervisory support) as a cause of satisfaction and has argued that high-performance work practices and thus a positive working climate foster employee satisfaction (Bowen, and Ostroff, 2004; Wright, Dunford, and Snell, 2001; Wright, Gardner, Moynihan, and Allen, 2005). This rationale is consistent with recent research on the impact of financial and non-financial incentives (e.g. training) on business-unit outcomes. For example, Peterson and Luthans (2006) used a quasi-experimental, control group design and found that both types of incentives had a significant impact on store profit, customer service, and employee turnover. Initially, the financial incentive had a greater effect on all three outcomes (as one might expect). But over time, however, the financial and non-financial incentives exhibited equally significant impacts on two of the three outcomes (the exception was employee turnover).

A Brief Comment on the Need for a Multidimensional Measure of Performance

Researchers have suggested that organizational effectiveness most likely reflects the combination and interaction of employee work behaviors that promote organizational performance (e.g. Ostroff, 1992). In other words, the definition of organizational performance may be too limited and narrow. Outcomes such as attendance, compliance, following of rules, cooperation, sabotage, and so on may also be important; however, such outcomes are usually not included in organizational performance criteria. Accordingly, we suggest that organizations wishing to explore the empirical connections between aggregated employee attitudes and organizational outcomes consider a wider range of performance-related outcomes.

Research Methodology

The survey was designed to deliver robust quantitative measures and also illustrative quality insight which was captured through employment of both qualitative and quantitative research methods. The study is Analytical in nature.

Researcher had conducted a survey of employees and to know the satisfaction level of employees in National Engineering Industries Ltd., Jaipur. The survey tool was in the form of a questionnaire developed by the consultant based on the issues investigated in the baseline survey. The researcher defined precisely the information desired and wrote a few questions as possible to obtain it. The aim was to obtain feedback from a small but representative sample of potential respondents. This activity involved more informal, open-ended interviews with several potential respondents as per the sample. The language of questionnaire is "Hindi" because the employees and workers of NEI are not much educated and not comfortable in English language that's why the questionnaire prepared in Hindi language.

Sample method was random sampling. Sample size was 210 respondents. The data generated was to test the employee satisfaction level and the employee perception on six factors. Each question was to be answered on a 5 point likert scale. All of the statements' used a scale that ranged across "Strongly Disagree", "Disagree", "neutral", "Agree", and "Strongly Agree".

Hypothesis

H_0: There is no significance difference between the factors affecting employee satisfaction in manufacturing industry.

Objectives

The objective of this study is to gain a deeper understanding about the employee's satisfaction level. The main objectives of research are:

- To know that which type of facilities/benefits provided by the manufacturing industry to their employees.
- Satisfaction level of employees in the manufacturing industry.
- To study the attitude of the employees towards their:

- Working conditions
- Compensation and Welfare
- Motivation
- Career Development
- Work Safety
- Training and Development

Data Analysis

Table 1: Work Environment for Employee Satisfaction

S.No.	Factors	Work Environment					
		Strongly Disagree	*Disagree*	*Average*	*Agree*	*Strongly Agree*	*Weighted Total*
1.	Cleanness	21	12	79	38	60	734
2.	Proper Ventilation	23	15	76	42	54	719
3.	Free from Voice Pollution	42	21	74	39	34	632
4.	Temperature	18	19	77	49	47	718
5.	Goods Availability	32	19	88	35	36	654
6.	Public Facility Available	48	18	82	34	28	606
7.	Work and Liability Knowledge	11	11	75	45	68	778
8.	Knowledge about Work Planning	16	15	78	46	55	739
9.	Mission and Vision	31	26	70	37	46	671
10.	Regular Presence	21	12	79	38	60	734
	Percentage	12.52%	8.00%	37.05%	19.19%	23.24%	Avg.-698.5

The data of work environment shows that the employees of manufacturing industry having a flexible workplace. The 23.24% and 19.19% of respondents are "strongly satisfied" and "satisfied" with work environment. The weighted average satisfaction of work environment is 698.5.

Table 2: Compensation and Welfare for Employee Satisfaction

S.No.	Factors	Compensation and Welfare					
		Strongly Disagree	*Disagree*	*Average*	*Agree*	*Strongly Agree*	*Weighted Total*
1.	Analysis and Justify of Work	41	41	81	20	27	581
2.	Extra Benefits	73	36	44	44	13	518
3.	Promotion	75	38	49	36	12	502
4.	Employee Value in Org.	46	36	61	43	24	593
5.	Award and Reward	45	28	68	35	34	615
6.	Work Evaluation	27	27	75	47	34	664
7.	Pension and Insurance Policy	73	36	46	36	19	522
8.	Medical Facility	53	30	57	41	29	593
9.	Safety Policy	41	41	81	20	27	581
	Percentage	25.08%	16.56%	29.74%	17.04%	11.59%	Avg-574.33

Majority of the employees felt that their pay package was competitive compared to other similar organizations, however only a few (28.63%) agreed that they understood how their salaries are determined by the organization. Some employees thought that the organization has a fair promotion policy while 25.08% and 16.56% were non-committal and disagreed respectively. Most employees disagreed that they were satisfied salary package. Majority of the employees (28.63%) agreed that they were satisfied with the benefits the organization extended to them. The value of weighted average is 574.33.

Table 3: Training and Development for Employee Satisfaction

S.No.	*Factors*	*Training and Development*					*Weighted Total*
		Strongly Disagree	*Disagree*	*Average*	*Agree*	*Strongly Agree*	
1.	Training Provided	50	20	77	30	33	606
2.	Increase Productivity	18	17	82	40	53	723
3.	Planning for Employee Development	35	30	64	41	40	651
4.	Increase Capacity and Knowledge	24	14	78	41	53	715
5.	Co-ordination Related to Work	17	19	80	51	43	714
6.	Relation with Co-workers	45	21	67	39	38	634
7.	Increase Lifestyle of Employee	50	20	77	30	33	606
	Percentage	16.26%	9.59%	35.71%	18.50%	19.93%	Avg-664.14

Respondents expressed satisfaction on the way the organization supports their work-related development and training. When asked if the industry is fair to provide training and development opportunities, 19.93% respondent are "strongly satisfied" with the opportunities for training.

Training and Development increase the productivity, career development, enhance knowledge and lifestyle of employees.

Table 4: Motivation for Employee Satisfaction

S.No.	*Factors*	*Motivation*					*Weighted Total*
		Strongly Disagree	*Disagree*	*Average*	*Agree*	*Strongly Agree*	
1.	Enhance Motivation	58	23	79	20	30	571
2.	Full Disclosure of Ability	12	19	61	52	66	771
3.	Good Behaviour of Supervisor	19	22	64	60	45	720
4.	Enhance Work Capacity	10	18	81	49	52	745
5.	Social Esteem	18	17	66	60	49	735
6.	Interest in Work	14	12	66	60	58	766
7.	Increase Productivity by Changing in Working Style	13	17	62	66	52	757
8.	Over Time Work	58	23	79	20	30	571
	Percentage	12.02	8.99	33.21	23.04	22.74	Avg-704.5

This table proves that the employees are satisfied with motivation factor. The supervisors and employers successfully motivate the employees and enhance their work capacity and interest, social esteem, productivity. 22.74% of respondents are "totally satisfied" and 23.04% of respondents are "satisfied". Only 12.02% of respondents are "strongly disagree" with this factor.

Table 5: Career Development for Employee Satisfaction

S.No.	*Factors*	*Career Development*					*Weighted Total*
		Strongly Disagree	*Disagree*	*Average*	*Agree*	*Strongly Agree*	
1.	Job Security	59	25	71	39	16	558
2.	Importance in Org.	19	25	84	43	39	688
3.	Perfect Organisation for Work	23	22	69	49	47	705
4.	Chances of Development	46	22	76	35	31	613
5.	Other Work Information	68	25	57	46	14	543
6.	Employee Development	74	28	51	38	19	530
7.	Promotion in Company after 5 yrs.	72	30	51	40	17	530
8.	Promotion Regarding Extra Work and Knowledge	59	25	71	39	16	558
	Percentage	25.00	12.02	31.55	19.58	11.85	Avg-590.62

The employees don't feel security and chances of development towards job in this industry. The level of "strongly dissatisfaction" is 25%, and 12.02% respondents are "disagree". 31.55% respondents are "average" or "neutral" to give the proper response. The value of weighted average of career development is 590.6.

Table 6: Work Safety for Employee Satisfaction

S.No.	*Factors*	*Work Safety*					*Weighted Total*
		Strongly Disagree	*Disagree*	*Average*	*Agree*	*Strongly Agree*	
1.	Safety to Avoid Accidents	45	22	84	33	26	603
2.	Maintenance of Machines	25	17	85	41	42	688
3.	Provide Good Facility	42	29	73	36	30	613
4.	Expectations from Employees	20	20	86	37	47	701
5.	Working Conditions are Stressfull	36	23	81	44	26	631
6.	Relation between Supervisor and Employees	50	16	81	39	24	601
7.	Realisation between Union and Management	49	20	82	40	19	590
8.	Need of Union	52	16	79	42	21	594
9.	Management Helps to Increase Profit	45	22	84	33	26	603
	Percentage	19.26	9.79	38.89	18.25	13.81	Avg-624.88

The safety management was measured with nine statement in which the respondents were to rank them on the level at which they agree with the statements. The employees are not satisfied with the work safety factor. Mostly responses of the respondent are "neutral". Only 13.81% respondents are "strongly satisfied" with their work safety. 19.26% and 9.79% of respondents not feel secure in the manufacturing industry.

Table 7: Overall Satisfaction Level of Employees

Parameters	*SD*	*D*	*N*	*A*	*SA*	*QT*
Work Environment	260	168	700	444	501	2073
Compensation and Welfare	469	304	511	356	224	1864
Training and Development	239	135	481	289	295	1439
Motivation	190	150	522	428	372	1662
Career Development	428	212	466	320	219	1645
Work Safety	351	174	670	352	277	1824
Total	1937	1143	3350	2189	1888	10507
Percentage	Strongly Disagree%	Disagree%	Neutral%	Agree%	Strongly Agree%	Q.T.
	18.4	10.9	31.9	20.8	18.0	

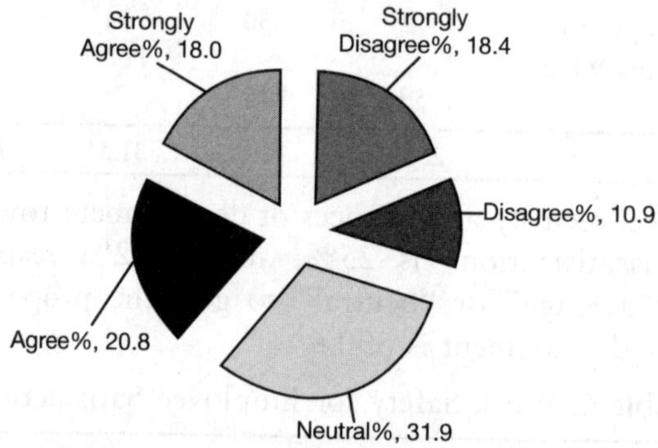

This section focuses upon findings from all respondents who were presented with the survey form. The survey questionnaire entailed a range of questions focusing on various attributes of employee satisfaction. They are work environment, compensation and welfare, training and development, motivation, work safety, career development. The employees are strongly satisfied with the work environment factor. Employees are not satisfied with the compensation and welfare policy of manufacturing industry.

Hypothesis Testing

H_0: There is not a significance difference between the factors affecting employee satisfaction in manufacturing industry.

S.No.	*Factors*	*Observed (Weighted total)*	*Expected*	*$(O_i - E_i)^2/E_i$*
1	Work Environment	6985	5464.667	422.9743
2	Compensation and Welfare	5169	5464.667	15.99709
3	Training and Development	4649	5464.667	121.748
4	Motivation	5636	5464.667	5.371802
5	Career Development	4725	5464.667	100.1171
6	Work Safety	5624	5464.667	4.645683
			Chi Square Value	670.854

The value of "Chi square test" is 670.85 and the "Chi square value" is 11 at the 5% significance level it shows that there is a very high significance difference between the employee satisfaction in manufacturing industry. So, in this research we are rejecting our hypothesis.

Conclusion

A recent study on employee satisfaction, where universe is 530 and sample size is 210, analysis upon the employee satisfaction using questionnaire. According to this analysis, most employees state that they are neutral with the responses every factor of employee satisfaction. The highest satisfaction level of employee could be observed in work environment is 79.48%. The lowest satisfaction is reported by employees in compensation and welfare policy and work safety.

The findings show that there is a very high difference between all these six factors of employee satisfaction in manufacturing industry.

To prove the hypothesis researcher apply "Chi square test". The test shows that there is very high significance difference between all the factors of employee satisfaction in manufacturing industry.

The result of this employee satisfaction survey provides feedback on employees' opinion about manufacturing industry. In the whole, the employees shows the levels of satisfaction.

The feedback from these surveys will help the industry to continue to improve on the way it manages employees and related issues.

Six factors have been chosen to analyze the satisfaction level of employees are: work environment, compensation and welfare, career development, training development, motivation, work safety.

Suggestions

- The manufacturing industry should develop clear compensation and promotion policies for it employees. The employees should be, if it's not against the industry way of operations, enlighten the employees on how their salaries are determined. The benefits given to employees should commensurate their dedication to their respective work. And give appraisal on their performance by giving award and reward.
- The industry should develop clear guidelines on determining/selecting prospective employees for various training and development opportunities and it may increase their productivity. Enhance employee morale and motivate them.
- The manufacturing industry should provide good facility, safety to avoid accidents, develop good relationship/co-ordination between supervisor and employees.

REFERENCES

Argyris, C. (1964). Integrating the individual and the organization. New York: Wiley.

Aydin, B. (2007). Faktor analizi yardimiyla performance olcutlerinin boyutlarinin ortaya konulmasi. The 8th Econometrics and Statistics Congress of Turkey, May, 2007, University of Inonu Malatya Turkey.

Bhatti, K., and Qureshi, T. (2007). Impact of employee participation on job satisfaction, employee commitment and employee productivity. *International Review of Business Research Paper.*

Bowen, D.E., and Ostroff, C. (2004). Understanding HRM-firm performance linkages: The role of "strength" of the HR system. *Academy of Management Review, 29*, 203-21.

Elmsford, NY: Pergamum Press.

Emery, R.E., and Trist, E.L. (1960). Socio-technical systems. In C.W. Churchman and M. Verhulst (Eds.), *Management Science Models and Techniques* (Vol. 2, pp. 83-97).

Erastus N. Njoka, Principal Chuka University College.

Gross, E., and Etzioni, A. (1985). *Organizations in Society*. Englewood Cliffs, NJ: Prentice-Hall.

Harter, J.K., Schmidt, F.L., and Hayes, T.L. (2002). Business-unit level relationship between employee satisfaction, employee engagement, and business outcomes: A meta-analysis. *Journal of Applied Psychology, 87*, 268-79.

Iaffaldano, M.T., and Muchinsky, P.M. (1985). Job satisfaction and job performance: A met analysis. *Psychological Bulletin, 97*, 251-73.

Likert, R.L. (1961). *The Human Organization*. New York: McGraw-Hill.

McGregor, D. (1960). *The Human Side of Enterprise*. New York: McGraw-Hill.

Organ, D.W. (1977). A reappraisal and reinterpretation of the satisfaction-causes-performance hypothesis. *Academy of Management Review, 2*, 46-53.

Ostroff, C. (1992). The relationship between satisfaction, attitudes, and performance: An Organizational Level Analysis. *Journal of Applied Psycholog* , 77, 963-74.

Peterson, S.J., and Luthans, F. (2006). The impact of financial and non-financial incentives on business-unit outcomes over time. *Journal of Applied Psychology, 91*, 156-65.

Ryan, A.M., Schmitt, M.J., and Johnson, R. (1996). Attitudes and effectiveness: Examining relations at an organizational level. *Personnel Psychology, 49*, 853-82.

Schneider, B., and Schmitt, N. (1986). *Staffing Organizations*. Glenview, IL: Scott, Foreman.

Schneider, B., Hanges, P.J., Smith, D.B., and Salvaggio, A.N. (2003). Which comes first? Employee attitudes or organizational financial and market performance? *Journal of Applied Psychology*.

Schneider, B., White, S.S., and Paul, M.C. (1998). Linking service climate and customer perceptions of service quality: Tests of a causal model. *Journal of Applied Psychology*.

Wright, P.M., Dunford, B. B., and Snell, S.A. (2001). Human resources and the resource-based view of the firm. *Journal of Management*.

Wright, P.M., Gardner, T.M., Moynihan, L.M., and Allen, M.R. (2005). The relationship between HR practices and firm performance: Examining causal order. *Personnel Psychology*.

Zohar, D., and Luria, G. (2005). A multilevel model of safety climate: Cross-level relationships between organization and group-level climates. *Journal of Applied Psychology*.

BIBLIOGRAPHY

Aswathappa K., *Human Resource and Personnel Management*, Tata McGraw-Hill.

Donald H. Mcburney and Theresa L. White, *Research Methodology*, Thomas wadsworth.

Densi and Griffine, *Human Resource Management*, Biztantra.

Gupta C.B., *Human Resource Management*, Sultan Chand and Sons.

Herbert J. Rubin, Irene S. Rubin, *Qualitative Interviewing: The Art of Hearing Data*.

Kothari C.R., *Research Methodology*, New Age International Publications.

Kulkarni, B.D., *Research Methodology*, Everest Publishing House.

Matthew, B. Miles, A. Michael Huber man, *Qualitative Data Analysis*, Sage Publications.

Mats Alvesson, Kaj Skoldberg, *Reflexive Methodology: Interpretation and Research*.

Pareek Udai and T.V. Rao, *Human Resource Systems*, Oxford and IBH Publishing Co. Pvt. Ltd.

Sadhu And Singh, *Research Methodology in Social Science*, Himalaya Publication House.

Seymour Sudman, Norman R. Bradburn, Norman Schwarz, *Thinking About Answers: Application of Cognitive Processes to Survey Methodology*.

Sharma, A.M., *Human Resource Management*, Himalaya Publications.

Tripathi, P.C., *Research Methodology in Social Science*, Sultan Chand and Sons.

CHAPTER 18

EMPLOYEE LOYALTY TOWARDS ORGANIZATION: A STUDY OF SMALL SCALE ORGANIZATIONS WITH REFERENCE TO SOUTHERN RAJASTHAN

–*Vineet Kumar Jain* and *Sakshi Chouhan*

ABSTRACT

Loyalty is a very powerful concept in today's business world. Employee loyalty can be defined as employees dedicated to the success of the organization. According to Woodrow T. Wilson, it is nothing unless it has its heart the absolute principle of self-sacrifice. Employee loyalty and commitment have attracted much attention due to the expectation that committed and loyal employees will act in the best interest of an organization (Fischer, 2004). Earlier it was thought that older employees stay longer as compared to younger employees who keep on switched frequently in search of better job opportunities. But times have changed and now every employee considers loyalty important in their professional career.

This research finding is based on the responses obtained from the employees working in various small-scale industries in Southern Rajasthan. This paper investigated the role of employer and those factors which actually help in building loyalty among employees. A total of 100 employees participated in this study. Data was collected through self-administered questionnaires including open and close ended questions that were randomly distributed to the employees. The study is done through Likert scale which provides a sufficient range of choice to test the correctness of the answer and show the attitude of the respondent. Suggestions have been provided to improve the situation.

Introduction

Employees are a vital resource for nearly all organizations. Every company keeps on investing in training and development, retention, healthcare plans, etc. But no one directly targets towards investing in increasing or maintaining employee loyalty. Employee loyalty is not very new. But was never considered as significant in an organization as it is intangible in nature and no contract is signed between the employer and employees with this respect. It is intangible because loyalty refers to employee's commitment towards the success of the organization and believing that working for this organization is their best option. Under this employees become so loyal where they plan to remain with their current organization and also they do not actively search for other alternative employment.

Loyalty is defined as a relationship between an employer and an employee often unwritten contract where the employer agrees to provide essential resources to the employee for accomplishing his task, and employee agrees to work at an optimal level to fulfill the goals of the company. Loyalty is like glue that ties an employee towards his organization. Most of the companies do not realize lose suffered due to loosing of efficient and loyal employees. Lack of employee loyalty may cost the company money, time, goals and lost customers. But when either party to this contact fails to fulfill their role, the contract that's hard to build in the first place gets broken. And then it's extremely difficult to rebuild the trust that existed between the employee and the boss. There are many factors which result in building a loyal employee such as trust, awards, honesty, retention, reward, etc. which are taken by employer. Awards and reward to employee loyalty explains that they are a valuable part of the organization and making success. This results in increases levels of commitment. This is seen as an example of a reinforcing cycle, whereby those who identify with the organization and are loyal will respond more favorably to organizations and increase their level of commitment and loyalty when they see that their organization actively considers levels of commitment and loyalty (Fischer, 2004).

Employees also feel lifetime loyal and like to continue in the same organisation because of the various retirement benefits and advancement opportunities along with salary/wages and health benefits. The cultures that value loyalty to the employer result in developing a kind of family relationship between employer and employee. Employee like to stay with one company till the time he thinks that it is mutually beneficial to the company and to him also. This relationship exists till that time. But when the opportunity moves around him such as to achieve new and a higher position, to move to a new world, or to find a new situation that is more suitable for his as well for his family, he then decides to leave that job. And hence the bond of loyalty breaks.

Rationale of the Study

In south Rajasthan, various small-scale industries exist producing different things like marble, granite, synthetic and polyester yarns, sanitary products, bricks, lime powder. Majority of these industries are not organized properly as they are not having a particular brand, not well recognized and a major reason being their output acts as input for various large-scale industries so it becomes all the more difficult for them to build their identity. Hence the policies and practices relating to HRM, finance and marketing are not very strong as big, well-established industries have for themselves. In these small-scale industries, some are of seasonal nature, hence do not operate for the whole year. Therefore, the policies are also not very sound. One major reason being the workers also mostly are illiterate or from a low educated background, and therefore are not aware of their rights. They are not aware of government policies for different industries, sectors and also are not able to fight for their rights in an organized manner. Either they are dependent on union leaders, political leaders or some workers at the high level who support them on different matters and specially in such situations. The employers also take undue advantage of the situation and try to avoid their welfare to some level and even exploit them in some cases.

Due to the majority of population being tribal people in the rural areas specially and low level of education, they face troubles. Dependance on agriculture does not provide full time involvement and low returns so they go for job in these industries to fulfill their needs for the majority of time and try to increase their earnings.

This study reveals the situation of the employee's trend regarding their loyalty towards the organization. Also suggestions are provided to the owners of the industry to increase employee loyalty towards them by some simple steps and some long-term high investment decisions which can help them to retain the potential employees as increase their loyalty.

Objective

This paper aims at highlighting the role of employer in building loyal employees as well as factors which results in making and increasing employee loyalty towards his company. It also suggests tips for improving the employee loyalty.

Research Methodology

The research methodology used here in this study is the Likert scale. A total of 100 employees participated in this study. Since here in-depth analysis of words has to be done, this scale provides a sufficient wide scale to quantify the word correctly and measure it. The five point rating provides a clear understanding of the aspects to be studied in the research. The scale provides the measurement as follows:

1. Strongly Disagree, 2. Disagree, 3. Neutral, 4. Agree, 5. Strongly Agree

Also a figure will be constructed to see the differences in the responses in the graphical form which provides a glance of the responses to all those who are not interested in the study at deep levels.

Analysis and Interpretation

The data collected was analyzed and interpreted in the following manner:

Table 1: Showing Factors Affecting the Employee Loyalty

S.No.	*Factors/Situation*	*Strongly Agree*	*Agree*	*Neither Agree nor Disagree*	*Disagree*	*Strongly Disagree*
1	I am happy with the working environment of my organization	60	7	12	6	15
2	I really feel like part of the family	40	2	17	11	30
3	I feel a strong personal attachment	42	12	15	13	18
4	When company has any problem, I think of it as my problem too	10	15	33	20	22
5	The company provides me with the information I need to make good decisions	60	5	15	12	8
6	The company listens to the grievances well and responds quickly	70	10	8	10	2
7	The company communicates openly and honestly	54	13	11	6	6
8	The company values my relationship, really cares about me, and invests in my success	45	19	15	11	10
9	The company attracts and retains outstanding employees and partners	10	23	18	35	14
10	I believe that company deserves my loyalty	63	20	10	2	5
11	Over the past years, my loyalty has grown stronger	10	13	18	29	30
12	Employee loyalty is appropriately valued and rewarded by the employer	57	10	15	2	6
13	People are fairly rewarded for their contributions to long-term success	33	12	23	18	14
14	The company treats me like a real partner	60	12	13	12	3
15	I would like to see my relationship with the company grow in the foreseeable future	10	5	17	27	51
16	I provide enthusiastic referrals for the company	45	9	16	10	20

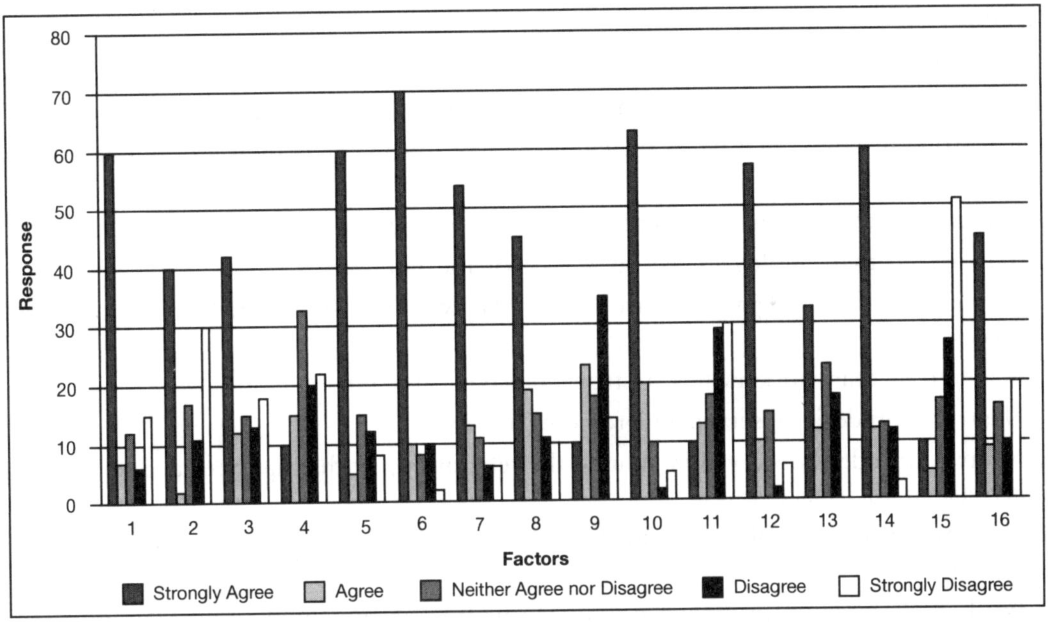

Fig. 1: Showing Factors Affecting the Employee Loyalty

Table 2: Average Calculation of the Above Factors

S.No.	*Factors*	*Sum of Scores (SS)*	*No. of Respondents (100)*	*Average score (SS/100)*	*Rank*
1.	I am happy with the working environment of my organization	209	100	2.09	10
2.	I really feel like part of the family	289	100	2.89	5
3.	I feel a strong personal attachment	253	100	2.53	7
4.	When company has any problem, I think of it as my problem too	329	100	3.29	3
5.	The company provides me with the information I need to make good decisions	203	100	2.03	11
6.	The company listens to the grievances well and responds quickly	164	100	1.64	15
7.	The company communicates openly and honestly	167	100	1.67	13
8.	The company values my relationship, really cares about me, and invests in my success	222	100	2.22	9
9.	The company attracts and retains outstanding employees and partners	320	100	3.2	4
10.	I believe that company deserves my loyalty	166	100	1.66	14
11.	Over the past years, my loyalty has grown stronger	356	100	3.56	2
12.	Employee loyalty is appropriately valued and rewarded by the employer	160	100	1.6	16
13.	People are fairly rewarded for their contributions to long-term success	268	100	2.68	6
14.	The company treats me like a real partner	186	100	1.86	12
15.	I would like to see my relationship with the company grow in the foreseeable future	434	100	4.34	1
16.	I provide enthusiastic referrals for the company	251	100	2.51	8

Interpretation

1. Employees strongly agree to see their relationship grow with the organisaton in future.
2. Over the past years the loyalty has grown stronger, strong agreement is observed.
3. It is strongly agreed that when the company has a problem, employees think it as their own problem.
4. It is agreed that company retains the outstanding employees and partners.
5. It is agreed that employees feel as a part of the family.
6. It is agreed that company rewards fairly the workers who contribute to long-term success.
7. It is agreed that workers feel a strong personal attachment.
8. Neutral attitude is observed in providing referrals.
9. Neutral attitude is observed in valuing the relationship with employees and very rarely invests for their success.
10. Neutral attitude is observed in feeling happiness with the environment of the organization.
11. Workers disagree on providing useful information by the company to take good and correct decisions by them.
12. Workers disagree on their treatment by the company as real partners.
13. Workers disagree on open and honest communication by the company regarding different matters.
14. Workers strongly disagree on the matter of the company deserving their loyalty.
15. Workers strongly disagree on the matter of listening to their grievances and taking action on it.
16. Workers strongly disagree on the matter of valuing their loyalty properly and rewarding it suitably.

Overall it can be said that

1. The workers are ready to provide their best output, but employer has to be considerate enough to make them motivated and keep their energy levels high.
2. Workers think the organization as a part of their family hence well knit with each other which results in good efficiency as well as their mental condition.
3. The employer should value the loyalty properly so that best output can be obtained and even best employees can be retained for a long time which will also provide mutual benefit to both the parties.
4. Grievances should be listened to and immediate action should be taken to provide strength to the worker and allow keeping his attention in the work.
5. Full information should be provided to the employees regarding necessary matters or those which affect the work directly so that they have the freedom to take proper action.

In addition to these steps, some more tips are provided which are as follows:

Tips for Improving Employee Loyalty

1. Awards and reward to the loyal employees simply boost the morale and motivate them to be loyal toward their organization in future also. If employees find that they are not appreciated for their work they will feel neglected in the organisation. While on the other hand management must also ensure that they are regularly promoting employees who deserve promotion and must not see that they are fighting for the promotions and increments. Some employees are also motivated to become loyal towards the organisation when they get new and more responsible or important task.
2. Encourage team-building activities, creating trust, building morale and feelings of unity among staff members through various informal get-together results in less tussles and more loyalty.
3. Employee satisfaction is a result of their happiness with the organisation. It is important to measure the level of their happiness so that they remain committed to their job and towards company. That's why the management must ensure that they are consistently satisfied and happy. It is also necessary to resolve conflicts immediately as soon as they appear. So that the employee work freely without any tension.
4. Management must also ensure the employee's works in a stress free environment and also get sufficient resources to do their job. Lack of proper resources with improper assistance and reasonable time can result in frustrated and disheartened. Management must also assure that employees are part of their organisation and must be included in decision making. They must welcome their thoughts, suggestions and ideas. This will make them feel that they are part of this family.
5. Company must offer fair compensation to its employees for the position with regular raises and evaluations. Along with the financial compensation, management must look at ways that the employees can benefit from remaining employed with them such as through health care plan, employee emergency fund, vacation plan, free gym memberships or club membership for them as well as for their family members.
6. Management must also keep in mind the importance of organizational goals as well as personal goals of the employees become it sometimes happens that due to non-achievement of personal goals that leave their job. It must remember employees are looking for the best place to work.
7. Applying the concept of work life balance in the organization make their job flexible and help in balancing the personal and professional life.

Conclusions

1. Employer has a great lot of efforts to do from his side to gain employee loyalty.
2. Employer should understand that if employees are loyal, the company can reach great heights.
3. Employer should create a favourable environment to get the best output from the employees.
4. Employer should take utmost care for the worker's grievances and satisfaction so that they remain happy and satisfied.
5. Employer should spare no effort to retain the good employees and keep their motivational levels high.

REFERENCES

Fischer, R. (2004), Rewarding Employee Loyalty: An Organizational Justice Approach, *International Journal of Organisational Behaviour*, Volume 8 (3), 486-503. Retrieved on 2012-07-01 from http://www.usq.edu.au/extrafiles/business/journals/HRMJournal/InternationalArticles/Volume%208/Vol8Fischer3.pdf

Gupta, S.P., *Statistical Methods*, Thirty-Eighth Edition (2008), Sultan Chand and Sons, New Delhi.

Kothari, C.R., *Research Methodology*, Vikas Publishing House, New Delhi.

www.loyaltyresearch.com

www.citehr.com/research-employee-loyalty3123309982-questionnaire-page1.htm

www.workforce.com/article/20021230/NEWS01/

CHAPTER 19 JOB SATISFACTION AND RETENTION OF MANAGEMENT FACULTY: THE NEED OF AN HOUR

–P. Annapurna

Empowering employees at all levels to do their best work can begin with something as simple as positive feedback and other gestures that show their efforts are appreciated. And it can help reduce staff turnover.

ABSTRACT

India has over 2000 business schools; the incidence of faculty turnover in most of the business schools is increasing day by day. Recruiting the management faculty is a major challenge to both new business schools and established institutions. Even though the demand for the business education has been growing steadily over the last decade, the production and trained faculty has not raise to satisfy the demand. The existing gap between demand and supply for the qualitative faculty is increasing drastically. The growth in the number of business schools, the financial lure of private sector and a stigma associated with doctorial qualification have lead to shortage of qualified faculty. Even the leading institutions are not immune to the challenges of faculty shortages. At present, the business schools in India face an acute shortage of qualified and competent faculty which leads to employee satisfaction and retention as being a major HR issue in the current scenario of business education. Retaining talents is not the choice of employer but it is a need of time, as management education is already at risk due to shortage of talent crisis. This paper focuses on identifying the levels of faculty satisfaction, various issues of faculty turnover and the retention strategies to be adopted by the business schools. The methodology adopted is an exploratory study through the survey of various business schools in Andhra Pradesh state and secondary date available in magazines, journals, research papers and websites.

Introduction

Over the past few years, the increasing number of institutes offering management education in India has helped the country produce more than 100,000 management graduates each year. As per All India Council for Technical Education (AICTE), in 2009, there were 1,608 institutes, which conducted AICTE-approved MBA program with an approved intake capacity of 1,28,947 students. There were another 391 institutes, which conducted AICTE-approved PGDM courses with an intake capacity of 44,318 students. According to Ranganath, director of National Assessment and Accreditation Council (NAAC), India has a dearth of about four lakh faculty members. He was speaking at the National Policy Dialogue 2012, which had been jointly organized by the Planning Commission and the British Council (Express India). Even though the number of business schools in India is increasing, there is tremendous shortage of good Ph.D. programs in the management sector creates faculty crisis. The shortage of faculty is severe that India will fail to accomplish the goal set in the field of higher education. A report which was released by the Central Government in 2011 shows that the lack of supply of Ph.D.'s along with slow recruitment activities and lack of incentives to attract and develop talents has led to a condition where 40 per cent of the faculty positions remain unfilled. If the faculty student ratio is considered against the standard set by the government, the positions are vacant by 54 per cent. This is the case of the higher education sector as a whole, which included management education too. The shortage is not restricted to Asian countries alone but also in developed countries as well to a limited extent. The management institutes which have a global reputation and based in India like IIMs, Great Lakes Management School, Indian School of Business (in collaboration with Kellogs Wharton) are all facing adequate faculty problems. The most intriguing aspect is on the retention of quality faculty members who are the right blend of academics, research and consulting as a big challenging to the b-schools. The teachers who can give the best of the academic inputs to the budding business professionals, imbibe professional values, can inspire the students/participants to be the business leaders of tomorrow is a rare species. The turnover rate of faculty members across the globe is an area of immense concern to the top echelons of the various b-schools. Some research agencies in India write that most Indian business schools "do not have the environment that motivates the faculty to do research. Unless the quality of research and knowledge created is of a high order, a paper can't be published in a top-ranking journal or get good citations. To write such a paper, faculty members will have to update themselves by reading about new developments in their area and interacting with the industry. This ensures they don't teach outdated stuff" (Premchand Palety). In order to counter the faculty shortage, business schools in India have been strengthening their doctoral programs and encouraging more students to take up research. According to the National Knowledge Commission, a high-level advisory body to the Prime Minister of India, the growth in higher education in India has not been accompanied by an equivalent growth in doctoral students (Ashok Kapoor). Raising the gross enrolment ratio (GER) would entail an additional enrollment of over 26 million in higher education and almost 1 million school teachers by 2020. "Thus, a concerted strategy to retain best talents in universities for faculty positions and preparing secondary teachers needs to be formulated. It would also require changes in strategies relating to open learning and technology enabled learning," said a ministry note in 12th five-year Plan. For faculty attraction and retention, the ministry is mulling Human Resource Planning and Management (HRPM) centre at the university level to assess teacher requirement and plan their professional growth research and faculty development program such as seminars, training, workshops, and incentive and award scheme.

Conceptual Framework

Job satisfaction can be defined as a positive feeling about one's job resulting from an evaluation of its characteristics a person with high level of job satisfaction holds positive feeling about job, while person who is dissatisfied holds negative feelings about the job. The theories of job satisfaction are many but most popular three are Edwin A. Locke's Range of Affect Theory (1976) is arguably the most famous job satisfaction model. The main premise of this theory is that satisfaction is determined by a discrepancy between what one wants in a job and what one has in a job. Further, the theory states that how much one values a given facet of work (e.g. the degree of autonomy in a position) moderates how satisfied/dissatisfied one becomes when expectations are/aren't met. When a person values a particular facet of a job, his satisfaction is more greatly impacted both positively (when expectations are met) and negatively (when expectations are not met), compared to one who doesn't value that facet.

Another well-known job satisfaction theory is the Dispositional Theory. It is a very general theory that suggests that people have innate dispositions that cause them to have tendencies toward a certain level of satisfaction, regardless of one's job. This approach became a notable explanation of job satisfaction in light of evidence that job satisfaction tends to be stable over time and across careers and jobs. Research also indicates that identical twins have similar levels of job satisfaction.

Hertzberg's two factor theory (also known as Motivator Hygiene Theory) attempts to explain satisfaction and motivation in the workplace. This theory states that satisfaction and dissatisfaction are driven by different factors—motivation and hygiene factors, respectively. An employee's motivation to work is continually related to job satisfaction of a subordinate. Motivation can be seen as an inner force that drives individuals to attain personal and organization goals. Motivating factors are those aspects of the job that make people want to perform, and provide people with satisfaction, for example achievement in work, recognition, promotion opportunities. These motivating factors are considered to be intrinsic to the job, or the work carried out. Hygiene factors include aspects of the working environment such as pay, company policies, supervisory practices, and other working conduit.

Employee retention is major HR issue in the organization. Retention of talent and maintaining a motivated and contended professors are perhaps the biggest challenges for the educational institutions. It has become more significance and assumes greater importance in era of open economy and cutting edge competition, colleges and education professionals are busy devising new and innovative management practices and ideas towards keeping their professors motivated, satisfied and always available for giving their best efforts towards achieving goals and objectives.

Faculty retention mainly depends upon four HR factors and such as university culture and policies, working environment, challenging opportunities and team work relationships (Mond H.R. Joarder). The academic administer plays a central role in successful retention of talented faculty members.

Employee retention involves taking measures to encourage employees to remain in the organization for the maximum period of time. Management institutions are facing a lot of problems in employee retention aspect. Hiring knowledgeable people for the job is essential for an employer. But retention is even more important than hiring. There is no dearth of opportunities for a talented person. There are many organizations which are looking for such employees. If a person is not satisfied by the job he's doing, he may switch over to some other more suitable job. In today's environment, it becomes very important for organizations to retain their employees.

Retention is a big and a constant challenge for every organization today whether to talk of any corporate sector or any educational institution. It is a cut-throat problem for most organizations in the modern era of globalization and competitive business. Successful organizations realize employee retention and talent management are integral to sustaining their leadership and growth in the marketplace

Employee retention is a challenge to the business schools to sustain in a knowledge market. Now Indian colleges are busy weaving out new strategies to attract and retain talent.

- Effective and sound remuneration policy must be constructed to attract, maintain and retain talented people in an organization.
- Empower the employees by enlarging an employee's job responsibility by conferring him the authority to get things done without becoming over burdened or distressed.
- Create a good quality work life by providing congenial work environment good organizational culture, values, company reputation, quality of people working, good working conditions, fostering employee development and growth.
- Effective reward and recognition of each faculty for their research initiates and provide time for research and publications.
- Optimize the work load per faculty.

Review of Literature

In a rapid developed markets, the traditional business education scaled up and stressfully to meet the strong demands for management education. There is a clear implication that to grow the developed markets the business schools either transform them to meet those demands or to weed out from the markets (Henery Granfold, 2005). In the current scenario of b-schools in particular are facing various challenges in various dimensions, the most intriguing aspect is on talent faculty who imbibe professional values and develop business leaders of tomorrow is decreasing drastically which cause a big challenge for b-schools to sustain in changing markets. (In book review of *The Business of in Business Schools*, Dr. V.R.K. Prasad stated that attracting and finding a faculty with right attitude and right abilities depending upon whether the business schools has a comprehensive manpower plan in place and how methodically it is put to practice and the efficiency of the plan depends on the validity of various methods followed. Indentify the need analysis of the faculty at various levels of teaching and identify appropriate training required and methods to impart required training to the faculty. Encourage the faculty in research and consultancy activities provides insights to stimulate and ensure capacity building among the faculty to take up the quality research and consultancy assignments with attractive compensation policies to sustain them. Compensation management plays a pivotal role in motivating faculty and propels their effects to make maximum contribution to the institution. Morale and motivation and organization culture gives the important guidelines on motivating the faculty by providing learning opportunities and creating the culture that triggers a desire to learn and to contribute to the organization. Managing attrition and retention of faculty in business schools is of paramount importance and it is difficult to replace the qualified faculty.

Objectives of the Study

- To determine the factors lead to faculty satisfaction in various b-schools.
- To identify the demand and supply of doctorial degrees and student: faculty ratio in various business schools.

- To determine the various reasons for faculty attrition in the business schools.
- To draw the implications to retain the faculty in the institutions.
- To suggest faculty retention and development strategies to the business schools.

Research Methodology

The present research paper is exploratory and empirical in nature with based descriptive analysis on the data of faculty satisfaction levels from various business schools in Andhra Pradesh state. And the sample size is 250 out of total population which means all management faculties from various business schools in Andhra Pradesh state. The primary data collected by the respondents through a structured questionnaire based on various dimensions of job-related factors and personal interviews of faculty about the causes of attrition and retention of faculty. Apart from this, the secondary data collected from publications, magazines, newspaper articles and through various websites.

Demand and Supply of Management Faculty

AICTE and UGC have given sanctioning and affiliation to large number of institutions but were unable to produce competent faculty to teach in management courses, which created a demand supply gap and resulted in low standard faculty. The business schools are the sources of developing managerial talents in various fields of business activity. It is very much surprising that 80% of b-schools deprive from faculty shortages. Recruit talent faculty is a major challenge to b-schools even though the demand for business has been growing steadily over the last decades the production of trained faculty has not rose to satisfy the demand. The situations are so bad that many schools manage their MBA program through a greater proportion of visiting and adjunct faculty. The root of the problem is the supply side that less candidates enroll in doctorial degree and those who enrolled they are not with a passion of learning, due to lack of opportunities in industrial sector and take part in academics. In some instances, there is a potential candidate to apply for doctorial degree but many universities had no facility to offer the service they focus on MBA degrees, there in a mask that it generates revenue to the institutes rather than doctorate degrees which is cost to the organization. If the demand and supply of talent faculty of 13 business is in this way and imagine there were more than 200 business in Andhra Pradesh and more than 2000 in the country.

Findings and Implications

Table 1: Demand and Supply of Management Faculty in AP B-schools

Dimensions	*Central university (1)*	*State universities (3)*	*Deemed universities (2)*	*Private B-Schools (8)*
Full Faculty strength	16	61	72	130
Master degree	1	0	37	108
Doctorate degree	15	61	35	22
Experience <=5	1	2	33	39
Age >56	6	6	5	7
Total no. of students	120	360	1060	960
Student: doctorate faculty ratio	1:8	1:6	1:30	1:43

Table 1 depicts that demand and shortage of talented management faculty in business schools. The data represents the fact that there are sufficient teachers to serve the students but the qualified and talented faculty is deficit that is the quantity of doctorial degree faculty is less in deemed universities and private institutions, student and qualified faculty ratio was not at par with the UGC standards and so these business schools should acquire the talented faculty to maintain the student and doctorial faculty ratio and to increase educational standards of students to satisfy demands of competitive business world appropriate measures taken to increase the faculty satisfaction and retention and faculty commitment to the organization.

Table 2: Job Satisfaction Levels of Faculty in Different Business Schools

Dimensions	*Central university (1)*	*State universities (3)*	*Deemed universities (2)*	*Private B-Schools (8)*	*Total*
Work autonomy	0.81	0.54	0.49	0.45	0.57
Recognition/appreciation	0.7	0.69	0.68	0.65	0.68
Responsibility	0.8	0.87	0.79	0.68	0.78
Nature of work	0.94	0.67	0.57	0.61	0.69
Relationships	0.76	0.81	0.81	0.82	0.80
Salary/benefits	0.31	0.22	0.25	0.23	0.25
Supervision	0.63	0.57	0.62	0.61	0.60
Working conditions	0.25	0.39	0.42	0.29	0.33
Job security	1.00	0.77	0.92	0.55	0.80
Carrier growth	0.08	0.06	0.07	0.04	0.06
Opp to use abilities	0.63	0.49	0.58	0.49	0.54
Authority/control	0.75	0.94	0.85	0.88	0.84
Org policies/procedures	0.64	0.59	0.67	0.57	0.61
Flow of information	0.64	0.65	0.66	0.60	0.63
Participatory managment	0.81	0.80	0.72	0.81	0.78
Teaching process	0.70	0.75	0.75	0.68	0.72
Research facilities	0.56	0.57	0.65	0.47	0.56
Stress	0.46	0.49	0.56	0.59	0.52
Coping strategies	0.01	0.04	0.03	0.01	0.02
Overall satisfaction	0.61	0.58	0.58	0.54	0.58

Table 2 represents a greater percentage of faculty satisfied with nature of work, recognition and appreciation, responsibility which includes individual and organizational, relationships in the organizations, supervision, authority and control, organizational policies and procedures, flow of information, participatory management, teaching process and job security. But the job security is low in private business schools compared with universities. And the average number of faculty satisfied in various facets like work autonomy, opportunities to use abilities at work and work autonomy. However, very less percentage of faculty tend to be satisfied in various dimensions like pay and fringe benefits, working conditions, carrier growth and development. The other issue is due to various positive and negative job-related factors half of the faculty was under stress and their coping strategies were very poor. Even though the overall motivational factors or satisfaction levels more or less same in all business schools, yet there is a difference in universities and private business schools on various dimensions like job security, working conditions, work autonomy, research facilities. At last there is only 58% of faculty satisfied with their jobs.

Issues of Faculty Turnover

Turnover is a function of perceived desirability of one's present job and ease with which the person between he or she can move to another job. The short supply of and high demand for doctoral qualified business faculty has resulted in a significant increase in turnover among faculty. This turnover involves the movement of talented and high qualified faculty from schools to schools and movement from academics to industry (M.K. Dash, 2011). The incidence of high faculty turnover in most of the b-schools have raised numerous issues relating to faculty work load, faculty research and publications, faculty development program and job security, etc. During data collection period in some of the private institutions when the faculty was interviewed about the causes of attrition of faculty in their institutions for which they stated that there is lack of carrier development opportunities, lack of job security, low wages, and work load in fact that administrative work is more than teaching activity and the faculty should participate in student promotion activities in most of the private business schools. If an organization requires the individuals put its best and present creativity for the organizational development which is not possible for an employee to give best effort. Imagine if a faculty giving a lecture on job satisfaction which he and she not satisfied with job and in a dilemma of what to do, in such situations how a faculty think of creativity and innovation at work (Rachit Gupta).

Suggestions

There are some of the strategies which elevate the present problem of the talent faculty shortage and protect the business schools form faculty crisis in future.

- Encourage monetary and non-monetary support and provide sufficient knowledge resources to Ph.D. scholars so they present a quality research work and number of talents enrolled in Ph.D.'s and develop a long-term commitment towards the organization.
- Hire the faculty trained in relative disciplines of management like sociology, psychology, commerce, economics and statistics and help them to refocus their research and teaching interests in management studies.
- Business schools administration manage their faculty in two distinct ways first those with a standard Ph.D. degree and strong academic profile with no business experience and other with no Ph.D. and with strong business and research profile.
- To address faculty shortage, India needs to remove barriers to hiring foreign nationals as permanent staff and provision of flexibility in faculty recruitment policies so that can hire more number of talents.
- Instead of increasing the regular work load to the faculty and offering double salaries for them, its better the business schools more importantly combine them with an offer reducing the work load those faculty who have talents to produce productive research papers in international a journals over last couple of years.

- Manage top performers and average performers both are require to run the organization and fine tune the talent persons there in sustain their competitive advantage.
- Motivate the students who show instead in teaching so they given an internship in teaching during MBA program with that they develop skill and knowledge in teaching profession. They should be introduced to the option of teaching as a profession and exposed to role models and provide the opportunities as teaching assistants after the MBA program.

Conclusion

Maintain the high employee satisfaction levels and retain talent in the organization is the challenging factor for all business schools. The organization should take the appropriate steps to acquire the talent resources and maintained them in long run in the organization. Shortage of talents in the business schools can be recovered by various suggested measures in the study. Employee satisfaction plays a prerequisite factor for employee retention and employee performance. In the present study, there are only 58% of employees satisfied with job-related factors which is the pre-indication for the business schools should be aware of faculty crisis in present and future. The business schools should focus on the faculty developmental programs and satisfy the needs of the faculty which in turn the organization extract knowledge from them and producing quality students to face the competitive business environment.

REFERENCES

Savitha, G.R. "A research paper on faculty supply chain in B-schools: Dynamics of current trend".

Anju Shukla, "Retention of talents and employee motivation challenge before the HR professionals".

Mohammad Ashraf, "Talent management and retention practices from faculty point of view, A case study". *Journal of Human Capital*, Vol. 1, 2009.

Rachit Gupta, "Faculty retention: challenge for business schools," *International Journal of Multidisciplinary Research*, Vol. 1, Issue 8, December 2011.

Nirmal Kumar "Taking stock of Indian management research", *Economic Times*, Feb. 2011.

Vipin gupta, "Quality of business education: A study of Indian context".

Vijay R. Kannan, "Business schools in India: Current challenges future opportunities" *Decision Line*, October 2008.

Mohoney et al., "Recouting and retaining sport management faculty: Factors affecting job choice", *Journal of Sport Manangement*, 2006, pp. 414-30.

Sanjeev Kumar, "Management education in India: Trends issues and implications", *Research Journal of International Studies*, Issue 18, Jan. 2011.

Ramesh R. Kulkarni and Dayavanti Dixit, "Pay pakage is a contemporary issue in retention of faculty in technical institutions—An empirical study of north Karnataka" 2012 international conference on management and innovation, *IPERDR*, Vol. 37.

Ken Starkey and Nick Tiratsoo, *Business School and the Bottom Line*.

V.R.K. Prasad, *The Business of HR in Business Schools*, Viva Book Pvt. Ltd.

Stephen H. Robbins, *Organization Behaviour*, pp. 95-103.

Websites

www.emerald insight.com; www.Economics Times.com; www.aide.com

www.aicte.ernet.in; www.ugc.com; www.indiamba.com

CHAPTER 20

JOB SATISFACTION—THE ESSENCE OF A MOTIVATED WORKFORCE

–Harvinder Soni

ABSTRACT

Employee job satisfaction has been targeted by research for almost one hundred years. The origin of these studies dates back to at least 1911, when Taylor began to study employees and their job duties to develop better ways to train worker (Taylor, 1911). Seven years later, the interest in job satisfaction had clearly arrived when Edward Thorndike examined the link between work and satisfaction in the *Journal of Applied Psychology* in 1918. One of the biggest preludes to the study of job satisfaction was the Hawthorne studies (1924-33), by Elton Mayo.

The study has been conducted at on 90 employees at working at Sawhney Export House, Noida which is leading and government reorganization in the field of readymade garments and accessories. The total number of 90 employees has been bifurcated into 50 workers and 40 supervisors. An attempt has been made to study the overall satisfaction of all level of employees working in Sawhney Export and to present a comparative analysis of the same. To assess the satisfaction level of employees Likert's five-point-scale has been used. On the basis of scores obtained average level of satisfaction of workers and supervisors has been calculated with the help of Arithmetic mean. Besides percentage-wise level of satisfaction of workers and supervisors for various components of job satisfaction has been calculated.

Analysis of data shows that overall these prevails dissatisfaction among the workers regarding their job, though the supervisors are satisfied overall. At the worker level, there is a need to improve the work-life balance provide job variety role clarity, quality of work life, promotion and development opportunities, autonomy and recognition and compensation and fringe benefits to increase the job satisfaction of employees. At the supervisory level again satisfaction level can be further improved in the area of work-life balance, role clarity, quality of work life and recognition.

An organization should regularly conduct employee surveys to assess the level of satisfaction of their employee with these aspects. This would enable the management to assess the areas of dissatisfaction of the employees. Removing the causes of dissatisfaction of employee will not only raise the motivational level of employees and help them to contribute optimally to the organization but will also enable the organization to deliver quality products and services and thereby survive in this highly competitive environment.

Introduction

People are the most important asset of an organisation. Like other materials and economic resources, they are also a resource to an organisation which represent an investment whose development and utilization requires efficient management. Human resources are the pivotal variable without which the inanimate assets are worthless. In fact, the success of an organization depends mainly on the quality of its manpower and hence its performance. For optimum performance of employees, their satisfaction with the job performed by them is a must.

The corporate world is today being buffeted by the winds of globalization, liberalization and innovation in technology. Organizations need to be dynamic to adapt to increasing pace of change. Human resources play a major role in the success of an organization. A talented skilled and satisfied and motivated workforce is required in an organization to sustain in the competitive global environment. In view of the current global meltdown, many companies are resorting to pay cuts and lay-off. In such a state of affairs, the question arises that how can a dissatisfied and demotivated workforce put in their optimum contribution for the growth of the organization.

Review of Literature

Employee job satisfaction has been targeted by research for almost one hundred years. The origin of these studies dates back to at least 1911, when Taylor began to study employees and their job duties to develop better ways to train worker (Taylor, 1911). Seven years later, the interest in job satisfaction had clearly arrived when Edward Thorndike examined the link between work and satisfaction in the *Journal of Applied Psychology* in 1918. Some experts in the field suggest that the study of job satisfaction can be traced back almost 200 years, when the industrial revolution had began to blossom in the United States. However, these initial studies were focused on maximizing worker productivity and the data was often muddled with vague construct such as "morale" which provided little conceptual clarity and results that were marginally useful.

One of the biggest preludes to the study of job satisfaction was the Hawthorne studies. These studies (1924-33), primarily credited to Elton Mayo of the Harvard Business School, sought to find the effects of various conditions (most notably illumination) on worker's productivity and conduct at the Western Electric Hawthorne Works in Chicago. These studies showed that lighting had little connection to worker productivity, creating the fundamental groundwork for future studies that asked about other factors that may have an impact on employees. The Hawthorne studies continued until 1932, and in the five-year interval, the research widened to include factors such as temperature, fatigue, breaks and working hours. Mayo's work may seem marginally relevant to job satisfaction today, but he discovered that the mere act of studying workers and providing them with more attention increased their motivation and productivity. Mayo had stressed upon the essence of human motivation marking a new era of humanistic job satisfaction research and revolutionizing the research and theories of job satisfaction.

Job satisfaction studies continue to emerge and the results are often valued for both humanistic and financial benefits. When employees are satisfied, they tend to care more about the quality of their work. They are more committed to the organization. They have higher retention rates and they are generally more productive. Spector (1997) suggests that job satisfaction data is helpful in evaluating the emotional wellness and mental fitness of employees and that organization can use the information to improve departmental policies and practices where dissatisfaction is expressed.

HR policy in one of the key steps to gain job satisfaction addressing the essentials including fair compensation policy, valuable benefits policy and the ability to balance work and life which are crucial components of an organization's overall retention strategy. Organizations must not only create a mix of benefits policy that retain and motivate what is often a very diverse workforce, but they must also continually fine-tune the mix policies with the job satisfaction.

Some factors of job satisfaction are universal and consistent. Both employees and HR professionals note that compensation and benefits are important to employee job satisfaction. However, research has shown that there are more important factors that contribute to job satisfaction such as relationship with immediate supervisor, management recognition of employee job performance, job clarity, job enrichment, career growth and advancement opportunities and autonomy. These factors have more to do with the organizational culture and working conditions in the company.

Case Study—Job Satisfaction of Employee at Sawhney Export House

Sawhney Export House is a government-recognized Export House and is situated in Noida (U.P.). From a modest beginning in 1973 as a merchant exports, Sawhney Export has sought to redefine excellence in vibrant line of readymade garments, high fashion in accessories and jewellery. At present the company has managed to attain a top notch position in high fashion, garments, accessories and jewellery under the able stewardship of Mr. N.P. Sawhney.

Its state-of-the-art manufacturing facility is equipped with latest imported machines from Japan and China. The company is never dependent on outside sources. The company's unfazed commitment to stick to the deadline without compromising on quality has earned a list of happy customers. Production schedules are always adhered to and deliveries are on time. Their wide range of product includes high fashion garments like shirts, tops, capri's kaftans, trousers, Bandanas/hats, evening 'N' beach boy scarves, shawls, jewellery, home furnishing, and gift items. Company customers are mainly big buying houses and countries like Italy, France, Germany, U.K., Spain, Sweden, U.S.A., etc.

The employee strength is 500. Total covered area of factory is 45000 sq.ft. The company has got in-house Dyeing and Printing unit. Company has got infrastructure and manpower to produce 1,00,000 pcs. per week.

Objectives and Scope

1. To assess the satisfaction of employees at Sawhney Export House with the quality of work life (QWL) and work-life-balance.
2. To analyse the aspect of role clarity and job variety in the work of employees.
3. To analyse the views of employees with respect of career growth and advancement opportunities, rewards and recognition and human relations in the organization.

4. To check the level satisfaction of employees with the pay/salary given to them.
5. To measure the overall job satisfaction of employees at Sawhney Export House.

The study has been conducted at on 90 employees at working at Sawhney Export House which is leading andgovernment reorganization in the field of readymade garments and accessories. The total number of 90 employees has been bifurcated into 50 workers and 40 supervisors. An attempt has been made to study the overall satisfaction of all level of employees working in Sawhney Export and to present a comparative analysis of the same.

Methodology and Procedure of Work

Sample Design : Non-Probability Purposive Type

Sample Size : A sample size of 90 employees has been taken. Out of 90 employees, 50 are workers and 40 have been taken from supervisory level.

Collection of Data

1. ***Primary Data***

For collection of primary data two techniques have been used:

- **Personal Interview**

  Structured interviews were conducted for collecting information about the company and assessing the attitude of the management and worker.
- **Questionnaires**

  Close-ended structured questionnaire was used to analyze the satisfaction level of various categories of employees, viz. workers' and supervisory level.
- **Analysis of Data**

(i) To analyse the job satisfaction of employees at Sawhney Export House. The following components of job satisfaction have been used in the questionnaire:

(a) Work-life Balance

(b) Job Variety

(c) Role Clarity

(d) Management – Employee Relations

(e) Quality of Work-life (QWL)

(f) Promotion and Development

(g) Autonomy

(h) Recognition

(i) Compensation of Job Security

(ii) To assess the satisfaction level of employees Likert's five-point-scale has been used. On the basis of scores obtained average level of satisfaction of workers and supervisors has been calculated with the help of Arithmetic mean.

(iii) Percentage-wise level of satisfaction of workers and supervisors for various components of job satisfaction has been calculated for each component of job satisfaction.

2. ***Secondary Data***

Secondary data has been taken from annual report and brochure of the company together with journals magazines and Internet.

Findings

(i) *Work-Life Balance*

The analysis shows that satisfaction level of employees at Sawhney Export House in respect of work-life balance is low. If we make a comparison of workers satisfaction with the satisfaction of supervisors then workers are more dissatisfied than the supervisors on this aspect. The average level of satisfaction of workers is six and that of supervisors is slightly higher, i.e. 10.85. 76% of the workers are highly dissatisfied whereas none of the supervisors are highly dissatisfied. However, 75% of the supervisors come into dissatisfied category.

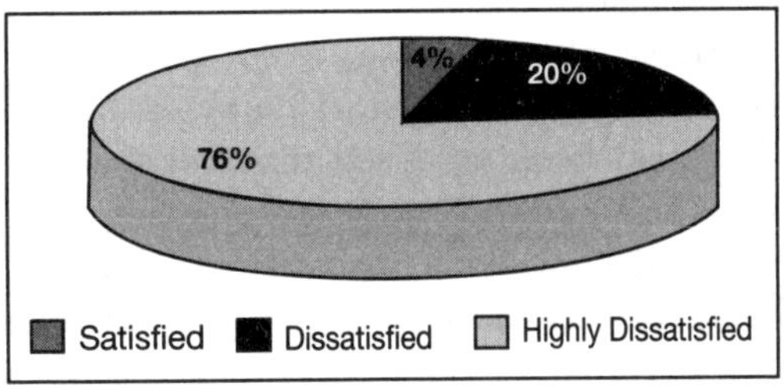

Fig. 1: Percentage-wise Level of Satisfaction of Workers with Work-Life Balance

Fig. 2: Percentage-wise Satisfaction of Supervisors with Work-Life Balance

(ii) *Job Variety*

Based upon data analysis, it can be interpreted that employees, i.e. both workers and supervisors in Sawhney Export are satisfied with job variety in their tasks. However, a comparison between satisfaction level of workers and that of supervisors shows the latter enjoy a higher satisfaction with job variety (mean value = 15.85) than the former (mean value = 13.96). It is interesting to note that though none of the supervisors come into the dissatisfied category, 16% of the workers are dissatisfied with their job variety. Besides, none of the workers come into highly satisfied category whereas 30% of the supervisors are highly satisfied and 65% are satisfied with their job variety. 84% of the workers come into the satisfied category.

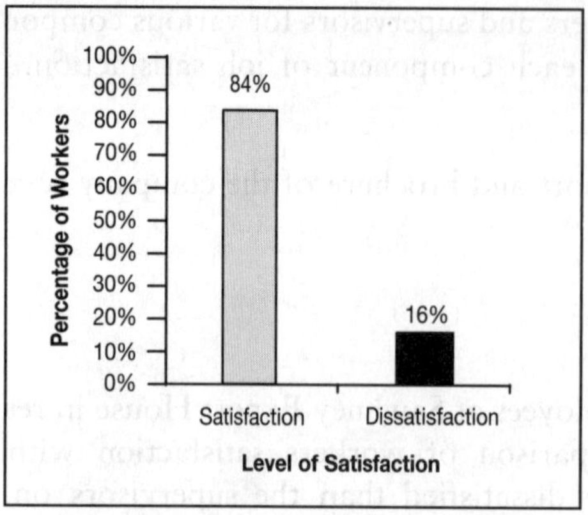

Fig. 3: Percentage-wise Satisfaction of Workers with Job-Variety

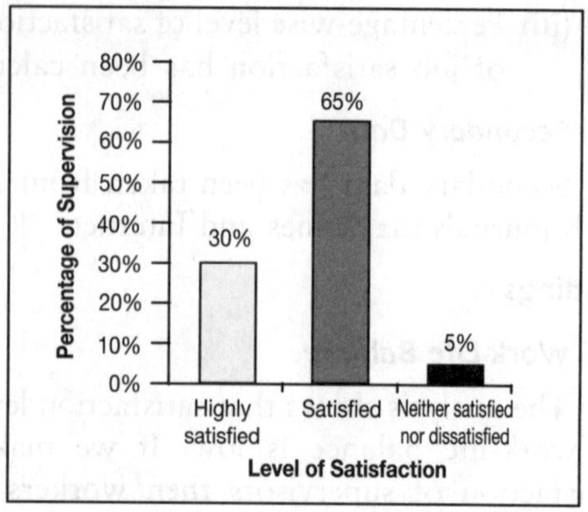

Fig. 4: Percentage-wise Satisfaction of Supervisors with Job Variety

(iii) *Role Clarity*

Under this aspect, an attempt was made to analyse how far the employees are clear about their duties and responsibilities in the organisation. The mean value calculated shows the average satisfaction level of supervisors as 11.72 and those of workers as 9.24. Hence, the workers enjoy a medium level of satisfaction whereas the supervisory staff enjoy a slightly higher level of satisfaction than that of workers. It has also been analysed that none of the supervisors come into the dissatisfied category whereas 36% of the workers come into this category. Besides, whereas 11% supervisors are highly satisfied and 68% are satisfied with their role clarity, in the workers category only 4% are highly satisfied and only 28% are satisfied with role clarity aspect.

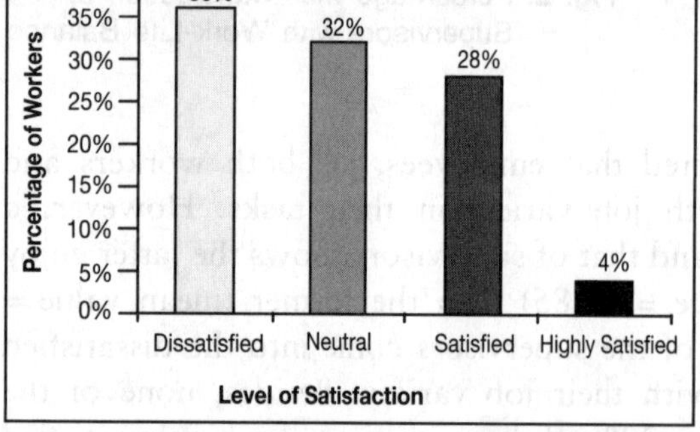

Fig. 5: Percentage-wise Satisfaction of Workers with Role Clarity

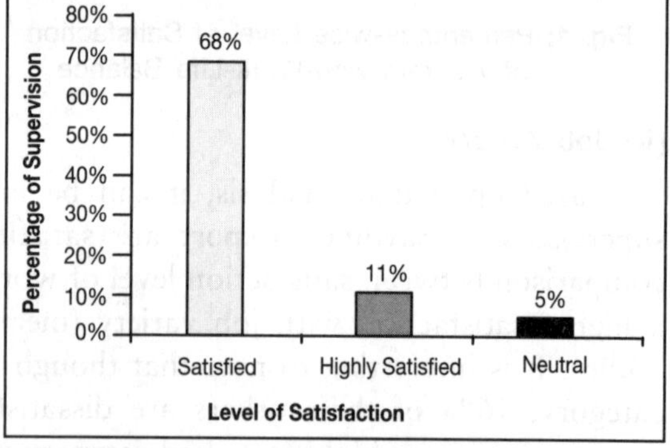

Fig. 6: Level of Satisfaction of Supervisors with Role Clarity

(iv) *Management Employee Relations*

In Sawhney Export House, healthy relation between management and employees prevails. This can be interpreted from the data analysis which shows that the average satisfaction level of workers with this aspect is 13.3 and of supervisors is 15.45. It can be interpreted that supervisory staff enjoy better relations with management because 30% of the supervisors are highly satisfied and 60% are satisfied with this aspect. On the other hand, among the workers none come under the highly satisfied category, though 68% are satisfied. Also 30% of the workers are dissatisfied whereas only 5% of the supervisory staff are dissatisfied regarding this aspect.

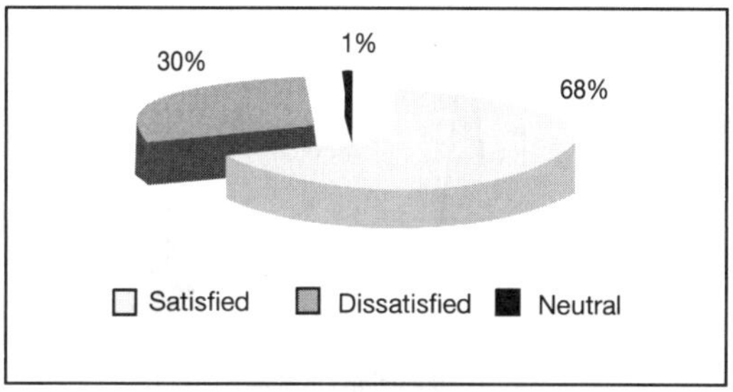

Fig. 7: Percentage-wise Satisfaction of Employees with Employer-Employees Relationship

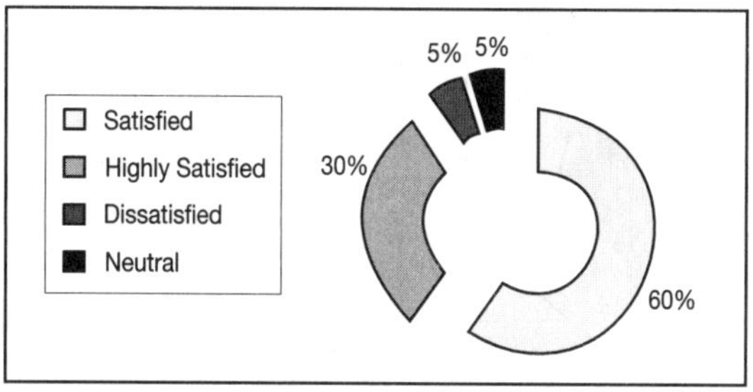

Fig. 8: Satisfaction Level of Supervisors with Management Employee Relations

(v) *Quality of Work Life*

An analysis of quality of work life of employee and their satisfaction level brings out the mean value of workers' satisfaction level 11.42 and supervisors satisfaction level at 11.37. 78% of the workers and 70% of supervisors are dissatisfied with the working condition and facilities provided to them. Hence, it can be interpreted that both the workers and the supervisory staff are dissatisfied with their quality of work life.

Fig. 9: Satisfaction Level of Workers with QWL in Sawhney Export House

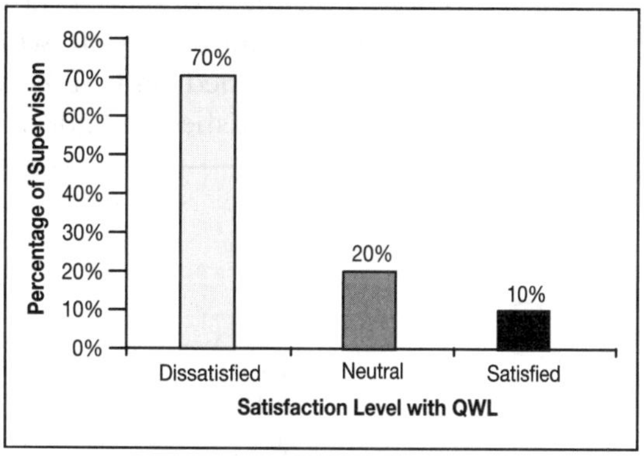

Fig. 10: Supervisors' Satisfaction Level with QWL

(vi) *Promotion and Development*

A comparison of the satisfaction level of workers and supervisory staff in Sawhney Export House brings out an interesting variation. The analysis shows that supervisors have a high satisfaction level of 16.5 whereas the worker class is dissatisfied with the promotion and development opportunities provided to them the mean value of satisfaction level being 8.12. 20% of the supervisors are highly satisfied and 80% come into the satisfied category. On the other hand, among the workers, 32% are highly dissatisfied and 64% are dissatisfied with this aspect 4% are neither satisfied nor dissatisfied and none of the workers are satisfied with the promotion and development opportunities provided to them.

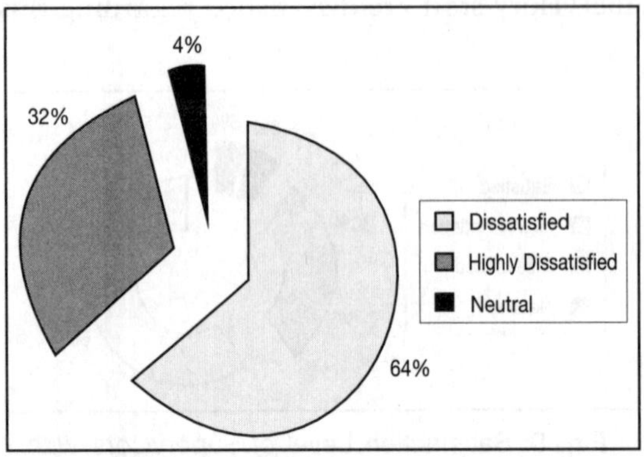

Fig. 11: Percentage-wise worker Satisfaction Level with Promotion and Development Opportunities

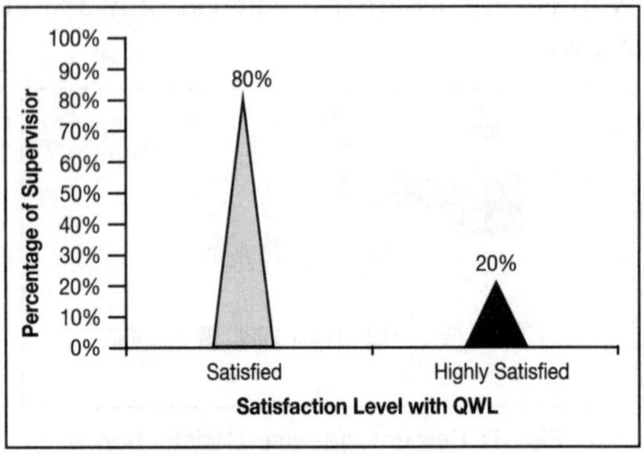

Fig. 12: Satisfaction Level Supervision with Promotion and Development Opportunities

(vii) *Autonomy*

Again, there is a conspicuous variation in the satisfaction level of workers and supervisors regarding autonomy. On one hand, the supervisory level of satisfaction is 12.55 which shows that a high satisfaction level prevails in Sawhney Export at this level. Also, 75% of the supervisors are highly satisfied and 20% are satisfied with their work autonomy.

On the other hand, the workers' level of satisfaction is 6.48 which shows dissatisfaction among the workers with autonomy at work. In fact, survey results show that 40% of the workers are highly dissatisfied and 52% are dissatisfied with the aspect. Only 8% of the workers come under the satisfied category.

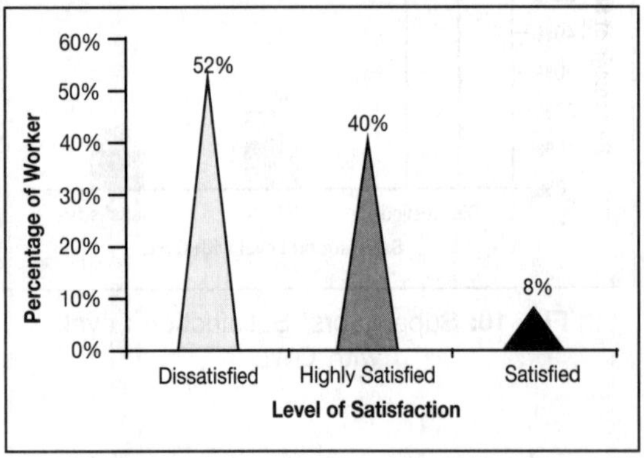

Fig. 13: Percentage-wise Level of Satisfaction of Workers with Autonomy

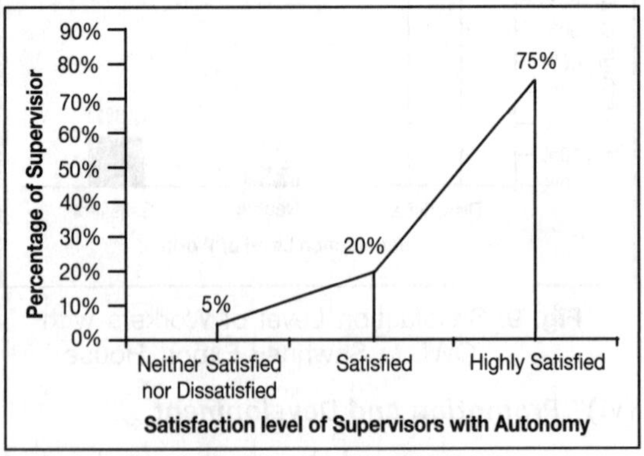

Fig. 14: Satisfaction Level of Supervisors Autonomy

(viii) *Recognition*

Data analysis shows that both the workers and supervisors are dissatisfied with the recognition given to them for their work. The average satisfaction level of supervisors is 5.1 and that of workers is 4.92. Hence, both the values show low satisfaction level. 52% of the workers have low satisfaction whereas 70% of the supervisors have low satisfaction with this aspect.

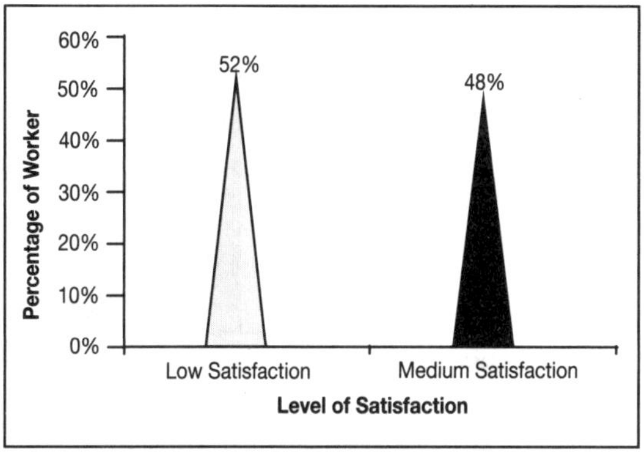

Fig. 15: Percentage-wise Level of Satisfaction of Workers with Recognition

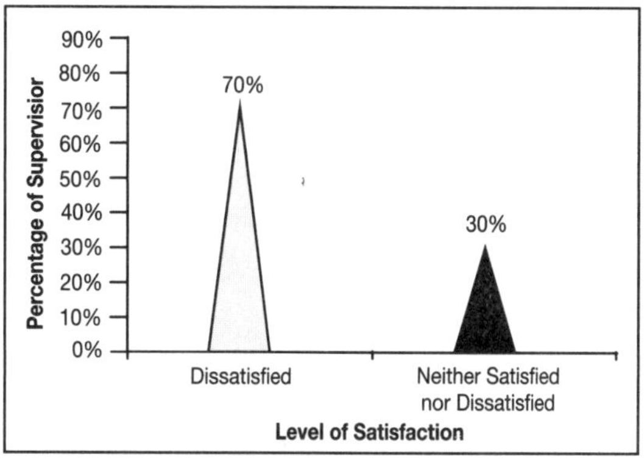

Fig. 16: Satisfaction Level of Supervisors with Recognition

(ix) *Compensation and Job Security*

Salary, benefits and job security form a very important component of job satisfaction. An analysis of the data shows again highly reverse results about the satisfaction level of supervisors and workers. The workers seem to be dissatisfied with their compensation and job security as shown by their average value of 8.92. On the other hand, the supervisor are satisfied with this aspect as depicted by their average value of 15.75.

5% supervisors are highly satisfied and 95% are satisfied with their salary and job security. On the other hand, none of the workers come into the satisfied or highly satisfied category. In fact, 20% workers are highly dissatisfied and 80% are dissatisfied with this aspect. Hence, there is a great variation in the satisfaction level of supervisors and workers.

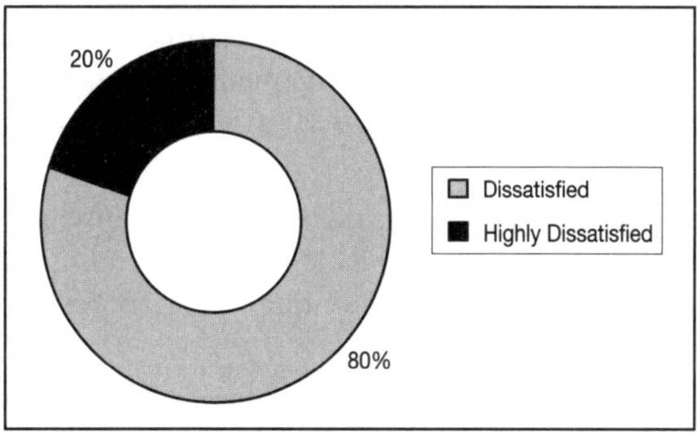

Fig. 17: Worker's Satisfaction with Compensation and Job Security

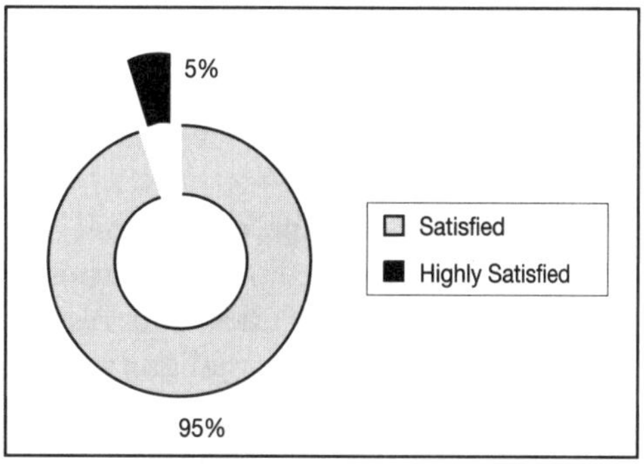

Fig. 18: Satisfaction Level of Supervisors with Compensation and Job Security

(x) *Overall Job Satisfaction*

At the final stage, an analysis of the overall job satisfaction of supervisors and workers was made. The workers' average satisfaction level is 1.96 and supervisors satisfaction level is 3.85 which shows that the workers are dissatisfied and supervisors are satisfied with their job overall.

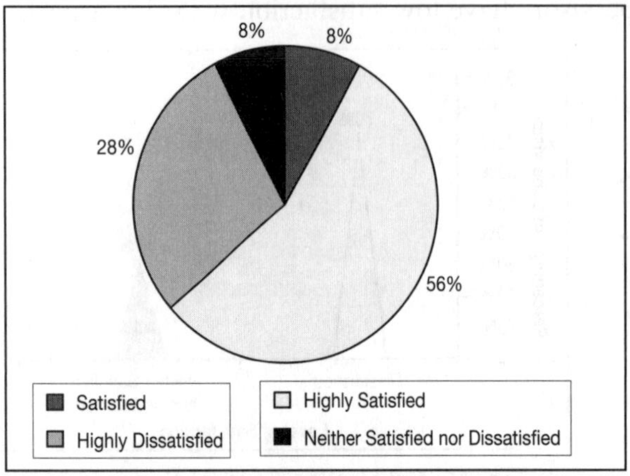

Fig. 19: Job Satisfaction Workers

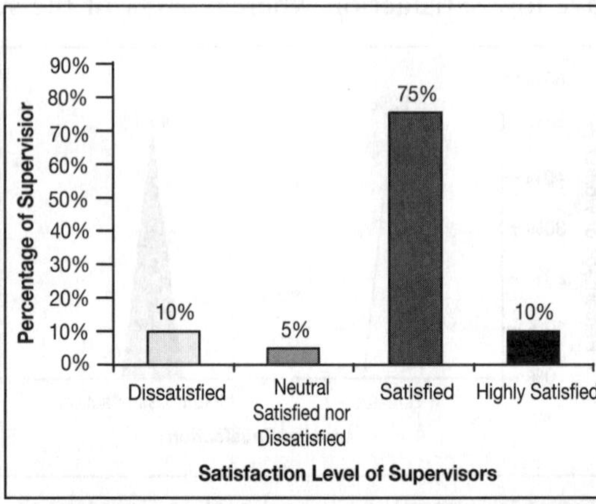

Fig. 20: Overall Job Satisfaction of Supervisors

Suggestions to Improve Job Satisfaction of Employees

1. It is recommended that Sawhney Export House should make some provision for alternative work schedules for the comfort and convenience of employees. These programmes may include working from home, reduced work-week, flexible working hours and part-time employment. These programs would provide leisure time to the employees and give them the opportunity to balance their personal and professional lives. The organization can conduct a 'Health of the Organization Survey' to know the problem and views of employee. All these steps will help to earn the loyalty of employees and also increase their job satisfaction.
2. The jobs can be made more challenging for the employees which helps to stimulate their intellect or personality. In the absence of any challenges, the employees might lose interest in a monotonous job. Also the job should offer something new to employees to avoid repetition and boredom. For this job enlargement, job rotation and job enrichment may be used for redesigning the jobs to offer variety and novelty to the employees.
3. There is a scope of improve the role clarity of supervisor and workers at Sawhney Export House. For this purpose, the company can adopt the Role Analysis Technique to clarity the duties and responsible of employees. This technique helps to resolve problems of role malignity and confusion.
   (a) In RAT, the role being defined is known as focal role. The incumbent of focal role attempts to analyse his role. He describes his formal duties and responsibilities in his role, the significance of the role to the organization and its place in achieving goals of the organization. The other members of the team give their suggestions

to the duties and behaviours described by the focal role incumbent. The discussion continues among team members till they arrive at a consensus on the role definition.

(b) The focal role incumbent describes the behaviour that he experts from other members of the team so that be can perform his role well.

(c) All the team members express the behaviour they expect from the focal role incumbent. The focal role incumbent may make some suggestions and subsequently, the entire team discusses and finalizes the expectations of focal role.

(d) The focal role incumbent prepares a written description of his role including the results of the above steps. It is known as the role profile. This can be done for every employee of the organization and duplication of work can be avoided by bringing about role clarity.

4. To further bring about harmonious relations between the management and employees, it is suggested that the company can develop a supportive culture and employee loyalty by encouraging workers' participation in management, using support groups, mentoring programs, diversity symposia, networking opportunities and host events to support diversity. Further, it can prepare policies, procedures and programs that emphasize the value of each individual employee.

5. Organizations should realize that their wealth lies in their employees and so providing a healthy work environment for employees should be their primary objective. To meet legal and humanitarian standards, Sawhney Export House should maintain the physical and psychological health of the work environment for the workers. The developments made in Ergonomics (Human Engineering) in the 1950s paved the way for promoting the physical and psychological safety of workers through the better layout of plant and improved equipment design. As per survey results, employees at Sawhney Export House find the working environment stressful. The outcomes of stress may be irritability, unstable behaviour, heavy smoking, psychosomatic pains, and depression, fatigue or drug abuse. Occupation stress may be due to the basic nature of work, hours of work, work environment, workers skills or lack of resources to accomplish the tasks. In Sawhney Export House, the HR manager should identify the factors that cause stress and efforts should be made to find ways to eliminate them. The necessity for leisure in employees life should be realized. Organization health programs should be designed to educate employees on way to improve and maintain their health. Diet control, stress release and relaxation techniques, physical exercise, yoga, etc. are examples of these programs. To encourage employees to adopt these program in their day-to-day lives, rewards can be offered to them. The other aspects that can be dealt with in this area are family planning, cardiovascular risk reduction, controlling hypertension, etc. The execution of health programs will help to reduce absenteeism of employees and bring down employee turnover.

6. At the worker level, there is a need for gearing up the career planning, training upgrading skills required for promotion, assigning challenging jobs with greater responsibilities that increase their abilities and knowledge. It should be ensured that

the work assignments that are given to an employee have a positive impact on the employees' self-esteem, motivate involvement and autonomy. When promoting employees to higher levels, the management should take extra care to encourage performance and talent. To avoid confusion, it should draw up clear promotional policies that match the organizational culture and foster healthy competition. Care should be taken to ensure that the promotional activities are executed fairly without any deviations. Deviation at the execution stage can lead to dissatisfaction among the employees and result in low level of job satisfaction.

7. It is advisable that at the worker level also some autonomy ought to be given based upon the skill and experience of the workers. This would give these workers a feeling of pride and recognition and increase their loyalty towards the organization. There should be some scope for experimentation and tolerance of mistakes to make the organization a learning organization.
8. The organization should take some measures to provide rewards and recognition to its employees. It can start the practice of monetary and non-monetary means of motivation to its employee like letters of appreciation, promotion based on merit, performance-based increments, reward.
9. At the worker level, dissatisfaction seems to have crept in regarding compensation and job-security. This shows that Sawhney Export needs to rethink on its compensation policy at the worker level. Many motivation theories conclude that fair and just compensation is a motivating factor for employees to perform better. Pay should be fixed on the basis of work done, responsibilities undertaken, individual skills, performance and accomplishments. The compensation should be designed to match the increase in the cost of living index and industry standards.

Conclusion

In the current scenario, where the corporate world is faced with the challenge of globalization and economic downturn, only those organizations will survive which are able to deliver quality products and deliver best service in the market. Skilled and efficient human resources play a major role in the success of an organization. A dissatisfied and demotivated workforce can never be expected to contribute to the growth of the organization.

The main determinants of job satisfaction are work-life balance, job variety, role clarity, management employee relations, quality of work-life, promotion and development, autonomy and recognition, compensation and job security. An organization should regularly conduct employee surveys to assess the level of satisfaction of their employee with these aspects. This would enable the management to assess the areas of dissatisfaction of the employees. Removing the causes of dissatisfaction of employee will not only raise the motivational level of employees and help them to contribute optimally to the organization but will also enable the organization to deliver quality products and services and thereby survive in this highly competitive environment.

REFERENCES

Anderson, Alan H. *Effective Personal Management,* Black Well UK, 1994.

Bakshi, Sunil *Industrial Relations and Labour Laws*, Galgitia Publisher NewDelhi, 2001.

Beck, Robert C. *Motivation Theories and Principle*, Person Education New Delhi, 2003.

Chauhan, Daisy *Managing Executive Stress* Excel Publisher New Delhi, 2002, Mamoria, C.B. and S.B. Mamoria *Dynamics of Industrial Relation*, Himalaya Publisher New Delhi, 2005.

Davar, R.S. *Personal Management and Industrial Relation*, Vikas Publisher New Delhi, 1996.

Dessler, Gary *Human Resource Management*, Prientice Hall New Delhi, 1997.

Fisher, Sharon G. *Performance Management*, Jaico Publisher House New Delhi, 2004.

Ghiselle, Edwin E. and Clarence W. Brown *Personnel and Industrial Psychology*, Tata Mcgraw Hill New Delhi, 1955.

Harrell, Thomas W. *Industrial Psychology*, Oxford and IBH Publisher New Delhi, 1958.

Kaila, H.L. and S. Ravishankar *HRM Practices in Industry*, Himalaya publisher New Delhi, 2005.

Miner, John B. *Industrial Organizational Psychology*, Tata McGraw Hill New Delhi, 1992.

Rao, P. Subba *Labour Welfare and Social Security*, Himalaya Publisher New Delhi, 2007.

Rao, T.V. et al. *Alternative Approaches and Strategies of H.R.D.* Rawat Publisher New Delhi, 2006.

Regis, Richad and S. Kayalvizhi *Managing Human Resource in Global Environment*, Vikas Publisher New Delhi, 2008.

Shrivastava, S.C. *Management Union Relation*, Vikas Publisher New Delhi, 2008.

Singh, Kuldeep and T. V. Rao *Selected Reading in HRD*, Tata McGraw Hill New Delhi, 1996.

Weightman, Lane *Managing Human Resource*, Jaico Publisher House New Delhi, 2003.

Well, Ian Bdited and Len Holden *Human Resource Management*, Macmillan New Delhi, 1995.

Wether, William B. and Keith Davis *Human Resource and Personal Management*, Tata McGraw Hill New Delhi, 1996.

Journals and Magazines

Effective-Executive, Volume 11 and No. 9, The ICFAI University Press, September 2008.

Human Resource Management Review, Volume 8 and No. 9, The ICFAI University Press, September 2008.

Organizational Behavior, Volume 7 and No. 4, The ICFAI University Press, October 2008.

Harvard Business Review, Volume 4 and No. 1, Living Media India Ltd., India Today Group, January 2009.

Effective Executive, Volume 12 and No. 02, The ICFAI University Press, February 2009.

Human Resource Management Review, Volume 9 and No. 02, The ICFAI University Press, February 2009.

Harvard Business review, Volume 4 and No. 2, Living Media India Ltd., India Today Group, February 2009.

Harvard Business review, Volume 4 and No. 3, Living Media India Ltd., India Today Group, March 2009.

CHAPTER 21

MGNREGA: AN EFFORT FOR EMPLOYMENT OF RURAL HUMAN RESOURCE (A STUDY OF TSP REGION OF UDAIPUR DISTRICT)

–*Rakesh Dashora* and *Nazma Banu*

ABSTRACT

When we talk about HR we think about companies, organizations, head-hunting companies, recruitment, placements, packages, etc. but have we ever thought what about the jobs of thousands of people who are unemployed in the country. Which HR department looks after it?

The Mahatma Gandhi National Rural Employment Guarantee Act (MGNREGA) is an Indian job guarantee scheme, enacted by legislation on August 25, 2005. The scheme provides a legal guarantee for one hundred days of employment in every financial year to adult members of any rural household willing to do public work-related unskilled manual work at the statutory minimum wage of ₹ 100 per day.

The choice of works suggested addresses causes of chronic poverty like drought, deforestation, soil erosion, etc. Effectively implemented, the employment generated under the Act will also build up the long-term livelihood asset base of rural India.

In this paper, we study the MGNREGA scheme and how this scheme helps in employment to thousand of unemployed rural people. Also this paper examines implementation of MGNREGA, its management and improvement in living conditions of tribal people. Tribal villages of Kherwara and Kotra tehsils from Udaipur district was selected for the study. Random sampling was used in choosing the panchayats. Both primary and secondary data were used for the study.

Introduction

Mahatma Gandhi National Rural Employment Guarantee Act (MGNREGA) belongs to a long history of wage employment programmes. The most significant features of NREGA are that it creates a rights-based framework and that it is a law. Backed by political will and adequate budget resources from the Government of India (GoI), the implementation of the Act has yielded encouraging results, despite an uneven performance across the country. Initial studies vindicate its effect in augmenting employment, increasing wage earnings, stemming distress migration, enhancing productivity and promoting equity, especially gender equity. This Act for unskilled manual labour is ushering in a new era of technology and financial inclusion for rural communities.

MGNREGA, designed primarily as a social safety net, has the potential to transform rural India into a more productive, equitable, connected society. MGNREGA is located in the policy response of the Indian government to a situation of poverty and inequality, by focusing on inclusive growth. There has also been a growing policy engagement with the rights regime witnessed by the formulation of rights-based laws as policy instruments.

The NREGA was passed by Parliament in August 2005 and received the Presidential nod on 5 Sept., 2005. The objective of NREGA is to enhance the livelihood security of the people in rural areas by generating wage employment through works that develop the infrastructure of the area.

The choice of works suggested addresses causes of chronic poverty like drought, deforestation, soil erosion, etc. Effectively implemented, the employment generated under the Act will also build up the long-term livelihood asset base of rural India. NREGA guarantees wage employment on public works to any adult who is willing to do unskilled manual work, subject to a guaranteed employment for 100 days per household per financial year. If employment cannot be provided, the applicant is entitled to daily unemployment allowance.

Panchayats will play a very important role as NREGA has designated them as the principal authorities for planning and implementation of schemes under the Act. With afore-stated governance business scope, initially in 200 districts which got subsequently extended to 330 and finally to all rural districts across the country.

This will require strong systems for the effective management and implementation of the schemes. The contemplated outlays are on an unprecedented scale and therefore transparency and accountability will be key issues. For successful implementation, potential beneficiaries need to be aware of their work entitlements and the essential elements of the schemes. Besides their roles and responsibilities, the implementing agencies also need to be aware of the legal implications, as employment has been guaranteed as a right. Productive assets have to be created so that the livelihood base of rural communities is built up to ensure long-term sustainability. NIC, along with Ministry of Rural Development and other stakeholders, conceptualized web-enabled management information system (i.e. NREGASoft) to address the planning and monitoring needs of scheme. The gram panchayats, block panchayats zilla panchayats, programme officers, district programme coordinators, engineers, bank/post offices, implementing agencies, state RD departments and Ministry of Rural Development and administrators in Government of India involved in implementation of the world's largest employment programme for rural human resource.

Udaipur district is the largest tribal populated district. There are twelve Tahsils. Tribal villages of Kherwara and Kotra tehsils from Udaipur district was selected for the study. The district is headed by a Deputy Commissioner who is over all in-charge of the administration in the particular district. He has to perform triple functions as he holds three positions: at once he is the Deputy Commissioner, the District Magistrate and the Collector. As a Deputy Commissioner he is the executive head of the district with multifarious responsibilities. As the District Magistrate he is responsible for maintaining the law and order situation in the district. As the Collector he is the Chief Revenue Officer of the district, responsible for revenue collection and recovery.

This is a big employment programe. It covers whole country's rural human resource for employment. It is a demand-driven employment programe not supply-driven. The Govt. of

India invested huge money on it. The study aims to critically examine the Mahatma Gandhi National Rural Employment Guarantee Act (MGNREGA) in tribal areas of Udaipur district as a rights-based legal framework for guaranteeing 100 days employment security to tribal households a research was conducted and tribal villages of Kherwara and Kotra tehsils from Udaipur district was undertaken to study the employability of the MGNREGA.

Methodology

Primary data was collected directly during the NREGA week that was observed in tribal areas of Udaipur district as well as through a schedule that was handed out later. The NREGA week generated tremendous field level experiences. A schedule was prepared containing a list of questions on the implementation of NREGA, which was distributed to generate data from the panchayats and the villages.

Random sampling was used in choosing the panchayats. The schedule primarily comprised of closed questions, though a few open-ended questions also existed to record the opinions and suggestions of the people.

Findings and Analysis

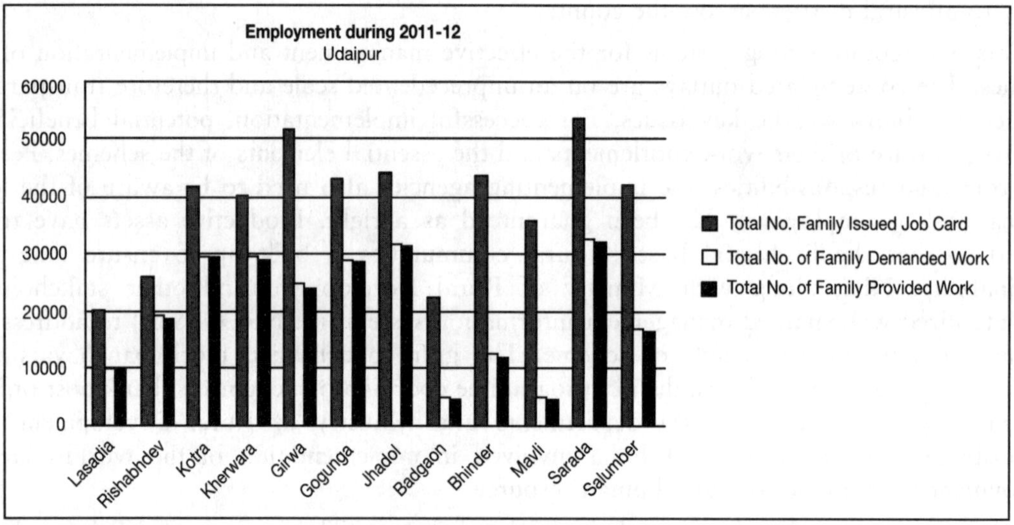

Fig. 1

Source: www.nrega.nic.in

Figure 1 represents the findings of employment in rural tesils of Udaipur district during 2011-12. The figure shows that more than 90% workers who demanded work under MGNREGA programe got work in 2011-12. The figure shows that the workers are aware about the Act and the number of issuance of job card in Udaipur district is impressive.

Table 1

Sr. No.	*Hypothesis*	*Response on MGNREGA*	
		Yes	*No*
1.	Is the MGNREGA provides 100 days of employment and are you aware about the act?	90%	10%
2.	How many people applied for manual labour under MGNREGA?		
	A. Less than 100	90%	10%
	C. More than 100	79%	21%
3.	Have all of them been employed?	80%	20%
4.	Implementation of MGNREGA scheme has brought better co-operation between people and administration (good communication system has been developed in villages because of MGNREGA)	69%	31%
5.	Improvement in the life of women folk because of MGNREGA	89%	11%
6.	MGNREGA provides food security to the workers	71%	31%
7.	What are the kinds of development taking place since the implementation of the scheme?		
	1. Infrastructural Development	95%	5%
	2. Seasonal Employment to the People	90%	10%
8.	MGNREGA has added sufficiently to the family income of workers	75%	25%
9.	MGNREGA has helped in reducing migration	65%	35%
10.	MGNREGA has bought socio-economic changes in the village level	62%	38%
11.	2011-12 has shown good development in standard of living in rural area	70%	30%
12.	NREGA scheme is a better alternative for them who don't have any other job in hand	90%	10%

Source: Field Data

These tabular findings are presented in the form of bar graphs below (Fig. 2).

Figure 2 represents the findings of workers' response regarding job guarantee of MGNREGA work. On an average, 90% of the workers in village are aware about the programe and 80% of the reported that this program gives them 100 days of job guarantee. This indicates the fulfillment of objective of the government machinery regarding employment to rural human resource under MGNREGA.

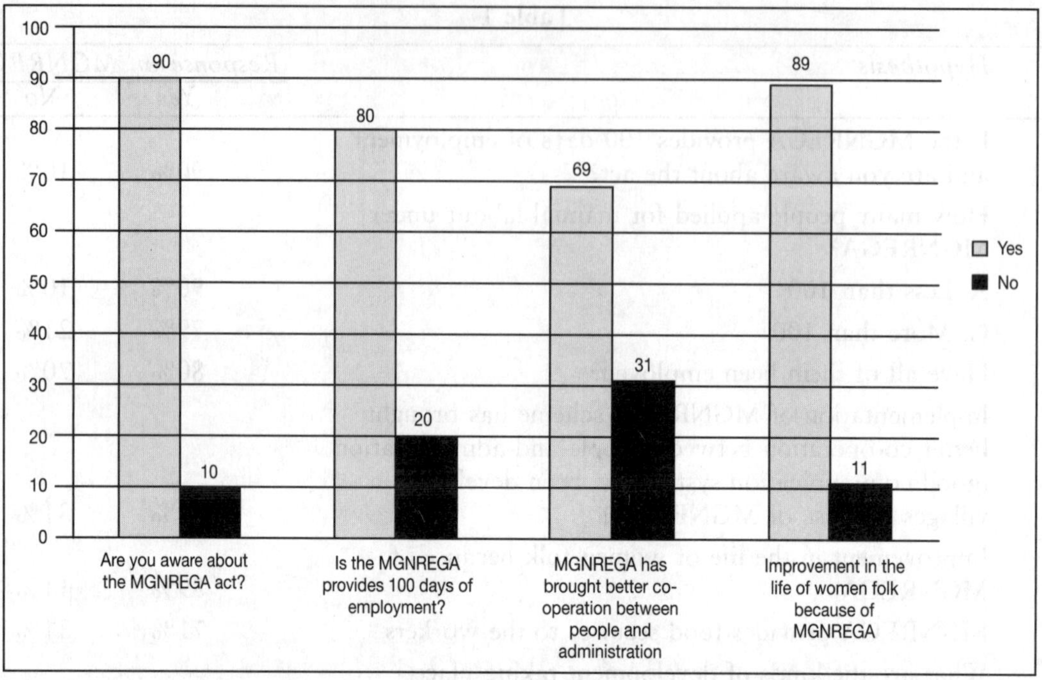

Fig. 2

79% agrees that it improves the communication between Implementation of MGNREGA scheme has brought better co-operation between people and administration (good communication system has been developed in villages because of MGNREGA). They also agreed that NREGA made social cohesion among them.

The child education ratio is also improved after implementation of MGNREGA in tribal villeges.

One of the most visible impacts of MGNREGA is promotion of women empowerment. The Act provides work to women and it improves women conditions. The provision of equal wages for men and women in the Act, working in MGNREGA has given an opportunity to workers particularly women workers to share information among fellow workers 89% women agree on it. This has led to knowledge empowerment in the tribal society. Similarly, MGNREGA has also brought in improvement in the health status of the women workers.

Figure 2 represents that more than 90% of the respondents states that there has been significant development in the standard of living of the people in the rural areas after implementation of act.

All the MGNREGA workers said that they have been able to arrange their households' daily food requirements after working in MGNREGA. 73% of the workers agreed that MGNREGA has given them sufficient additional income, as result of which, their primary and secondary activities have improved. Primary activities refer to the primary occupation of the workers like farming, agricultural labor, small business, etc. Secondary activities are those activities that add to the income of the people besides their primary activities.

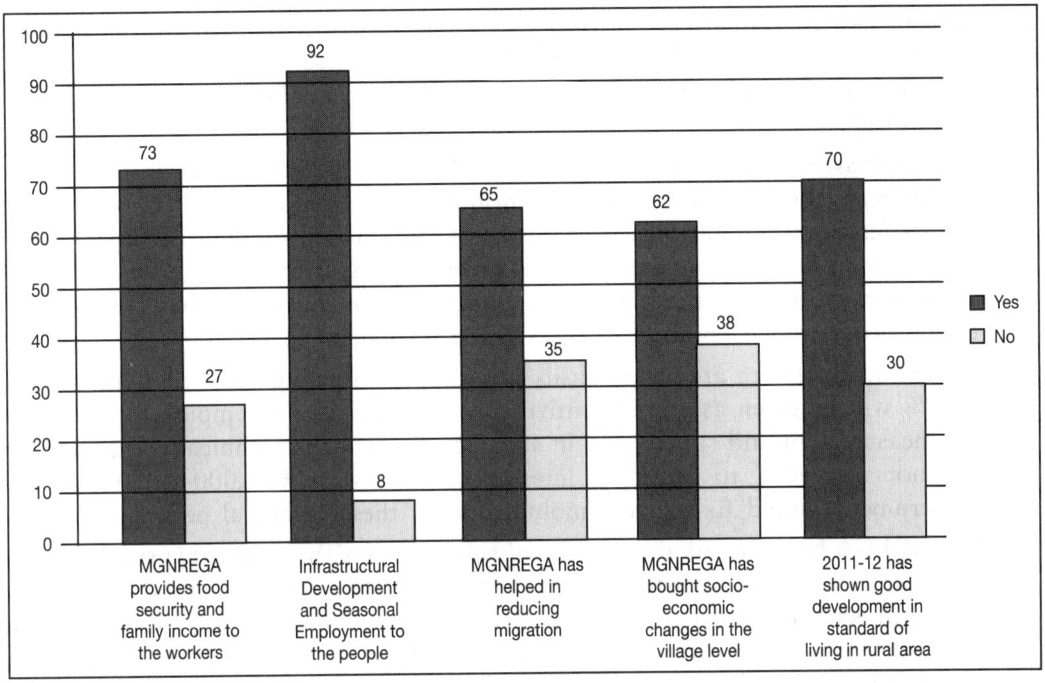

Fig. 3

By working in NREGA, the workers have been able to improve their primary and secondary activities because of their extra income and savings from NREGA.

The Act also curbed migration of people from rural to urban area in search of employment. This is another induced impact of MGNREGA, i.e. reduction in migration. MGNREGA scheme is a better alternative for them who don't have other job in hand.

They agree that infrastructural development and seasonal employment have taken place in the village. 62% said that MGNREGA brought socio-economic changes the village level.

2011-12 has shown a huge employment and good development in standard of living in rural areas.

Conclusions and Suggestions

Based on findings and analysis of quantitative and qualitative data, the conclusions and suggestion are as follow:

1. MGNREGA was initiated as a short-term intervention strategy for creation of employment in the rural society wherever there is no such scope. However, ultimate long-term success of MGNREGA lies in creating the required economic, social, and environmental empowerment and social capital in the rural society so that it graduates from one stage of development to next higher stage.
2. MGNREGA is world's largest rural employment programme in terms of financial commitment and coverage. It requires adequate and sufficient time on the part of the implementing officers. However, it is observed that supervising and implementing

officers like BDOs, project directors and district collectors are overburdened with other administrative and developmental works. These officers, thus, do not find enough time for this programme, which affect its quality of implementation and monitoring.

3. The process of implementation of MGNREGA in the state of Rajasthan is largely transparent across regions. This is primarily due to the well-conceived in-built transparency and monitoring mechanisms of the Act and subsequent improvements in it. Rajasthan Government's transparent governance system integrated with a well ICT (Information and Communication Technology) and e-governance has also contributed to the better implementation of the scheme in that state.
4. Kotra and Kherwara are tribal tehsils and happen to be high cost economies. Amount of 4% will be given as administrative cost is insufficient to employ technical people for measurement and supervision in such economies. The technically qualified people are not interested to work in interior villages with ₹ 4,000-6,000 per month. Government should fix proper emoluments for these technical persons.
5. MGNREGA has ensured a strong social safety net for the vulnerable rural poor in the tribal areas of Udaipur district. It has brought in significant income diversification in the rural economies of both these tehsils. This inference is strongly established when we find that about 80% of the workers working in NREGA are from BPL category. This has been possible because of the supplementary income and off-season employment that the predominantly tribal people earn by working in MGNREGA. The economies of the both these tehsils happen to be predominantly agrarian. However, since the cultivation practices are traditional, irrigation infrastructure is much underdeveloped (vis-à-vis the country) and the cultivable land-man ratio is very low; the rural areas in these states have a long spell of agricultural off-season. Wage employment through MGNREGA has thus become a boon for the rural people of these two tribal areas.
6. One of the most visible impacts of MGNREGA is promotion of women empowerment. The Act provides work to women and it improves women conditions. The provision of equal wages for men and women in the Act, working in MGNREGA has given an opportunity to the workers particularly women workers to share information among fellow workers. This has led to knowledge empowerment in the tribal society. Similarly, MGNREGA has also brought in improvement in the health status of the women workers.
7. MGNREGA is a right s-based demand driven programme. It requires adequate flow of funds all through the year in response to the job demand. However, flow of funds is not normal. It is skewed towards the first few months and finishing two months of the financial year. In such situation, the officers/GP/AEC officials in-charge of implementation of the programme find it difficult to implement the programme properly.
8. One of the important objectives of MGNREGA is to promote financial inclusion and empower workers socially and economically. To realize this objective and to make the payment system transparent, MGNREGA stipulated for 100% payment through

banks/post offices. Although the problem of wage payment through banks/POs is difficult in some of the interior gram panchayats/villages in tribal areas, this practice of non-payment through banks/post offices should become a norm.

9. More than 70% of the workers agreed that MGNREGA has given them sufficient additional income, as result of which, their primary and secondary activities have improved. Primary activities refer to the primary occupation of the workers like farming, agricultural labor, small business, etc. Secondary activities are those activities that add to the income of the people besides their primary activities. By working in MGNREGA, the workers have been able to improve their primary and secondary activities because of their extra income and savings from MGNREGA. All the workers who working in NREGA said that they have been able to arrange their households' daily food requirements after working in MGNREGA.
10. There has been a improvement although marginal in school enrollment after introduction of the MGNREGS in their areas respectively have stated that there has been a slight reduction in the school drop-out rate.
11. Another visible impact of NREGA has been arresting of distress migration from rural areas. The impact is significant in the tribal areas. MGNREGA has curbed migration of people from rural to urban area in search of employment. MGNREGA has become a boon to them in overcoming their destitution caused by the unilateral divorce of them by their husbands and forcing them earlier to migrate to nearby towns/villages in search of employment so as to bring up of their children. MGNREGA scheme is a better alternative for them who don't have other job in hand. Most of them agreed on it. It give income and job security for 100 days to them.
12. MGNREGA has facilitated convergence. It has provided and made it imperative for line Departments like RD, Horticulture, Irrigation and Flood Control to work together to maximize the linkage effect. the development infrastructure of villages through road connectivity, irrigation, etc. Finally, NREGA has the potential to promote sustainable development through participation. NREGA works and the three elements of sustainable development, i.e. (i) environmental sustainability (via land terracing and overcoming environmental degradation caused by sand quarrying), (ii) social sustainability (through women empowerment, distress migration, social capital formation) and (iii) economic sustainability (through wage income generation).

REFERENCES

Adhikari, Anindita Bhatia, Kartika "NREGA Wage Payments: Can We Bank on the Banks?" *Economic and Political Weekly*, Vol. 45 No. 1, 2 Jan 2010.

Agarwal, Harsh (2010). "National Rural Employment Guarantee Act—A review" policyproposalforindia.com

Basu, A.K. et al. (2009). "A theory of Employment Guarantees: Contestability, Credibility and Distributional Concerns": *Journal of Public Economics.*

Chhabra, Sangeeta Sharma, G.L. "National Rural Employment Guarantee Scheme (NREGS): Realities and Challenges", *LBS Journal of Management and Research*, Vol. 6, No. 1-2, Dec. 2008.

Chandrashekhar, R. (2006). *Common Services Centres: A Strategic Cornerstone of NeGP,* Workshop on Knowledge Centre Initiatives, Jaipur.

Dreze, Jean Oldiges, Christian "NREGA: Progress Report", *Frontline*, Vol. 24, No. 14, 14 July 2007.

Fernandez, Grace Sudarshan, M. Ratna Bhattacharya, Rina, "Women's Participation in the NREGA: Some Observations from Fieldwork in Himachal Pradesh, Kerala and Rajasthan", *IDS Bullein*, Vol. 41, No. 4, Jul 2010, pp. 77-83.

Gopal, K.S. "NREGA and the Budget", *Labour File*, Vol. 6, No. 3, June 2009.

Government of India, April 2009. State and district administration, second administrative reforms commission 15th report.

India, MoRD 2005. *The National Rural Employment Guarantee Act 2005 (NREGA): Operational Guidelines*. New Delhi, India: Ministry of Rural Development, Department of Rural Development.

Jha, Raghbendra and Gaiha, Raghav and Shankar, Shylashri "*Targeting Accuracy of the NREGA: Evidence from Rajasthan, Andhra Pradesh and Maharashtra*". Working Paper. Australia South Asia Research Centre.

Manavalan, D.K., Jain, S.C. and Chatterji, Anish and Kumar, Ajit and Ekka, Pramod and Augustine, Thomas Sunil "*Infrastructure Development and Beyond: Exploring the Scope for Sustainable Livelihood Support under NREGA—A Study of Schemes implemented under NREGA*" a study commissioned by united nations development programme (UNDP) with the Support of Ministry of Rural Development, Government of India submitted by Action for Food Production (AFPRO) New Delhi www.undp.org.in www.afpro.org.

Ministry of Communication and Information Technology, March *2012 National e-Governance Plan*, http://www.mit.gov.in/

Narayanan, S. 2008. Employment guarantee, women's work and childcare. *Economic and Political Weekly*, 43 (9).

Raabe, Katharina and Birner, Regina and Sekher, Madhushree and Gayathridevi, K.G. and Shilpi Amrita and Schiffer, Eva "*How to Overcome the Governance Challenges of Implementing NREGA—Insights from Bihar Using Process-Influence Mapping*" April 2010 IFPRI Discussion Paper.

Saxena, N.C. (2007) "Rural poverty reduction through centrally sponsored schemes", Samya-Centre for Equity Studies, New Delhi, India.

State Government of Madhya Pradesh, *Intranet in Tribal District of Dhar* [http://www.gyandoot.nic.in/].

Vanaik, Anish "NREGA and the Death of Tapas Soren", *Economic and Political Weekly*, Vol. 42, No. 30, 26 Jul. 2008.

CHAPTER 22 COLLISION OF HR PRACTICES ON EMPLOYEES PRODUCTIVITY: A COMPARATIVE STUDY BETWEEN PUBLIC AND PRIVATE BANKS IN INDIA

–R.S. Meena

ABSTRACT

Employee productivity is a particularly important issue to managers and supervisors as the primary purpose of their job is to get the most out of the people they that are responsible for. The success of any organization depends on the ability of its human resource to utilize other resources such as capital, equipment and land for the achievement of organizational objectives. Human resource thus requires the necessary attention in order to achieve corporate objectives. Over recent years there has been an increasing interest in the field of human resource management. Currently, the literature encourages the consideration of human resources as strategic factors, not only because they play important role in strategy implementation, also because they are beginning to be reckoned as sources of sustainable competitive advantage. Relationships between human resource management and productivity have been studied from different perspectives. This study is an attempt to investigate the extent to which banks differ on aspects of human resource management practices and their contribution in employees productivity.

Introduction

Human resource management is a dynamic discipline that keeps changing with the change in the external environment. In the fiercely competitive modern business world, employees are considered as a key resource, which provides a sustainable competitive advantage. This has led to an increased demand for high performing individuals. This has also necessitated the need for improved human resource practices that address the issues of employee satisfaction, motivation, commitment and work culture. The HR practices might not have a direct impact on the bottom line of a company, but increased employee productivity and a better work environment as a result of innovative human resource practices, can certainly have a favourable impact on the bottom line. An organization is made up of a number of people who strive to achieve the organization's goals. Human resources have a significant bearing on the profitability, efficiency and overall organizational effectiveness. Human beings differ from one another in their basic mental abilities, skills, approaches, qualifications and also behaviour which account for their complex behaviour patterns and psychological makeup. Such difference gets multiplied when they interact with one another in a group or in an organization. This generates different styles of management, values, feelings, beliefs and opinions of the employees. They must be groomed in order to take risks, think innovatively, and handle new problems. In the competitive environment, employees of any business organization are the key factor for deciding the success of the firm. It is understood that cooperative banks approach human resource management (HRM) from the wrong perspective and their financial performance suffers as a result. Instead of focusing on how to execute strategy through the performance of the employees in banks, the first priority is cost control and the focus often begins with the HR function. No organization can exist unless the human capital is of a quality capable of properly exploiting the material resources to generate surplus for survival, growth and diversification into new fields keeping in view the environment in which it operates. This is true of banking and marketing organizations, where physical capital is only a fraction of the total resources mobilized by the organization. These are service organizations where human capital makes the difference between success and failure. World over, the technology driven channels such as ATM, net banking and mobile banking have reduced walk-in-customers at the bank branches. However, in India, it is observed that the customers still find it difficult to use these technology-based channels and they are more comfortable in traditional banking over the counter personally to ensure error—free and risk—free banking service. While struggling to provide better and efficient service at the counters, the staff is also confronted with various regulatory norms to mitigate risks in operations. This clearly establishes that employees of cooperative banks play a vital role in managing not only the 'transaction' of a customer but also future long-term relationship with them. There are several reasons for the new approaches to the management of staff. Firstly, infrastructural problems with growth in the bank and over staffing, secondly, the increasing competitive pressure in banking had led to greater attention to controlling labour costs and increasing labour productivity. Thirdly, the nature of change had moved the emphasis towards being a market-driven rather than an administratively driven organization and the importance of staff quality was being emphasized.

Literature Review

Since the beginning of the 1980s, a vast literature has been developed calling for a more strategic role for human resources (Guest, 1987; Miller, 1987; Armstrong, 1991). A research is available on the impact of HR practices on perceived employee performance. Huselid (1995) took eleven human resource management practices which are personnel selection, labor management participation, incentive compensation, performance appraisal, grievance procedures, information sharing, job design, attitude assessment, recruitment efforts, promotion criteria and employee training. He found a significant relationship between high work practices such as compensation and employees outcomes.

Barn (1991) felt that firms could develop strategic capability and for attaining this, the strategic goal will be to create firms, which are more intelligent and flexible than their competitors. Aurora and Malhotra (1997) tried to give some idea about factors determining customer satisfaction, the level of customer satisfaction and some marketing strategies in both private and public sector banks in India. They have found six factors of customer satisfaction in public sector banks, viz. routine operations, price, situational, environmental, technology, and interactive. But in private sector banks, there exists seven factors in total, having staff factor as the first ranked and situational factor as the lowest ranked items. As compared to public sector, private sector bank customers' level of satisfaction is comparatively more. Proper training and development of bank staff, regular market survey, personalizing the service, efforts to avoid long queues in bank, and attractive environment in public sector bank. The uniqueness of HR requires a totally different type of attention from management. The HR function has the characteristics that provide the greatest challenges as well as opportunities. The increased probability of having to manage in an international situation demands the conduct of more comparative HRM research (Boxall, 1995; Brewster et al., 1996; Budhwar and Debrah, 2001; Budhwar and Sparrow, 2002).

HR practices can be viewed as strategic personnel management emphasizing on acquisition, organization and motivation of human resources (2000). The role of HR practices towards employee productivity has been discussed by number of researchers and practitioners through human resource projects and conferences taking responsibility for evaluating employee productivity which incorporated HR management domains. HR is to monitor as well as measure and employee productivity (2000) have outlined HR role into human resource knowledge management strategies, creating productivity measures accordingly. Employees are more pivotal in high-involvement organizations because these firms are employee centered by design; information and decision-making power is dispersed throughout the organization with employees at all levels taking on greater responsibility for the operation and success of the organization. To facilitate this approach, high involvement organizations use human resource practices which develop and support a workforce which is self-programming and self-managing (1992).

Objectives of the Study

1. There is ample need to banks employee productivity base from HR practices perspective.
2. To Finding out banks employee productivity impact from HR based functions.
3. To Relating to several theories and applications of HR practices in accordance to employee productivity.
4. To identify the needs of employee through which they can work effectively.
5. To examine and compare the human resource practices followed by the banks in India.
6. To find out human resource practices contributing to employee productivity in these banks.
7. To find out the HR needs of bank employee productivity.

Research Design

The present study is based on primary data. The survey was carried out in the banks working in Varanasi Region Eastern UP. For this purpose, various HR practices, which are perceived to affect the employee productivity has been identified and selected on the basis of their relevance to the banking sector.

Sample

For conducting this study 50 sample were drawn from each public and private sector banks, located in Varanasi Region Eastern UP.

1. HDFC Bank
2. ICICI Bank
3. Punjab National Bank
4. Oriental Bank of Commerce.

Procedure for Data Collection

Each subject was approached individually and was assigned the questionnaire it was emphasized that the results of the study would be utilized only for research purpose. The 12 HR practices have been included and the employee productivity has been taken as dependent variable. The questions have been designed to facilitate the respondents to identify major strength and weakness of the banks. They were requested to answer all the statements honestly and truthfully and not to leave any questions or statement unanswered.

Research Instrument

Questionnaire is used as a research instrument. The respondents have been requested to use their best judgment on a five point Likert scale. Five point scale indicated as 1. Strongly disagree, 2. Disagree 3. Neither agree nor disagree 4. Agree 5. Strongly agree. These points show the opinions of employees in regard to each question.

Tools

The data were analyzed through statistical package for social sciences (SPSS). The main tests conducted for the data analysis are mean, standard deviation, T-test and multiple regression tests is applied to test the significance of the results wherever it is considered to be necessary.

Hypothesis

Keeping in mind the above discussion, this research or study is designed to test the following hypothesis:

H_1: Employee's productivity affects organizational effectiveness.

H_2: Employee's productivity leads to organizational effectiveness.

H_3: Employee's performance factor affects organizational effectiveness.

Data Analysis and Results

In order to compare various human resource practices among the respondents of two banks, various tests have been carried out in the present study. The following tables show all the factors statistically.

Table 1: Comparison of Various Factors among the Respondents of Banks

Factors	*Bank1 (N=50) (Private)*		*Bank2 (N=50) (Public)*		*t-value*
	Mean	*SD*	*Mean*	*SD*	
Manpower Planning	4.2	0.80	3.8	1.12	1.64
Recruitment and Selection	3.8	1.03	3.6	1.16	0.81
Motivation	4.1	0.80	3.6	0.89	2.78
Reward System	3.9	0.76	3.4	1.09	2.57
Training and Development	4.3	0.66	3.8	1.18	2.30
Team Building	3.8	0.91	3.9	0.89	–0.88
Employee Participation	4.2	0.94	3.5	0.99	3.81
Employee Behavior	4.4	0.50	3.1	0.94	8.61
Incentives	3.8	0.82	3.3	0.84	3.23
Employee Productivity	4.4	0.73	3.1	1.05	6.35
Creativity	3.7	0.90	3.4	1.16	1.07
Promotion	4.4	0.64	2.9	0.93	9.00

Table 1 provides the descriptive statistical information like mean, standard deviations and comparative analysis followed by both types of banks. It discusses that there is a significant difference between the banks. Both the public and private sector banks differ from each other in providing incentives, reward system and promotion. Employee motivation will ultimately increase the employee performance, employee participation, employee behavior and the employee productivity. Most important ingredient of human resource practices is reward system and incentives, which at present does not have any linkage to skills and performance. Incentives are provided for motivation in some of the organizations. From the table, it is clear that employees performance is directly influenced by their motivation. The outcomes of the training and development to any type of organization are increased productivity of employees. Promotion is also directly related to the employee productivity. And in the end all these factors will lead to make a positive affect over the organization.

Table 2: Multiple Regression Analysis Private Sector Bank [N = 50]

Independent Variables	*Dependent Variables: Employee Productivity*		
	Beta	*R square*	*t-value*
Motivation	–074	.006	–.51
Employee Participation	–.88	.008	–.61
Creativity	.180	.033	1.27
Promotion	.123	.089	.84
Training and Development	.072	.005	.50
Incentives	.042	.002	–.29
Team Building	–.162	.026	–1.13
Employee Behavior	.053	.003	.36

Results of multiple regression analysis and independent variables (HR factors) with the dependent variables (employee productivity) for private banks are shown in Table 2. From the table (private sector bank), we observe that all independent variables are positively related with employee productivity. Beta of several factors in the regression equation is statistically significant. Employee creativity (Beta value = .180, t-value = 1.27) is highly significant contributor to the employee productivity and the second largest contributor is promotion (Beta value = .123, t-value = .84) to the employee productivity and other human resource practices shows negative sign like motivation (Beta value = –.074, t-value = –.51), employee participation (Beta value = –.088, t-value = –.61), incentives (Beta value = –.042, t-value = –.29), team building (Beta value = –.162, t-value = –1.13) are affecting employees productivity.

Table 3: Multiple Regression Analysis Public Sector Bank [N = 50]

Independent Variables	*Dependent Variables: Employee Productivity*		
	Beta	*R square*	*t-value*
Motivation	–.153	.023	–1.07
Employee Participation	–.272	.074	–.1.95
Creativity	–.203	.041	–1.43
Promotion	.123	.089	.84
Training and Development	–.098	.010	–.68
Incentives	.303	.092	2.19
Team Building	–.235	.055	–1.67
Employee Behavior	–.145	.021	–1.01

Table 3 shows the results for multiple regression analysis of the relationship between human resource practices and employee productivity of public sector bank. Results of multiple regression analysis of bank in the table indicate that out of eight HR practices affecting employee productivity like incentives (Beta value = .303, t-value = 2.19) has come as highly significant contributor and creativity (Beta value = .138, t-value = .96) has the second largest contributor to employee productivity. The other contributors to employee productivity in bank are motivation (Beta value = –.153, t-value = –1.07), employee participation (Beta value = –.272, t-value = –1.95), promotion (Beta value = –.203, t-value = –1.43), training and development (Beta value = –.098, tvalue = –.68), team building (Beta value = –.235, t-value = –1.67), employee behavior (Beta value = –.145, t-value = –1.01) show the negative sign. The results signify that the employee participation necessary for the high performance of the firm.

Conclusion

Human resource management in cooperative banks is more sensitive, personalized and cannot be managed through a set of predefined techniques. The HRM performance link that has been demonstrated in the Western hemisphere also exists in the Indian context. Five critical motivational issues in banking today are: (1) performance management, (2) equal pay demands for comparable worth, (3) training and development, (4) how to best motivate individuals, and (5) providing competitive compensation beyond the bounds of one's own industry. This study focused on employee productivity, HR practices and organizational effectiveness. The result of this study indicates significant relation of employee productivity with human resource practices including motivation, selection, training and development, promotion and incentives. Effective organization depends on having the right system of HR policies and practices in place to recruit, select, motivate, training and development, promote or send away employees. In private sector, banks employee productivity is highly dependent on high motivating environment in the bank. In public sector banks, it perceives that all independent variables are essential for employee productivity. Banks are among the many organizations experimenting with alternative reward and benefit programs, including several innovative compensation plans. This paper concludes that HR practices implemented successfully, they could achieve the maximum contribution of their employees.

REFERENCES

Barney, J.B. (1991). Firm Resources and Sustainable Competitive Advantage. *Journal of Management*, Vol. 17, pp. 99-120.

Bedeian, A.G. (1993). *Management*, 3rd Edition, New York, Dryden Press.

Ben-Ner, A. and Jones, D. (1992). "An New Conceptual Framework for the Analysis of the Impact of Employees Participation, Profit Sharing and Ownership on Firm Performance," Papers 92-10, Minnesota—Industrial Relations Center.

Brunello, G. (1989). "Bonuses, Wages and Performance in Japan: Evidence from Micro Data," Papers 359, London School of Economics—Centre for Labour Economics.

Budhwar, P. and Sparrow, P. (2002). An Integrative Framework for Determining Cross-National Human Resource Management Practices. *Human Resource Management Review*, Vol. 12, No. 3, pp. 377-403.

Casey Ichniowski, Kathryn Shaw and Giovanna Prennushi (1995). "The Effects of Human Resource Management Practices on Productivity," NBER Working Papers 5333, National Bureau of Economic Research, Inc.

Derek, C. Jones and Jeffrey Pliskin (1988). "The Effects of Worker Participation, Employee Ownership and Profit Sharing on Economics Performance: A Partial Review," Economics Working Paper Archive No. 13, Levy Economics Institute.

FitzRoy, Felix R. and Kraft, Korenelius (1987). "Cooperation, Productivity, and Profit Sharing," *The Quarterly Journal of Economics*, MIT Press, Vol. 102(1), pp. 23-35, February.

Freeman, Richard B. (1976). "Individual Mobility and Union Voice in the Labor Market," *American Economic Review*, American Economic Association, Vol. 66(2), pp. 361-68, May.

Freeman, Richard B. and Weitzman, Martin L. (1987). "Bonuses and employment in Japan," *Journal of the Japanese and International Economies*, Elsevier, Vol. 1(2), pp. 168-194, June.

Herzberg, F., Mausner, B., and Snyderman, B.B. (1959). *The Motivation to Work*. New York: John Wiley and Sons.

Huselid, M.A. (1995). The Impact of Human Resource Management Practices on Turnover, Productivity, and Corporate Financial Performance. *Academy of Management Journal*, Vol. 38, No. 3, pp. 635-72.

Jones, Derek C. and Kato, Takao (1995). "The Productivity Effects of Employee Stock-Ownership Plans and Bonuses: Evidence from Japanese Panel Data," *American Economic Review*, American Economic Association, Vol. 85(3), pp. 391-414, June.

Khera, S.N. (2010). Human Resource Practices and their Impact on Employee Productivity: A Perceptual Analysis of Private. *Public and Foreign Bank Employees in India DSM Business Review*, Vol. 2(1), 45-78.

Kruse, Douglas L. (1992). "Profit Sharing and Productivity: Microeconomic Evidence from the United States," *Economic Journal*, Royal Economic Society, Vol. 102(410), pp. 24-36, January.

Kumbhakar, Subal C. and Dunbar, Amy E. (1993). "The elusive ESOP—productivity link: Evidence from U.S. firm-level data," *Journal of Public Economics*, Elsevier, Vol. 52(2), pp. 273-83, September.

Malik, E., Ghafoor, M., and Naseer, S. (2011). Organizational Effectiveness: A case study of telecommunication and banking sector of Pakistan. *Far East Journal of Psychology and Business*, Vol. 2(1), 93-109.

Masanori Hashimoto (1990). "The Japanese Labor Market in a Comparative Perspective with the United States," Books from Upjohn Press, W.E. Upjohn Institute for Employment Research, number jlm, Febrero.

Nakamura, Masao and Nakamura, Alice (1991). "Risk behavior and the determinants of bonus versus regular pay in Japan," *Journal of the Japanese and International Economies*, Elsevier, Vol. 5(2), pp. 140-59, June.

Paauwe, J. and Boselie, P. (2003). Challenging Strategic HRM and the Relevance of the Institutional Setting. *Human Resource Management Journal*, Vol. 13, No. 3, pp. 56-70.

Ramu, N. (2008). Human Resource Management in Cooperative Banks in India: Issues and Challenges, July-September.

Sparrow, P.R., and Budhwar, P. (1997). Competition and Change: Mapping the Indian HRM Recipe against World Wide Patterns. *Journal of World Business*, Vol. 32, No. 3, pp. 224-42.

Tracy, Joseph S. (1986). "An Investigation into the Determinants of U.S. Strike Activity," *American Economic Review*, American Economic Association, Vol. 76(3), pp. 423-36, June.

Wadhwani, S. and Wall, M. (1988). "The Effects of Profit-Sharing on Employment, Wages, Stock Returns and Productivity: Evidence from UK Micro-Data," Papers 311, London School of Economics—Centre for Labour Economics.

Yukl, G. (1999). An evaluation essay on current conceptions of effective leadership. *European Journal of Work and Organizational Psychology*, Vol. 8(1), pp. 81-102.

CHAPTER 23 | IMPACT OF "SICK BUILDING SYNDROME" ON EMPLOYEE WELL-BEING: A CASE STUDY OF SELECTED PRIVATE SECTOR EMPLOYEES OF UDAIPUR CITY

–*Dimpy Jain* and *Ankita Jain*

ABSTRACT

This paper deals with the "Sick Building Syndrome" (SBS). Automation and technology explosion has distanced us today from our natural physical environment and as a result we now live in a concrete jungle being further detached from our natural surroundings. What primarily started as a means for sheltering protection from extremes of mother nature, gradually took us a way to far and aloofed us from our natural atmosphere and thereby making us victims of artificial dwellings. SBS can be described as a cluster of health problems that can occur in the occupants of a office, home or other buildings. This syndrome can be majorly attributed to poor Indoor Air Quality (IAQ). There is a strong association between work environment and job as it has the potential to impact efficiency of an organisation and to affect its profits. Sick Building Syndrome is a critical issue and needs urgent attention of the Human Resource Manager of concerned company. The important thing is to take action to have a suspected sick building investigated as soon as possible as it is likely that the problem will only get worse if not addressed. This paper attempts to explicate the causes, preventive measures and corrective strategies which must be attended urgently to minimise the effects of the same.

Objectives of the Study

1. To understand the concept of SBS.
2. To analyse its impact on employee well-being.
3. To study its impact on employee's job/productivity/stress levels/performance/satisfaction/absenteeism.

Introduction

Swift Technological Developments of, this century, has distanced today's mankind from its natural physical habitat in which we have long existed. As a appalling outcome we have, further drifted apart from our natural surroundings, and now find ourselves locked in buildings that completely disconnect us from the external environment. At the outset it all occurred to seek protection from extreme weather conditions but, as a matter of fact, slowly and gradually people got entangled in the fine web of this artificially created environment and thereby started the mutiny of falling health and other ailments. Many experts are now beginning to question this artificial separation, as it is taking a toll on human health. The point in case is that when we are indoors, at home, in a factory, shopping mall, cinema, hospital or any other environment—

we should feel a fresh, healthy atmosphere in the same way as we would feel if we were in a green field.

As people in today's modern world spend about 90% of their life indoors, mostly at home. The working population spends about 20% of the time at work. Human reactions to the indoor environment can be divided into three main categories. First, the most common effects of indoor air pollution are complaint reactions due to poor Indoor Air Quality (IAQ). Secondly, there are some diseases that may be caused by factors in the indoor environment. Finally, patients may report certain medical symptoms with unclear cause, but with a possible relation to the indoor environment. The term 'sick building syndrome' (SBS) has been used to describe such symptoms.

What is Sick Building Syndrome?

"Sick building syndrome" is a worldwide problem but in India it is only recently gaining recognition as a public health concern. The concept SBS is used when the symptoms of a significant number of people occupying a particular building, are associated with their presence in that building. Over the last two decades, there have been an increasing number of instances where the occupants of a building have complained of a general feeling of being unwell, in most cases sick building syndrome occurs in office buildings. However, the symptoms usually disappear when they are away from the building. This phenomenon is called "Sick Building Syndrome". It describes a situation in which building occupants experience acute health and comfort effects that appear to be linked to time spent in a building, but no specific illness or cause can be identified. The complaints may be localized in a particular room or zone, or may be widespread throughout the building.

Sick building syndrome is a broad label that covers a range of symptoms from specific symptoms such as itchy eyes, skin rashes, and nasal allergy symptoms, to more vague symptoms such as fatigue, aches and pains, and sensitivity to odours.

The term "sick building syndrome" was coined in 1983 by the World Health Organisation (WHO) and is currently defined by that body as:

> the occurrence of specific symptoms with unspecified aetiology, and are experienced by people while working or living in a particular building, but which disappear after they leave it. Symptoms include mucous membrane, skin and eye irritation, chest tightness, fatigue, headache, malaise, lethargy, lack of concentration, odour annoyance and influenza symptoms. SBS usually cannot be attributed to excessive exposure to known contaminants or to a defective ventilation system. (WHO, 2000)

According to the US Environmental Protection Agency (EPA), sick building syndrome is assumed when the following circumstances are present:

- Symptoms are temporally related to time spent in a particular building
- Symptoms resolve when the individual is not in the building
- Symptoms recur seasonally
- Co-workers, peers have noted similar complaints.

The American Society of Heating, Refrigeration and Airconditioning Engineers (ASHRAE, 1998) states that:

> The term "sick building" is used to describe a building in which a significant number (more than 20 per cent) [emphasis added] of building occupants report illness perceived as being building related. This phenomenon, also known as "sick building" is characterised by a range of symptoms including, but not limited to, eye, nose and throat irritation, dryness...mucous membranes and skin, nose bleeds, skin rash, mental fatigue, headache, cough, hoarseness, wheezing, nausea and dizziness. Within a given building, there will usually be some commonality among the symptoms manifested as well as temporal association between occupancy in the building and appearance of symptoms.

So, it can be said that SBS occurs when people in a particular building or part of it feel their health is being affected by the building's environment. Typically, the occupants attribute their unwell feeling to poor Indoor Air Quality (IAQ). SBS has become prevalent since the 1970s, following the energy crisis, when many buildings were sealed in order to be more energy efficient. This resulted in less natural ventilation. For this reason, SBS is also known as "tight building syndrome".

Symptoms of Sick Building Syndrome

The sick building syndrome comprises a group of symptoms which are varied, but symptoms may occur singly or in combination with each other.

1. **Nasal manifestations.** The symptoms most frequently experienced are nasal irritation with a blocked or stuffy nose.
2. **Ocular manifestations.** Dryness and irritation of the mucous membrane of the eye.
3. **Orooharvngeal manifestations.** Dryness and irritation of the throat.
4. **Coetaneous manifestations.** Dryness and irritation of the skin, associated with a rash on exposed skin surfaces.
5. **General manifestations.** A general feeling of tiredness and lethargy is often the most prevalent symptom. It usually starts within a few hours of coming to work, and improves within minutes of leaving the building.

Few of the symptoms can be clubbed in the table below:

Asthma	Fatigue	Loss of concentration
Allergies	Nausea	Dry cough
Irritation of the eyes	Lethargy	Cold and flu
Headaches	Memory impairment	Sensitivity to odours

Source: www.who.int

Causes of Sick Building Syndrome

In many SBS cases, poor building design, maintenance, and ventilation system may be at fault. The ventilation system in particular is often found to be at the heart of the problem, and can itself be a source of irritants. Interior design factors such as the arrangement of individual offices and cubicles, may also interfere with efficient functioning of ventilation systems. Essentially, poor office design can amplify the negative health effects.

The following is the list of the various indoor pollutants that can contribute to making a building 'sick':

I. Chemical Pollutants

1. **Combustion Pollutants:** Various chemical pollutants that can affect the health of a building's occupants are produced when heating systems or gas-fired appliances such as stoves are poorly maintained, and thus don't burn fuel efficiently, or don't vent exhaust correctly.

   The main pollutants from this source are:

   Carbon Monoxide (CO)—CO is known as the 'silent killer' as it is colourless and odourless. When it is breathed in CO binds to red blood cells preventing them from carrying oxygen and essentially suffocating the victim.

   Sulphur Dioxide (SO_2)—is a colourless gas with a strong odour. Sulphur dioxide is an irritant to the respiratory system and exposure to high concentrations for short periods of time can constrict the blood vessels in the lungs and increase mucous flow, making breathing difficult.

   Nitrogen Dioxide (NO_2)—is another toxic gas produced from combustion of fuels. Long-term exposure makes people more susceptible to respiratory infections such as pneumonia and influenza.

   Volatile Organic Compounds (VOCs)—Volatile organic compounds are organic (carbon-based) compounds that evaporate at ambient temperatures within a building. These compounds often have effects on health from irritating the eyes, nose, and throat, to causing breathing difficulties, to increasing the risk of developing cancer.

2. **Building Construction:** Modern buildings with modern materials suffer the most from VOCs. Carpeting is another major source of VOCs in many buildings since a large number of chemicals are used in their manufacture in the form of glues, backing materials and dyes. These chemicals are all known to cause irritation and effect breathing. Finishes such as paints and varnishes can also increase the VOC content of a building or room.

3. **Chemicals Used within a Building:** The various chemical-based products routinely used inside a building can be an equally large source of VOCs. Products that contain VOCs range from chemical products used to clean a building to marker pens and printer ink, common in an office environment.

4. **Heavy Metals:** Older buildings still contain a significant amount of the highly toxic substances. The two most common heavy metals present in buildings are lead and mercury. Lead and mercury can cause severe neurological damage and a host of other problems.

II. Biological Pollutants

There are many sources of biological pollution that can affect a building, the following are the main sources of this form of pollution:

1. **Toxic Black Mold**—is reported to be the leading cause of sick building syndrome. Mold grows rapidly in warm and damp environments. If the indoor environment is too humid or if water damage occurs through leaks or rising damp, mold growth is very likely to occur.
2. **Viruses and Bacteria**—are common in every building, especially high occupancy buildings such as offices. These micro-organisms can make a significant contribution to causing SBS.
3. **Dust Mites**—are highly allergenic and thrive on the constant supply of shed human skin cells that accumulate in carpeting, soft furnishings, and other areas.
4. **Pollen**—is another allergy causing substance that can accumulate in a building if proper ventilation and filtering is not maintained.
5. **Moisture**—Moisture from unvented or poorly vented kitchens and bathrooms.

III. Other Factors that may Contribute to Sick Building Syndrome

Besides the more obvious chemical and biological pollutants that are commonly present in buildings and can lead to SBS, there are a number of more factors that can also contribute, sometimes significantly. The most common of these are:

1. **Fluorescent Lighting and Electrical Equipment**—People commonly report feeling unwell after spending time in buildings lit entirely with fluorescent strip lighting. Many people also complain of feeling unwell when they spend time close to computer screens and other electrical equipment.
2. **Temperature**—If the temperature is too hot for prolonged periods, people can become dehydrated with potentially serious consequences for their health.
3. **Humidity**—Again can put a strain on the body a very humid environment can lead to dehydration and associated problems.
4. **Noise**—It is an equally important factor. Too much noise can be draining and produce headaches and other symptoms. It also makes it hard to concentrate.
5. **Bad Office Design/Ergonomics**—A badly designed workplace can cause numerous health problems. A office with uncomfortable furniture can result in injuries such as those to the back.

Sick Building Syndrome and its Impact on Human Resources of an Organisation

The human resource manager needs to be aware of the environment in which employees work as the work environment has the potential to impact efficiency of an organisation and to affect profits. Today, the technological developments have provided societies with considerable benefits. Even in developing societies like India, we have become much more dependent on creating artificial environments. This all primarily started with good intentions, to improve our comfort in often complex environments. However, history has shown that technological developments can have negative impacts on human health. Often the undesirable impacts are not immediately evident, but slowly and gradually our over dependence on artificially created indoor environments make their mark felt. The consequences can manifest in form of poor quality air to breathe thereby causing severe health problems and drastically affecting the productivity level of employees. This feeling of ill-health even increases sickness and absenteeism among the employees. As a result, this adds a potential cost to the company. Thus, it can be said that the work environment is of concern to the human resource manager since there is a perceived link between productivity and the workplace. So, if the workplace is restricting productivity then this translates into significant inefficiency. The point is that an inefficient premises lead to inefficient organisational performance.

Sick building syndrome is a crucial issue and it is the role of human resource manager to ascertain whether employee's job satisfaction and productivity are affected by external factors in the environment.

Research Methodology

Research Design: The research type for this survey is exploratory because of the flexibility of research design.

Research Approach: For this study, the approach used is survey based, as it was best suited to know the impact of SBS and employee reactions for the same.

Data Collection Techniques: Primary data has been collected using questionnaires from selected private sector employees.

Secondary data has been collected from various newspapers, magazines and websites.

Area of Study: It covers the employees working in private sector of Udaipur City.

Sampling Size: Sampling size is 75 office employees who were randomly selected from different private sector companies of Udaipur.

Sampling Procedure: The technique used is convenience sampling.

Data Analysis and Interpretation: This part presents the analysis of collected data. All aspects mentioned for study in objectives were included for analysis.

Table 1: Shows Awareness about the Concept of "Sick Building Syndrome"

Do you understand about SBS?	*Yes*	*No*
	50	25

Interpretation

Many employees were aware about the concept of sick building syndrome and understood it.

Table 2: Shows Air Circulation in Office

Do you experience lack of air circulation in your office?	*Never*	*Sometimes*	*Mostly*
	10	40	25

Interpretation

More than half the employees have sometimes felt lack of air circulation in office.

Table 3: Lists Symptoms Related to SBS

Have you experienced any of the following while in office?

Symptoms	*Yes*	*No*
Headache	45	30
Chest Congestion	25	50
Sneezing	55	20
Cough	40	35
Tiredness and Drowsiness	55	20
Watery Nose	20	55
Cold and Flu	30	45
Irritation of eyes, skin and nose	40	35

Interpretation

A good number of people have experienced SBS related symptoms such as headaches, sneezing, tiredness, etc. at some point of time while at work in the office.

Table 4: Shows the Frequency of the Occurrences of Symptoms

Do the above-mentioned symptoms disappear as soon as you leave the office premises?	*Yes*	*No*
	55	20

Interpretation

In the majority of employees, the major part of these ailments diminish substantially when the inhabitants of those polluted interior spaces have left the premises for over several hours.

Table 5: Shows Complaints Related to the Upsetting Factors at the Workplace

Does any of the menace is present in your office premises?

Menaces	*Yes*	*No*
Dust in air	60	15
Smoke of cigarette	25	50
Disturbing noises	20	55
Foul odours	40	35
Poor lighting	45	30
Leaking walls	20	55
Uncomfortable office furniture	50	25

Interpretation

A number of above factors are causing menaces in the office premises. Like say dust in air can be attributed to the floor carpeting, likewise, foul odours from canteen waste and poorly maintained toilets can be very distressing. The office furniture should be designed ergonomically to provide maximum comfort to the employees at the workplace.

Table 6: Exhibits the Link between SBS and Performance and Productivity Levels of Employees

Does the poor work environment at workplace affect your productivity and performance level?	*Never*	*Sometimes*	*Often*
	5	35	35

Interpretation

SBS does often interfere with the productivity and performance of office employees. The meagre working conditions at the workplace divert the employees and restrict their limit to attain maximum productivity level and superior performance.

Table 7: Shows Relation of Stress Level to SBS

Does SBS increase your stress level at the workplace?	*Never*	*Sometimes*	*Mostly*
	10	40	25

Interpretation

Employees at the workplace do sometimes feel increased stress level while experiencing sick building syndrome.

Suggestions for Solution of Sick Building Syndrome

If employees working in the same building experience health problems that seem to only be present when they are in that building, or at least get much worse, then it is reasonable to suspect sick building syndrome. A thorough inspection of the building should be carried out to determine possible causes for the occupant's health complaints. There are many measures that can be taken to rectify the situation. A combination of some of the factors is discussed above.

1. **The Initial Walkthrough**—should be first done by human resource manager to develop some possible explanations for the complaint. At this point, the manager should collect sufficient information about the problem.

2. **Technical and Hygiene Investigations**—Human resource manager must carry out a hygiene and technical review of the type and severity of the indoor problems. Technical survey of the building is also performed in order to decide the relevant actions to be taken. A simple questionnaire concerning symptoms about different factors is distributed to a randomly selected sample of employees. The questionnaire should clearly distinguish between symptoms experienced in the building and those experienced when away from the building.

3. **Inspection and Guiding Measurements**—The following aspects should be observed:
   - Tobacco smoking.
   - Building and furnishing materials.

- Odours. Characterize them and identify sources.
- Cleaning level.
- Dust on floor carpets, bookshelves, etc.
- Presence of green plants.
- Water damage, water stains.
- Inlet and exhaust openings. Are they clean or blocked with dirt?
- Use of sun shielding.
- Number of employees in the offices. Are there more than planned?

  Also the factors which in the questionnaire are mentioned as disturbing and upsetting (e.g. noise or lighting) should be checked.

4. **Measurements of Ventilation, Climate Indicators and Other Implicated Factors**—The following factors should be investigated:

- **Ventilation:** Increase the ventilation rates and air distribution. The heating, ventilation and air-conditioning systems should be designed to meet ventilation standards in the local building codes. The HVAC system should be operated and maintained properly to ensure that the desired ventilation rates are attained. If there are strong pollutants, the air may need to be directly vented to the outside. This method is especially recommended to remove pollutants that accumulate in specific areas such as rest rooms, copy rooms and printing facilities.
- **Air Quality:** Again indoor air quality indicators like carbon dioxide, carbon monoxide and air temperature should be measured. In situations where poor cleaning is suspected or where large quantities of paper are being handled, the dust content in the air and on the floor should be measured. An evaluation of the composition of the dust may be of importance.
- **Lighting Measurement**: Even in the absence of complaints. Visual display users may have lighting problems that are not recognised.

5. **Education and Communication**—These are important elements in both remedial and preventive indoor air quality management programs. When building occupants, management, and maintenance personnel fully communicate and understand the causes and consequences of problems, they can work more effectively together to prevent problems from occurring, or to solve them if they do. Good communication between workers, occupational health staff, and building service managers and their plant staff is fundamental to improving existing sick buildings.

Conclusion

Human resource management is the management of people. It is specifically aimed at getting the best effort from people in an organisation, getting the best people for the job initially and providing the environment required that will enable people to give their best. An important part of human resource manager's role is dealing with the environment in which employees work as this has the potential to impact on the efficiency of the employees. Human resource managers can assess the workplace environment in a variety of ways and it is at this point that the role of human resource manager plays a crucial role in ensuring job satisfaction and employee efficiency, key issue of concern in human resource management. The effect of working in sick buildings can be seen on employee's productivity, performance and stress levels. SBS seriously affects the employee well-being. Human resource managers should play proactive role in promoting environmental health at the workplace.

REFERENCES

Åke Thörn, The Emergence and Preservation of Sick Building Syndrome, KI 1999.

Brasche, S., Bullinger, M., Bronisch, M. et al. Eye and skin symptoms in German office workers-subjective perception vs. objective medical screening. *Int J. Hygiene Environ Health*, 2001; 203:311-16.

Burge, P.S., Hedge, A., Wilson, S. et al. Sick building syndrome: A study of 4373 office workers. *Ann Occup Hyg* 1987; 31:493-504. First major study looking at a wide range of buildings including those with natural ventilation.

Carmichael, A.J., Roberts, D.L. Visual display units and facial rashes. *Contact Dermatitis*, 1992; 26(1):63-4.

Case Study: Sick Building Syndrome in a Humid Climate Richard J. Shaughnessy and Estelle Levetin Center for Environmental Research and Technology. The University of Tulsa 600 South College Ave.Tulsa, OK 74104.

Charlotte Brauer, The Sick Building Syndrome Revisited, Copenhagen 2005.

European Concerted Acllon Indoor Air Quality and Its Impact On Man Cost Project 61 3 Environment and Quality of Life Report No. 4 Sick Building Syndrome A Practical Guide Commission.

European Concerted Action Indoor Air Quality and Its Impact On Man Cost Project 61 3 Environment and Quality of Life Report No. 4 Sick Building Syndrome A Practical Guide.

Franck, C. Eye symptoms and signs in buildings with indoor climate problems ("office eye syndrome"). *Acta Opthalmologica* (Copenhagen), 1986; 64:306-11.

Franck, C., Skov, P. Evaluation of two different questionnaires used for diagnosing ocular manifestations in the sick building syndrome on the basis of an objective test. *Indoor Air*, 1991; 1:5-11.

Franck, C., Skov, P. Foam at inner eye canthus in office workers, compared with an average Danish population as control group. *Acta Opthalmologica* (Copenhagen), 1989;67: 61-8.

Human Resource Management Journal, Volume 21, Issue 1, pp. 14–27, January 2011.

Indoor Air Facts No. 4 (revised) Sick building syndrome. Available from:http://www.epa.gov/iaq/pubs/sbs.html

Joshi, Sumedha M. The sick building syndrome, Indian Journal of Occupational and Environmental Medicine, August 1, 2008, Volume 12, Issue 2, p. 61.

Legislative Assembly Standing Committee on Public Works Report Sick Building Syndrome Report, Parliament House Macquarie St Sydney 2000.

Martin-Gil et al. Hospital Management International. Sterling Publications Limited; Outcome of research into a sick hospital.

Martín-Gil, J., Yanguas, M.C., San José, J.F., Rey-Martínez and Martín-Gil, F.J. "Outcomes of research into a sick hospital". Hospital Management International, 1997, pp. 80-82. Sterling Publications Limited.

Michelle Murphy, Sick Building Syndrome and the Problem of Uncertainty, 2006.

Muzi, G., dell'Omo, M., Abbritti, G. et al. Objective assessments of ocular and respiratory alterations in employees in a sick building. *Am J Ind Med*, 1998; 34:79-88.

Niosh Guidance for Indoor Air Quality Investiations, Cincinnati, OH, January, 1987.

Purushottam, K. The sick building syndrome. *Indian J Occup Health*, 2001; 44:36–40.

Rycroft, R.J.G. Low humidity and microtrauma. *Am J Ind Med*, 1985;8:371-73.

Sick building syndrome, From Wikipedia, the free encyclopedia.

Sick Building Syndrome, P.S. Burge Downloaded from oem.bmj.com on August 22, 2012—Published by group.bmj.com

Statistics USA (SBS): Compiled by WHO statistics available on the their website www.who.int

Sundell, J., Lindvall, T., Stenberg, B. et al. Sick building syndrome in office workers and facial skin symptoms amongst VDT-workers in relation to building and room characteristics. Two case-referent studies. *Indoor Air*, 1994; 4:83-94.

United States Air and Radiation (6609J) Research and Development Environmental Protection (MD-56) Agency February 1991 Indoor Air Facts No. 4 (revised) Sick Building Syndrome.

World Health Organization, "Indoor Air Pollutants: Exposure and Health Effects"; EURO Reports 8 Studies 78. Report on a meeting of the Working Group on Assessment and Monitoring of Exposure to Indoor Air Pollutants, Copenhagen; World Health Organization, Regional Office for Europe, 1983.

CHAPTER 24

LABOUR UNREST AT MARUTI SUZUKI LTD.: ALARM OF LABOUR REFORMS IN INDIA

–*Mahendra Singh*

ABSTRACT

Indian auto industry is sunrise industry of India. Indian market is considered to be fastest passenger car market home for fifth largest commercial vehicle manufacturer. Genesis of Indian automotive is 1940 but the growth started after 1970. In the decade of 1985 to 1995, Maruti Udyog and other Japanese players were introduced in India. Automobile industry is considered big employer in India. Specially four wheeler manufacturer and allied industry is employing a big whole some skilled, semi-skilled and unskilled labours too. This paper is about the alarming situation of labour unrest in India which was indicated recently in strike by labors of Maruti Suzuki at their Manesar plant. The objective is to examine causes which led this kind of situation at Maruti Suzuki Ltd., and consequences resulted by situation directly to Maruti Suzuki Ltd. and indirectly to Indian automobile industry.

Introduction

Indian auto industry is sunrise industry of India. And is fastest passenger car market home for fifth largest commercial vehicle manufacturer. Start-up of Indian automotive is 1940 but the growth started after 1970. In the decade of 1985 to 1995, Maruti Udyog and other Japanese players were introduced in India. Automobile industry is big employer in India. Specially four wheeler manufacturer and allied industry is employing a big whole some skilled, semi-skilled and unskilled labours too.

Workforce Structure of Automobile Majors in India

According to SIAM reports, the Indian automotive sector will be requiring about 25 million additional workforce including downstream and upstream activities. The pie of workforce is about management-28%, skilled workers-62% and unskilled workers-10%. As the industry have adverse impact over competitiveness and labour economy, there are 45 central acts and 16 associated rules which effect employment with certain others too. Most of the automobiles major employing workers by different modes like: permanent, temporary, ad-hoc, part time, and contract. Outsourcing of skilled and unskilled labours through agencies is also in practice in Indian automobile sector.

HR Policies in Practice

The Contract Labour (Regulation and Abolition) Act, 1970 permits to provide fixed term contractual employment. Contract labours are allowed to work in primary areas for fixed time period. At MSL the recruitment policies being practiced are

- MSL always lookout for ambitious, hardworking and innovation driven professionals.
- Provide good career opportunities that are second to none.
- Maruti Suzuki adheres to certain norms for any vacancy. Given below is a list of norms that they follow.
- Fresher, just out of college applicants are recruited only through campus recruitments from select empanelled campuses.
- Laterals, applicants having more than three years of experience are only considered.
- Good academic track record with minimum 60% throughout in all full-time qualifications is mandatory.
- Applicants working in any of our business associates as employee (dealers, vendors, JVs, etc.) are not considered.
- Applicant should not have been interviewed in Maruti Suzuki in the last one year.

Maruti Suzuki believes that a positive attitude and proactive nature takes person miles ahead. The person should be flexible and should have a never ending zeal to learn and innovate. Hard work, commitment and persistence are essential for any candidate to perform in Maruti Suzuki. The work culture have the roots of Maruti Suzuki are the discipline, integrity and honesty that it brings in its every process.

The HR Values Flow at Maruti Suzuki Ltd.

MSL have a performance and result-oriented culture which requires commitment from every person. Its culture breeds good employee bonding and a self-starter approach. Maruti Suzuki is a family and they take care of their people. The company provides good canteen facility and superannuation and medical insurance policy to its employees. At MSL they value their people and understand their needs for personal growth and career. Providing people with appropriate environment and resources for growth, learning and confidence is priority. MSL conduct various development programs to train their people with the latest technologies and developments of the industry in line with their business requirement. The programs are conducted on the basis of the training needs identified. There are different programs for different people.

Key programs of training are:

(a) Foreign training done in Japan in collaboration with SMC.

(b) Annual training plan comprising management and technical programs.

(c) Outbound training for enhancing team building skills and rejuvenate.

(d) Technical training

(e) Soft skills training.

Strike: A Weapon for Labours

(a) *Strike in Indian Industries*

A devil seems to be scolding India these days, the trouble of industrial unrest. In the recent several months, there have been a series of strikes in automobile manufacturing units across the country. GM, Hyundai, Ashok Leyland, and the most recent and long-drawn one in Maruti Suzuki's Gurgaon units. Nowadays, the automobile industry is zooming growth rate and globalized connections, this has pitch forked the rather humdrum issue of industrial relations right on to the centre stage. Outside this high-profile industry too, there are signs of deep stirring within India's vast and scattered workforce in Indian automobile industry.

There has been deep trouble on both sides of the divide, the industrialists and the trade unions. As now the first time, there is unity across the spectrum among central trade unions in Indian industry from the BJP-backed Bharat Mazdoor Sangh and Congress-backed Indian National Trade Union Congress to the Left-led All India Trade Union Congress and CITU. All have called for a *jail bharo andolan* demanding drastic policy changes to:

1. Controlling price rise,
2. Stopping privatization of public sector units,
3. Ending the system of contract workers,
4. Better work conditions, and
5. Establishing same policies at all sister concerns/ancillaries of the big units.

Among other things, their leaders are raring to go, promising serious action in the coming months.

(b) *Types of Strike*

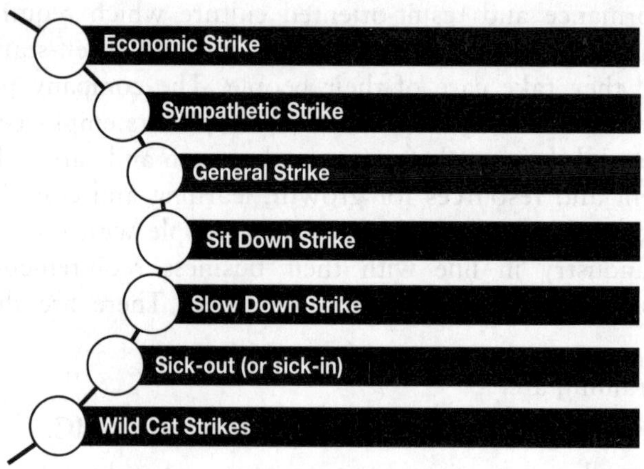

(c) *Strike Guidelines by ILO*

(i) *Objectives of Strikes*

The strikes can be seen as essential in some cases for labour issues. For discussing objective of strike, reference should be made at the outset to Article 10 of Convention No. 87 which, for the purposes of the Convention, defines worker organizations as any organization "for furthering and defending the interests of workers". This definition is clearly of fundamental importance not only in that it sets down guidelines for differentiating such organizations from those of other types, but also because it specifies the purpose of such organizations is for "furthering and defending the interests of workers"—thereby demarcating the boundaries within which the rights and guarantees recognized by the Convention are applicable, and consequently protected insofar as they achieve or seek to achieve the stated objectives. The nature of the demands pursued through strike action may—

1. Occupational (seeking to guarantee or improve workers' working or living conditions),
2. Trade union (seeking to guarantee or develop the rights of trade union organizations and their leaders),
3. Political.

(ii) *Conditions for Exercising the Right to Strike*

The Committee on Freedom of Association has specified that such conditions "should be reasonable and in any event not such as to place a substantial limitation on the means of action open to trade union organizations" (ILO, 1996d, para 498). The large number of committee decisions in this connection may be attributed to the fact that some 15 per cent of the cases submitted to it concern the exercise of the right to strike.

The Committee on Freedom of Association has accepted the following prerequisites:

1. The obligation to give prior notice (*ibid.*, para(s) 502-504).
2. The obligation to have recourse to conciliation, mediation and (voluntary) arbitration procedures in industrial disputes as a prior condition to declaring a strike, provided that the proceedings are adequate, impartial and speedy and that the parties concerned can take part at every stage (*ibid.*, para(s) 500-501).
3. The obligation to observe a certain quorum and to obtain the agreement of a specified majority (*ibid.*, paras, 506-513).
4. The obligation to take strike decisions by secret ballot (*ibid.*, paras 503-510).
5. The adoption of measures to comply with safety requirements and for the prevention of accidents (*ibid.*, paras 554-555).
6. The establishment of a minimum service in particular cases (*ibid.*, paras 556-558).
7. The guarantee of the freedom to work for non-strikers (*ibid.*, para 586).

(iii) *Body of Principles on the Right to Strike*

Committee on Freedom of Association regards the right to strike.

1. Consideration of the right to strike as a fundamental right to be enjoyed by workers and their organizations (trade unions, federations and confederations), which is protected at international level, provided that the right is exercised in a peaceful manner.
2. General recognition of the right to strike for workers in the public and the private sectors, with the sole possible exceptions being members of the armed and police

forces, public servants who exercise authority in the name of the state and workers employed in essential services in the strict sense of the term (the interruption of which could endanger the life, safety or health of the whole or part of the population), or in situations of acute national crisis.

3. The principles of freedom of association do not cover strikes of a purely political nature, although they do cover those which seek a solution to major issues in economic and social policy.
4. A blanket ban on sympathy strikes could lead to abuse. Workers should be able to enjoy the right to take such action when the initial strike they are supporting is itself lawful.
5. A minimum safety service may be imposed in all cases of strike action when such minimum services are intended to ensure the safety of persons, the prevention of accidents and the safety of machinery and equipment.
6. A minimum operational service may be established (in the undertaking or institution in question) in the case of strikes in public utility services and in public services of fundamental importance; employers' and workers' organizations and the public authorities should be able to participate in determining this minimum service.
7. The obligation to give prior notice, the obligation to engage in conciliation, have recourse to voluntary arbitration, ply with a given quorum and obtain the agreement of a given majority where this does not cause the strike to become very difficult or even impossible in practice and the secret ballot method to decide strike action are all acceptable conditions for the exercise of the right to strike.
8. Restrictions on picketing should be confined to cases in which such action ceases to be peaceful, and picketing should not interfere with the freedom to work of non-strikers.
9. Requisitioning of the workers of an undertaking or institution in the event of a strike is admissible only in the case of a strike in an essential service or under circumstances of utmost gravity and in situations of acute national crisis.
10. The hiring of workers to replace strikers seriously impairs the right to strike and is acceptable only in strikes in an essential service or in situations of acute national crisis.
11. Legal provisions regarding wage deductions for days of strike give rise to no objection.
12. Appropriate protection should be afforded to trade union officials and workers against dismissal and other detrimental acts at work for organizing or participating in a legitimate strike, in particular through prompt, efficient and impartial procedures, accompanied by sufficiently dissuasive remedies and sanctions.
13. The protection of freedom of association does not cover abuses in the exercise of the right to strike involving failure to comply with reasonable requirements regarding lawfulness, or consisting of acts of a criminal nature; any sanctions imposed in the event of abuse should not be disproportionate to the seriousness of the violations.

Strike at Maruti Suzuki

Maruti Suzuki's Manesar plant in Haryana 1800 workers (1500 according to the management) have refused to leave the plant since they stopped work on the fifth day of strike. According to the agreement with the management on 1 October 2011, it was understood that all employees would be allowed to resume work. However, only permanent employees were allowed to enter the plant and others which includes 1200 contract workers were on *dharna* outside the premises were not allowed to go inside premises. This was third strike since June at Maruti Suzuki.

The strikes and stoppage of production have hit the company hard. The problems MSL had since June has cost about 51,000 cars which translates to loss of turnover worth ₹ 1500 crore, as per company estimates. The Haryana Government issued a breach of settlement notice to the Maruti Suzuki workers. The condition of striking workers inside the plant remained unknown as no media (or other workers) were allowed inside by the security personnel. A temporary kitchen has come up outside the plant to supply food to workers inside. Some of the workers who have fallen ill were seen giving samples for blood test across the fenced wall.

Causes and Effects of Strike

(i) *Strike Fire Spreads to Aiding Units Too*

Suzuki Powertrain (a plant of Suzuki company and has two plants in Manesar) was also on strike in their support. Loudspeakers inside the premises was heard making a recorded announcement calling for an immediate end to the strike, only to be greeted by boos and songs of protest by the workers inside and outside. Labour officer of the Haryana Government, Ajay Pal, who was at Manesar's Suzuki Powertrain Casting plant on one evening to mediate talks with workers who've also been on strike since 7 October in solidarity with Maruti Suzuki workers, maintained that the "process of conciliation was carried on. The second and longest strike, since troubles first started in June, lasting 33 days ended after a hard-fought negotiation that led to the 1 October agreement, which both parties are now accusing the other of breaching. The one of the workers who was out of 44 terminated workers said the agreement was that barring the 44 workers who had been suspended, all workers would be allowed to resume work. But the management didn't allow 1200 contract workers to resume work. Only 1800, which include permanent employees, were taken back. This is a violation. Our demands now are that the management take back the 44 previously suspended workers and also the 25 who were suspended on 8 October. The false cases of inciting strikes that have been lodged against them be taken back.

The company officials showed other case of situation. The number of permanent employees at the plant is 950. Barring the 44 who were suspended, that is 906 employees were admitted into the plant. The 1200 workers being referred to are contract workers and the agreement has nothing to do with them. But it was explicitly communicated at the time of the agreement that the contract workers would be taken back over the next couple of weeks. There was no confusion on this and the contract workers is a complete non-issue as per the company officials. The heart of the conflict is the issue of establishing a second workers union to represent the Maruti's Manesar plant workers. Maruti has another plant at Gurgaon. "In December, the management said that there would be union elections. When the workers who wanted to contest were discouraged by the management and mentally tortured and harassed. Until June, no elections happened. The management does not want to hold elections here. Workers then decided that they should have another union that will represent the welfare of Manesar plant workers. On 3 June, they applied for the registration of the Maruti Suzuki Employees Union at Chandigarh.

Table 1: Industrial Conflicts (1970-95)

Year	*Number of Disputes*			*Number of Workdays lost to Disputes (thousands)*		
	Strikes	*Lockouts*	*Total*	*Strikes*	*Lockouts*	*Total*
1970	2598	291	2889	14749	5814	20563
1971	2478	274	2752	11803	4743	16546
1972	2857	386	3243	13748	6796	20544
1973	2958	421	3370	13862	6764	20626
1974	2501	428	2929	33643	6619	40262
1975	1644	299	1943	16706	5195	21901
1976	1241	218	1459	2799	9947	12746
1977	2691	426	3117	13410	11910	25320
1978	2762	425	3187	15423	12917	28340
1979	2709	339	3048	35804	8050	43854
1980	2501	355	2856	12018	9907	21925
1981	2245	344	2589	21208	15375	36583
1982	2029	454	2483			74615
1983	1993	495	2488			46858
1984	1689	405	2094			56025
1985	1355	400	1755	11487	17753	29240
1986	1458	434	1892	18824	13925	32749
1987	1348	451	1799	14026	21332	35358
1988	1304	441	1745	12530	21417	33947
1989	1397	389	1786	10695	21968	32663
1990	1459	366	1825	10640	13446	24086
1991	1278	532	1810	12428	14000	26428
1992	1011	703	1714	15132	16127	31259
1993	914	479	1393	5615	14686	20983
1994	808	393	1201	6651	14332	20983
1995	732	334	1066	5720	10570	16290

Source: Bhattacharjee (1999)

Strike Settlement

Maruti Suzuki Ltd. management was trying to cool down the fire of strike at their plant as it was hampering their production a lot. But the major problems they faced for settling it down early was the big bundle of demands made by the group of agitating workers. The labour leaders were demanding for job security issues of contract labours which were not allowed to premises few days ago. MSL management tried for two-way discussions between the aggrieved party but it failed many times. The tripartite negotiation was machinery used for settlement. Talks between the MSI management and workers in the presence of Haryana Labour Department officials was carried on after workers broke down on October 18. Hopes of an agreement were raised later, but an agreement could not be reached as both sides stuck to their stands. The 14-day-long strike at the plant, causing an estimated over ₹ 700 crore loss, was called off following a tripartite agreement that reinstated 64 dismissed permanent workers and took back 1,200 casual workers. However, 30 permanent workers remain suspended.

Controversies

1. The battle at Manesar is all about relevance of trade unions

Industry experts said the crisis at Maruti is a combination of labour militancy combined with rising aspirations of the working class and politics inter mingling. The unrest at Maruti is not an industry problem but a "problem of rival unionism problem in a newly industrialised area where people have not got into industrial mindset". It is said that the real battle at Manesar is more about the relevance of trade unions than an issue of contract vs. permanent labourers.

2. Does the hero sell them out?

The employee which led this all rise to fame some would say notoriety and fall from grace has been equally spectacular. He always looked like a reluctant union guy no red flags for him, no fiery slogans either. And he was not overly bothered about the conflict between labour and capital. For him, workers cause had a different meaning.

Till a few months back, this ITI-trained man from Jhajjar was not seen as a potential troublemaker by the management of Maruti Suzuki's factory at Manesar in Haryana. Forced to quit school following the death of his father. He joined the factory in July 2006. Over the next five years is attendance averaged more than 98%; he won the best operator award and the managing directors trophy for best employee. Then two incidents, says he, changed his attitude towards the multinational. When some workers met with an accident and did not get any support from the company, he took up their cause. Later, when a colleague's mother died, he was pulled up for asking other workers to observe two minutes silence. This made me realize that the management doesn't care for us. They treat us like robots. So I decided to stand up for the workers as the official union was not doing anything, he told Sunday Times days before he suspiciously disappeared, allegedly after taking a hefty amount from the management to shut up and scoot.

After he decided to contest election for the illegal union, the management tried to stop him. But it didn't work. Comrade won and began a strike for the workers right to form an independent union. As the company went into a tailspin lockout at Manesar plant, trouble in other factories, record fall in profits his stature grew by the day. And when Maruti decided to shift its operations to Gujarat, he became a giant slayer the man who drove Maruti out.

But just the other day came reports that he and his associates had quietly left the company after a settlement of ₹ 14 lakh each. The workers are fuming. He was not serious about our problems. He didn't know anything about labour laws. He made some populist demands and took us all for a ride, says a worker at the Manesar plant. Guilty or not, he must be a lonely man today.

3. Major cause is wage vs. worth

In the decade between 1998-99 and 2008-09, net value added by workers increased from about ₹ 2 lakh per worker to Rs 6 lakh, according to the latest available ASI reports. In the same period, wages as a proportion of net value added declined steeply from about 18% to 11%. This means, in essence, that workers are creating more profit than before, yet getting paid less and less. It is often argued that the productivity of Indian workers is low because of, among other things, restrictive regulation. But recent figures from the labour ministry's annual report show that productivity of the Indian worker was growing at over 7% in 2007 compared to just short of 4% a decade earlier. Only China, with a remarkable 11% growth rate, was ahead among major countries on this count.

It is obvious that equilibrium of sorts was achieved by industry through local settlements in the absence of policy reform at the national level. In some cases, industry acted more generously, in others they were more flexible, and thus they assuaged the unions and workers, he explains.

This appears to reflect in the number of strikes and lockouts reported by the Labour Bureau, a government body. In the last five years, the lost because of strikes and lockouts have declined from about 300 lakh in 2005 to a mere 16.9 lakh in 2010. Although these figures often underestimate industrial disputes because of incomplete reports from states, and they do not include smaller units, the declining trend is clear.

4. The impact on neighboring business

The Gurgaon plant of Maruti Suzuki was the face of the city for over two decades, before IT industries started investing and opening offices to make Gurgaon, a Millennium City. However, with reports about Maruti rethinking its expansion and moving out of Gurgaon, villagers and industrial workers have been a worried lot.

The villagers around IMT Manesar have come out in the open against the 'unruly behaviour' of the striking Maruti workers, who have greatly affected the lives and finances of the landless villagers who depend on the rentals from industrial workers for their sustenance. Occasional panchayats have been held in various villages to work out a solution to the ongoing crisis. Panchayats have made it clear that the striking workers should not be given an opportunity to return to the plant since they are unwilling to resolve the matter and have stretched it too far. Speaking about the Maruti crisis, sarpanch of Manesar village, which has over 25,000 tenants and over 30,000 original residents (excluding the tenants) said, "We don't have any land left for farming. Some are engaged in small time businesses like running a grocery shop, while most offer one-room accommodation on rent. Our major source of income has been severely affected."

According to a localite doctor, who has 35 rooms on rent in a Manesar village, "Land was acquired by the state for as low as ₹ 2.5 lakh per acre and a job for each family in the industrial set-up was promised. However, not a single villager has got a job and we are dependent on the rental income. My clinic has also been affected due to the strike."

"Youths from outside the state, like Rajasthan, UP, Bihar want to return to work as the protest has severely affected their livelihood and financial condition back home.

5. Others are reaping the peace dividend

Gujarat in the west and Bengal in the east took opposite stands on the politics of labour. And it reflected on their economic growth rates. Call it a culture thing or merely good politics, but theres a simple statistic behind the Gujarat success story: a sharp, almost three-fold decrease in cases of industrial unrest over the last decade. In 2001, the state lost 2,24,132 man-days because of strikes and lockouts in 53 establishments. By 2010 the number had progressively declined to a mere 41,128 man-days lost and 18 strikes and lockouts, according to state labour commissioner.

Underlying all these figures is the fact that Gujarat has never had a tradition of militant trade unionism. The states Majur Mahajan Sangh, founded by Mahatma Gandhi in 1921, was historically the mainstay of all union activity. It worked for the welfare of the workers and followed the Gandhian principle of trusteeship. And while its influence has waned, the tradition continues.

In effect, this has helped Gujarati entrepreneurs keep wages low compared to many other states, both for regular and daily workers. According to National Sample Survey data released in June, the average wage per day in Gujarat for regular employees is ₹ 276.48 for men and ₹ 213.10 for women. The national average is ₹ 332.37 and ₹ 253.02 respectively. And the average urban wage for casual labour in the state is ₹ 106.17 (all-India it is ₹ 121.83). These are lower than wages in states such as Karnataka, Maharashtra, Chhattisgarh, Tamil Nadu, Andhra Pradesh, Haryana and Kerala.

Also, much of Gujarat's industrial progress is being fuelled by high capital-intensive investment by entrepreneurs. This has impacted the growth of industrial labour. Organized employment in Gujarat grew by merely 0.5% per year between 1995 and 2008, while the state domestic product (SDP) showed more than 8% growth. In a recent study, senior economist Indira says that the increasing capital intensity of the industrial sector is a striking feature in Gujarat. In 2007-08, Gujarat ranked first among the 20 major Indian states in capital investment, second in total invested capital and fourth in total number of factories, but ranked 18th in labour-capital ratio.

Incidentally, Gujarat is among the few states which strongly favour an exit policy and want the Centre to make the necessary changes in labour laws. It became the first state to implement an amendment in the Central law which allows states to have their own labour laws in special economic zones (SEZs), with powers to entrepreneurs to hire and fire workers at will.

Measures and Suggestions for Avoidance of Strikes

(i) *Labour Reforms and Work Conditions*

The recent Maruti experience and the rumblings among unions have caused industry bodies to sit up and renew their long-standing demand for reform in labour laws. B.P. Pant, head of the labour bureau at FICCI, says that India's labour laws were mostly designed in the British times when conditions were quite different and workers needed protection. Laws relating to registration of trade unions, participation of non-employees in unions, restrictions on closing factories, contract labour and strikes need major changes, he adds.

Dipankar Mukherjee, secretary of Citu, is dismissive of these demands. They want to do away with whatever limited industrial democracy exists in India today and bring back feudal rule, he says. Only about 8% of India's workforce is covered by labour laws, as the majority of workers are in the informal sector, he points out.

Leaving regulatory issues aside, industrial workers are facing a host of problems. Their worsening economic condition is a source of deep discontent. Economist Surajit Mazumdar of Ambedkar University, Delhi, points to data collected by the Annual Survey of Industries (ASI) under the ministry of statistics that shows the share of wages in industrial expenditure has dipped alarmingly over the years even as the value created by labour has increased.

(ii) *Issue of Unsocial Contract*

But there is a flip side to this its underbelly. A very large number of workers even in big industrial units and the public sector are now working as contract workers. They are technically employed by contractors. Thus, the principal owners have washed their hands of them. The wage differences between regular and contract workers are huge. In Maruti's new plant at Manesar, there are about 1,000 permanent workers who get between ₹ 13,000 and 17,000 a month. But the 1,200 contract workers get only about ₹ 6,500. Contract workers are also denied other benefits like provident fund and medical insurance. Since they are not on the rolls of the company, contract workers can be removed at will. They are treated like sheep. The same story is repeated across the country, in innumerable factories, big and small. So, despite labour reforms not taking place, a *de facto* change has set in. Industrial relations have been largely quiescent but under the seemingly calm waters, there is simmering discontent. Reeling under rising prices and harsh living conditions, and with no hope of support from a crisis ridden agricultural hinterland, a whole generation of workers more educated and skilled than their predecessors is looking for a way out and not finding it. Whether this will end in organized protest or anarchy or a farsighted policy solution only time will tell.

6. Conclusion

The unsolved issue of industrial relations is suddenly centre stage. Indian automobile companies are again talking of labour reforms. Trade unions are flexing their muscles. And a whole generation of workers is looking for a better deal with employers.

The Indian automobile industry employs a big ratio of workers on contract. The contract terms and condition are the big cause for the labour unrest in the Maruti Suzuki Ltd., and others automotive manufacturers and allied industries too. Even though Maruti Suzuki has very good human resource policies which helps to attracts best talent for them. By providing good working conditions they are able to retain good talented workforce also. The issue which caused big loss too Maruti Suzuki Ltd. was the dismissal of contract worker from duties. Which shows poor contract conditions in the companies and further this fire was given air by political and other communities.

The analysis shows that labour unrest causes downgrading in all over aspects. Maruti Suzuki Ltd. was under loss of their production lines and image in customers also. The discussion of wage and worth of work done is the area where Indian employers have to think for.

REFERENCES

Bernard, G., Alberto, O., Horacio, G., ILO Principles concerning the right to strike.

Hodges-Aeberhard, Jane ; Odero de Dios, Alberto, 1987. "Principles of the Committee on Freedom of Association concerning strikes", in *International Labour Review* (Geneva), Vol. 126, No. 5 (Sep.-Oct.), pp. 543-63.

ILO 1998a: Record of Proceedings, International Labour Conference, 86th Session, 1998, Geneva.

Report of the Committee of Experts on the Application of Conventions and Recommendations: General report and observations concerning particular countries. Report III (Part 4A), International Labour Conference, 86th Session, 1998. Geneva.

Report of the Committee of Experts on the Application of Conventions and Recommendations: General report and observations concerning particular countries. Report III (Part 4A), International Labour Conference, 85th Session, 1997. Geneva.

Subodh Varma; Forces of labour: Times Insight Group.

Shobhan Saxena; Man of moment: Did the hero sell them out Times News network.

Atul Thakur; Indian worker has always come cheap: Times Insight Group.

Rajiv Shah; Reaping the peace dividend: Times News Network.

Ajanta Chakraborty; Work as usual Cholbey na: Times News Network.

http://ibnlive.in.com/news/maruti-strike-ends-30-workers-leave-company/199102-7.html

Tanushree Roy Chowdhury; Maruti strike: Villagers angry with protesters as income hit, TNN Oct. 21, 2011.

CHAPTER 25 HR STRATEGIES IN UTILISING MAXIMUM OUTCOME FROM THE WORKFORCE BY TEAM BUILDING

–Kritika Joshi and Ashish Mathur

ABSTRACT

Human resources are most critical because these are the only active resources and the effective use of other resources depends on these. Today is the world of competition, and the organizations which want to stay competitive in the years to come must strategically redefine their operations to work harmoniously with the changes. In the new economy, fluid business models are rewarded, and inflexible models are pummeled. Organizational structures, leadership and management styles are evolving in recognition of this reality and with them, new strategies to manage talent are emerging. With the current circumstances in dynamic scenario for employees, flexible work arrangements may be an option that can meet the needs of both the organization and the employees. This paper is an attempt to understand the team effectiveness as a proven and practical diagnostic tool for assessing team effectiveness and improving work group performance.

Introduction

Potential of human resources can be utilized effectively by employee cross training method. Employee cross training is a training and development program to assist staff employees to increase the effectiveness of their performance in their present positions and to encourage and provide opportunities for employees to obtain skills, knowledge and abilities which may improve their chances for career advancement within the organization. The employees has the primary responsibility for individual career development and should, therefore, make career interests known to the supervisor and initiate the request to participate in the employee cross training program. Employee cross training program helps in acquiring employees and enhancing their skills, knowledge and abilities. It also assists in enhancing employee's opportunities for mobility and advancement within the organization. Training may allow employees to be minimally qualified for the position in which they are cross-trained.

Work Team

Team building is a critical function for effectiveness in organization. Better understanding of team work can make more effective employee and give an extra edge in corporate office. A team building success is when team can accomplish something much bigger and work more effectively than a group of the same individuals working on their own. In real life, team work success rarely happens by itself, without focused team building efforts and activities. There is simply too much space for problems. When team members work well together there is little they cannot accomplish. For example, different personalities, instead of complementing and balancing each other, may build up conflicts. Even if the team goals are clear and accepted by everyone, there may be no team commitment to the group goals or no consensus on the means of achieving those goals. There may be a lack of trust and openness that blocks the critical communication and leads to loss of coordination in the individual efforts. Employees have a strong synergy of individual contributions. But there are two critical factors in building a high performance team. The first factor in team factor in team effectiveness is the diversity of skills and personalities. When people use their strength in full, but can compensate for each other's weaknesses. When differently personality types balance and compensate each other. The other critical element of team work success is that all the team efforts are directed towards the same clear goals, the team goals. This relies heavily on good communication in the team and the harmony in member relationships.

The Flexible Workforce

The flexible workforce is an innovative strategy that provides the responsiveness, cost-effectiveness and resilience organizations need to survive while leveraging the strength of a diverse workforce and enhancing employee satisfaction. Just-in-Time (JIT) have also proved very effective technique to reduce fixed inventory costs, deployed supply chain management to gain flexibility and control production factors, outsourced noncore functions to minimize overhead and utilized the contingent workers for low level clerical and administrative roles. But the management and the professional workforce didn't fit well into this model. There is no easy way to maintain flexibility or apply JIT techniques, organization still stocked seldom used resources to ensure they had them when needed. Companies are beginning to appreciate the need for flexibility in all talent expenditures including those at professional and management levels—recognizing the value and cost savings that can be realized by adding expert staff in increments as needed. The flexible staffing model offers benefits in many areas like:

- Cost Saving
- Expertise
- Flexibility and Agility
- Workers Satisfaction

By deploying expert just-in-time talent at all levels of the organization to work along with full time staff, flexible staffing models combat increasing recruiting and retention problems while enabling companies to accommodate volume fluctuations, maintain leaner permanent head counts and access the expertise they need, when they need it. More and more companies are viewing the contingent workforce as a vital component of their human capital strategies to remain competitive in 21st century.

Literature Review

An extensive review of extant literature establishes a credible theoretical basis for team building interventions as a tool for OD but reveals problems and barriers to evaluation, which hamper its application. Frameworks for evaluation are critically analyzed and suggested applications within the context of purpose are suggested. Primary research centered on a sample population of central Scotland organizations (both public and private sector), proves the hypothesis, revealing that most organizations evaluate the benefits and outcomes of team building interventions at a superficial level. Analysis of the data reveals that organizations are concentrating on criteria such as participant reaction, the perceived quality of the event and the performance of the provider, rather than evaluating the more fundamental issues of change in participant behavior and the subsequent impact on organizational performance. The conclusions consider the competitive advantage and other benefit that may be gained by the authors, employing company through extending their service to assist clients in the evaluation team building events. The initial search identified that the specific area of team building, through the medium of the activities is poorly addressed in textbooks and journals. The few articles that did exist were mainly found in trade journals and perhaps expectedly, were superficial, general, biased and lacking in any degree of academic rigor. It was necessary, therefore, to investigate more broadly and identify existing areas of study that could contribute to the purpose of this dissertation:

- Current thinking on employee development and OD.
- Establishing the basis for the credibility of team building.
- Concepts, content and processes of development interventions.

The literature review in this area identified only seven relatively contemporary textbooks on the subject of evaluating training (Bramley, 1996; Easterby-Smith, 1994; Phillips, 1990; Jackson, 1989; Kirkpatrick, 1976; Hamblin, 1974, Warr *et al.*, 1974.) Two of these, Warr *et al.* and Easterby-Smith more specifically; address the subject of evaluating management development training. Despite this specialization these texts were considered to be a source of valid contribution to the investigation of team building, as the concepts and tools discussed therein are common to and have application in training as a more general concept. There are, however, many peer-reviewed journal articles that refer to instruments of evaluation as specifically applicable to team building and these are heavily drawn upon in this review. In addition to these sources of specific review, many of the more general texts on training and development pay considerable notice to the role of evaluation as part of the systematic training cycle as described by Stewart (1999). Hamblin's (1974) framework has close similarity to that of Kirkpatrick's (1976), in that it suggests that a multi-level framework is useful in the evaluation of employee development. In Hamblin's model, it is argued that the five levels of evaluation reflect a causal chain of consequences for a training event and that outcomes at each level can be measured. The literature review concentrated on three main areas; examination of current thinking on employee development and OD; team building as an instrument of OD and examination of the research into the evaluation of development interventions. The first area for review revealed that defining the terms associated with OD is fraught with ambiguity. As such describing a team building intervention in precise terms is difficult and very much depends on the context in which they are applied. The underpinning theories of team building as a valid and beneficial intervention are generally agreed, however, this is subject to certain caveat, namely that in order to be effective other organizational conditions must be present and indeed a checklist has been developed to assist in the practical application of this. The majority opinion discovered suggests that team building events can result in benefit to the team and to the organization. The models of team development and the team performance curve offer a framework for the observation, description and assessment of the development of teams.

The review covered the literature that considers the concept, content and process of evaluation and identified two ubiquitous frameworks, the first of which can assist in the understanding and application of assessing to what extent an intervention has affected the individual, team and organization. The second framework for evaluation looked at the components of a development intervention, rather than the effects, which may result. The application of these frameworks can be influenced by the purposes of the evaluation process.

The purposes of evaluation can range from establishing the extent to which the participants have enjoyed the event to attempting to prove that the activity has generated a financial benefit in excess of the investment.

Many authors recognize that the practical application of evaluation is problematic. The major barriers to applying evaluation techniques are attributable to the inherent subjectivity of any measurement values and the inability to isolate the effects of intervention from a myriad of uncontrollable variables which exist in the workplace. The potential bias of the evaluator is also flagged as a barrier to definitive evaluation.

Factors Influencing Effective Team Work

Factors that pay an impact and influence the working of a team effectively could be as follows:

(1) **Clear Expectation:** Has executive leadership clearly communicated its expectation for the team's performance and expected outcomes? Do team members understand why the team was created? Does the work of the team receive sufficient emphasis as a priority in terms of the time, discussion, attention and interest directed its way by executive leaders?

(2) **Context:** Do team members understand why they are participating on the team? Do they understand how the strategy of using teams will help the organization attain its communicated business goals? Do the teams understand where its work fits in the total context of the organization's goals, principles, vision, values, etc.?

(3) **Commitment:** Do team members want to participate on the team? Do team members feel the team mission is important? Are members committed to accomplish the team mission and expected outcomes? Do team members expect their skills to grow and develop on the team? Are team members excited and challenged by the team opportunity?

(4) **Control:** Does the team have enough freedom and empowerment to feel the ownership necessary to accomplish its charter? At the same time do team members clearly understand their boundaries? How far may members go in pursuit of solutions?

(5) **Communication:** Are team members clear about the priority of their tasks? Is there an established method for the teams to give feedback and receive honest performance feedback? Does the organization provide important business information regularly? Are necessary conflicts raised and addressed?

(6) **Creative Innovation:** Is the organization really interested in change? Does it value creative thinking, unique solutions and new ideas? Does it reward people who take reasonable risks to make improvements? Does it provide the training, education, access to books and films and field trips necessary to stimulate new thinking?

(7) **Collaboration:** Does the team understand team and group process? Do members understand the stages of group development? Are team members working together effectively interpersonally? Do all team members understand the roles and responsibilities of team members? Team leaders? Team recorders?

(8) **Charter:** Has the team taken its assigned areas of responsibility and designed its own mission, vision and strategies to accomplish the mission. Has the team defined and communicated its goals; its anticipated outcomes and contributions, its timelines, and how it will measure both the outcomes of its work and the process the team followed to accomplish their tasks?

Research Methodology

Research methodology comprises the research design, sample design, sources of data, selection of data, various designs and techniques used for analyzing the data. The methodology used for the study at hand is as under:

Research Design

The research design used for the research problem in hand is causal research as the objective is to determine which variable might be causing certain behavior, i.e. whether there is a cause and effect relationship between variables. In order to determine cause and effect, it is important to hold the variable that is assumed to cause the change in the other variable, constant, and then measure the changes in the other variable. This type of research is very complex and the researcher can never be completely certain that there are not other factors influencing the causal relationship, especially when dealing with people's attitudes and motivations.

Sample Design

The sample design adopted for the research problem in hand is convenience random sampling. The following points are also included in sample design for the purpose of the study:

The sample size for the study was 200. The sample unit of the study includes male and female employees of sample area. The sample area for the study in hand was Jodhpur city of Rajasthan.

Methods of Data Collection

For the study in hand, both the primary and secondary data were collected. The sources of collecting both the data are as follows:

- **Sources of Primary Data:** The primary data for the study was collected directly from target respondents through structured questionnaire. This questionnaire includes the personal information about the respondents. The questions asked to respondents were related to their leader's behavior on workplace.
- **Sources of Secondary Data:** The secondary data for the study was collected from different sources such as technical and trade journals, articles, newspapers, magazines,

Internet, periodicals, books, reports and publication of associations related to consumer durable industry.

Tools for Analysis of Data

Along with the usual statistical tools such as tables, percentages, Chi-square test was used for analyzing the data which helps in arriving at sound conclusions.

Results and Interpretations

Hypothesis

Null Hypothesis

H_0: There is no significant difference between all the factors influencing effective team work, i.e. all the factors have equal role in influencing the team work.

Alternate Hypothesis

Ha: There is significant difference between all the factors influencing effective team work, i.e. all the factors do not have equal role in influencing the team work.

Impact on	*Factors influencing effective team work*								*Total*
	Factor 1	*Factor 2*	*Factor 3*	*Factor 4*	*Factor 5*	*Factor 6*	*Factor 7*	*Factor 8*	
	No.	No.	No.	No.	No.	No.	No.	No.	
Productivity	22	28	25	25	24	26	27	23	200

df = 7, Result is highly insignificant ($p < 0.01$)

The above table indicates that there is insignificant difference between the factors influencing team work. The calculated value of chi-square is much greater than the table value which means that the calculated value cannot be said to have arisen just because of chance. It is insignificant. Hence, the null hypothesis is accepted and alternate hypothesis is rejected.

Conclusion

Executives, managers, and organization staff members universally explore ways to improve business results and profitability. Many views team-based, horizontal, organization structures as the best design for involving all employees in creating business success. No matters how the team-based improvement efforts, continuous improvement, and total quality, lean manufacturing or self-directed work teams, striving to improve results for customers. Few organizations, however, are totally pleased with the results their improvement efforts produce. Organizations that want to stay competitive in the years to come must strategically redefine their operations to work harmoniously with these changes. In the new economy, fluid business models are rewarded, and inflexible models are pummeled. Organization structures, leadership and management styles are evolving in recognition of this reality and with them, new strategies to manage talent are emerging.

REFERENCES

"What is team building?". BusinessDictionary.com. Retrieved 15 May 2012.

"Creative Team Building Activities and Exercises". Managerial Skills. Retrieved 15 May 2012.

Heathfield, Susan M. "How to Build Powerfully Successful Work Teams". About.com. Retrieved 15 May 2012.

LaFasto, Frank M.J.; Larson, Carl (August 2001). *When Teams Work Best.* Thousand Oaks, CA: Sage.

Hackman, Michael Z.; Craig E. Johnson (2009). *Leadership: A Communication Perspective* (Fifth ed.). Long Grove, Illinois: Waveland Press, Inc.

Hackman, Michael Z.; Craig E. Johnson (2008). "7". *Leadership: A Communication Perspective* (Fifth ed.). Long Grove, Illinois: Waveland Press, Inc.

Heathfield, Susan M. "Keys to Team Building Success". Retrieved 26 March 2012.

Henry George Liddell, Robert Scott, *A Greek-English Lexicon*, on Perseus Digital Library.

The Saylor Foundation. "Unemployment Rate." pp. 1[1] Retrieved June 20, 2012.

http://data.bls.gov/PDQ/servlet/SurveyOutputServlet?data_tool=latest_numbers&series_id=LNS11300000&years_option=specific_years&include_graphs=true&to_month=1&from_month=2

http://data.bls.gov/PDQ/servlet/SurveyOutputServlet?data_tool=latest_numbers&series_id=LNS11300002&years_option=specific_years&include_graphs=true&to_year=2006&from_month=3

Breaking down the male participation rate by age bracket shows a marked decline in participation among men 55 and over from approximately 71% in 1948 to 44% in 2005 [2]. Among younger age groups a decline is noticeable, but not nearly as drastic.

Peter Barth and Dennis Heffley "Taking Apart Taking Part: Local Labor Force Participation Rates" University of Connecticut, 2004.

Seager, Joni, 2008. The Penguin Atlas of Women in the World. 4th ed. New York: Penguin Books. Part 5.

http://en.wikipedia.org/wiki/Informal_sector

CHAPTER 26

MANAGING HUMAN RESOURCES IN TEA INDUSTRY: NEW CHALLENGES IN NEW ERA

–*Sanjib Bhattacharjee*

ABSTRACT

Tea industry is one of the most important export-oriented industries of India. The industry is having a history of more than 170 years and for the last 150 years India is maintaining its command as the market leader. Tea industry provides employment of more than one million workers. It is a labour-intensive industry and more than ninety per cent of the workers are unskilled and are paid very low rates of wages. The Human Resource Management (HRM) in tea industry shows its indifferent and unique approaches which are being challenged in the new era. A micro level study on three tea estates under Indian Tea Association shows that there is no steady recruitment policy to acquire the best human resources, nor such practice is there to allow promotion and development of workers. The HRM practice in tea industry also does not encourages workers' participation in management.

The age-old practice of human resource management in tea industry is facing challenges in the new era as evident from the reported cases of deplorable industrial relation over the last few years. The challenges faced by tea industry are evolving with the ever transforming scenario in the globalised business world. It is urgently necessary that a total change in the perception and practice should be made so that the existence of every worker is recognized and a congenial corporate environment is to be developed for further growth of the industry.

Introduction

India accounts for 27 per cent of world production of tea and 13 per cent of world tea trade.[1] Tea industry occupies a very important place in Indian economy. It is also one of the traditional industries of the country, which for a long time has remained an important export-oriented industry of India. It was in the early part of the 19th century, the British merchants had initiated tea plantation in Assam. Later on, tea cultivation was started in the States of West Bengal, Tamil Nadu and Kerala. Since 1938, India is exporting tea to other countries. Having a history of 170 years,[2] tea industry is the only industry, where India is maintaining its command as market leader for the last 150 years.[3]

The export of tea is around 20 percent of domestic production. The country produces around 850 million kg tea per annum.[4] With a total annual turn over of 1000 crores,[5] tea industry provides direct employment of more than one million workers.[6]

Keeping in view the century old history of the industry and its command in the national economy; and also the vast number of human resources engaged in the industry, this paper is designed to make an in-depth study on some issues of HRM in tea industry as being characterised by increased number of qualified workers, their changed perception, globalisation and the advancement in information technology.

HRM is the planning, organizing, directing and controlling of the procurement, development, compensation, integration, maintenance and separation of human resources to the end that individual, organizational and social objectives are accomplished.[7]

HRM, or as it was semantically termed as personnel management is the application of management functions and principles. The functions and principles are applied to acquisition, developing, maintaining and remunerating employees in organization.[8] HRM is a vast subject. All the major activities relating to the working life of a worker from the time of his or her entry in the organization until he or she leaves , comes under the purview of HRM. Specifically, the activities include human resource planning, job analysis and design, recruitment and selection, orientation and placement, training and development, performance appraisal and job evaluation, creative remuneration, motivation and communication, welfare, safety and health, industrial relation and the like.[9]

Among all the objectives of HRM, development of workers is one of the most important one. Development of workers refers to those learning opportunities designed to help employees grow.[10] Development is most primarily skill oriented. Instead, it provides general knowledge and attitude which will be helpful to employees in higher positions. Development of workers can be achieved by training. Training indicates any attempt to improve current or future employee performance by increasing his ability to perform through learning, usually by changing the employee's attitude or increasing his or her skills and knowledge.[11] Training brings development among workers. Development is expected to be reflected not only on the improved skills; or only for a worker to be better position for a placement in a higher post or position; but also an attitudinal change towards the organization. Positive attitudinal change improves the sense of belongingness towards the organization, which will bring in better industrial relation, better understanding in conflict solution among workers and management.

Keeping in view the large number of human resources encourages engaged in tea industry, which is having a century-old history, it has become necessary to study the important issues of HRM as being practiced over the years; and the problems and challenges being faced by the industry in the new era.

Human resources engaged in tea industry are mainly of four categories, viz. management or executive level, administrative or clerical, technical or skilled and non-technical or unskilled or semi-skilled.

The non-technical unskilled or semi-skilled staff consist of more than ninety per cent of the total workforce engaged in the industry. These workers perform mainly the following functions:

(a) **Cultivation:** As an agro-based industry, cultivation is a continuous activity in tea industry. These activities include chilling, levelling, weeding, forking, cleaning creepers, deepening drains, cleaning drains, manuring and sickling, etc.

(b) Spraying of foliar, weedcide, pesticide, insecticide, etc., which remains a continuous activity in tea industry.

(c) **Shed Nursery and Tea Nursery:** These include planting sheds, making beds, staking, transplanting, sorting, weeding, bag filling, etc. It is mainly the male workers who are engaged in such activities.

(d) **Infilling Tea:** These include infilling plants, carrying plants, digging pit, staking, etc., such activities are also done by male workers.

(e) **Prunning:** This is mainly a seasonal activity, which is necessary for keeping tea plants in proper size. Though dominated by male, yet female workers are also engaged in this activity.

(f) **Plucking:** This is the day-to-day activity of tea industry. Baring the dry off season, plucking is the activity which is done on routine basis. This activity is dominated mainly by female workers. But a sizeable number of adolescents, both boys and girls are also found to be engaged in plucking.

Considering the variety of activities being undertaken by more than ninety per cent of the workforce, it is interesting to make analysis of the human resource practice being followed in tea industry over the years. A micro level survey has been conducted in three tea estates of Assam, viz., Doloo, Bicrampore, and Jellalpore. Our survey highlighted the following, which may be considered as sufficient to give an insight view about the HRM practice being followed in tea industry.

1. **Recruitment Policy:** Recruitment is the process of finding and attracting capable applicants for employment.[12] Recruitment represents the first contact that a company makes with potential employees.[13]

   It is found in our study that in all the three tea estates under the Indian Tea Association, which employ individually one thousand workers; and majority of them, both males and females, are employed as adolescent workers, on casual basis. On attaining the age of majority, they are generally inducted as permanent employees. There is a total absence of employment notification or open interview system. Each individual tea estate has its own colony of workers, whose forefathers were originally employed by the then British planters. Children of the workers are inducted as tea garden labourers when they grow up. This is the age-old recruitment practice of the tea industry.

2. **Training Facilities:** Training is an attempt to improve current or future employee performance by increasing an employee's ability to perform through learning, usually by changing the employee's attitude or increasing his or her skills and knowledge.[14] Training need to bring development of employees. Development refers to those learning opportunities designed to help employees grow.[15]

   But none of the tea estates in our study does have any formal training arrangement or system. Workers, when inducted, are generally put in to workplace under a senior worker. After a period of two to three months, they are expected to be competent workers.

3. **Development of Workers:** Developmental programmes are meant for employees in order to make them competent to hold higher positions in future. But this concept of development is found almost absent in tea industry. The workers, known as labourers, are appointed as labourers to be retired as labourers only. No such instance is noticed in any of the tea estates where a labourer is promoted to an executive or supervisory cadre. However, the system of promotion or development is not totally uncommon to administrative or executive staff. But as far as the labourers are concerned, a total mental set up has been apathetically developed to born as labourers, live as labourers and to die as labourers only. System of job evaluation or performance analysis is not practiced in tea industry.
4. **Motivation:** Motivation means the set of forces that cause people to behave in certain ways. It is the result of process, internal or external to the individual, that arose enthusiasm and persistence to pursue a certain course of action.[16] There are different approaches to motivate the employees. But, in tea industry, the only motivational approach being followed is the carrot and stick approach. No work, no pay is the strict policy being followed over the years. The workers are to work to meet their physiological needs only. Such an approach followed in tea industry cannot be considered as conducive to motivate the workers. Tea industry, in our micro-level study shows, is yet to actualise the fact that highly motivated workers are more productive than apathetic workers.
5. **Workers' Participation in Management:** Workers' participation in management, in actual practice, amounts to the workers having a share in the reaching of final managerial decisions in an enterprise.[17] There are different modes of participation. But this concept of human resource management is almost absent in tea industry. Business decisions are taken by the management; and there is no scope for the unskilled workers to have their participation in decision making. However, in case of reported disputes regarding economic as well as non-economic matters, some instances of collective bargaining have been reported. The trade unions generally represents the workers in the matters of disputes. However, collective bargaining is not well encouraged in tea industry according to the opinion of trade unionists.

The micro-level study on the three tea estates points out some important facts relating to the HRM practice in the age-old tea industry, which may be pointed out as follows:

(a) The recruitment policy followed in tea industry is conventional, unique of its own way and does not follow any accepted principle of human resource planning.

(b) There is, as such, no policy of employee training and development and because of this the motivational level of workers in tea industry is not encouraging.

(c) The existing human resource management policy of tea industry allows very limited scope of promotion and development of workers.

(d) The vertical organizational structure followed in tea industry does not encourage group cohesiveness.

(e) There is a total absence of workers' participation in management in tea industry.

The age-old HRM policy followed in tea industry is to induct workers on daily wage basis. A labourer, once joins in a tea estate can be promoted at best, to the level of 'sardar' or group leader. Development of workers in proper sense hardly takes place; which shows the indifferent ways of human resource management in tea industry. This principle is responsible for the workers to believe that they are dependant on others and that their own effort will have little impact on performance. This powerlessness contributes to the frustrating experience of low self-efficacy.[17]

The age-old practice of HRM in tea industry is facing a tremendous challenge in the new era as evident from the reported cases of deplorable industrial relation over the last few years. Labour unrest is increasing day by day and the management is failing terribly to handle the labour problems. As a result, the industry is suffering, not only in terms of total production, but also in terms of its long-standing reputation as an export-oriented industry.

Actually, the approach in the new era has brought about new challenges for human resource management. David Ulrich,[19] renowned HR expert and practitioner has identified some issues for this change like:

- globalisation
- managing the value chain for business competitiveness
- profitability through cost and growth
- capability focus
- organizational change
- technology; and
- transforming the organization.

An industry like tea which can provide direct employment of million of people and which has its product for trading in international market will obviously be affected by all these issues of human resource management characterised by new era.

Human Resource Management today has become more complex as India is more strategically positioned in the global corporate map;[20] and so also the scenario of tea industry. It is necessary that human resource elements in tea industry, wherever placed in the hierarchy should work towards the vision, mission and goals of the organization. The challenges faced by human resource management in tea industry are evolving with the ever-transforming scenario in the globalised business world.

The age-old practice of classification of people according to the work done should be replaced by talent-based and quality-based work distribution among the people so that existence of everyone is recognized giving him the appropriate and congenial corporate environment for continuous growth.

NOTES

1. www.teaauction.com (accessed on 17th January, 2010).
2. www.teaboard.gov.in (accessed on 19th January, 2010).
3. www.stockmarketsreview.com (accessed on 7th January, 2010).
4. P.K. Dhar (2005): *Indian Economy—Its Growing Dimension,* Kalyani Publishers, New Delhi.

5. www.teaauction.com (accessed on 17th January 2010).
6. P.K. Dhar (2005): *op cit.*
7. Edwin B. Flippo (1984): *Personnel Management,* Fourth Edition, McGraw Hill, New York, p. 5.
8. K. Aswathappa (2003): *Human Resource and Personnel Management—Text and Cases,* Third Edition, Tata McGraw Hill Publishing Co. Ltd, New Delhi, p. 4.
9. Lallan Prasad and A.M. Bannerjee (1997): *Management of Human Resources,* Starling Publishing Private Ltd, New Delhi.
10. John H. Barnerdin and Joycee E.A. Russel (1993): *Human Resource Management—An Experimental Approach,* McGraw Hills, New York, p. 297.
11. Randall S. Schuler. *et al.* (1989): *Effective Personnel Management,* Third Edition, West Publishing, New York, p. 385.
12. William B. Werther and Keith Davis (1993): *Human Resource and Personnel Management,* Fourth Edition, McGraw Hills, New York, p. 195.
13. K. Aswathappa (2003): op cit. p. 114.
14. Randall S. Schuler *et al.* (1989): *op cit.*
15. John H. Bernerdin and Joycee E.A. Russel (1993): *op cit.*
16. J.L. Gray and F.A. Starke (1988): *Organisational Behaviour—Concepts and Application,* Merril, Columbus, p. 104.
17. K. Aswathappa (2003): *op. cit.* p. 363.
18. John W. Newstorm and Keith Davis (2005): *Organisational Behaviour,* Tata McGraw Hills, New Delhi, p. 265.
19. www.citehr.com (accessed on 10th July 2012).
20. www.chillibreeze.com (accessed on 10th July 2012).

CHAPTER 27

COMPETENCY MAPPING: A TOOL FOR EMPLOYEE PERFORMANCE

–*Sweta Modi*

ABSTRACT

Competency mapping is a process of identifying key competencies for a company and the job and functions within it. The objectives of the present study are to develop competency calendar and map the competency level of the workforce in automobile industry and also assess the training need identification of workforce. Gaps has been identified in the competency level of automobile workforce working in two Indian companies. A total of 20 dimensions have been used to assess the performance level and identify the gaps. It is found that performance level of Hero Motor Corps employees are higher when compared to the employees of Maruti Udyog Ltd. The gaps are found to be high among the employees the Maruti Udyog Ltd. in most 20 dimensions.

Introduction

The current globalization of economy necessitates innovative approaches in managing the workforce. The fast changes happening in the demography and social systems thereof have given breathing space for various HR practices enhancing the employee productivity and growth. And one of the most commonly used HR practices is competency mapping for development of the employees. Identifying and development of the competencies in organization enable better performance management as well as reward and recognition systems leading to career and succession planning programmes. Also competency mapping is a strategic HR framework for monitoring the performance.

Human resource management is a process of bringing people and organizations together so that the goals of each other are met. Nowadays, it is not possible to show a good financial or operating report unless your personnel relations are in order. Over the years, highly skilled and knowledge-based jobs are increasing while low-skilled jobs are decreasing. This calls for future skill mapping through proper HRM initiatives. Indian organizations are also witnessing a change in systems, management cultures and philosophy due to the global alignment of Indian organizations. There is a need for multi-skill development. Role of HRM becomes more important.

Competency mapping is a process of identifying key competencies for a company or an organization and the jobs and functions within it. Competency mapping is important and is an important activity. Every well-managed organization should have well-defined roles and list of competencies required to perform each role effectively. Competency mapping analysis individual's

SWOT for better understanding and this helps to improve his career growth. This identifies the gap for improving knowledge to develop.

Every industry in the present scenario is trying to achieve high efficiency and effectiveness in order to survive in this cut-throat competition. Industry is basically classified into production and service sector. They try desperately to improve the efficiency of their system. All the methods and approaches for improving the performance and efficiency of their operations points to a basis key factor—"Skill and Competency". Skills and competency, therefore, becomes a focal point of companies, which aims at improving their performance. Every industry, especially production industries, emphasizes on skill and competency. It becomes mandatory for any production company, aiming at improving their performance, to map the skill level of their workers.

With increased importance to operational efficiency, cost-reduction, higher productivity norms and managing with fewer employees than before by corporate, brings competency as the most important yardstick for all HR-related decisions like selection, assimilation, development, growth charting and promotion, etc. The competence approach focuses on linking business strategies to individual performance efforts. It also encourages employees to develop competencies which can be used in diverse work situations rather than being boxed into the job. Development of employees focuses on enhancing their competencies rather than preparing them for moving to jobs. In this way, they can develop capabilities useful throughout the organization as it changes and evolves.

Fundamental Characteristics

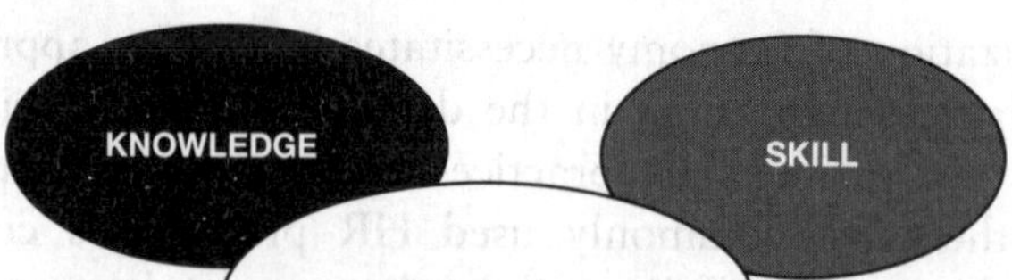

Knowledge, skill are surface competencies, which can be easily developed. Attitude, motives, and traits are core competencies which are most difficult to develop.

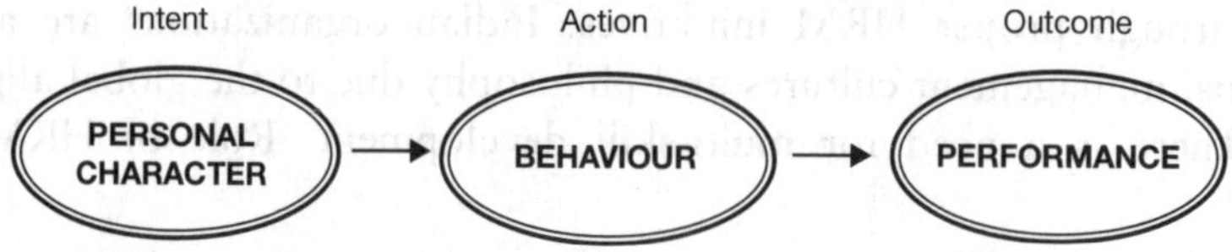

Objectives of the Study

Primary:

To map the competency level of the workforce for two different automobile companies.

Secondary

To develop the competency calendar of workforce in automobile companies.

To assess the training need identification of the workforce in the company.

To offer the suggestions to the organization for the betterment of the workforce and organization.

Hypothesis

H_0^1 : The competency level in each one of the 20 dimensions is same among automobile workforce with two different automobile companies.

H_1^1 : The competency level in each one of the 20 dimensions is not the same among automobile workforce with two different automobile companies.

H_0^2 : The competency gap in each one of the 20 dimensions is same among automobile workforce with two different automobile companies.

H_1^2 : The competency gap in each one of the 20 dimensions is not the same among Automobile workforce with two different automobile companies.

Research Methodology

The following methods are used in combination for competency mapping:

Interviews, Group work, Task Forces, Questionnaire, Use of Job descriptions, Performance Appraisal Formats, etc.

Sampling Method

Simple Random Sampling was adopted for the study. Tools like t-test were used to identify the present competency levels and the competency gap.

Data Source

Primary Data

The first-hand primary data was collected through questionnaires. In addition to it, discussions were held with the immediate supervisors and the managers of each department.

Secondary Data

The secondary data was collected through the company profile, the company manuals, and previous year records.

Need of the Study

There are some useful benefits of using competency model for the company, managers and employees as well.

For the Company:

- Support corporate objective, strategy, vision, mission and culture.
- Establish performance appraisal by a systematic approach for career growth which results in improved job satisfaction and better employee retention.
- Increase the effectiveness of training and professional development programs by linking them to the success criteria.

- Provides clear two-way communication process.
- Better understanding of roles and responsibilities.
- Provide common standards and same kind of work at equal levels that enable employees to move and work at different parts of the organizaton.

For Managers:

- Identify performance level to improve the accuracy of selection process.
- Provide more objective performance standards.
- Provide good communication.
- Develops employer-employee relationship.
- Reduces career-related issues.

For Employees:

- Identify the critical skill to perform in the organization.
- Targets, roles and responsibilities are very clear.
- Identifies the gap for improvement.
- Provides a systematic approach to improve the skill level.
- Improved job satisfaction.

Table 1: t-test for Competency (Performance) Levels of the Respondent's Present Position in each one of the 20 Dimensions as Assessed by the Respondents Themselves, Compared with Two Different Companies

Name of the Organisation	*Hero MotoCorp N=145*			*Maruti UdyogLtd. N=150*			*t test for equality of means*	
Dimensions	*Mean*	*SE*	*SD*	*Mean*	*SE*	*SD*	*t*	*Sig.(2-tailed)*
Drive for results	77.43	1.01	12.14	74.53	.85	10.36	2.211	.028*
Process management	77.43	1.01	12.14	74.53	.85	10.36	2.211	.028*
Functional expertise	79.52	1.17	14.06	76.20	1.00	12.24	2.163	.031*
Personal effectiveness & ability to influence	77.43	1.02	12.27	74.56	.91	11.13	2.108	.036*
Innovation	79.03	1.11	13.35	75.27	.97	11.91	2.560	.011*
Team effectiveness	77.07	.96	11.60	74.83	.86	10.58	1.731	.085
Customer service	78.32	1.04	12.52	74.56	.95	11.69	2.665	.008*
Self-development orientation	79.45	1.11	13.37	76.76	.88	10.83	1.904	.058
Analytical thinking	78.00	1.32	15.93	74.33	1.10	13.43	2.134	.034*
Physical ability	75.72	1.20	14.47	76.33	1.05	12.82	–.382	.703
Knowledge	80.90	1.12	13.43	75.20	1.01	12.35	3.793	.000*
Aptitude	80.64	1.09	13.18	75.73	.82	10.08	3.586	.000*
Motivation	96.07	.05	.59	96.26	.04	.55	–2.884	.004*
Communication	96.10	.05	.60	96.24	.04	.51	–2.117	.035*
Leadership	96.14	.05	.64	96.29	.05	.56	–2.127	.034*
Managerial ability	78.75	.91	10.94	76.52	.78	9.59	1.860	.064
Negotiations	77.79	1.07	12.89	74.49	1.00	12.25	2.257	.025*
Personal values	79.26	.94	11.32	74.75	.91	11.13	3.449	.001*
Social skills	77.91	.96	11.55	75.76	.74	9.12	1.772	.077
Technical Competence	78.55	1.20	14.43	77.00	1.04	12.68	.982	.327

Source: Primary Data; Note – * indicates significance at 5% level.

Analysis and Interpretation:

Research questions were designed to identify differences if any, in the permanent workforce based upon several criteria.

Drive for results, process management, functional expertise, personal effectiveness and ability to influence, innovation, team effectiveness, customer service, self development orientation, analytical thinking, physical ability, knowledge, aptitude, motivation, communication, leadership, managerial ability, negotiations, personal values, social skills, technical competence.

Table 1 provides competency levels found among the different levels of competency of respondents in each one of the 20 dimensions. All statements listed in each one of the twenty dimensions are assessed using a five point Likert Scale. The averages of all the statements listed under each dimension are computed and compared for two different automobile companies.

Null hypothesis are tested using t-test. Table 1 provides Mean gaps, Standard Errors of the means of the respondents' on the competency levels of the employees of the two automobile companies in the twenty dimensions considered. Table 1 also provides t-values and the significance of the mean scores. From it is apparent that the significance value is less than 0.05 in the following dimensions: Drive for Results (0.028), Process Management (0.028), Functional Expertise (0.031), Personal Effectiveness and ability to influence (0.036), Innovation (0.011), Customer Service (.008), Analytical Thinking (0.034), Knowledge (0.000), Attitude (0.000),

Table 2: t-test for the Competency Gap in Each One of the 20 Dimensions among the Automobile Workforce in Two Different Companies

Name of the Organisation	*Hero MotoCorp N=145*			*Maruti UdyogLtd. N=150*			*t test for equality of means*	
Dimensions	*Mean*	*SE*	*SD*	*Mean*	*SE*	*SD*	*t*	*Sig.(2-tailed)*
Drive for results	22.57	12.14	1.01	25.47	10.36	.85	–2.211	.028*
Process management	22.57	12.14	1.01	25.47	10.36	.85	–2.211	.028*
Functional expertise	20.48	14.06	1.17	23.80	12.24	1.00	–2.163	.031*
Personal effectiveness & ability to influence	22.57	12.27	1.02	25.44	11.13	.91	–2.108	.036*
Innovation	20.97	13.35	1.11	24.73	11.91	.97	–2.560	.011*
Team effectiveness	22.93	11.60	.96	25.17	10.58	.86	–1.731	.085
Customer service	21.68	12.52	1.04	25.44	11.69	.95	–2.665	.008*
Self-development orientation	20.55	13.37	1.11	23.24	10.83	.88	–1.897	.059
Analytical thinking	22.00	15.93	1.32	25.67	13.43	1.10	–2.134	.034*
Physical ability	24.28	14.47	1.20	23.67	12.82	1.05	.382	.703
Knowledge	19.10	13.43	1.12	24.80	12.35	1.01	–3.793	.000*
Aptitude	19.36	13.18	1.09	24.27	10.08	.82	–3.586	.000*
Motivation	3.93	.59	.05	3.74	.55	.04	2.884	.004*
Communication	3.90	.60	.05	3.76	.51	.04	2.117	.035*
Leadership	3.86	.64	.05	3.71	.56	.05	2.127	.034*
Managerial ability	21.25	10.94	.91	23.48	9.59	.78	–1.860	.064
Negotiations	22.21	12.89	1.07	25.51	12.25	1.00	–2.257	.025*
Personal values	20.74	11.32	.94	25.25	11.13	.91	–3.449	.001*
Social skills	22.09	11.55	.96	24.24	9.12	.74	–1.772	.077
Technical competence	21.45	14.43	1.20	23.00	12.68	1.04	–.982	.327

Source: Primary Data; Note – * indicates significance at 5% level.

Motivation (0.004), Communication (0.035), Leadership (0.034), Negotiation (0.025), Personal Values (0.001). So it is inferred that the mean levels are not the same among the automobile workforce with different companies. Also from Table 1 it is clear that Null Hypotheses are not to be rejected in the following dimension: Team effectiveness, Self Development orientation, Physical ability, Social skills, Technical Competency, since the significant value is more than 0.05. In all the dimensions where significant differences are found, the employees of Hero Motor Corp. scored higher values compared to Maruti Udyog Ltd. employees.

Table 2 provides Competency Gaps found among the respondents in each one of the 20 dimensions. All statements listed in each one of the twenty dimensions are assessed using a five point Likert Scale. The averages of all the statements listed under each dimension are computed and compared for two different software companies.

Null hypothesis are tested using t-test. Table 2 provides Mean gaps, Standard Errors of the means of the respondents' on the competency gaps in both the automobile companies in the twenty dimensions considered. Table 2 also provides t-values and the significance of the mean scores. From Table it is apparent that the significance value is less than 0.05 in the following dimensions: Drive for results (.028), Process Management (.028), Functional Expertise (.031), Personal Effectiveness and ability to influence (.036), Innovation (.011), Customer Service (.008), Analytical Thinking (.034), Knowledge (.000), Aptitude (.000), Motivation (.004), Communication (.035), Leadership (.035), Negotiation (.025), Personal Values (.001). So it is inferred that the mean levels are not the same among the Automobile workforce in different companies. Also from Ttable 2, it is clear that Null Hypotheses are not to be rejected in the following dimension: Team Effectiveness, Self-Development orientation, Physical ability, Managerial ability, Social skills, and Technical Competence since the significant value is more than 0.05. In all the dimensions where significant differences are found. The gaps are found to be higher among the employees of Maruti Udyog Ltd. compared to the employees of Hero Motor Corp.

Conclusion

Skill development by competency mapping is one of the most accurate means in identifying the job and behavioral competencies of an individual in an organization. Competency mapping should not be seen as rewards. All the stakeholders must see in the exercise an opportunity for long-term growth. Competency mapping is not only done for confirmed employees of an organization and it can also be done for contract workers or for those seeking employment to emphasize the specific skills which would make them valuable to a potential employer.

Competency is a set of knowledge, skills and attitudes required to perform a job effectively and efficiently. A competency is something that describes how a job might be done excellently; a competence only describes what has to be done, not how. Core competency is something which cannot be copied and it is the pillar upon which individual rest.

The present study has been attempted to identify gaps in the competency levels of automobile workforce working in two Indian companies. A total of 20 dimensions have been used to assess the performance level and identify the gaps. It is found that the performance levels of Hero Motor Corp. employees are higher when compared to the employees of Maruti Udyog Ltd. The gaps are found to be high among the employees of Maruti Udyog Ltd. in most of the

20 dimensions. These could be developed by giving training and personality development classes for the employees.

REFERENCES

Adelaide Wilcox King, Sally Fowler W. and Carl Zeithaml P. Managing organizational competencies for competitive advantage: The middle-management edge, *The Academy of Management Executive.* (2001), Vol. 15, No. 2, pp. 95-106.

Adrian Furnham, A Question of Competency, *Personnel Management* (1990), Vol. 22, No. 6, p. 37.

Alessandro Margherita and Giustina Secundo, Competency management in support of organizational change, *International Journal of Manpower* (2009), Vol. 28, No. 3/4, pp. 260-75.

Amir Aczel D. and Jayavel Sounderpandian, *Complete Business Statistics*, Sixth Edition, Tata McGraw Hill Publishing Company Limited (2006), pp. 375-81.

Amir Aczel D. and Jayavel Sounderpandian, *Complete Business Statistics*, Sixth Edition, Tata McGraw Hill Publishing Company Limited (2007), p. 278.

Anderson, T.W., *Introduction to Multivariate Analysis*, John Wiley, New York (1998).

Andrew, May, Developing management competencies for fast – changing organization, *Career Development International* (1999), Vol. 4, No. 6, pp. 336-39.

Anne, Lara E., *Using competency management as foundation for employee development in a global information technology company*, Proquest Thesis, Section 1517, Part 0688 (Ed. Dissertation), Wilmington University (Delaware), United States – Delaware, Publication Number: AAT 3362629 (2009), 100 pages.

Anup kumar Das, *A project report on Strategic issues in training and development in the IT service industry at Kolkata Region: A study*, Submitted to Indira Gandhi National Open University, http://etdindividuals.dlib.vt.edu:9090/303/1/Das_AK_MBA_Dissertation.pdf(2008)-accessed on 03-02 2008, (2005), pp. 7-8.

Aswathappa, *Organisational Behaviour*, Seventh Edition, Himalaya Publishing House (2007), pp. 249-50.

Bai-Chuan Yang, Bing-Eng Wu, Pei-Gi Shu and Ming-Hsien Yang, On establishing the core competency identifying model: A value-activity and process oriented approach, *Industrial Management and Data Systems* (2006), Vol. 106, No. 1, pp. 60-80.

Bergenhenegouwen, G.J., Ten Horn, H.F.K. and Mooijman, E.A.M., Competence development—A challenge for HRM professionals: Core competences of organizations as guidelines for the development of employees, Journal of European Industrial Training (1996), Vol.20/9, pp. 29-35.

http://www .Strategicmanagement.com

http://www.addedv.com

http://www.allmbastuff.blogspot.com

http://www.buzzle.com/articles/leadership-and-management

http://www.citehr.com

http://www.financialexpress.com/news/competency-mapping

http://www.hrmba.blogspot.com

http://www.jagooindia.com

http://www.scribd.com

http://www.Wikipedia.com

CHAPTER 28

EMPLOYEE PERCEPTION OF TALENT MANAGEMENT PRACTICES IN INDIA

–*Shivani Kapoor* and *Madhu Jasola*

ABSTRACT

Attrition in India is in double digits in all the sectors and is maximum in IT sector that is 31%. Talent management was initially designed to improve the process for recruiting and developing people with the required skills but today due to high attrition rate, especially in growing economies like India, talent retention has become a major concern for HR heads. This paper examines the effect of HR practices—career development, training and development, competitive compensation, quality of work life, flexi-time, leadership, conducive environment, participative culture, challenging work role on the decision of the employee to stay with the organisation. A questionnaire was developed using a five point likert scale. A sample of 100 was collected from the employees of IT companies from Delhi NCR. Statistical tool was applied to study the link between these HR practices and employee intention to stay with the organisation. All the variables except one, was found to have positive impact on the employee intention to stay with the organisation.

INTRODUCTION

Employee Perception of Talent Management Practices in India

In the present rapidly changing, dynamic and highly competitive global market, organizations worldwide are facing major decisions and challenges in global talent acquisition and retention. Indeed, there has been growing interest in talent management among senior managers and academics alike since the late 90s when McKinsey consultants coined the phrase "the war for talent" (McDonnell, 2011; Scullion and Collings, 2011). Talent is an individual characteristic that singles out some individuals from others on the basis of their level of possession of that characteristic (Glastra and Martha, 2012).

Talent management was initially designed to improve the process for recruiting and developing people with the required skills and aptitude to meet current organizational needs (Bhatnagar, 2007). But today with high attrition rate especially in growing economies like India, talent retention has become a major concern for HR heads. Attrition in India is in double digits in all the sectors. It is highest in the IT/ITeS sector at 31%, followed by telecom 26%, banking and financial services 23%, aviation and hospitality 22%, real estate 15%, FMCG 21%, automobile and manufacturing 19% (*Business Today*, 2012).

Competition and the lack of availability of highly talented and skilled employees make finding and retaining talented employees major priorities for organizations (Fegley, 2006). There has been a shift from job security and lifelong employment to lifelong learning, employability and talent management (Nilsson and Ellström, 2012). Consulting agency PricewaterhouseCoopers (PWC) recently published their 15th Annual Global CEO Survey which states that one in four CEOs said that they were unable to pursue a market opportunity or have had to cancel or delay a strategic initiative because of talent challenges.

Objectives of the Study

The objective of the study is to understand the employees perception of talent management practices adopted by the organisation. To check the effect of HR practices—career development opportunities, training and development opportunities, competitive compensation, quality of work life, flexi-time, leadership, conducive environment, participative culture, challenging work role on the decision of the employee to stay with the organisation.

Research Methodology

The area covered under the study is Delhi and NCR. A pilot study was conducted with the help of questionnaire. A five-point likert scale was used in the questionnaire to find out how strongly respondents agree or disagree with the statements. The reliability was tested and Cronbach's alpha value was calculated $\alpha = .812$. The sampling unit for this study consists of employees of the IT company. The sample size taken is 100.

Analysis

1. **Leardership has no impact on the employee retention.** The calculated value of $x^2 = 63.02$ at 5% level of significance which is more than the tabulated value thus the null hypothesis is rejected and alternate hypothesis is accepted. That is leadership has an impact on the employee retention.

2. **Flexi-timing has no impact on the employee retention.** The calculated value of $x^2 = 92.02$ which is greater than the tabulated value hence H_0 is rejected, thus we conclude that flexi-timing has a positive impact on employee intention to stay with the organisation.

3. **Competitive compensation has no impact on the employee retention.** The calculated value $x^2 = 13.57$ at 5% level of significance which is greater than the tabulated value. Thus, null hypothesis is rejected. Therefore there is a positive association between competitive compensation and employee retention.

4. **Cooperative and conducive environment has no impact on the employee retention.** The calculated value is greater than the tabulated value, $x^2 = 23.95$, thus H_0 is rejected. So we can conclude that cooperative and conducive environment of the organisation has an impact on the employee intention to stay with the organisation.

5. **Company as a brand has no impact on the employee retention.** The calculated chi square value ($x^2 = 13.57$) is greater than the tabulated value. H_0 is rejected and alternate hypothesis is accepted, that is, the brand name of the organisation has a positive impact on the employee retention.

6. Global exposures has no impact on the employee retention. The calculated value of x^2 = 20.97 at 5% level of significance. The calculated value is greater than the tabulated value, H_0 is rejected. Therefore, there is an impact of global exposures on employee retention.

7. Quality of work life has no impact on the employee retention. At 5% level of significance, the calculated value of chi square is 19.79. Since the calculated value is greater than the tabulated value, H_0 is rejected. So we conclude that quality of work life has an impact on the employee willingness to stay with the organisation.

8. Career development opportunities provided by the organisation has no impact on the employee retention. The calculated value is greater than the tabulated value, x^2 = 35.41, at 5% level of significance thus H_0 is rejected. Therefore, career development opportunities have an impact on the employee retention.

9. Challenging tasks provided by the organisation has no impact on the employee retention. The calculated chi square value (x^2 = 35.3) is greater than the tabulated value. H_0 is rejected, thus we conclude that an employee would like to stay with an organization that provides challenging task to its employees.

10. Ongoing feedback provided by the organisation has no impact on the employee retention. The calculated value x^2 = 6.34 is less than the tabulated value. H_0 is accepted and alternate hypothesis is rejected. Ongoing feedback provided by the organisation has no impact on the employee retention.

11. Performance-based reward system in the organisation has no impact on the employee retention. The calculated value of x^2 = 36.47 which is greater than the tabulated value. H_0 is rejected. Hence, we conclude that performance-based reward system in the organisation positively effects the employee intention to stay with the organisation.

12. Participative culture in the organisation has no impact on the employee retention. The calculated value of x^2 = 31.71 at 5% level of significance. Since the calculated value is greater than the tabulated value, H_0 is rejected. Thus, the participative culture has impact on the employee retention.

13. Training and development opportunities in the organisation have no impact on the employee retention. The value of x^2 = 39.26, since the value is more than the tabulated value, H_0 is rejected. Thus, we infer that training and development opportunities have an impact on the employee willingness to stay with the organisation.

Conclusion

Thus, we see that leadership, flexi-time, competitive compensation, cooperative and conducive environment, brand name of the company, global exposure, quality of work life, career development opportunities, challenging work role, performance-based reward systems, participative culture and training and development all had an impact on the employees intention to stay with the organisation and the only factor which did not show any impact is regular feedback. Earlier studies also show similar out-comes, one of the best predictors of turnover is whether an employee had recently received training (Cohn et al., 2005). Other studies confirm that executives who feel they have been made to wait longer for promotions are more likely to become disenchanted and quit (Phillips, 2009).

Future Research Agenda

This research paper recognises that talent retention is a major challenge for the HR heads and highlights the factors which influence employee decision to continue with the organization. There is also an urgent need for more empirical research on global talent management strategies and decision making in the emerging markets due to the rapid growth of these markets and the dearth of empirical research in these areas (Tymon et al., 2010). Study of talent management is still a relatively new and evolving area of research and more empirical studies are required especially in developing economies like India to better understand the perception of employees regarding their intention to stay with the organization. Also recent researches suggest that there is growing evidence that corporate social responsibility (CSR) activities are becoming an increasingly important way to attract and retain high potential staff (Macey and Schneider, 2008). Future research should examine the links between CSR and talent management (Kim and Scullion, 2011) and this could be particularly fruitful in some of the emerging markets like India.

REFERENCES

Bhatnagar, J. (2007), "Talent Management Strategy of Employee Engagement in Indian ITES Employees: Key to Retention", *Employee Relations*, Vol. 29, Iss: 6, pp. 640-63.

Cohn, J., Khurana, R. and Reeves, L. (2005), "Growing Talent as if Your Business Depended on It", *Harvard Business Review*, Vol. 83, No. 10, pp. 62-70.

Fegley, S. (2006), Talent Management Survey Report, SHRM Research, Alexandria, VA, pp. 5-36.

Glastra, J.F. and M. Martha (2012), "Developing Ethnic Talent in the Dutch National Tax Administration: A Case Study", *European Journal of Training and Development*, Vol. 36, Iss:1, pp. 105-24.

Kim, C.K. and Scullion, H. (2011), "Exploring the Links Between Corporate Social Responsibility and Global Talent Management: A Comparative Study of the UK and Korea", *European Journal of International Management*, Vol. 5, No. 5, pp. 501-23.

Macey, W.H. and Schneider, B. (2008), "The Meaning of Employee Engagement", *Industrial and Organizational Psychology*, Vol. 1, pp. 3-30.

McDonnell, A. (2011), "Still Fighting the War for Talent? Bridging the Science Versus Practice Gap", *Journal of Business and Psychology*, Vol. 26, No. 2, pp. 169-73.

Nilsson, S. and Ellström, P.E. (2012), "Employability and Talent Management: Challenges for HRD Practices", *European Journal of Training and Development*, Vol. 36, Iss: 1, pp. 26-45.

Phillips, D.R. and Roper K.O., (2009), "A Framework for Talent Management in Real Estate", *Journal of Corporate Real Estate*, Vol. 11, Iss: 1, pp. 7-16.

Scullion, H. and Collings, D. (2011), *Global Talent Management*, Routledge, London.

Tymon, W.G., Strumpf, S.A. and Doh, J.P. (2010), "Exploring Talent Management in India: The Neglected Role of Intrinsic Rewards", *Journal of World Business*, Vol. 45, No. 2.

http://businesstoday.intoday.in/story/india-inc-may-see-attrition-rates-as-high-as-31-per-cent/1/24519.html Accessed on June 25, 2012.

http://www.pwc.com/gx/en/ceo-survey/key-findings/hr-talent-strategies.jhtml, 15th Annual Global CEO Survey, Accessed on August 6, 2012.

CHAPTER 29

ESSENCE OF TALENT MANAGEMENT—ORGANISATIONAL CONTEXT

–Rajesh Kumar Pandey

ABSTRACT

"Talent Management" in the present day business environment has gained the never before momentum. In today's organisational context Talent Management is a commitment to recruit, retain, and develop the most talented and superior candidates available in the job market. Traditionally, in the employee attitude and satisfaction surveys, the areas covered used to be job satisfaction, compensation, career opportunities, working conditions, etc. However, with time the trend is changing as today's survey also includes areas like understanding business strategy and organisational direction, goal alignment, customer focus, quality of life, etc. Primarily from talent management perspective, we look into the performance and potential of the employees that leads to their self-development and eventually development of the organisation. The proponents of the thought that talent management leads to the success of the organisation, believe in adopting practices that are inclined towards betterment of the employees. In order to gain the desired results, organisations have to focus on the skill set development and competency management that leads to tapping talent in the workforce. This paper attempts in highlighting the significance of talent management and feasible process to experience talent management at the organisation. The paper put forwards an effective talent management model towards organisational efficiency. The study further highlights the Threat & Opportunity Profile (TOP) pertaining to talent management. The research design includes a survey among the randomly selected working professionals from the organisations in the region of the Union Territory of Dadra & Nagar Haveli. The study facilitates the understanding of the core concept of talent management in the light of the organizational context.

Introduction

Management aspects are deep rooted in the organisational context and majorly the management is required for the four Ms, i.e. Money, Materials, Machine and Men. The Human Resource is considered as the most vibrant element of the all the resources used in the organisations. One of the important measures of human resource is their capability to perform. The individuals perform based on their learning, experience, competencies and more over based on their talent that assists to gain all these three (learning, experience, competencies). Pertaining to Human Resource Management, it all starts with appropriate hiring leading to satisfactory performance while ensuring adequate measures to retain the workforce. Talent has become measure criteria in terms of a candidate's recruitment and existence in the organisation. While an individual shall always have the impetus to gain more of talent, however it has become a prime importance for the organisation to judge the proper talent and take every measure to ensure enhancement of talent in the employees. Talent management in the organisational context is the commitment to recruit, retain, and develop the most talented and superior candidates available in the job market. The ability of hiring, retaining, deploying and engaging talent at all levels is really the high-quality competitive advantage an organization will look forward to in its business domain. The talent management process and practices have the potential to enhance the capabilities of the overall workforce and ensure the success of the organisation.

Research Design

Essence of Talent Management—Organisational context is a descriptive research paper with an analytical study by the help of *primary data* collected through a structured questionnaire. Random sampling technique was adopted with a sample size of 100 respondents from both manufacturing and service sector representing different strata of age group and tenure at the organisations. The literature review and theoretical understanding was gathered through Secondary data in the form of the related books, magazines & journals and websites listed in the references section of the paper. The scope of the study is the employees at the Organisations in the region of the Union Territory of Dadra & Nagar Haveli. The researcher has considered the industries at large rather any specific organisation which may be a major limitation of the study.

Literature Review

Talent management is an essential aspect in organizational context. It can be referred as an important measure to value human capital at the workplace. There has been literary work done in this regard and the following sources have been referred by the author:

V.V. Ramani through the book *Effective Talent Management* has compiled the literary work of various authors on the theme Talent Management. In the words of *Parish Mishra*, the common reason for attrition today is shaping out to be the dissatisfaction with the bosses. Gregory C. Kesler says, "People are certainly the most valuable assets at the organisation. But a market where competition for managers is growing rapidly, attracting, developing and retaining key executives is possible through a critical weapon called *Succession Planning*". P.V.L. Raju suggests, "The competitive advantage for the firm is unmistakably through the quality of the workforce".

Garima Bardia in her paper "Making Talent Count" has mentioned that out of the four Ms (Money, Machine, Material & Men) only the fourth M, i.e. men that cannot be replicated and can be taken as a lasting weapon of competitive advantage. In order to tackle the pace of globalization and proliferation of competitors, it is the responsibility of the organisations to make, build and nourish their talent pool to ensure survival in the long run.

Dr. Pranab Kumar Bhattacharya through his article on "Talent Management: An Agile Edge over Competition" considers that in today's highly competitive global economy, the war for talent has transacted regional and national boundaries and has evidently become global. He states that to enhance organisational efficiency, talented employees must be provided with the liberty for change, challenge and creativity at the workplace.

Talent Management: Defined

Talent management is an organization's commitment to recruit, retain, and develop the most talented and superior candidates available in the job market. The process of attracting and retaining profitable employees, as it is increasingly more competitive between firms and of strategic importance, has come to be known as "the war for talent". Development Dimensions International (DDI) defines talent management as a mission critical process that ensures organizations have the quantity and quality of people in place to meet their current and future business priorities. The *Oxford Dictionary* defines talent as a natural ability or skill. This conceptual definition curtails the scope of acquiring talent however the growing aspirations and anxiousness of human force makes this concept as a learning tool for individuals and organisations at large. Talent is a natural ability but may be acquired with practice.

Cultivating talent is about making people undergo training and development activities and embedding learning and knowledge sharing into the fabric of day-to-day business operations. No wonder that the organisations today prefer different ways of imparting training and executing developmental plans. The survey conducted for the study highlights that 63% of the respondents (Fig. 6) consider training and development as the major source of enhancing skills. To accomplish appreciating results in the organisations, we require thought leaders who can transform opportunities in the human capital to possibilities. Effective leadership style leads the operations to success. The survey suggests that majority of the respondents (50%, Fig. 3) experience both autocratic and participative leadership styles in the organisation.

Careful planning is required for talent management to become deep rooted in an organization's culture and practices. A fair talent management planning benefits both the organisation and the employees. The survey suggests that 53% of the respondents experience training programmes as the part of talent management aspects at the organisation with 18% respondents indicate job delegation. The other possible aspects of talent management at the organisations may include employee counseling and educations tie ups (Fig. 2). The key benefits that an organisation fetches through these aspects includes boost in the productivity level, possible reduction in attrition figures, synergy between the stakeholders and growth of the human capital assets. The employee reaps the benefits in the form of better growth prospects, enhancement of their skills, self-motivation and over all satisfaction from the work. Talent management encourages the affiliation and recognition of the employees with the organisation.

Exhibit I: Snap Shot of the Survey

Table 1

Sr. No.	*Questions to Respond*	*Agree and Highly Agree Responses*
1.	I am completely aware of the organization's objectives, mission and vision	80%
2.	I get challenging tasks at my organisation	71%
3.	My annual goals/targets at work are defined and explained by my supervisor	73%
4.	My performance appraisal motivates me to do better job	72%
5.	Employees get an opportunity to get trained in the area they need improvement	66%
6.	Growth opportunities are available for employees at my organisation	67%
7.	My job profile at present matches the job description considered while hiring me	82%
8.	I find a proper work-life balance between my personal and professional life	56%
9.	Reward & Recognition (R&R) scheme at the organisation boosts my morale	72%
10.	I am provided with necessary labour welfare facilities like drinking water, washrooms (toilets), lighting, first aid, canteen facility, spittoons, etc.	74%
11.	I am overall satisfied with my job at the organisation	74%

The study was intended to establish opinions on the relevant attributes pertaining to the Talent Management aspects. Work life balance is an essential aspect towards talent management. The analysis highlights a good 44% respondents do not find a proper work life balance, which shall eventually affect their performance. A significant portion of 33% respondents lack growth opportunities in the organisations. Referring to the concept of talent management, the best observation in the survey was pertaining to awareness of objectives, mission and vision, wherein 80% of the respondents agreed that they are aware of the objectives, mission and vision.

Note: The survey results here are a representative figure and may not be exhaustive in nature.

Talent Management: Significance

In the organisational context talent is termed as the optimization of an inherent potential attained through the organisational efforts. The organisations today look forward to solution of problems from marketers rather just selling the products. A production manager today concentrates on innovations in operations and enhancement of productivity rather only manning the operations. A finance manager today emphasizes more on learning and understanding of the capital management rather only earning revenues and the overall organisation today looks beyond the possible and meets the impossible through product innovations, qualitative outputs and competitive instincts. The all-round grooming of the employees leads to success. The survey conducted for this study stated that 74% of the respondents (Fig. 5) received both personal and professional grooming at the organisation, which certainly is an impressive approach. The organisations today require highly productive employees who are multi-skilled, self-motivated and possess out of the box thinking quality. This outlines the significance of the talent management at the organisations.

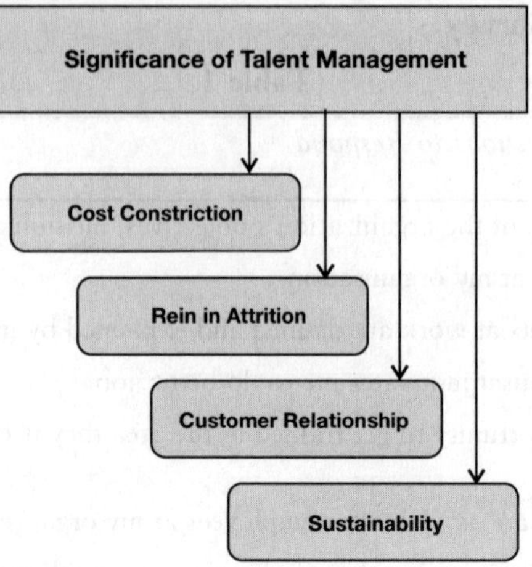

Fig. 1

✓ Cost Constriction

HRM is the function attracting more of the cost pertaining to recruitment, training, retention, motivation, etc. The fear for the organisation gets established when trained employee leaves the organisation. The cost constriction is that part of the management aspect where you have the fear of losing hence safe guarding the cost is very essential.

✓ Rein in Attrition

Attrition in the organisations today is the real time trouble. To curtail the attrition, numerous efforts have been taken in the organisations in the form of retention techniques. One of the major techniques is the employee engagement either on the job or off the job. The employees get acquainted to challenging atmosphere that eventually enhances their potential. Their inherent qualities and skills get a boost leading to effective talent management for the organisation.

Exhibit II: Impact of Age Group on Talent Management Aspects

Table 2

Sr. No	*Questions to Respond*	*Agree & Highly Agree Responses*		
		Up to 25 Years	*26 to 35 Years*	*Above 35 Years*
1	I am completely aware of the organisation's objectives, Mission & Vision	85%	77%	75%
2	My performance appraisal motivates me to do better job	73%	73%	63%
3	I find a proper work-life balance between my personal & professional life	67%	57%	63%
4	Reward & Recognition (R&R) scheme at the organisation boosts my morale	58%	66%	56%
5	I am overall satisfied with my job at the organisation	76%	68%	63%

The study reflected the responses from the various age groups of Employees. The aim was to establish if there is a correlation between the age group and the talent management aspects. The respondents of the age group below 25 years who would have relatively lesser experience as compared to other age group looked more positive on certain aspects like alignment with organization's objectives, mission & vision, self motivation, job satisfaction and work life balance. The respondents who were above the age of 35 years and certainly with more experience than other respondents looked skeptical through their responses. Especially, the results in case of job satisfaction and R&R aspect were inferior in their case. The conclusion may be obtained that the age factor and experience does have an impact on talent management aspects at the organisations.

✓ **Customer Relationship**

A set of well-equipped employees in terms of their abilities and potential helps the organisation to meet the Public Relation (PR) commitments. Talent management helps in this respect. It emphasizes on the fact that the hidden potential of the employees have to be nurtured in order to get the best of the performances on and off the shop floor.

✓ **Sustainability**

The highly competitive environment in the industrial segment today highlights the importance of distinctive strategies. Along with all the resources at the organisation, human resource also needs to be nurtured to achieve the distinctive feature. A business sustains its growth and prosperity when the mind behind the business grows. Talent management supports the sustainability factor for organisations.

Process of Talent Management

Talent management is often referred to as Human Capital Management (HCM) which is essentially a process of hunting certain selective human resources who would take the ownership to bring in the competitive advantage of an establishment. The major resource in any organisation today is the smart, sophisticated workforce that is technologically literate, globally alert and professionally responsive. Talent management is an attempt for end to end process of planning, recruiting, developing, engaging, managing and compensating employees in the organization with the aim to find the right person to the right position. The major input for a talent management process would be the best of the breed hiring and the obvious output would be a workforce with a differentiating feature leading to successful attainment of the organisational goals. The in-between process of talent management is detailed below:

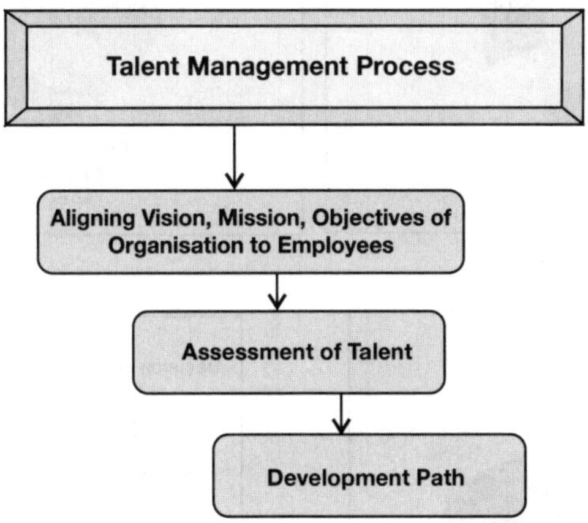

Fig. 2

✓ **Aligning Vision, Mission, Objectives of Organisation to Employees**

The new recruits need to go through an induction programme pertaining to the values of the organisation which would lead to alignment of organisational instinct to Employees expectation. The vision, mission and objectives of the organisation need to be clearly explained to the employees in order to experience a like-minded environment.

✓ **Assessment of Talent**

The inducted employees need to go through a progressive assessment of the talent. Talent is the inherent quality of people, which may undergo a series of modulation to achieve the best of the human potential. The thought process and knowledge gained in the journey of learning are the two core determiners of the capacities or the capabilities of an employee. This shall now lead to formation of roles and responsibilities.

✓ **Development Path**

Once the goal alignment is accomplished and the assessment is completed through the assignment of roles and responsibilities, it is the time to plan the further developmental path of the employee. Growing up the ladder will never be achievable if the scope of expectation is not raised. The organisations go for the career development plans including the succession planning route. This collective effort of the organisation and the employee shall lead to the outstanding performance.

Exhibit III

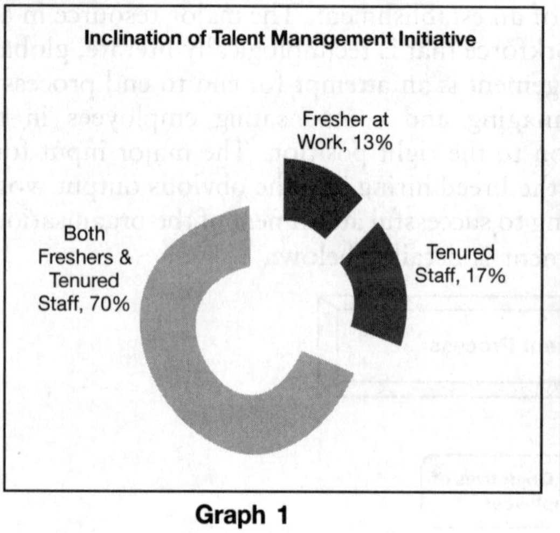

Graph 1

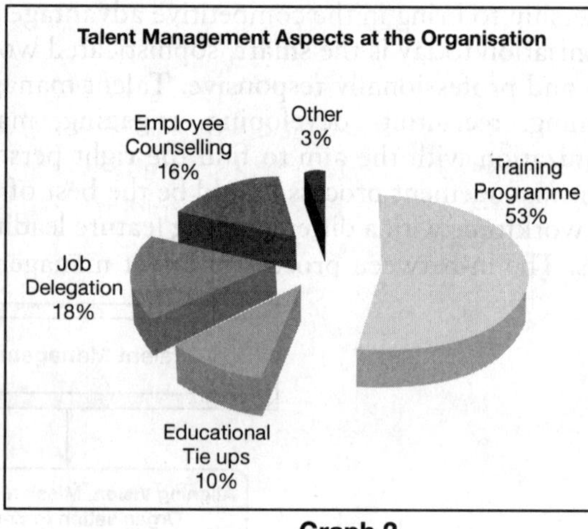

Graph 2

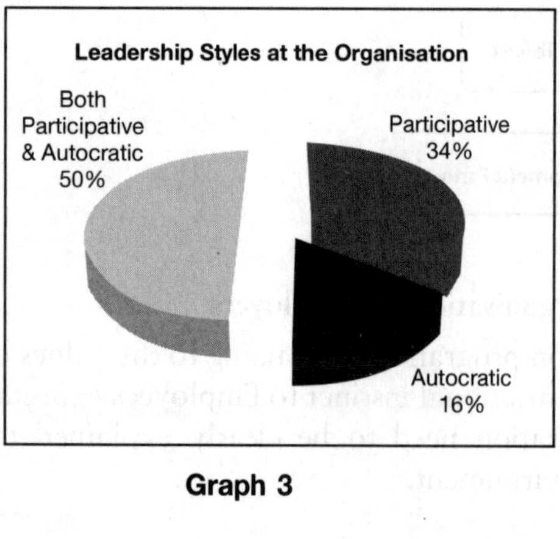

Graph 3

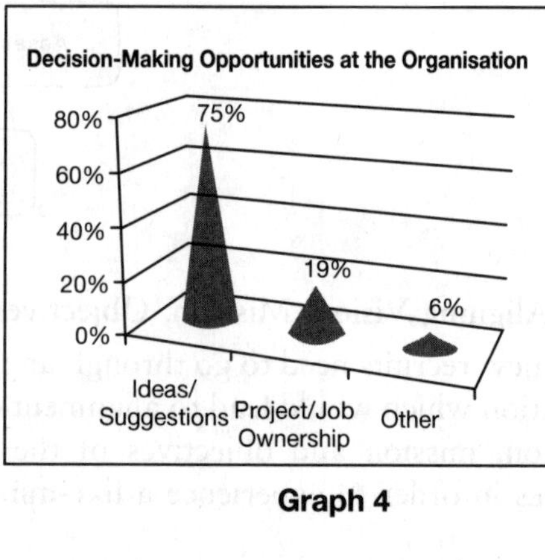

Graph 4

Effective Talent Management Model

The effective talent management will have to undergo the following exercise in order to achieve the desired level of human excellence at the organisations:

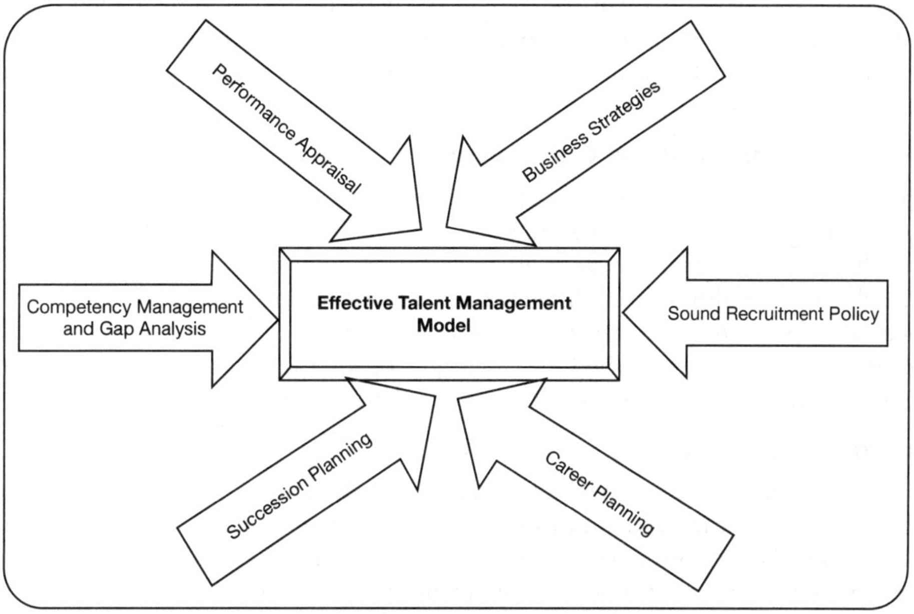

Fig. 3

✓ **Business Strategies**

The individual goals at the organisations need to be aligned to the business goals in order to reach the desired results. As per the survey 80% respondents (Table 1) were aware of the organization's objectives, mission and vision, which signifies a positive sign. People development and progress may be the centre of the business strategies to boost the talent management aspects at the organisation.

✓ **Sound Recruitment Policy**

Recruitment is the first touch point of the employee with the organisation. A sound policy in this regard shall lead to future gains for organisations. Employee referrals are the preferred source of recruitment today as it gives a feel of belongingness to the Employees as well and they refer the best of the breed for recruitment. Talent management becomes pretty achievable when the hiring goes hand-in-hand with the business strategies and policies.

✓ **Career Planning**

In the organisational context, it is the employee's career that the management plans and develops a module to empower the employees. Career planning involves core process of determining the pathway for the employees to grow and mature in the organisation with added flavor of qualification, competency and job excellence. The major ways of career planning includes internal job postings (IJPs), educational tie ups, training and development, etc. Effective career planning proves as a catalyst to talent management.

✓ **Succession Planning**

Succession planning is to identify, develop and make the people ready to occupy higher level jobs as and when they fell vacant. Organisations appraise employee potentialities, identify competency gaps and develop them for higher and varied jobs. A proper mentoring helps in developing subordinates and employees at lower level and make them eligible for higher level jobs. Succession planning helps in boosting the morale of the employees and enhances the overall productivity at the organisation.

✓ **Competency Management and Gap Analysis**

Competency management relates to the supervision of the skills and abilities in employees. The current gaps and potential improvements in the performance of the employees need to be addressed. This paves the path towards effective talent management. While an employee may enhance the skills and abilities through tenure and experience however as per the survey 63% of the respondents (Graph-6) have considered training and development as the key measure for enhancement of skills. An established gap shall get tackled through competency management exercise which in turn shall signify the essence of talent management.

✓ **Performance Appraisal (PA)**

Controlling is an essential aspect of management function. PA is a kind of controlling measure with respect to the tasks and job assigned to the employees. It helps in recording the observations from the performance of the employees and a periodical feedback mechanism helps in rectifying deviations, if any, and enhancing the performance. It is a good opportunity for an employee to interact with the supervisor and skip and seek feedback to further improve the performance. As per the survey a good 84% (Table 3) of the respondents have experienced PA in their organisations and nearly 65% (Table 4) experience it on a yearly basis. The employer's dedication towards PA practice show cases its intent towards tapping the talent.

Exhibit IV: Snap Shot of the Survey

Table 3

Opportunities at the Organisation	*Ratio with Positive Response*
Performance Appraisal	84%
Decision Making	74%
Activities Other than Work	74%
Skills Enhancement	84%

Table 4

Frequency of Performance Appraisal	*Response*
Monthly	9%
Quarterly	6%
Half Yearly	20%
Yearly	65%

Table 5: Modes of Overll Appreciation at the Organisation

Monetary Mode	
Annual Bonus	32%
Quarterly Incentives	15%
Monthly Incentive Schemes	22%
Vouchers	9%
Cash Rewards	22%
Non-Monetary Mode	
Hall of Fame	7%
Gift Hampers	23%
Team Outings (Picnics/Parties)	23%
Public Applaud	17%
Appreciation Letters/Cards	30%

Note: The figures in percentage represent the responses during the survey. Majority of the respondents have suggested Annual Bonus as the Major Appreciation in Monetary Terms while Appreciation letters or cards are the major mode of non-monetary appreciations at the organisations.

Talent Management: Threat and Opportunity Profile (TOP)

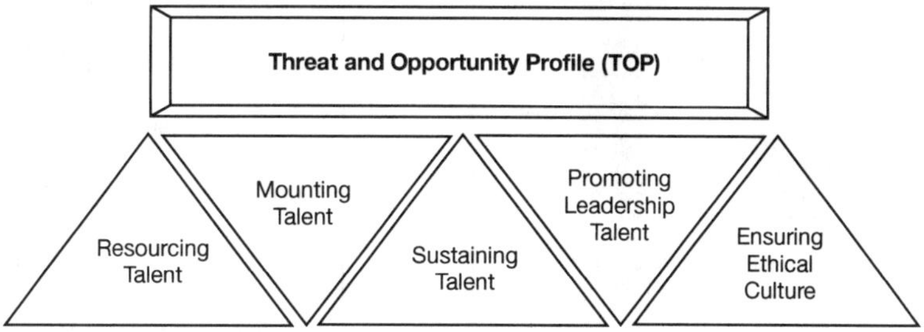

Fig. 4

Resourcing Talent

The organisations experience a major threat today in the form of acquisition of effective human resource and further more retaining them in the turbulent business environment. It is the influence of talent management to get such people on onboard, who are enterprising and ensure that an organization doesn't suffer for the same.

Mounting Talent

Mounting talent is a new challenge for the organisation. It has grown as an opportunity to train resources and seek the desired benefits. Developmental aspects range from the core process training (technical aspects) to the high-end assessment programmes leading to self-developments.

Sustaining Talent

Retaining the top guns in the organisation is the priority today. The organisations at times may look for headcount reduction however it must ensure that rightsizing shouldn't be a source of demotivation among those who are retained. It is essential to maintain a psychological contract with employees those who have been fired as well as those who have been retained. Investing on people development in crisis is the best thing an organization may do to retain its top talent.

Promoting Leadership Talent

Leadership in action means ability to deal with crisis situation, aim for certainty, set goals and driving change to ensure that the business momentum is maintained. Identifying growth prospects in employees is a critical talent management challenge. This is an opportunity for the organisation to build the force of leaders of tomorrow.

Ensuring Ethical Culture

Organisations may ensure ethical culture by setting standards for ethical behavior, increasing transparency, reducing job complexities and developing a culture of reward and recognition. These aspects boost the ownership feel in employees and are certainly an opportunity for effective talent management at the organisation.

Exhibit V

Talent Management Activities Intended Towards

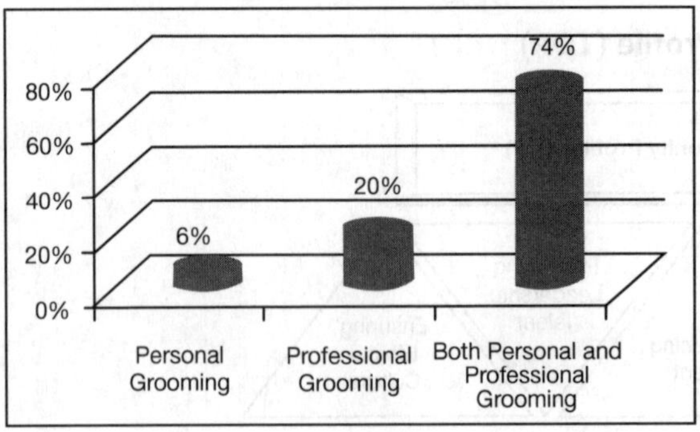

Graph 5

Enhancement of Skills Through

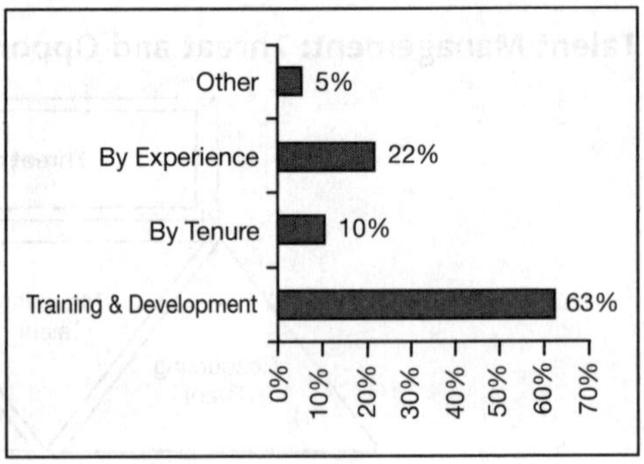

Graph 6

Employees Participation in Activities Other than Work

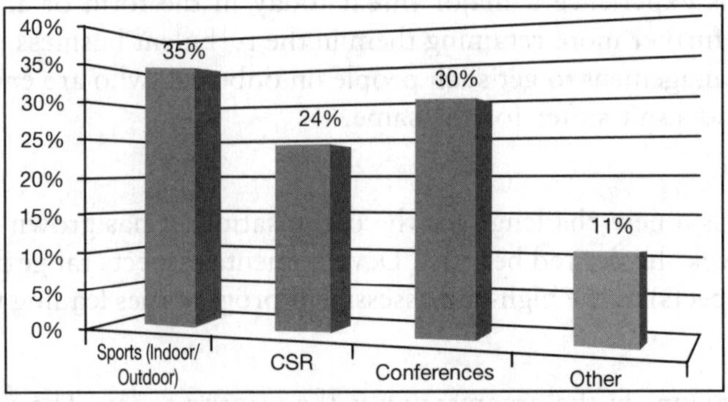

Graph 7

Conclusion

Talent management essentially is a key business process which converts a set of inputs into desired outputs. It is aimed to develop team capabilities through nurturing individual capacities.

In order to enhance organisational efficiency talented employees must be provided with the liberty for change, challenge and creativity at the workplace. With rapidly changing skill sets and job requirements, talent management becomes a progressively more difficult challenge for organizations. Implementing an effective talent management model may help to ensure that the right people are in the right place at the right time, as well as ensure organizational readiness for the future. Businesses have bright prospects with talent management as their key practice towards achieving human excellence at the organisations.

REFERENCES

Books and Magazines Referred

Armani, V.V., *Effective Talent Management*, The ICFAI University Press, 2004.

Bardia, Garima, "Making Talent Count", IUP Publications, *HRM Review*, August 2010.

Bhattacharya, Dr. Pranab Kumar, "Talent Management: An Agile Edge over Competition", IUP Publications, *HRM Review*, May 2011.

Jha, Ratish, "Innovation in Tapping Leadership Talent", *Human Capital*, Vol. 16, No. 1, June 2012.

Webliography

http://articles.economictimes.indiatimes.com/keyword/talent-management

http://www.halogensoftware.com/resources/reference-library/talent-management-during-downturn.php

http://www.managementstudyguide.com/talent-management-opportunities-and-challanges.htm

CHAPTER 30

HUMAN RESOURCE DEVELOPMENT IN HOTEL INDUSTRY

–Basant Mehta and Priyanka Daya Choudhary

ABSTRACT

Hotel industry is one of the core industries of the country. It is the main pillar of Tourism Industry. It plays vital role in the development of the country. Historically viewed as an industry providing a luxury service valuable to the economy only as a foreign exchange earner, the industry today contributes directly to employment and indirectly facilitates tourism and commerce. The success of any hotel depends on the synergy created by its human resources. The human resources appreciated in value through increased knowledge, experience and efficiency. Therefore, Human Resource Development has become very popular in the recent years. Many hotels spend considerable effort and skill in planning the purchase, installation and maintenance of machinery and often pay little attention to the need for planning their manpower requirements. New hotels and restaurants are built and almost as an afterthought, management applies itself to the recruitment and training of human resources. There are some hotels where future needs to various categories of human resource are considered and plans are set in hand for their training and development.

The present investigation is an attempt to study the Human Resource Development in five-star hotel industry. The paper highlights main findings and suggestions in the light of research conducted.

Introduction

The Hotel Industry comprises a major part of the Tourism industry. The hotel and tourism industries are complementary, and are also highly connected by the country's overall economic performance. There are many different sectors in the tourism industry, and one of these is the hotel industry. Without an adequate development of hotel resources, all the national scenery, all the climate virtues and all sporting and recreational facilities will not suffice to sustain a good volume of tourist's trade. The expansion of tourism will inevitably bring about the development of the hotel industry. Travelers are taking new interests in the country which leads to the upgrading of hospitality sector. Indian tourism and hospitality sector has reached new heights today.

Growth and Development of Tourism and Hotel Industry

The development of hotel industry goes back to 19th century. Hotel industry also known as travel and tourism industry. The travel and tourism industry encompasses lodging operations, transport activities, F&B operations and retail stores. According to World Tourism Organization (WTO) Madrid, tourism has now become the world's largest industry, ahead of automobiles and petroleum products. The hotel industry has a direct impact on rural development. The industry has encouraged cottage industries in many ways—handlooms for furnishing, carpets, handicrafts, etc.

Tourism in the World—The world tourism has faced various ups and downs during 2006 to 2010. In past few years, it was affected by outbreak of H_1N_1 influenza virus, terrorism attacks and natural disasters. Among top ten countries of the world in terms of growth rate of foreign tourist arrivals, France was recorded with 77.90 mn. foreign tourist arrivals and ranked first. France, USA, Spain and China were top four countries in 2010 with highest number of foreign tourist arrivals.

Tourism in the Country—Tourism has been one of the most profitable industries in the country. This industry contributes to substantial amount of foreign exchange also. Foreign tourist arrivals in Indian increased from 2.29 mn. to 5.58 mn. from 1996 to 2010. However, the year 2009 shows decline in foreign tourist arrivals in India for various reasons such as global slowdown, terrorism attacks and natural disasters, etc.

Tourism in the Rajasthan State—Rajasthan is famous for textiles, semi-precious stones and handicrafts. The attractive designs of jewellery and clothes are eye-catching and invite shoppers. Rajasthani furniture has intricate carvings and bright colours. Rajasthani handicrafts are in demand due to the intricate work on them.

Rajasthan's almost 80% of the places are regarded as the places of tourist interest; attracts domestic and foreign tourist.

The above attractive tourists destinations and culturally rich festivals are center of attraction for tourists in Rajasthan state. Every year domestic as well as foreign tourists turn up Rajasthan State to enjoy these beautiful places and festivals. Owing to tourist which arrivals, demand of hotel industry increases.

Growth and Development of Tourism in the State of Rajasthan—Rajasthan attracted 14% of total foreign visitors during 2009-10 which is fourth highest in all states of India. It positioned fourth place also in domestic tourist visitors. The rate of growth of tourism in Rajasthan has been sustained at around 5-7% per annum in the last few years. Domestic tourist in Rajasthan increased from 73.70 lakh to 255 lakh from 2000 to 2010. Foreign tourists increased from 6.23 lakh to 13 lakh in the same period.

Tourism in the Gujarat State—Gujarat also known as the Manchester of the East was famous for textile industries from the medieval times is visited by numerous big and small business travelers to make trade; they form the bulk of the patrons in hotels. Gujarat has undertaken extensive efforts to develop tourism activities and to attract greater number of tourists. Gujarat has immense potential to become a major tourist destination. The state has many enchanting tourist places, memorable historic monuments and sacred pilgrimages, depicting the glorious cultural heritage, which attract lot of tourist and increases development opportunities for hotel industry in Gujarat State.

Growth and Development of Tourism in the State of Gujarat—The State Government decided the year 2006 as "Tourism year", keeping in view the importance of tourism industry as an important factor of the development process and generator of large-scale employment. The number of tourist (domestic and foreign) who visited Gujarat in 2002-03 was only 66.69 lacs which increased by 85.84 lacs in 2003-04. Number of tourists increased from 121.48 lacs to 206.37 lacs during slab of 2005-06 to 2009-10.

Human Resource Development

Human Resource Development in hotel industries is a countrywide issue and the subject of human resource development is everlasting value. It has unending facets and one cannot say with certainty as to what ideal theme of developing of human resource. Human resource development is the frameworks for helping employees develop their personal and organizational skills, knowledge, and abilities. Human resource development includes such opportunities as employee training, employee career development, performance management and development, coaching, succession planning, key employee identification, tuition assistance, and organization development. The focus of all aspects of human resource development is on developing the most superior workforce. Since hotel industry is one of the most important service industries of an economy, it requires efficient workforce to render quality services to its customer. Every customer expects quality of service and value of money he/she pays, it becomes crucial for hotel management to maintain cordial manpower to meet these expectations. To train, motivate and to develop competent and proficient manpower, human resource department is essential to hotel industry.

Hotel Industry

The Indian hotel industry was a slow-growing industry, but in recent years, the hotel sector has grown at a faster rate than GDP (Gross Domestic Product). Some countries have an official body with standard criteria for classifying hotels, but in many regions there are none. There have been attempts at unifying the classification system so that it becomes an internationally recognized and reliable standard but large differences exist in the quality of the accommodations within one category of hotel.

Research Methodology

Objective

The objective of this research paper is to study the human resource development in hotel industry.

Locale of Study

The study was conducted at Rajasthan and Gujarat States.

Method of Data Collection

Questionnaire was prepared to collect the primary data.

The Sample

The sample size of 300 employees was selected for our study out of which we randomly screened out 240 employees from Cambay Hotel (Udaipur) and Inder Residency Hotel (Ahmedabad).

Findings

Some of the findings of research paper are as follows:

1. The respondents from Cambay and Inder Residency Hotels were asked a question related to functions performed by human resource department by their hotel. Maximum numbers of respondents from both hotels considered all the HRD functions were performed by their hotels. When the above functions are compared, recruitment, selection and placement rank first in order of preference for respondents from both the hotels. Career planning and development was least performed by human resource department.

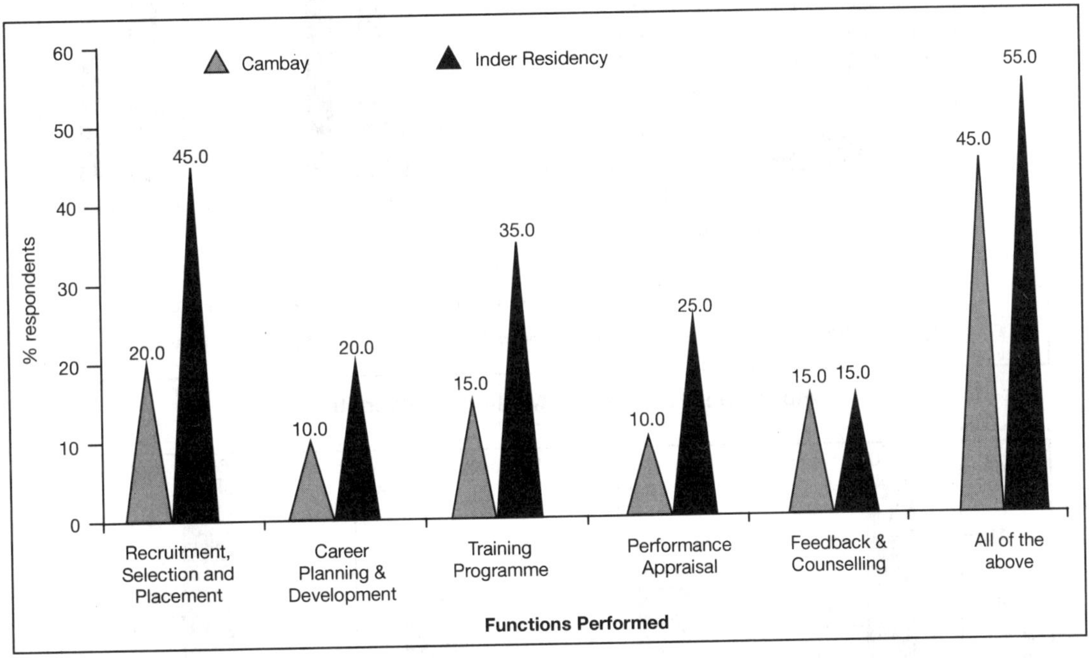

Fig. 1: Functions Performed by Human Resource Department in Hotels

2. In Cambay, "Employee Referrals" (36%) and "Placement Agency" (29%) is the best method for recruitment of employees while in the opinion of employees of Inder Residency "Placement Agency" (40%) and "Advertisement" (32%) is the best method for recruitment.
3. The employees of Cambay responded that "Reference" (60%) and "Through Investigation" (25%) was the worst method for recruitment while in Inder Residency employees state that "Employment Exchange" (33%) and "Reference" (25%) was the worst method.
4. Cambay Hotel more focus on academic qualification of employees rather than experience in selection of employees while Inder Residency more focus on experience of employees compare to their academic qualification.

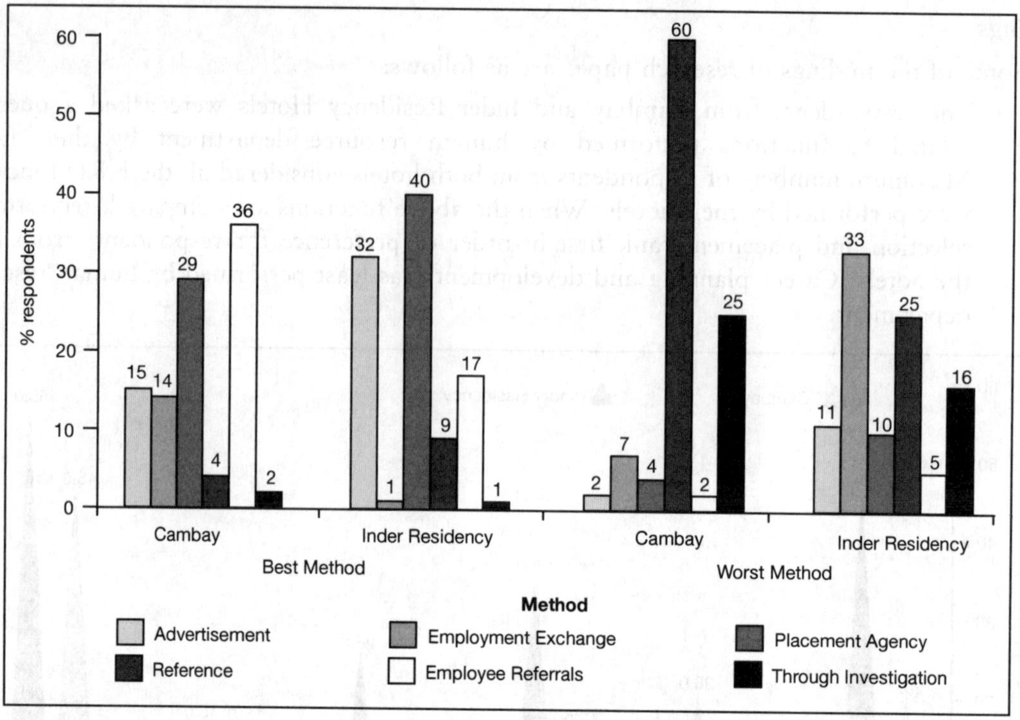

Fig. 2: Best and Worst Method of Recruitment

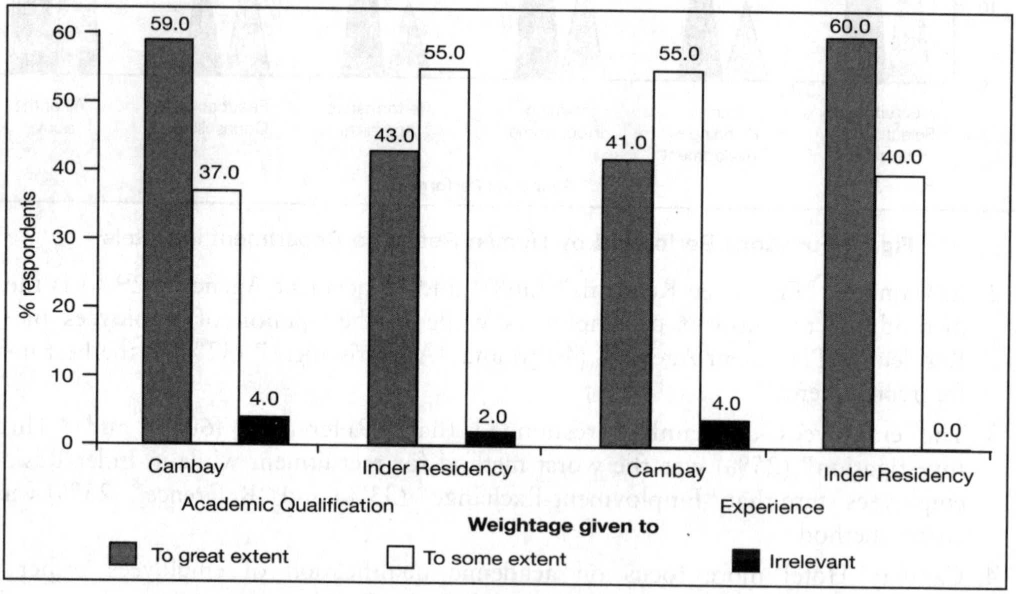

Fig. 3: Weightage Given to Academic Qualification and Experience in Selection of Employees

5. 66% employees of Cambay Hotel reported that management often appreciated to them for increasing productivity while 72% employees of Inder Residency felt that management normally appreciated to them for increasing productivity.

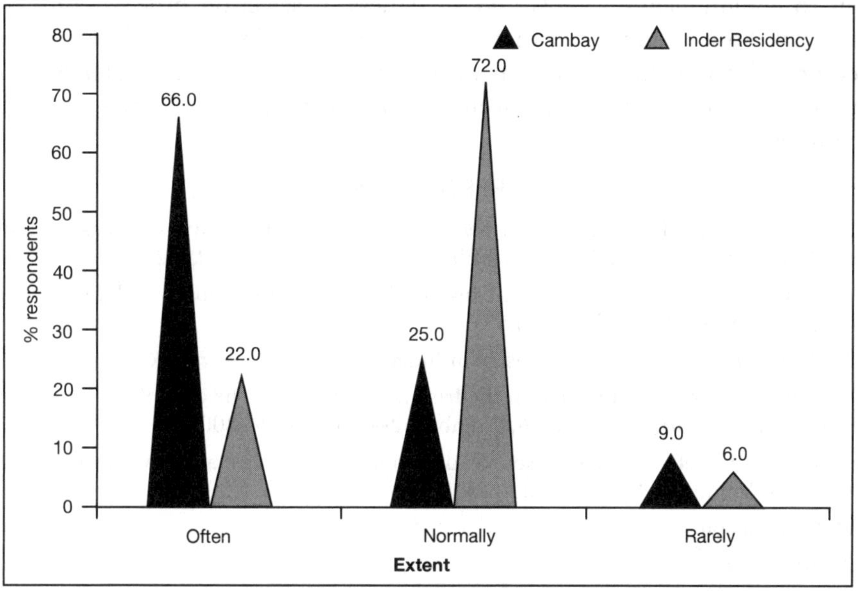

Fig. 4: Employees Appreciated for Increasing Productivity

Testing of Hypothesis

Table 1: Testing of Hypothesis

Sr. No.	*Hypotheses*	*Result*
Ha : 1	"Advertisement is the best method of recruitment than any other method of recruitment."	Rejected
Ha : 2	"Motivation method adopted by hotel management increases productivity in hotels."	Accepted

Suggestions

- According to 5% of employees of Cambay and Inder Residency feedback and counseling and career planning and development was least performed by human resource department. Therefore, it is suggested that human resource department of both the hotels should include feedback and counseling and career planning and development among their various functions. Career planning and development application can help employees in furthering their careers and also facilitate finding qualified internal employees for new job openings. Since these functions are backbone of successful human resource department, therefore, due consideration should be given. Other suggestion to improve situation with career planning is to use more personal approach such as counseling employees by department's managers about the career development opportunities.

- Cambay Hotel has given more emphasis on academic qualification than experience in selection process whereas Inder Residency more emphasized on experience than academic qualification in selection process. In Cambay Hotel, more weightage was given to communication skills and smartness in selection process compared to Inder Residency. So it is suggested that Inder Residency Hotel should give more weightage to communication skills and smartness and both Cambay and Inder Residency Hotels should consider experience as well as qualification for selecting the managers and employees.

REFERENCES

Jithendran, K.J., Baum Tom, "Human resources development and sustainability—The case of Indian tourism". *International Journal of Tourism Research*, Volume 2, Issue 6, pp. 403-21 (2000).

Olsen, Michael D.; Chathoth, "Forces Driving Change in the Hospitality Industry in India." Prakash; Sharma, Amit, *Journal of Services Research* (2001).

Kuthiala, S.K., "Tourism and Hospitality Industry in India." *Journal of Services Research* (2001).

Ciara Nolan, "Human resource development in the Irish hotel industry: The case of the small firm" *Journal of European Industrial Training*, Volume 26, Numbers 2-4, pp. 88-99 (2002).

Grant Cairncross Stephen Kelly, Human resource development and 'casualisation' in hotels and resorts in Eastern Australia. Volume: 14 pp. 367-85 (2008).

www.hospitalitybizindia.com

www.financialexpress.com

www.expresshospitality.com

www.ezinearticles.com

www.bestwestern.com

CHAPTER 31

ROLE OF ORGANIZATIONAL CULTURE AND METHODOLOGICAL APPROACH IN IMPLEMENTING THE KNOWLEDGE MANAGEMENT ACTIVITIES

–*Vijay Shrimali* and *Nidhi Maheshwari*

ABSTRACT

The importance of knowledge management has already been accepted by the corporate world in enhancing the productivity and capabilities of the organization. That is why, it is very important to understand the contributing factors at the organizational front which support the knowledge activities. In this direction, this research is an effort to understand the impact of organizational cultural factors as well as systematic approach of the organization on successfully implementing the knowledge management. For this study, the data is collected from the hundred executives from where the knowledge management is already implemented. The study was conducted in two years and the data was collected through questionnaire.

The analysis of the collected data shows that willingness of the employees and the systematic approach of implementation are the two important factors for successful implementation of knowledge management. Keeping these two factors in mind the researcher has identified three approaches, i.e. culture driven, targeted methodical and management driven of knowledge management.

With the help of data analysis, it was identified that the targeted methodical approach is more effective than the other two approaches for successful implementation of knowledge management.

This study is very useful for those organizations who are trying to get the benefits of knowledge management by enhancing the organizational capabilities. Further, the organizations must understand that the knowledge management is not merely a technical function but it is more a people function as sharing, transferring and implementing all knowledge activities are people-oriented activities.

Introduction

In the highly competitive environment, knowledge management has been indicated one of the key factors to the organizational success (Davenport and Prusak, 2000; Nonaka and Takeuchi, 1995; Desouza and Evaristo, 2003; Desouza and Awazu, 2006). This field is continuously growing and number of research studies has already established the relevance of knowledge as a foundation for competitive advantage and operational efficiency (Skyrme and Amidon, 1997; KPMG Management Consulting, 1998; Pricewaterhouse Coopers and World Economic Forum, 1999).

Those organizations that are successful in leveraging knowledge have seen improvement in customer service, cost reduction, improvement in decision-making processes, innovative and improved corporate agility (Hansen and Oetinger, 2001; Skyrme and Amidon, 1998).

Furthermore, to enhance the competitiveness many organizations have automated the operational activities and allowed the workforce to utilize their time to produce new work capabilities by utilizing individual knowledge and organizational knowledge. Organizations which are leveraging the advantages of individual and organizational knowledge can survive for longer duration due to using the competitive knowledge produced by knowledge management systems (Lee and Choi, 2003; Riege, 2005).

But to nurture the environment of knowledge management, a culture of trust and collaboration is the prime requisite for knowledge sharing and organizational effectiveness (Ruggles, 1998; De Long and Fahey, 2000). A particular culture for creating, sharing and utilizing critical knowledge is a must condition for knowledge management (De Tiene and Jackson, 2001; Ford and Chan, 2003). The negligience of this sort of culture makes knowledge-sharing processes more difficult and incomplete (Pauleen and Mason, 2002; Simonin, 1999).

The failure of efforts of many organizations in successful implementation of knowledge management has enhanced the inquisitiveness of the organization to understand the important factors and practicality for successful implementation of the knowledge management to enhance the organizational knowledge to improve the competitive capabilities.

The process of effective knowledge management implementation depends on effective knowledge creation, transfer and recycling. Two important aspects besides knowledgeable workforce for successful implementation of knowledge management in any organization is willingness of the people involved and facilitation by the organization. Willingness comes from those aspects of organizational culture where the employees are allowed and motivated to do experimentation. Facilitation comes in the form of resource allocation like infrastructure facilities, R&D labs, etc. But if the implementation is not done by following a particular methodology, i.e. the use of particular procedures and concepts then there is increased risk that the project of knowledge management implementation will not achieve its desired goals.

Our research in 30 companies pursuing knowledge activities had shown that the important hurdle in successful implementation of knowledge management is the organizational culture as the knowledge creation, transfer and recycling is completely people-driven activity. The objective of the paper is to identify the what kind of culture is more effective in implementing the knowledge management activities. In brief, we try to provide to the organizational world a different perspective to understand the linkage between organizational culture and smooth implementation of knowledge activities. Further, we try to facilitate the managers to understand which sort of culture is favorable to knowledge activities.

Literature Review

The number of organizational studies has been conducted in which the interest has been shown for the processes in which the knowledge is created by the organization. Knowledge management is the process through which organizations generate value from their intellectual and knowledge-based assets. Defined in this manner, it becomes apparent that knowledge management is concerned with the process of identifying, acquiring, distributing and maintaining knowledge that is essential to the organization. So to facilitate the processes of knowledge management, it is appropriate to understand the role of organizational culture.

Organizational Culture

De Long and Fahey put forward that organizational culture is a major barrier to leveraging intellectual assets. In their research work, they focused on four ways in which culture influences organizational behaviors central to knowledge creation, sharing, and use (De Long, David W. and Fahey, Liam, 2000). Gupta and Govindarajan had identified the six cultural factors that impact knowledge management activities within organizations. These factors are: (1) information systems, (2) organizational structure, (3) reward systems, (4) processes, (5) people, and (6) leadership and examined how these factors impact knowledge creation, acquisition, retention, and sharing in Nucor Steel Corporation, the most innovative and fastest-growing steel company for the past 30 years.

Bill Martin (2000) examines the difficulty in managing knowledge because of its intangible nature and because existing management practices focus primarily on managing tangible resources. Martin argues that organizational culture holds the key to successful organizational learning and knowledge management, and that leadership plays a critical role in creating and sustaining this culture.

Prabandh N. Rastogi (2000) supports the importance of organizational culture in knowledge management by positing that knowledge management cannot be accomplished in the absence of a social environment that is built on trust, cooperation, sincerity, goodwill, help and care, shared values and vision. Literature states that companies aimed at achieving KM objectives should align them to organizational culture (De Long and Fahey, 2000; Lo´pez et al., 2004). Besides, it may be more effective to align the KM system with the organizational culture than to attempt to change its culture (Park et al., 2004).

The review shows that the important aspect of knowledge management implementation is associated with organizational culture. Further it inspired the researcher to explore the factors related to workforce and organizational structures in the successful implementation of knowledge management and running the knowledge management activities.

Knowledge Management Activities

Knowledge is created through continuous, dynamic interactions between explicit knowledge and tacit knowledge (Nonaka, 1994; Nonaka et al., 2000). This kind of interaction is called "knowledge conversion" or SECI (socialization, externalization, combination, internalization). Knowledge management is being defined (Rastogi, 2000) as a systematic and integrative process of coordinating organization-wide activities of acquiring, creating, storing, sharing, diffusing, developing, and deploying knowledge by individuals and groups in pursuit of major organizational goals. In general, the required activities for knowledge can be thought of as being of four kinds, transferring, diffusing, storaging, and innovating of domain knowledge (Berztiss, 2001; Chua, 2004). In simple terms, the knowledge management activities are those activities and processes which ignite and facilitate the creation of knowledge. These activities include identification, capturing, using and leveraging the knowledge required for competitive advantage.

Organizational Culture and Knowledge Activities

Employee knowledge is one of the most important assets of any organization. But this asset is not utilized in full capacity by most of the organizations. This is the knowledge challenge. Organizations contain vast reservoirs of untapped core knowledge and enabling expertise. The problem is that top management usually does not know who has what information. Few top executives are aware of where core and enabling knowledge reside and how to enable this knowledge to flow through the organization. This is the very purpose of knowledge management.

Knowledge cannot be managed but it can only be enabled. That is why rather than managing the knowledge the concept of enabling the knowledge is more relevant as knowledge creation is based on human action (von Krogh, Georg, Ichijo, Kazuo, and Nonaka, Ikurijo, 2000). The term management is more control oriented and knowledge enabling refers to all the activities which functionally affect knowledge creation. Further, knowledge management depends on a situation and people involvement rather than only on absolute truth or hard facts. The organizational knowledge repository is created by people working people working together, knowledge creation relies on cultural factors and human interaction.

Conceptual Model and Hypotheses

The review of literature has clarified that number of studies have been conducted which shows organizational culture as a major causes of the failure of KM initiative (Rooney, 2005). Davenport and Prusak (1998) assume that there are many kinds of cultures, which might hinder the knowledge conversion process. Therefore, it is essential to understand the organization's culture and its influence on knowledge activities.

The successful implementation of knowledge management always requires the commitment and involvement of the employees of the workforce and it is equally true that the involvement comes with willingness of the employees. Further, the willingness comes from those aspect of corporate culture which allows its employees to contribute by providing them motivation for their initiatives and a value system which encourages trust, openness, experimentation and proactiveness.

The successful knowledge transfer depends on using and reusing of the existing knowledge, that is why another factor which is needed for successful implementation of knowledge management is methodology which includes the use of particular procedures and concepts in knowledge management.

By emphasizing on these two factors willingness and methodology, three approaches can be thought off for successful implementation of knowledge management. These approaches are culture driven, targeted methododical and management driven approach.

Culture-driven Implementation Approach

Here the open culture allows the employees to take voluntary actions to create, rather than deliberate application of specific methods. Sharing knowledge with others is considered secondary. Since knowledge is considered as power by the employees, they perceive that knowledge is the key point of success, i.e. knowledge is the way to advance in personal rank and job position. But more than 'knowledge is power' the concept of sharing knowledge is important for knowledge management we hypothesized:

Hypothesis 1: Culture-driven implementation approach will negatively affect knowledge activities

Targeted Methodical Approach

Under this approach, the organization values creativity and innovation. The defined structure and procedure facilitates the flow of knowledge. People are willing to contribute and share as they are motivated and they get the environment to experiment. Due to the willingness and structured procedures, knowledge activities such as developing, sharing, coordinating and recycling knowledge would highly take place within such organization. Therefore, we hypothesis:

Hypothesis 2: Targeted methodical approach will positively affect knowledge activities

Management-driven Approach

The major concern is with this type of approach is structure rather creativity of the people. It focuses on targets and system is more valued than the willingness of people. People are not very personally involved. In this kind of culture, organization emphasizes on procedures which results that technical people are admired more. Non-flexible and absence of openness demotivate people to take voluntary actions and this kills experimentation.

Therefore, we propose:

Hypothesis 3: Management-driven approach will negatively affect knowledge activities

Keeping the above three approaches in context, this study try to find out the impact of willingness aspect of corporate culture and methodology aspect of organizational structure in successful implementation of organizational culture. Therefore, this study examined what kind of implementation approach of organizational culture out of the above-mentioned approaches would benefit the most to the implementation of knowledge management. The below-mentioned figure shows the the utilized research model for this study:

Hypothesis 1: Culture-driven implementation approach will positively affect knowledge activities

Hypothesis 2: Targeted methodical approach will negatively affect knowledge activities

Hypothesis 3: Management-driven approach will negatively affect knowledge activities

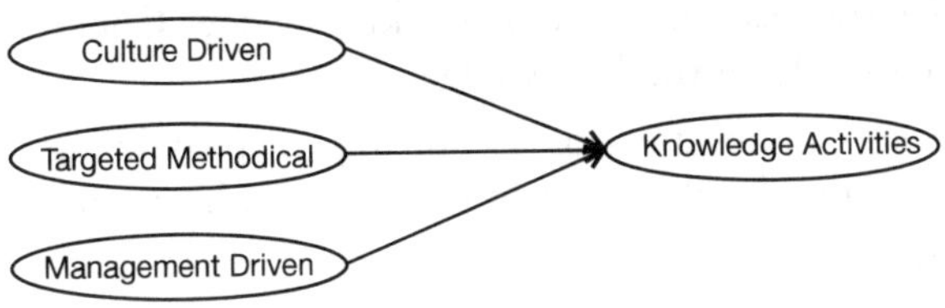

Research Methodology

Participants were senior manager who were selected randomly the organizations from Delhi and NCR region of India who had already implemented or in the process of implementing the knowledge management.

A cover letter explaining the study objectives and a stamped return envelope were enclosed. Follow-up telephone calls were made after the first mailings.

A total of 100 usable questionnaires were returned, for a response rate of 15.25 per cent. Approximately, 50 per cent of the participants were banking and financial circles and rest were from telecommunication circles (22 per cent), and others for remainder, including construction, thermal power and transportation circles.

Measures

For this study, researcher had selected the items from the previous studies conducted all constructs were measured multiple items in a five-point Likert-type scale (1 – disagree strongly, 5 – agree strongly). All the survey items have been shown in the below-mentioned table. We differentiate organizational culture into three types: culture-driven implementation approach, targeted methodical approach, management-driven approach culture.

There are four items preset what meaning of targeted methodical approach, culture-driven approach and management-driven cultures have two items for each (Wallach, 1983; Harris, 1982; Cameron, 1985; Kotter and Heskett, 1992; Randolph and Sashkin, 2002; DeSanctis et al., 2002). And knowledge activities were measured using eight items described (Bourdreau and Couillard, 1999; Roberts, 2000; Berztiss, 2001 and Chua, 2004).

Constructs and Definition

Culture Driven: High degree of voluntary actions rather than specific methodology is followed here and sharing knowledge is secondary and all are engaged to create the awareness of the importance of knowledge. Open culture is there but no structured is followed for sharing and reusing the knowledge. Creativity is admired but no structure is predefined to share the knowledge within the organization. People are willing to contribute but not very systematic in approach.

Targeted Methodical Culture: In this sort of culture sharing of knowledge is there and appropriate methods and procedures are introduced to focus creative potential on the organizational strategic goals. Sharing and transferring is more important and valued in this culture. People are willing to follow the procedures as they are motivated and impressed with the organizational value system.

Management-driven Culture: Here the organization is very formalized and structured and completely structure driven. For everything strict adherence is admired and no scope for creativity is there. People are less willing to share knowledge. Concrete methods are available but people are not willing to share the knowledge.

Knowledge Activities: Capabilities of acquiring, externalizing, and reusing pertinent knowledge, and stimulating the development of new knowledge to achieve the vision and ideals.

Data Analysis and Results

Means, standard deviations, kurtosis, and skewness for the four measured variables are shown in Table 1. Data were checked for normality, which is a critical assumption underlying the maximum-likelihood procedure used in this study. Results indicated univariate normality for all measured variables (Kline, 1998).

Tabel 1: Descriptive Statastics

	KNOW A	*MOA*	*CDA*	*TMA*
Mean	3.6900	3.3300	3.5300	3.8600
Std. Error of Mean	.11254	.09326	.09995	.10638
Std. Deviation	1.12542	.93263	.99955	1.06382
Skewness	–.835	–.405	–.611	–.999
Kurtosis	.377	.107	.324	.723

Note: N = 100, KNOWA = Knowledge Activity, MOA = Management-Oriented Approach, CDA = Culture-Driven Approach, TMA = Targeted Methodical Approach

To understand the relationship of knowledge activity and organizational cultural approach eight items describing three constructs for different cultural-driven approach were chosen. These constructs were management-oriented approach, cultural-driven approach and targeted methodical approach. Another construct, knowledge activities has eight items to describe what status in organization.

To understand the dependability of successful implementation of knowledge management, the above-mentioned hypothetical relationship is examined by conducting the regression analysis. For data analysis multiple linear regression analysis is done with the help of SPSS and the results has been shown in Table 2, Table 3 and Table 4.

The probability of the F statistic (21.13) for the overall regression relationship is <0.001, less than or equal to the level of significance of 0.05. We reject the null hypothesis that there is no relationship between the set of independent variables and the dependent variable ($R^2 = 0$). We support the research hypothesis that there is a statistically significant relationship between the set of independent variables (organizational cultural approach) and the dependent variable (knowledge activities). The Multiple R for the relationship between the set of independent variables and the dependent variable is 0.631, which would be characterized as strong using the rule of thumb than a correlation greater than 0.40 greater than 0.60 strong.

Table 2: Model Summary

Model	*R*	*R Square*	*Adjusted R Square*	*Std. Error of the Estimate*
Dimension 1	.631a	.398	.379	.88693

a. Predictors: (Constant), TMA, CDA, MOA

The F ratio (in the Analysis of Variance Table 3) is 21.33 and significant at p = .001. This provides evidence of existence of a linear relationship between the knowldge activities and three exploratory organisational cultural approach variables.

Table 3: ANOVAb

Model	*Sum of Squares*	*df*	*Mean Square*	*F*	*Sig.*
1 Regression	49.872	3	16.624	21.133	.000a
Residual	75.518	96	.787		
Total	125.390	99			

a. Predictors: (Constant), TMA, CDA, MOA b. Dependent Variable: KNOWA

For the independent variable cultural-driven approach, the probability of the t statistic (–.283) for the B coefficient is >0.001 to the level of significance of 0.01. We accept the null hypothesis and conclude that there is a statistically not significant relationship between cultural-driven approach and successful implementation of knowledge activities. Similarly for the management-driven approach also the relationship is not significant but for the targeted methodical approach the t statistic (7.724) is for the B coffeicient .663 is significant and we accept that there is a significant relationship exists between targeted methodical and successful implementation of knowledge management.

Table 4: Coefficientsa

Model	*Unstandardized Coefficients*		*Standardized Coefficients*		
	B	*Std. Error*	*Beta*	*t*	*Sig.*
1 (Constant)	1.307	.593		2.205	.030
CDA	–.025	.089	–.022	–.283	.778
MDA	–.026	.098	–.022	–.269	.788
TMA	.663	.086	.627	7.724	.000

a. Dependent Variable: KNOWA

Conclusion and Implication for Managers

This research contributes to the literature review that for implementing the knowledge activities, culture plays an important role. As the knowledge activities are people-driven activities that is why if people are not willing to share, participate and transfer the knowledge it appears that all the organizational efforts will be futile. That is why it is required rather it is a pre-condition to motivate people to contribute willingly in order to successfully implement the knowledge management activities.

Another key factor in the successful implement of knowledge management is a methodological approach on the organizational part. Methodology highlights the use of particular procedure and concepts in knowledge management. Creative and innovative methods are always required but high degree of voluntary actions are not supportive to knowledge management. It is clear from the study that targeted methodical approach of organisational culture is directly and positively related to knowledge activities implementation, as hypothesized (Table 5).

Organizations fostering targeted methodical approach culture are more proactive and aware of changes in their environment.

Its main features are that focused methods for implementation is applied which steer the flow of management between all the employees of the organization. This approach concentrates on generating, developing and evaluating knowledge in line with organizational strategy.

This paper concludes that the managers must understand that willingness of the employees and specific use of appropriate methods are the two key factors for the successful implementation of knowledge management.

REFERENCES

Berztiss, A.T. (2001), "Dimensions of the knowledge management process. Database and expert systems applications, 2001", Proceedings of the 12th International Workshop on September 3-7, pp. 437-41.

Cameron, K.S. (1985), "Cultural congruence strength and type: Relationship to effective", in Quinn, R.E. (Ed.), *Beyond Rational Management*, pp. 142-43.

Chua, A. (2004), "Knowledge management system architecture: A bridge between KM consultants and technologists", *International Journal of Information Management*, Vol. 24, pp. 87-98.

Davenport, T.H. and Prusak, Laurence (2000). *Working Knowledge: How Organizations Manage What They Know*. Boston, Massachusetts: Harvard Business School Press.

De Long, D.W. and Fahey, L. (2000), "Diagnosing cultural barriers to knowledge management", *Academy of Management Executive*, Vol. 14, No. 4, pp. 113-27.

De Sanctis, G., Glass, J.T. and Ensing, I.M. (2002), "Organizational designs for R&D", *Academy of Management Executive*, Vol. 16, No. 3, pp. 55-66.

Desouza, K.C. and Awazu, Y. (2006), "Knowledge management at SMEs: Five peculiarities", *Journal of Knowledge Management*, Vol. 10, No. 1, pp. 32-43.

Desouza, K.C. and Evaristo, J.R. (2003), "Global knowledge management strategies", *European Management Journal*, Vol. 21, No. 1, pp. 62-67.

De Tiene, K.B. and Jackson, L.A. (2001), "Knowledge management: Understanding theory and developing strategy", *Competitiveness Review*, Vol. 11, No. 1, pp. 1-11.

Fahey, L. and Prusak, L. (1998), "The 11 deadliest sins of knowledge management", *California Management Review*, Vol. 40, No. 3, pp. 265-76.

Ford, D.P. and Chan, Y.E. (2003), "Knowledge sharing in a multi-cultural setting: A case study", *Knowledge Management Research and Practice*, Vol. 1, No. 1, pp. 11-27.

Gupta, A.K. and Govindarajan, V. (2000). Knowledge Management's Social Dimension: Lessons From Nucor Steel. *Sloan Management Review*, 42(1), 71-81.

Hansen, M.T. and Oetinger, B.V. (2001), "Introducing t-shaped managers: Knowledge management's next generation", *Harvard Business Review*, Vol. 79, No. 3, pp. 107-16.

Harris, D.G. (1982), "How national cultures shape management styles", *Management Review*, July, pp. 58-61.

Kotter, J.P. and Heskett, J.L. (1992), *Corporate Culture and Performance*, The Free Press, New York, NY.

KPMG Management Consulting (1998), Knowledge Management Report, available at: http://kpmg.interact.nl / publication/kmsurvey.shtml

Lee, H. and Choi, B. (2003), "Knowledge management enablers, processes, and organizational performance: an integrative view and empirical examination", *Journal of Management Information Systems*, Vol. 20 No. 1, pp. 179-228.

Lo´pez, P.S., Peo´n, M.M.J. and Orda´s, V.J.C. (2004), "Managing knowledge: The link between culture and organizational learning", *Journal of Knowledge Management*, Vol. 8, No. 6, pp. 93-104.

Martin, B. (2000). Knowledge Management within the Context of Management: An Evolving Relationship. *Singapore Management Review*, 22(2), 17-37.

Nonaka, I. and Takeuchi, H. (1995). *The Knowledge-Creating Company: How Japanese Companies Create the Dynamics of Innovation*. New York, New York: Oxford University Press.

Park, H., Ribie're, V. and Schulte, W. (2004), "Critical attributes of organizational culture that promote knowledge management technology implementation success", *Journal of Knowledge Management*, Vol. 8 No. 3, pp. 106-17.

Pauleen, D. and Mason, D. (2002), New Zealand Knowledge Management Survey: Barriers and Drivers of KM Uptake, *New Zealand Knowledge Management*, available at: http://nzkm.net/

Pricewaterhouse Coopers (1999), "Inside the mind of the CEO: The 1999 Global CEO Survey", Paper presented at World Economic Forum 1999, Annual General Meeting, Davos, p. 139.

Randolph, W.A. and Sashkin, M. (2002), "Can organizational empowerment work in multinational settings?", *Academy of Management Executive*, Vol. 16, No. 1, pp. 102-15.

Rastogi, P.N. (2000). Knowledge Management and Intellectual Capital—The New Virtuous Reality of Competitiveness. *Human Systems Management*, 19(1), 39-49.

Riege, A. (2005), "Three-dozen knowledge-sharing barriers managers must consider", *Journal of Knowledge Management*, Vol. 9, No. 3, pp. 18-35.

Rooney, D. (2005), "Knowledge, economy, technology and society: The politics of discourse", *Telematics and Informatics*, Vol. 22, No. 4, pp. 405-22.

Sanchez, R. (1997), "Managing articulated knowledge in competence-based competition", I Sanchez, R. and Heene, A. (Eds), *Strategic Learning and Knowledge Management*, Wiley New York, NY.

Simonin, B. (1999), "Transfer of marketing know-how in international strategic alliances: An empirical investigation of the role and antecedents of knowledge ambiguity", *Journal of International Business Studies*, Vol. 30, No. 3, pp. 463-90.

Skyrme, D.J. and Amidon, D. (1997), "The knowledge agenda", *Journal of Knowledge Management*, Vol. 1, No. 1, pp. 27-37.

Skyrme, D.J. and Amidon, D.M. (1998), "New measures of success", Journal of Business Strategy, Vol. 19 No. 1, pp. 20-4.

Von Krogh, G., Ichijo, K. and Nonaka, I. (2000). *Enabling Knowledge Creation: How to Unlock the Mystery of Tacit Knowledge and Release the Power of Innovation.* New York, New York: Oxford University Press.

Wallach, E.J. (1983), "Individuals and organizations: the cultural match", *Training & Development Journal*, February, pp. 29-36.

http://www.innovation.at/wp-content/uploads/2011/02/An_illustrated_Guide_to_Knowledge_Management.pdf

CHAPTER 32

INNOVATION THROUGH MINDFULNESS IN THE WORKPLACE

–*Jayant Sharma* and *Kanti Mohan Saini*

ABSTRACT

Purpose—This paper seeks to outline one approach "mindfulness" as a prerequisite in bringing innovation in the workplace and to derive conclusions and suggest implications for research and practice.

Methodology—The paper uses the descriptions and views from existing literature to outline and discuss the definition, components of mindfulness and its functions. Based on this, it describes conclusions and implications for research and practice.

Findings—The paper finds that the "mindfulness" approach, with its definition and components emphasizes on mastery of components via mindfulness interventions to facilitate innovation in the workplace.

Research Implications—Inputs from the present paper will help future research to specify and select various interventions based on mindfulness to facilitate workplace innovations.

Practical Implications—The paper can inform HR practitioners in implementing mindfulness efforts in the organizations to facilitate creativity and innovation.

Originality/Value—Mindfulness in the workplace is at a formative stage. Thus, various inputs outlined in the research implications part of the paper, for further development of body of knowledge will be valuable contribution to mindfulness research. And hopefully this paper is a small step in that direction.

Introduction

Companies regularly face the rituals of markets in the form of competitor's rivalry, customer demand, or the fact that the firm will lose that perfect business opportunity. For instance organizations face the challenges of operating with limited number of employees in the workplace across different geographies and diverse set of employees. The sales are nose-diving and competitors are waiting for opportunities to crop customers due to workplace innovations, viz. technological and socio-economic trends. These concerns keep creeping in for enterprises and for their management and firms generally do not reinvent them when it really counts. In turn, these hassles create distraction for top management from "employees"—its key resource.

Creating environment, giving support and breeding an organization culture to encourage creativity and innovation can help enterprises on any given opportunity or even in the face of challenge to accomplish uniqueness.

In this paper, we attempt to confer one simple intervention 'mindfulness' as a perquisite to foster creativity and innovation in the workplace. As outlined above, the present paper seeks to contribute to workplace innovation via mindfulness research by focusing on the definition, components and facilitation of mindfulness at work. This paper is organized as follows. First, two approaches to innovation at workplace is outlined. Next, innovation at work and obstacles to innovation are outlined by drawing on description from our experience and literature review. Subsequently, mindfulness as novel practice at work is discussed to foster creativity and innovation in the work setting. Thereafter, some of the conclusions emerging from this paper are outlined. Finally, implications of this paper for future research on workplace innovation via mindfulness and for practice are outlined.

Relevance of This Paper to HR Domain

The germaneness of this paper to the topics of HR which are the focus areas of the conference can be assessed by considering some of the views in the existing literature about the outcomes of mindfulness at work. Thus, in the following section, drawing on some of the exiting literature various work-related outcomes of mindfulness are outlined and subsequently various views about the relationship between mindfulness and innovation are outlined.

Approaches to Understand Innovation at Work

It is the organizations and their leaders' job to pose instances for their employees to discuss and propose alternative approaches to existing management practices. For example, Manish, what is your opinion about our desired and actual corporate performance? Rajiv, is there any other way we could do our marketing campaign? Ashish, from our present employee satisfaction survey will you have a different opinion on human resource policy? These simple questions on periodic basis can bring surprising prospects and could enhance a company's processes and performance. Ardent creation of occasions will shape an environment where people share and invest their time, and, energy into unconventional way of doing things. Eventually, employees will be satisfied, loyal and ingenious.

To answer the above business risks, the focal affair essentially is innovation in the workplace, where enterprises and working managers come across ways to innovate the products, processes, and services even more than before to make people and organization productive. In our understanding managing and creating a place of innovation and performance for diverse set of employees in the work setting requires a meticulous plan. To surmount these issues related to workplace, the enterprises can do two simple things: first, understand the employees, and, second develop insights into innovation and performance.

First: Understanding the Employees

In this universe, every human being is unique. The individuality of each person is one, single whole without any division. To understand the individuality of human beings, we may need to understand the working of mind. Mind is a complex information processing machine, which has capacity to think. All the essential and tremendous work of human mind is being done by intellect. Man has made all progress and advancements in this world, by its ability to think and reason. All science and technology are the creation of human intellect. All intellect and reasoning has a utility in our life, viz. in education, social system and for the physical progress in the world.

But unfortunate part of all this progress is that too much focus is given to the mind. And mind has its own wisdom. For example, the process of thinking done by human mind. If the thinking process would have been in the hands of man, life would have become a miracle. Every minute would be filled with creativity, innovation, joy and prosperity. Unfortunately, over these mental processes man has no control. It is only because of intellect, which has become the master and has impounded mind in every aspect of life.

What is then being totally ignored? The answer is consciousness. The consciousness has a totally different centre for its functioning—the wisdom. Consciousness does not know about rules by the book but it has its own wisdom. Consciousness sees things as they are to put simply unfiltered perception (Hunter and McCormick, 2008). The lives of great thinkers, scientists reveal that they have gone beyond the mind and have seen more than what normally human mind cannot see. For example, Buddha, Jesus Christ, Albert Einstein, Henry Ford, Mahatma Gandhi, Stephan Hawking and Thomas Alva Edison.

We want to emphasize that whenever a person is fully conscious, sees things beyond his mind then innovation happens naturally with a spark of wisdom. Since this is the stage where consciousness starts functioning with a realm of its own wisdom. No matter how often groundbreaking workshops, management games or classroom trainings are delivered, they generally end up in discussion. The fundamental reason is that innovation is something forced in the companies where as it is naïve. It requires a quality of curiosity, internal motivation and consciousness among the people to be creative and performing in their work. They should know about the insight of innovation, which is discussed consequently.

Second: Insight into Innovation

Innovation is spontaneous and unconventional. People rarely innovate when they simply follow instructions. Professional life of most of the executives is more or less entangled and surrounded by a set framework of rules, procedures and systems. The lines have to be followed. So, most of executives are stuck with set norms in their mind. They do not realize the hidden traps of mind (Hammond, Keeney and Raiffa, 1998). This leads the mind to function in a mechanical way, just like a robot or computer which functions according to the feeded programs. But the executives have to go outside the rules and closed patterns. They have to break the walls of mind and think beyond.

The executives who understand the hidden traps of mind understand the functioning of their mind. And that is why sometimes they insist on not following the set pattern of lines, just for the sake of following. For example, when somebody asked Thomas Edison that you have failed again, then he said, no I did not fail. I found 10,000 ways of not doing things this particular way. This illustration portrays how exclusively human mind functions, how one person has insight into innovation and that how people (innovators) make a distinction between them and the others. And then, it always recompensed to the innovators. Literally, everybody is aware about the history of Thomas Edison. It is repaid because it always brings the person to a new territory, perhaps to his own being, the consciousness. And whenever a man reaches his innermost core of consciousness, the innovation happens surprisingly. So innovation is spontaneous and unconventional.

Innovation in Workplace

In today's global environment, the survival and growth of most of the companies largely depend on developing new technologies, products, services and most importantly their 'employees'. While many organizations acknowledge that innovation is important to their growth and success, the construct "innovation" is still without a consistent definition in the business world.

Freeman (1982) suggests that it is "an idea, a sketch or model for a new or improved device, product, process or system.... An innovation in the economic sense is accompanied with the first commercial transaction involving the new product, process, system or device, although the word is used to describe the whole process." Similarly, Drucker (1985) defines innovation as the specific instrument of entrepreneurship...the act that endows resources with a new capacity to create wealth; whereas Schumpeter (1942) states innovation as "creative destructive". To recap, innovation in the workplace can be defined as doing things in novel ways to discover new paths and methods to create economic value.

Innovation is sustainable when it turns into performance and becomes one of the most important keys to success for the companies, what Roger (1983) defines as "diffusion of innovation". Propagation of Management by Objectives, McKinsey's 7S framework, Boston Consulting Group's growth share matrix, Hay Groups Spectrum for job evaluation and balanced scorecard are remarkable examples of workplace innovations and performance that helps in harvesting earnings from innovation and performance.

Overcoming Obstacles to Innovation

It is hard to get people along onto the same page as the organization objectives. Additionally, complexities of languages, geographies, culture, religion, mental disposition, work deadlines, personal concerns mediate the communication between organization and its workforce. And without intentional steps from proactive managers innovation and performance cannot occur in the workplace.

Innovation is imperative, and it is what the firms need most to triumph over the performance hazards. Innovation can be transpired anywhere in the corporation, precondition is crystal-clear objectives, uncomplicated management processes and collaboration of all resources. For example, when Larry Page of Google wanted Steve Jobs advice, he was told by Jobs to, "Figure out what Google wants to be when it grows up. It's now all over the map. What are the five products you want to focus on? Get rid of the rest, because they're dragging you down" (*Times of India*). This is a brilliant example of having the cogent focus on objectives.

In spite of everything, the companies get swayed as things do not work. This question always leads to the analogous answers: the management is not encouraging, performance measures are not known, problem of resource allocation, incentives for novel ideas are not exciting and the classic and my favorite employees are not interested.

One of the most powerful ways to overcome these differences for an organizational leader is to create cognizant picture of aspiration. Careful plan envisaging hurdles with deep understanding keeps innovation alive with promising pay back. This is done once ground work is done to build a realistic case for renovation. Once that happens, apt allocation and collaboration of resources is exclusively realized for the workplace reinvention indispensably.

Mindfulness as HR Intervention to Facilitate Innovation

One of the simplest initiatives to instill creativity and innovation in the work setting is through the mindfulness practice. Mindfulness refers to "being attentive to and aware of what is taking place in the present moment" (Brown and Ryan, 2003), relating to positive individual focus and attention. Consistent with this definition, Bishop et al. (2004) state mindfulness as "process of regulating one's attention to bring awareness to have orientation towards curiosity, openness and acceptance towards one's experience". Similarly, Shapiro (2009) note mindfulness as "the awareness that arises through intentionally attending in an open, accepting, and discerning way to whatever is arising in the present moment". Hence, enquiry of mindfulness involves the presence of acceptance of facts, attention towards facts, present focus thoughts, feelings and sensations, and awareness of thoughts, feelings, sensations. Similarly, Glomb et al. (2011) highlight "mindfulness as a state of consciousness characterized by receptive attention to and awareness of present events and experiences without judgment and cognitive filters.

Therefore, according to the definitions of mindfulness, a mindful individual is one who is aware and alert of every moment. This will facilitate in being malleable towards workplace challenges ensuing hard work which is a characteristic of motivation theory (Vroom, 1964). Ample of empirical researches have reported benefits of mindfulness at work (Giluk, 2010; Glomb et al., 2010; Shao and Skarlicki, 2009; Tipsord, 2009). For instance, Langer, Hefferman, and Kiester (1998) note that increase in mindfulness resulted in increased creativity because we think that the ability of seeing things as they are (Kabat-Zinn, 1990) or unfiltered perception (Hunter and McCormick, 2008) creates insight into the nature of mind and people can avoid bias towards status quo.

Empirical evidence on mindfulness suggests that mindfulness can be increased via several interventions (Kabat-Zinn, 1982, 2003). To exemplify, mindfulness will be critical where diverse set of employees interact with each other. Social relationship is vital aspect of organizational life and mindful individuals will be able to adapt themselves better (Giluk, 2010; Glomb et al., 2010; Tipsord, 2009). Since they are mindful, their behavior is concurrent with inherent values and interests (Brown and Ryan, 2003).

Eventually, people can be effective organizational members. This will facilitate innovation via mindfulness in the workplace with positive individual and organizational outcomes. Thus, mindfulness is potential human resource intervention (Shao and Skarlicki, 2009) to facilitate creativity and innovation at work.

Bottom Line

Innovation does not mean doing something exceptional like harvesting stars or it does not mean to do something which nobody has done ever. It is something incremental which simply means to take small progressive steps towards existing ways with novel approaches. In short, it requires a conscious and determined effort on the part of organizational leaders to create environment for creativity and innovation, and reinforce it as company's culture.

If innovation disseminates, organization will not only be reaping the socio-economic rewards but also be exemplifying a culture that promotes and rewards innovation in the workplace. In spite of that if diffusion does not happen, employees will be satisfied and totally effective since their and organization actions are conscious.

Conclusion

We conclude that workplace innovation via mindfulness is vital for organization success. Explanation of innovation alongside understanding employees and insights into innovation is important for many functions that we employ in our vocation. For many years, organizations have not only contemplated but also given their attention for cultivating creativity and performance among their workers.

As the industry and customers become more demanding, extra attention will be diverted towards instances of innovation phenomenon. Under such circumstances, great strides are like to be made in organization initiatives towards creativity and innovation in the place of work. One such initiative is practice of mindfulness for employees to increase their consciousness for better creativity and performance.

This paper outlined two simple aspects, viz. understanding people, insights into innovation to facilitate innovation at workplace. This was done based on the definition and components of mindfulness in the existing literature which outlined manifestations of mindfulness within the work contexts. This paper by discussing mindfulness and its approach as an intervention for innovation is hopefully one step towards research in workplace innovation.

Implications for Research

The descriptions of mindfulness, approaches to understand innovation and mindfulness as HR intervention outlined in this paper provides some directions for future mindfulness research at work. In light of the conclusions in the preceding part of the paper that the approaches to facilitate workplace innovation, one direction for future research emerging from this paper is to explore and specify more comprehensive range of various forms or types of approaches to understand innovation at work.

Therefore, conceptually derived terms or empirically derived taxonomies can provide avenues to specifying classification of various approaches to understand innovation at work settings. For illustration, future research can propose conceptual classification of approaches to innovation at work. Another possibility is to formulate a taxonomy or empirical classification of the approaches to workplace innovation facilitation based on the concept of mindfulness in organizational settings.

Implications for Practice

The existence of two approaches to workplace innovation facilitation outlined in this paper may inform the practice in its efforts to implement workplace innovation interventions via mindfulness practice. Thus, considering mindfulness as potential HR intervention (Shao and Skarlicki, 2009) is reasonable.

To illustrate, it may indicate the nature of available options that can be explored for implementing interventions for creativity at work. Such approaches may facilitate attainment of transformations of individual employees, and, reasonable connection between mindfulness and individual creativity for positive organization outcomes.

Limitations

While the coverage of only approach to workplace innovation facilitation may reflect a limitation in this paper, the following points may need to be noted to appropriately view the inevitability of this limited coverage and the utility of this paper even with the limited coverage. First, to the best knowledge of the author, this is the first attempt to suggest mindfulness as an intervention for facilitating innovation at work. Second, the mindfulness approach covered in this paper may possibly yield reasonable options for future research. Thus, this paper takes possibly the first step in facilitating innovation via mindfulness at work setting.

REFERENCES

Baer, R.A. (2003). *Mindfulness Training as a Clinical Intervention: A Conceptual and Empirical Review.*

Bishop, S.R., Lau, Ma, Shapiro, S.L., Carlson, L., and Anderson, N.D. (2004). Mindfulness: A proposed operational definition. *Clinical Psychology: Science and Practice*, 11, 230-41.

Brown, K.W., Ryan, R.M., and Creswell, J.D. (2007). Mindfulness: Theoretical Foundations and Evidence for its Salutary Effects. *Psychological Inquiry*. Vol. 18, No. 4, pp. 211-37.

Brown, K.W., and Ryan, R.M. (2004). Perils and Promise in Defining and Measuring Mindfulness: Observations from Experience. *Journal of Clinical Psychology: Science and Practice*, Vol. 11 (N3), pp. 242-48.

Collins, J. and Porras, J.I. (2004). Built to Last: Successful Habits of Visionary Companies. Harper Business.

Christensen, C. (1997). The Innovators Dilemma: When New Technologies Cause Great Firms to Fail. Harvard Business Review Press.

Davidson, R.J. (2010). Empirical explorations of mindfulness: Conceptual and methodological conundrums. *Emotion*, 10, 8-11.

Deci, E.L., and Ryan, R.M. (2008). Self-Determination Theory: A Macrotheory of Human Motivation, Development and Health. *Canadian Psychology*. Vol. 49, No. 3, pp. 182-85.

Drucker, P.F. (1985). Innovation and Entrepreneurship. Practice and Principles. HarperCollins.

Freeman, C. (1982). *The Economics of Industrial Innovation*. The MIT Press. See www.wikipedia.org retrieved between 15 march to 29 march, 2012.

Joseph Schumpeter, (1942). *Capitalism, Socialism and Democray*. See www.wikipedia.org retrieved between 15 march to 29 march, 2012.

Roger, E.M. (1983). Diffusion of Innovations. New York: Free Press. See www.wikipedia.org retrieved between 15 march to 29 march, 2012.

Times of India, see the link following link. <http://articles.timesofindia.indiatimes.com/2011-10-24/hardware/30315633_1_tim-cook-steve-jobs-google-ceo> retrieved between 15 march to 29 march, 2012.

Thomas Edison see the following link. http://www.brainyquote.com/quotes/authors/t/thomas_a_edison.html retrieved between 15 march to 29 March, 2012.

Giluk, T.L. (2010). Mindfulness-based stress reduction: Facilitating work outcomes through experienced effect and high quality relationships. Doctoral Dissertation. Available at Iowa Research Online.

Glomb, T.M., Duffy, M.K., Bono, J.E., and Yang, T. (2011). Mindfulness at Work. *Research in Personnel and Human Resource Management*, Vol. 30, 115-57.

Grabovac, A.D., Lau, M.A., and Willett, B.R. (2011). *Mechanisms of Mindfulness: A Buddhist Psychological Model.*

Grossman, P., Niemann, L., Schmidt, S., and Walach, H. (2004). Mindfulness-based stress reduction and health benefits: A Meta analysis. *Journal of Psychosomatic Research*. Vol. 57, pp. 35-43.

Hammond, J.S., Keeney, R.L., and Raiffa, H. (1998). The Hidden Traps in Decision Making. *Harvard Business Review*.

Homan, A.C., Hollenbeck, J.R., Humphrey, S.E., Knippenberg, D.V., Ilgen, D.R., and Van Kleef, G.A. (2008). Facing Differences with an Open Mind: Openness to Experience Salience of Intragroup Differences, and Performance of Diverse Work Groups. *Academy of Management Journal*, Vol. 51, No.6, 1204-22.

Hunter, J., and McCormick, D.W. (2008). Mindfulness in the Workplace. An Exploratory Study. Presented at the 2008, Academy of Management Annual Meeting, Anaheim, CA.

Kabat-Zinn, J. (1982). An outpatient program in behavioral medicine for chronic pain patients based on the practice of mindfulness meditation: Theoretical consideration and preliminary results. *General Hospital Psychiatry*. 4 (1).

——. (1990). Full catastrophe living: Using the wisdom of your body and mind to face stress, pain and illness. New York, N.Y.: Delacorte Press.

——. (2003). Mindfulness based Interventions in Context: Present, Past and Future. *Journal of Clinical Psychology Science and Practice*, Vol. 10, pp. 144-56.

——. (2006). Coming to our senses: Healing ourselves and the world through mindfulness. Hyperion Books.

Kahya, E. (2007). The Effect of Job Characteristics and Working Conditions on Job Performance. *International Journal of Industrial Ergonomics*. Vol. 37, pp. 515-23.

Lafley, A.G., and Charan, R. (2008). The Game Changer: How You Can Drive Revenue and Profit Growth with Innovation. Crown Business.

Langer, E.J. and Moldoveanu, M. (2000). The Construct of Mindfulness. *Journal of Social Issues*, Vol. 56, No. 1, 1-9.

Levinthal, D., and Rerup, C. (2006). Crossing an Apprarent Chasm: Bridging Mindful and Less-Mindful Perspectives on Organizational Learning. *Organization Science*. Vol. 17, No. 4, pp. 502-13.

Martin, R. (2007) Opposable Mind: How Successful Leaders Win Through Integrative Thinking. *Harvard Business Review Press*.

Rapgay, L. and Bystrisky, A. (2009). Classical Mindfulness: An Introduction to Its Theory and Practice for Clinical Application. Longevity, Regeneration, and Optimal Health: Ann. N.Y. *Acad. Sci*. 1172: 148-62.

Shapiro, S.L., Brown, K.W., and Biegel, G.M. (2007). Teaching self-care to caregivers: Effects of mindfulness-based stress reduction on the mental health of therapists in training. *Training and Education in Professional Psychology*, Vol. 1, 105-115.

Stross, R.E. (2007). The Wizard of Menlo Park: How Thomas Alva Edison Invented the Modern World. Crown Publishing Group.

Shao, R. and Skarlicki, D.P. (2009). The Role of Mindfulness in Predicting Individual Performance. *Journal Behavioral Science*, Vol. 41, No. 4, 195-201.

Shapiro, S.L. (2009). The Integration of Mindfulness and Psychology. *Journal of Clinical Psychology*, Vol. 65 (6), pp. 555-60.

Shapiro, S.L., Brown, K.W., Thoresen, C., and Plante, T.G. (2011). The Moderation of Mindfulness-based Stress Reduction Effects by Trait Mindfulness: Results from a Randomized Control Trial. *Journal of Clinical Psychology*. Vol. 67 (3), 267-77.

Tipsord, J. (2009). The effects of mindfulness training and individual difference in mindfulness on social perception and empathy. Unpublished doctoral dissertation, University of Oregon, Portland, OR.

Vroom, V.H. (1964). *Work and Motivation*. New York: Wiley.

Weick, K.E., and Putnam, T. (2006). Organizing for Mindfulness: Eastern Wisdom and Western Knowledge. *Journal of Management Inquiry*, 15 (3).

CHAPTER 33

KNOWLEDGE MANAGEMENT: RELISHING ECONOMY TO PROSPERITY

–Ashish Mathur and *Aarti Khanchandani*

ABSTRACT

Knowledge is a significant source of wealth at all levels of any economy. Most of new jobs and wealth creation are fuelled by the international competitiveness of new knowledge-based industries. The knowledge economy is often taken to mean only high-technology industries or information and communication technologies (ICTs). The time is very opportune for India to make its transition to the knowledge economy—an economy that creates, disseminates, and uses knowledge to enhance its growth and development.

Introduction

One of the world's largest economies, India has made tremendous strides in its economic and social development in the past two decades and is poised to realize even faster growth in the years to come.

Knowledge is basically valuable information. It is important because it is a source of wealth at all levels of an economy. Most new jobs and wealth creation are fuelled by the international competitiveness of new knowledge-based industries. The knowledge economy and the growth of knowledge management, as an essential competency of organizations, provides new opportunities for various industries and information specialists to expand existing roles and utilize the skills they have honed to meet corporate objectives. The key information management role of both internal and external information, alongside the contribution to information competence and the ability to contextualize information, contributes to organizational excellence, customer benefit and competitive advantage which can be achieved more effectively through collaboration and partnership.

Embracing the Knowledge Economy

The time is very opportune for India to make its transition to the knowledge economy—an economy that creates, disseminates, and uses knowledge to enhance its growth and development. The knowledge economy is often taken to mean only high-technology industries or information and communication technologies (ICTs). It would be more appropriate, however, to use the concept more broadly to cover how any economy harnesses and uses new and existing knowledge to improve the productivity of agriculture, industry, and services and increase overall welfare. In India, great potential exists for increasing productivity by shifting labor from low productivity and subsistence activities in agriculture, informal industry, and informal service activities to more productive modern sectors, as well as to new knowledge-based activities—and in so doing, to reduce poverty and touch every member of society.

Knowledge Economy in India

In the world where change is a universal fact, only Darwinism follows in every field/sphere of the life. If one remains aloof from the rest of the world in terms of knowledge then their survival will be at risk. The same rule applies to both individual and organization. As a result of the 1998/99 World Development Report on Knowledge for Development, the topic of the knowledge economy gained prominence with policymakers worldwide. In 2001, the K4D (Knowledge for Development) program held a high-level policy forum to share knowledge strategies among key stakeholders from Brazil, India and China—potential knowledge superpowers representing 45 per cent of the world's population. India has many of the key ingredients for making this transition. It has a critical mass of skilled, English-speaking knowledge workers, especially in sciences. It is the largest democracy in the world. Its domestic market is one of the world's largest. It has a large and impressive Diaspora, creating valuable knowledge linkages and networks. The list goes on: macroeconomic stability, a dynamic private sector, institutions of a free market economy, a well-developed financial sector, and a broad and diversified science and technology infrastructure. In addition, the development of the ICT sector is remarkable. India has created profitable niches in information technology and is a global provider of software services. Building on these strengths, India can harness the benefits of the knowledge revolution to improve its economic performance and boost the welfare of its people. The some of the key constraints and emerging possibilities confronting India on four critical pillars of the knowledge economy:

- Empowering the economic and institutional regime
- Developing educated and skilled workers
- Creating an efficient innovation system
- Building a dynamic information infrastructure

Growth of Knowledge Management in India

The systematic process of finding, selecting, organizing, distilling and presenting information, improves an employee's comprehension in a specific area of interest. Knowledge management helps an organization to gain insight and understanding from its own experience. Specific knowledge management activities help focus the organization on acquiring, storing and utilizing knowledge for problem solving, dynamic learning, strategic planning and decision making. It also prevents intellectual assets from decay, adds to firm intelligence and provides increased flexibility. Indian organizations are more 'innovative' in applying new Internet-based tools to effectively share and reuse knowledge in an increasingly global workplace.

Apart from it, knowledge economy has some great significance in other areas too. The basis of knowledge economy is IT and infrastructure which must be in integration with each other.

Government Policy for Knowledge Economy

IT firms in India have focused on developing and delivering IT services to advanced economies. In a nation with over a billion people, this constitutes but a dent in the employment statistics.

A social planner should be concerned not just with the creation of wealth, but also with its distribution across social divides. The IT industry holds limited potential for wealth to trickle down to the poorer sections of society. Unlike a steel plant, IT engenders few opportunities for the uneducated. Any transfer of wealth from the IT sector (for example, by taxing the IT sector to fund social spending) would be achieved through the heavy hand of government. This represents, at best, a dubious economic proposition. In fact, the rapid growth of IT is leading to a digital divide, where the rich and educated are empowered and enriched by IT and the poor are oblivious to its impact.

Before embracing IT, Indian policy planners must carefully evaluate whether investments in other areas would yield higher, and more equitable, returns. For example, consider the jute industry. This industry sustains over five million Indian households.

Indian policy planners frequently overlook two important points. First, the creative application of IT in a range of manufacturing and agricultural industries can yield much greater returns at a societal level, compared with software production and export. Second, not all technology is information technology—traditional R&D related to design and manufacturing remains extremely important. Such R&D can be enhanced by IT (for example, via virtual collaboration and computer-aided design), but not substituted by it.

The country needs to be particularly careful not to give short shrift to the manufacturing sector. China is not known for its strengths in IT, although it now has some presence in the area. But what China has accomplished in terms of its core industrial base is striking.

Many countries like Taiwan, Malaysia and South Korea have prospered their economy using knowledge economy. The knowledge economy helps in creation of jobs in a nation for both skilled and unskilled manpower. For example, exporting footwear employs millions of jobs for the manpower who lacks sophisticated skills. These jobs have improved living standards in an economy. According to some reports, a total of 34 million export-related jobs have been created in China, with exports to the U.S. alone accounting for over 20 million jobs in the last decade. It is a lesson that we should learn from China that manufacturing sector can aid in strengthening the economic growth.

The above-mentioned statement has clearly emphasized on the impact of manufacturing sector on economic growth of an economy. But some argued the above by saying that the manufacturing sector is inherently less appealing because it may involve some physical labor. In the more advanced economies, a skilled factory floor worker is frequently paid more than a call-centre employee. Empowered with technology, the factory worker can add value at a remarkable rate. In India, the reverse often holds. Mundane call-centre jobs, often outsourced from more developed economies, absorb well-educated, English-speaking workers whose abilities could be employed much more productively elsewhere.

In contrast with manufacturing, the direct benefits to IT (such as employment in IT jobs) are likely to flow to the few who already have the benefits of education. The trickle-down effects of IT (such as cleaning and maintenance staff for IT firms) are likely to be modest or non-existent outside the large cities. The benefits of IT implementation across other industrial sectors (such as employing IT to make transportation and supply chains more efficient) will likely be substantial, but Indian industrial policy does not point in this direction at the moment.

The emphasis on IT would be less objectionable if it did not contrast sharply with the treatment meted out to other industrial sectors. The actions of governments in India tend to be biased in favour of the IT sector. For instance, software taxes levied in Karnataka were removed within a week in response to pressure from IT companies. Many workplace inspection procedures have been suspended for IT companies, while other sectors are subjected to myriad regulations, many of which have not been re-evaluated for relevance and effectiveness for decades. The government needs a more balanced policy, one that ensures that the core industrial sector is not ignored in the rush toward IT.

Research Methodology

It is the description explanation and justification of various methods of conducting research. It involves various steps adopted by research in studying the research problem along with the logic behind them. The whole study was basically based on collection of data from primary sources but secondary sources were also used. Research methodology deals with the efficient plan and decisions on sources of gathering the needed on data, research instrument to be used-and research design.

Research Design

It is the conceptual structure within which research is conducted; it constitutes the blueprint for the collection, measurement and analysis of data.

Data Collection Method

Secondary Data: In order to have a proper understanding an in-depth study was done from the various books, magazines, articles written on the subject. A lot of data has also been collected from these and also from websites on the topic.

Primary Data: The primary data was collected by means of a survey.

Hypothesis: Impact of all the key constraints and emerging possibilities confronting India on four critical pillars of the knowledge economy are insignificant

Impact on	Key constraints and emerging possibilities confronting India								Total
	Empowering the economic and institutional regime		Developing educated and skilled workers		Creating an efficient innovation system		Building a dynamic information infrastructure		
	No.	%	No.	%	No.	%	No.	%	
Knowledge economy	45	22.5	75	37.5	45	12.85	35	17.14	200

Chi sqr = 18.4; df = 3; Results = highly significant ($p < 0.001$)

The above table indicates that there is a clear effect of the key constraints and emerging possibilities confronting India on four critical pillars of the knowledge economy. The calculated value of chi-square is much greater than the table value which means that the calculated value cannot be said to have arisen just because of chance. It is significant. Hence, the hypothesis does not hold good. This means that all the key constraints and emerging possibilities confronting India do not have equal role in knowledge economy. One factor, i.e. developing educated and skilled workers plays major role in knowledge economy.

Conclusion

The Indian vision of a knowledge-based economy will be realised only when it is based on the foundation of a robust industrial economy. To be truly beneficial, the rain of IT must fall at the right place, in the right quantity, at the right time and for the right purpose. The Indian software industry has compiled an impressive track record over the past decade. Entrepreneurs, bureaucrats and politicians are now advancing views about how India can transform itself into a knowledge-based economy by riding the information technology (IT) bandwagon.

REFERENCES

AIMA (All India Management Association). 2003. *India's New Opportunity, 2020: Report of the High-Level Strategic Group*. Prepared with the Boston Consulting Group. Mumbai and New Delhi, India.

Barro, Robert J., and Jong-Wha Lee 2001. "International Data on Educational Attainment: Updates and Implications." *Oxford Economic Papers*, 3: 541-63.

Front Line; Volume 19- Issue 02, Jan. 19- Feb. 01,2002; India's National Magazine from the publishers of The Hindu.

2002a. *Tenth Five-Year Plan 2002–2007*. New Delhi.

http://planningcommission.nic.in/plans/planrel/fiveyr/welcome.html

2002b. *Report of the Steering Committee on Communication and Information for the Tenth Five-Year Plan (2002–2007)*. New Delhi.

http://planningcommission.nic.in/aboutus/committee/strgrp/stgp_candi.pdf

http://planningcommission.nic.in/reports/genrep/pl_vsn2020.pdf

http://www.telegraphindia.com/1050117/asp/knowhow/story_4249252.asp

Huang, Yasheng, and Tarun Khanna 2003. "Can India Overtake China?" *Foreign Policy*. July-August.

India, Planning Commission. 2001. *India as Knowledge Superpower: Strategy for Transformation*. New Delhi.

Kalam, A.P.J. Abdul and Y.S. Rajan 2002. *India 2020: A Vision for the New Millennium*. New Delhi: Penguin Books India.

"Knowledge Management: A Tool to Prosper Economy", [pg no. 01-07], Gupta Vandana, Patni Dr. Priyadarshi, *International Journal of Management and Tourism Trends*, Vol. 2, Special Issue.

Maddison, Angus 2001. *The World Economy: A Millennial Perspective*. OECD, Paris.

Mudur, G.S. 2005. "Reverse Drug Design." *The Telegraph*. 17 January. Calcutta, India.

The Tata Group 2005. "40 Hours Is All It Takes to Teach an Indian to Read." http://www.tataliteracy.com

CHAPTER 34

EFFECTIVE MANAGEMENT THROUGH SUCCESSION PLANNING

–*Bharti Pandya*

ABSTRACT

Purpose—This paper seek to present brief description of Succession Planning, its Significance, Steps of Succession Planning and how it affects management.

Design/Methodology/Approach—Review of history of succession planning, publications, journals, websites and reference books.

Findings—The paper suggests that it has become a necessity to have viable succession plan in place to face the changing economies and to keep operations unaffected due to unstable leadership. Succession planning is mandatory for long-term success of an organization.

INTRODUCTION

Attracting talent from the competitor has become a tedious exercise. It has not remained a viable option anymore. Not only is this costly, but studies conducted by the Center for Creative Leadership has revealed that a staggering 66 per cent of senior managers hired from the outside usually failed within the first 18 months. The smart way for organization professionals to combat the looming leadership succession crisis is to identify and develop the internal talent needed for key executive positions and start now. This indicates the importance of succession planning as the vital tool for effective management. Selection of wrong CEOs could lead to downfall of companies.

Succession Planning

Succession planning is defined as "a means of identifying critical management positions, starting at the levels of project manager and supervisor and extending up to the highest position in the organization. Succession planning also describes management positions to provide maximum flexibility in lateral management moves and to ensure that as individuals achieve greater seniority, their management skills will broaden and become more generalized in relation to total organizational objectives rather than to purely departmental objectives."

According to William J. Rothwell, succession management is more than "replacement planning," or simply filling openings as they occur. Comprehensive succession management integrates talent management with organizational strategic planning. It anticipates changes in management.... A strategic business plan can only be realized when the *right people* are in the *right place* and at the *right times* to do the *right things*. Having the necessary intellectual capital to compete is a given in today's fast-paced world. Throughout his book, Rothwell (2005) indicates that organizations lacking a formal succession plan find that:

- Key positions will not be filled in a timely manner,
- Key positions can only be filled by external candidates due to lack of development of internal candidate,
- There are only a few people prepared for the key positions,
- Key positions face frequent and unpredictable turnover,
- The potential replacements lack the necessary skills,
- The most qualified talent continues to leave and look elsewhere for advancement.

Schein (1997) has defined "Succession Planning and Management as a purposeful and systematic effort made by an organization to ensure leadership continuity, retain and develop knowledge and intellectual capital for the future, and encourage individual employee growth and development."

Review of Literature

In the 2009 edition of their book, *Execution: The Discipline of Getting Things Done*, Larry Bossidy and Ram Charan make a case that "one of the most important parts of an executive job is to pass the knowledge he has acquired over the years to the next generation of leaders. It's how an executive gets results today and leave a legacy that the executive can take pride in when he moves on" (Bossidy, 2009, p. 74). It further discusses the importance of "developing the leadership pipeline through continuous improvement, succession depth, and reducing retention risk," and a leadership assessment matrix to identify those who are ready for a bigger role vs. those who need to be replaced (Bossidy, 2009, p. 150).

In *Succession Planning—Key to Corporate Excellence*, Arthur X. Deegan II notes that the specific purpose of succession planning is to provide an organized approach for the most effective identification and utilization of the organization's management resources (Deegan, 1986, p. 7). In the Sixth edition of the book *Leadership—Research Findings, Practice, and Skills*, Andrew J. Dubrin notes that in a well-managed organization, replacements for executives who quit, retire, or are dismissed are chosen through leadership succession, an orderly process of identifying and grooming people to replace managers (*Leadership*, 2010, p. 461).

In the 13th edition of *Human Resource Management*, Robert L. Mathis notes that succession planning must include a well-designed employee development system to reach its potential. Succession planning is the process of identifying a plan for the orderly replacement of key employees.

As more Baby Boomers near retirement age, the impact of their departure becomes more pronounced within the executive ranks of both private and public sector organizations (Grace Endres, *Organization Development Journal*, Summer 2006, p. 24). The loss of knowledge due to the retirement of Baby Boomers and an overall aging workforce is what Thomas Calo calls a "perfect storm" that managers will have to endure for many years. He notes that the previous methods of acquiring talent may not be effective in the future. A 2006 study published in *McKinsey Quarterly* noted that, while companies view the ability to manage talent effectively as a strategic priority, research indicates that senior executives largely blame themselves and their business line managers for failing to give the issue enough time and attention. Many companies do not conduct succession planning until it is too late, and cope with the inconvenience of conducting it during a crisis (Stensgaard, 2005). Regrettably, succession planning is not conducted until it is too late, after vital personnel leave the organization and no one is present to fulfill the leadership positions (Ibarra, 2005). According to Evangelista (2003), succession planning is a key component in leading businesses that were identified by a group of CEOs. Those companies were recognized as "world class" due to the financial and resource commitment to professional development, recruiting and training. With this commitment, it demonstrated a great propensity for top leadership coming from within the organization, rather than 3.5% of CEOs that were hired from the outside. "Succession Planning is mandatory for the long-term success of the organization" (Wolf, 2006, Conclusion section).

In summary, the reviewed literature has established a need and importance of having succession planning in an organization for long-term effective management.

METHODOLOGY

An applied research methodology was followed to collect information for this paper. Research performed is of a subjective category. Information was gained through literature reviews in academic research engines, Google Scholar and direct Internet searches using primary keywords that included "succession planning", "leadership development", "effective management", replacement planning", "leadership development", "transition planning", and "organization success through succession plans". Library searches were also conducted at university and public libraries for journal articles, books and book chapters, and popular magazine articles. Few citations are provided in text; key articles are included in the bibliography and are provided for closer reading.

RESULTS/ANALYSIS

Significance of Succession Planning to Management

Management faces several challenges that can be addressed by effective succession planning. Some of these challenges have been summarized by InfoHRM and Bersin are listed below:

- **Gaps in Leadership**—Succession planning helps in identification of needs and development of key skills and competencies for effective current and future leaders.
- **Executive Recruitment is Producing Uninspiring Results**—Succession planning recruiting internally groomed successors who understands the unique organizational agenda and environment.
- **Filling Key Positions**—Succession planning helps planning ahead leading to development of leaders in timely fashion.
- **Rapid Recruitment to Meet Growth Needs**—Succession planning provides job ready talent pool.
- **Impending Retirement of Key Leaders**—Succession planning facilitates successors who are ready to take their new roles.

- **Inadequate Career Paths and Ineffective Line Management**—Succession planning can assist with filling in positions, as well as assist in smooth transitions for those departing. It helps in lateral moves, job assignments and secondments to address career path ambiguity.
- **Talent Programs Lack Corporate Oversight**—Succession planning endorsed and supported by the CEO/MD and executive team.
- **Retention Problems/Key Talent a Turnover Risk**—According to Karaevli and Hail (2003), succession planning helps in development of initiatives, ongoing challenges and learning opportunities will motivate high potential employees. Job satisfaction is the most important contributor to the retention of high performing individuals. Talented people appreciate projects that stretch their abilities and a work environment that encourages ongoing development.
- **Developing Young Workers**—The succession planning development framework extends to all levels of organizations.
- **Downsizing the Workforce**—Succession planning assists in knowing the type of person who will succeed in the future and therefore worth investing in despite the possible obsolescence of their current role.

Steps Involved in Succession Planning

There are seven steps involved in succession planning. As per SHRM, they are:

1. **Identifying Legal and Diversity Issue to Consider**—In this step, management should avoid "like-me" approaches while positioning employees for succession. Many organizations prefers those employees to key positions who closely resemble incumbents in ways such as age, education, leadership style, industry experience, career trajectory, race and gender. This may lead to diversity issues. For such biased selection practices, assessment tools can be used. Discrimination laws require inclusion of all qualified employees regardless of race or gender.
2. **Establishing Present and Future Leadership Roles and Objectives**—In this step, management must probe into future critical business operations; growth prospects of business; impact of process improvement, technology or reengineering on future business; consolidation of job functions; projected workload volume; changes in staffing levels and matching skills and abilities.
3. **Selecting Key Employees**—In this step, the top management identifies employees available for succession into their positions. Profile of these candidates is then developed. A history of performance reviews and accomplishments, including years of relevant experience, education and credentials are compiled for profiles. Cross-departmental leadership/key decision makers must be involved in the plan throughout the process to represent their selections and discuss concerns with one another. Identifiable gaps need to be temporarily or permanently closed in the event of an emergency replacement of a candidate in another department. Selection is based on available candidates. There will be some available candidates who are ready while there will be some who will not meet the demands of critical positions and in some

cases there will be no identifiable candidate for succession at all. A common method used to chart the available candidates and their readiness level to succeed is a 9-box grid. The 9-box grid helps management to visualize the available successors along with the strengths/weaknesses in the plan.

Potential	*Satisfactorily Placed*	*High Professional*	*High Potential*
→→→	Remain at current level of organization, in current or similar role; has likely achieved highest career level.	Able to do the work of bigger jobs at the same management level in the next 1 to 2 years.	Able to do the work at the next management level in 3 to 5 years or sooner.
↑	**Box 4**	**Box 2**	**Box 1**
Outstanding/ Excellent	Highly valued, seasoned professional in current role; remain at current level.	Does extremely well at current job with potential to do more, give stretch assignments to help prepare leader for next management level.	Consistently performs well in a variety of assignments, prime targets for recruitment by other companies.
↑	**Box 7**	**Box 5**	**Box 3**
Effective	Probably solid performers in current roles. Could progress higher in specialty and become a box 4.	These individuals should be considered for a bigger job at the same level if they can deliver better results.	Current role may still provide opportunity for growth/ development; focus should be on helping them improve performance.
↑	**Box 9**	**Box 8**	**Box 6**
Needs Improvement	Consider reassignment, reclassification or exit.	Tight performance management is crucial, consider helping leader manage time more effectively.	Maybe job mismatch, new hire with lots of potential, or new assignment. May require coaching to improve performance.

**Source*: Motorola 9 Box Grid Definitions

4. **Evaluating the Strengths, Weaknesses and Readiness for Succession in Key Employees—** Once candidates have been identified for succession and skills required for current and future succession have been identified, assessment tools may be used to determine skill deficiencies that may presently exist. There are a number of approaches which may include 360 surveys (can include feedback from peers, direct reports, line management and other relevant sources—such as clients, customers, vendors and/or suppliers); leadership evaluations by independent third party consultant; and existing performance review information and feedback from management.
5. **Planning for the Individual Development of and Ways to Retain Key Employees—** Once strengths and weaknesses have been identified, action plans for development of strengths and reduction of weaknesses should be created. Common action plans include leadership development programs and skill specific educational programs such as finance for non-financial managers, but may also include an internal mentoring program. Samples of documents used in steps 4 and 5 follow.

6. **Identifying "Emergency" Positions Without Successors**—Emergency positions are those where no successor is available or no successor with developmental potential exists. Emergency positions are critical because the organization has already determined the key roles and future organizational needs. When a succession plan has a vacancy, the organizational operations may be at risk in the event of a departure. In the case where no developmental potential exists in an employee, organizations need to ask themselves whether this employee has the ability to bring value to the organization. In some cases, an exit plan may be appropriate.
7. **Planning for Positions that cannot be Filled Internally**—Where no successor exists, the organization will need to consider external recruitment strategies and develop a recruitment plan and in the interim consider cross-departmental succession opportunities. This situation can be beneficial in that it presents the opportunity for the organization to bring fresh and diverse talent into the organization.

Georgia's Flexible Model of Succession Planning

1. **Pre-plan.** This step has several components, which include creating a succession planning team, establishing program objectives, establishing measures of success, establishing program design, and developing an implementation plan.
2. **Communicate Plan.** Inform stakeholders about the purpose and value of succession planning and the objectives and specific contents of the agency's program. The sub-steps include determining communication goals and measures, identifying target audiences, and determining communication methods.
3. **Identify Leadership Characteristics.** Particular emphasis is placed upon the concepts of leadership levels, the demands of each level, and capacity to meet those demands. Each is discussed in terms of competencies and results required of each leadership level. Because leadership is multilevel, different leadership characteristics are needed in order to successfully perform at each level. In this step, three leadership characteristics are identified for each leadership level: competency levels, competency scope of impact, and leadership results. The intensity and impact dimensions of competencies are introduced, and their assessment is explored. A measure of "balanced leadership results" is presented. These characteristics are used as the basis for assessing, developing, and selecting future leaders. The importance of leadership competency models and their use in assessing candidates' match to the demands of leadership is addressed.
4. **Assess Bench Strength and Other Pre-Measures.** The concept of bench strength is presented, and its importance as both a primary goal and an assessment of succession planning validity is discussed. Bench strength is defined as the number of critical leadership positions that have at least one person ready to successfully assume the role and responsibilities of each of these positions. Bench strength assessments can serve as a baseline measure of an organization's ability to fill positions from within. In such cases, organizations evaluate the effectiveness of a succession planning program by comparing the number of positions that have someone ready to successfully move into them before and after implementation of the succession planning program. Other pre- and post-measures of succession planning success are suggested.

5. **Assess Talent.** The identification of leadership potential and its measurement is explored in detail. The tutorial introduces "the potential-results matrix" and demonstrates its use in differentiating leadership talent and identifying high potential. This step involves assessing employees on multiple dimensions and comparing them with successful characteristics that have been determined to be associated with a specific leadership level. The results of these assessments provide useful information regarding employees' potential to take on greater leadership responsibilities and their strengths and areas for development. Employees who demonstrate appropriate competency levels, scope of impact, and a history of getting successful results are identified as having high potential and may be selected to participate in a structured set of activities to rapidly prepare them for higher leadership positions.
6. **Develop Talent.** In this step, development strategies are outlined for members of the succession planning pool based upon the results of the assessment in the previous step. Development strategies for each member of the pool should be based on information gathered during the talent assessment process. The potential-results matrix is converted into a "development matrix", and its implications for structuring developmental actions are illustrated. The relative value of various developmental methods is compared, and methods for identifying priority developmental assignments are shared. Different approaches to development may be necessary to address issues related to competency levels versus issues related to scope of impact or results. Although many strategies are available to develop employees, the key is to identify the right combination of strategies that prepares them to successfully take on higher leadership roles within the organization. Effective in developing future leaders are key assignments, developmental feedback, mentoring, coaching, formal classroom training, and professional membership. The pivotal importance of key assignments, their identification, and the removal of blocks to key assignments are emphasized.
7. **Evaluate Succession Planning.** This step involves measuring the impact of the succession planning program upon established objectives. After sufficient time following implementation, program processes and results should be periodically reviewed to assess whether program objectives have been achieved and to identify areas for improvement. Once the evaluation has been completed, modifications to the program should be made as appropriate. There are many approaches to program evaluation, which vary in complexity. Measures used to evaluate the effectiveness of programs may range from simple methods such as an assessment of stakeholder satisfaction to more sophisticated processes such as a return on investment or cost-benefit analysis.

Effects of Succession Planning on Management

Success of any program, plan or project depend the measurement of the outcome. For effective management, it is important to understand how a success of succession planning can be measured. Busine and Watt (2005) and other researchers have suggested the numerous ways in which it can be done. These are:

- The number of job-ready people to fill senior jobs when they become vacant.
- The percentage of jobs filled by internal candidates.

- Cost of turnover and demotivation inside the organization when an external hire is made.
- Time it takes for an outside hire to get up to speed.
- Turnover of external hires.
- Turnover of identifies pool members/high potentials.
- Frequency of external CEO searches
- Size and quality of cross-functional or international talent pools.

Any succession plan's success depends on how efficiently key positions are identified, how involved and committed is the top leadership, is this plan owned by line management and supported by human resources, how integrated is the plan with firm's strategic direction and initiatives, whether it is linked to unit development, whether the system is compatible with the organization's culture and whether it is treated as an ongoing process.

CONCLUSION

Review of literature and significance underscores the necessity of succession planning in an organization. For effective succession planning, it is important to understand organization's long-term goals and objectives, identifying effective leaders and their developmental needs and analyzing human resources forecasting. Most often succession planning becomes very costly and arduous process resulting in rush filling of key positions and instability of business operations. A good succession plan should develop a diverse workforce in line with organization's future. Thoughtful and culturally adapted succession planning/management systems are keys to any organizations success. There are seven important steps in succession planning, which followed devotionally will lead to development of workable succession plan which should later be kept current and be communicated to all employees.

REFERENCES

Bersin. J. (2007), *The Business Case for Performance Management Systems: A Handbook for Human Resources Executives and Managers*, Bersin and Associates.

Bossidy, L. et al. (2009). "Execution: The Discipline of Getting Things Done." New York: Crown Business.

Busine, M. and Watt, B. (2005), "Succession management: Trends and current practice", *Asia Pacific Journal of Human Resources*, Vol. 43, No.2, pp. 225-37.

Beverly, Behan. (2009). "Lessons from BofA: Avoiding a Succession Debacle." *Business Week*.

Caruso, K.N., Groehler, L. and Perry, J. (2005), *Current Trends in Succession Planning and Management*, viaPeople, Inc.

Cedar, Crestone (2008), CedarCrestone 2008-2009 HR Systems Survey: HR Technologies, Service Delivery Approaches, and Metrics. 11th Annual Edition.

Conger, J.A. and Fulmer, R.M. (2003), "Developing your leadership pipeline", *Harvard Business Review*, Vol. 81, No. 12, pp. 76-84.

Deegan II, A.X. (1986). "Succession Planning—Key to Corporate Excellence." John Wiley and Sons.

Dubrin, A.J. (2010). "Leadership—Research Findings, Practice and Skills." Mason: South-Western Cengage Learning.

e-Corporate Buy-Sell Handbook: An Essential Guide to Business Succession Planning. By Stephan Leimberg, Joseph Yohlin, and Morey Rosenbloom (Dearborn Trade, 1992).

Evangelista, E. (2003). Succession planning: Effective strategies for transitional corporate leadership. *Contingency Planning and Management*, 8 (1), 18-21.

GSA (2001). "Succession Planning Guide." Washington, DC: GSA Office of Government Policy.

Ibarra, P. (2005). Succession planning: An idea whose time has come. *Public Management*, 87 (1), 18-24.

InfoHRM (2008), Talent Management Survey: Talent Management in Challenging Times.

Karaevli, A. and Hall, D.T. (2003), "Growing leaders for turbulent times: Is succession planning up to the challenge?" *Organizational Dynamics*, Vol. 32 No. 1, pp. 62-79.

Rothwell, W.J. (2005), *Effective Succession Planning: Ensuring Leadership Continuity and Building Talent Within*, 3rd ed. New York, AMACOM.

Stensgaard, A.B. (2006). Why is succession planning important. AME Info, retrieved August 3, 2006 from http://www.ameinfo.com/news/Detailed/59276.html

Somerville, P. (2006), "Successful succession", *HR Monthly*, September 2006.

Wolf, Dennis (2006), Succession Planning: Mentoring and educating younger fire officers for the chief's position.

CHAPTER 35

TALENT MANAGEMENT IN SOCIAL MEDIA: EMERGING TRENDS

–*D. Mehta, Shruti Jain* and *Naveen K. Mehta*

ABSTRACT

Amidst the process of globalization, organizations have become more competitive to attract and retain pool of talented employees. Now, it is quite apparent that the organizations are utilizing optimum benefits from social media network to strengthen and promote their employees development programmes. These programmes are referred as the most cost-effective source of attracting qualified talent. Through the help of social media networking, organizations can approach a large number of aspirants and select the best aspirants which fulfill their organization requirements. This paper is an attempt to study the emerging trends of talent management in social media.

Introduction

It is a well-known fact that talent management is all about managing the ability, competency and power of employees within an organization. It is not just limited to attract the best people from the industry but a continuous process that involves sourcing, hiring, developing, retaining and promoting them while meeting the organization's deadlines as well. On the other hand, social media networking tools have transformed our lives. Facebook, Twitter, Google+, etc. have changed the way we work. Now we can connect, share, and communicate with people, like never before on 24 × 7 bases from any corner of the world.

It seems that organizations are exploring the value proposition via social media. As Talent Management Solutions integrating with social media networks, it is easier to launch, collect and evaluate data from candidates and employees through social networks. Use of social media sites such as Facebook has grown immensely to more than 400 million users which are more than the population of the United States and Canada combined.

Talent management is targeted to recruit, retain, and develop the most talented and superior employees available in the job market. Talent management is being continously adopted, as more organizations come to realize that their employees' talents and skills drive their business success. Such organizations develop plans and processes to track and manage their employee talent, including, attracting and recruiting qualified candidates with competitive backgrounds, managing and defining competitive salaries, training and development opportunities, performance management processes retention programs, promotion and transitioning. In India, many companies are still using the second gen (2G) approach to talent management. There are a few companies which have incorporated the 3G of talent management like Infosys that provides some best-in-class benchmark for other companies to follow.

Table 1: Social Media Used by Internet Users: A Worldwide Perspective

Social Media Websites	*2010*		*2011*	
	Professional	*Personal*	*Professional*	*Personal*
LinkedIn	62%	33%	86%	48%
Twitter	13%	11%	76%	62%
Digg	10%	10%	68%	63%
Delicious	12%	9%	68%	58%
Second Life	6%	6%	56%	59%
YouTube	34%	55%	51%	85%
Facebook	18%	35%	36%	93%
My Space	8%	27%	19%	91%

Source: Face time Communciations "The Collaborative Internet Usage Trends, End User attitude and IT Impact, Seventh Annual Survey" March 3, 2012.

Literature Review

According to McKinsey, talent is "the sum of a person's abilities...his or her intrinsic gifts, skills, knowledge, experience, intelligence, judgement, attitude, character and drive. It also includes his or her ability to learn and grow" (Michaels et al., 2001). Ashton and Morton (2005) see TM as a strategic and holistic approach to both HR and business planning or a new route to organizational effectiveness. Talent, to their mind, should be a strategic balance between performance and potential. David Ulrich (2006) uses a holistic approach to talent. To his mind, talent equals competence time's commitment time's contribution.

Jäger's (2009 concluded that TM is a new, overarching key process of HRM. He differentiates direct and indirect personnel functions. According to Scullion et al. (2010) as well as McDonald et al. (2010), GTM has gathered mainstream acceptance in the professional community as a key management activity. In their opinion, this key strategic issue in this relatively new field of investigation is particularly critical for MNCs for several reasons. Tymon et al. (2010) who focused on GTM in the emerging economy India as these types of countries play a more and more important role in the world economy. Attracting, managing, and retaining reflect a continuing challenge for India.

Hambrick and Mason (1984), Miller, Burke and Glick (1998) observed recent emphasis on talent management represents a paradigm shift from more traditional human resource related sources of competitive advantage literature such as those that focus on organizational elites, including upper echelon literature and strategic human resource management (SHRM). Huselid et al. (1997), Wright and McMahon, (1992) said that the management of talent specifically suited to today's dynamic competitive environment. While the context may have shifted significantly since the latter part of the last century, the notion of talent management remains important.

Research Methodology

Objectives

- To study the impact of social media on talent management.
- To study the emerging trends of talent management in social media.

Data Collection

Since it is a secondary data-based study, the secondary data have been collected from magazines, books, Internet, industry journals, etc. Literature review has shown prior research work done in this area. All the available secondary data have been studied and analyzed by the researchers.

Emerging Trends

In the present economic scenario of recession, despite of compressed budgets, organizations continue to hire and nurture talent. One factor that appears to occupy most of the discussion is social media. It is quite apparent that Facebook, LinkedIn, and Twitter will play a dominate role.

Global Demand—The global war for talent will remain continue in major regions of industries and organizations. While growth has slowed somewhat in China, Australia, Southeast Asia and India also but the demand for skilled talent will still be continue.

Learning is a 24 × 7 Process—Crowd sourcing is the best method for effective social learning where people can learn from each other in a more virtual environment. Social media helps learning to become a continuous process and not dependent on specific time and place.

Retention Issues—It is quite striking to note that a majority of employees are willing to quit their current jobs as soon as a better opportunity comes along. The turnover rates in high, demand of occupations will increase by 25% during the next year. Rate of retention could turn out to be the highest-economic-impact area in all of talent management.

Presence Factor—Today, most of the firms are vying to rope the social media but unfortunately the trial-and-error approach used by most has not yielded expected results. Adapting social media tools for the business purpose will allow a more focused approach that directs the effort of all employees.

Remote Working—The continuous development of technology, social media, and easy communications now makes it possible for most knowledge work and team activities to occur remotely. Allowing top talent to work "wherever they want to work" improves retention and enables recruiting much easier.

Now, managers and talent management leaders have realized that teamwork, learning, development, recruiting, and best-practice sharing can now successfully be attained by using remote methods. Firms like IBM have paved the way in eliminating barriers to remote work.

Social Media Policy—Some organizations still remain skeptical about social channels' security and integrity. Every organization should have a well-drafted 'social media policy' implemented for their employees. HR has to work closely with IT/security departments to minimize potential risks and losses.

Employee Referrals—With proper coordination, employee relationships can easily be turned into employee referrals. This realization will lead to a shift away from recruiters and toward relying on employees to build social media contacts and relationships.

Emergence of Forward Looking Metrics—At present times, all talent management and recruiting metrics are backward looking, in that they tell us what happened in the past. Other business functions like supply chain, production, and finance have long championed the use of "forward-looking" and the time has already arrived when talent management leaders will have to shift their metrics emphasis. Forward-looking metrics cannot only improve decision-making but they can also enable to prevent or mitigate future talent problems.

Internet Freedom and Content Regulation Aspects—According to experts, the wide spectrum subscribers' data base has the potential to raise concern about the Internet freedom, unacceptable content as well as threat to national security issues. TM experts have to remain alert after the Arab Spring, exodus from the people of North-East and mobilization of right public opinion because no provocative information should be allowed to spread if the talent management experts consider networking sites as blessings. Thus, TM and social media experts should look into such issues that either of them is not misused.

Indian Scenario

The last two years have witnessed unprecedented growth of social media in our country. According to a report by iCRossing, nearly 6 million people use Facebook out of which nearly 50% users are aged below 50. Estimates for 20120 show that micro blogging sites like Twitter and LinkedIn have nearly 15 million users in India. Countries like India need to encourage young talented professionals to push up constructive debates on issues like environment, wild-life conservation, gender justice , human rights, education and tirades against cyber pornography, terrorism, trade and business affairs, then only both will justify their right usage.

Concluding Remarks

Talent management is a dynamic process that has to be continuously reviewed to ensure that organisational requirements are still being met in the light of changing business priorities. Ultimately, organisational success is the most effective evaluation of talent management. Harvard Business Review points out that, in the best of talent management programs, organizations "integrated talent management, succession planning and leadership development into the company's strategic business processes".

Talent management can be a major part of acompany's value proposition and a distinct competitive advantage. When it comes to talent management, Indian companies need to adopt the next-gen method of talent management—aligning talent to business capability and strategy execution. To accomplish success in business, it's very important to recognize the organization talent and clubbing it with the social media. Talent management and social media experts should also try to pay attention towards the recent developments of hounding of Julian Assange, a 41 year old founder of WikiLeaks that how the values of freedom, equality and democracy can be put on the acid test and new generation talent, governments, policymakers and industry wizards should also learn hard ethical lessons and various types of risk involved in dealing with social media.

It will not only provide the best talents to the organization but will also help take it to the highest level. So in this cut-throat competition where survival is a big question mark, talent management has emerged as a never-ending opportunity for talent. It is hoped that social networks will continue to be the best way to form strong relationships with prospective employees. In this changing scenario, the impact of social media networks can't be overlooked on talent management.

REFERENCES

Ashton, C. and Morton, L. (2005). 'Managing talent for competitive advantage', *Strategic HR Review*, 4, pp. 28-31.

Becker, K.H., and Haunschild, A. (2003). The impact of boundaryless careers on organizational decision making: An analysis from the perspective of Luhmann's theory of social systems. *International Journal of Human Resource Management*, 14, 713-27.

Cappelli, P. (2008a). Talent on Demand, Boston, MA, Harvard Business School Press.

Cappelli, P. (2008b). "Talent Management for the Twenty-First Century." *Harvard Business Review*, March: 74-81.

Jäger, W. (2009), 'Talent Management is Personal management', In Jäger, W. and Lukasczyk, A. (Eds.), *Talent Management—Strategien, Umsetzung, Perspektiven*, 15-24, Köln: Luchterhand.

Lewis, R.E. and Heckman, R.J. (2006) "Talent Management: A critical review", *Human Resource Management Review*, 1.

McDonnell, A., Lamare, R., Gunnigle, P. and Lavelle, J. (2009), 'Developing tomorrow's leaders—Evidence of global talent management in multinational enterprises', *Journal of World Business*, 45, pp. 150-60.

Michaels, E., Hanfield-Jones, H. and Axelrod, B. (2001), 'War for talent', Boston: Harvard Business School Press.

Rao, H. and Drazin, R. (2002) "Overcoming resource constraints on product innovation by recruiting talent from rivals: A study of the mutual fund industry, 1986-94", *Academy of Management Review*, 45, 491-507.

Scullion, H., Collings, D.G. and Caligiuri, P. (2010), 'Gobal Talent Management', *Journal of World Business*, 45, pp. 105-08.

Somaya, D. and Williamson, I.O. (2008) "Rethinking the 'war for talent'", MIT Sloan Management Review, 49, 4, 29-34.

Tymon, W.G., Stumpf, S.A. and Doh, J.P. (2010), 'Exploring talent management in India: The neglected role of intrinsic rewards', *Journal of World Business*, 45, pp. 109-21.

Ulrich, D. (2006), 'The talent trifecta', *Workforce Management*, pp. 32-33.

DNA, "Social Media Becoming Double Edged Sword", 22 August, 2012, Page 8 Danik Bhaskar Publication, Indore.

DNA, "Social Media Being Misused", 22 August, 2012, Page 12 Danik Bhaskar Publication, Indore.

CHAPTER 36

TALENT MANAGEMENT

–*S.S. Aggarwal* and *G.M. Saxena*

ABSTRACT

Globalization has brought on dynamic markets and competition, and with that obliged companies to focus on long-term strategies and a greater focus on attracting, developing and retaining its employees. The present hunt for talent can be entitled as talent management, a concept that nowadays cannot be avoided. Talent management is identifying recruiting, hiring and encouraging people with strong potential to succeed in an organization and the timeframe for implementing this varies according to the size o f the organization. Many organizations speak about the importance of retaining their talent, but workplace analysts point out that few organizations with a mature plan have implemented talent management which addresses the entire cycle from hire to retire.

Introduction

Talent management implies recognizing a person's inherent skills, traits, personality and offering him a matching job. Every person has a unique talent that suits a particular job profile and any other position will cause discomfort. It is the job of the management, particularly the HR department, to place candidates with prudence and caution. A wrong fit will result in further hiring, re-training and other wasteful activities.

Talent management is beneficial to both the organization and the employees. The organization benefits from increased productivity and capability; a better linkage between individuals' efforts and business goals; commitment of valued employees; reduced turnover; increased bench strength and a better fit between people's jobs and skills. Employees benefit from higher motivation and commitment; career development; increased knowledge about and contribution to company goals; sustained motivation and job satisfaction.

In these days of highly competitive world, where change is the only constant factor, it is important for an organization to develop the most important resource of all—the human resource. In this globalized world, it is only the human resource that can provide an organization the competitive edge because under the new trade agreements, technology can be easily transferred from one country to another and there is no dearth for sources of cheap finance. But it is the talented workforce that is very hard to find. The biggest problem is how to retain the present workforce and stop them from quitting?

Increasing Knowledge: The knowledge era has necessitated the retaining of those talents which have the ability to assimilate new technologies and knowledge, which are growing at a pace never seen before.

Getting the right people with the right skills into the right jobs, a common definition of talent management is the basic people management challenge in organizations. While the focus of talent management tends to be on management and executive positions, the issues apply to all jobs that are hard to fill.

Decisions about talent management shape the competencies that organizations have and their ultimate success, and from the perspective of individuals, these decisions determine the path and pace of careers. Talent management practices can have a crucial impact on society as well. The lifetime employment model of the post-WW II generation, for example, provided the economic stability that created middle-class society.

The concept of talent management has evolved into a common and essential management practice and what was once solely attached to recruitment now covers a multitude of areas including organisational capability, individual development, performance enhancement and succession planning.

There are a range of views about the usefulness of the specific term—and indeed its meaning. However, broadly speaking it can be understood as referring to the "identification, development, engagement/retention and deployment of those employees who are particularly valuable to an organisation—either in view of their 'high potential' for the future or because they are fulfilling business/operation-critical roles."

The business case for taking a strategic approach to talent management is strong and persuasive. CEO's as well as HR directors are now likely to number talent management among their key priorities.

Methodology

This research study is one of the industry's most in-depth study of trends, best-practices, and industry solutions in corporate talent management. It clearly identifies how to best apply talent management programs, processes, and systems for the greatest business impact. This research program studied more than 60 organizations business, talent, and HR processes and includes in-depth analysis of 10 best-practice processes, in eight functional areas:

- Workforce planning
- Performance management
- Competency management
- Leadership development
- Succession planning
- Learning and development
- Compensation
- Talent management software systems.

Using Bersin and Associates what works research methodology, we analyzed data elements to identify key business drivers, trends, and best practices. We also interviewed some vice-presidents and directors of HR to develop specific examples and case studies throughout this report.

This groundbreaking research study is designed to give corporate HR managers and executives specific, actionable recommendations which deliver high-impact business results.

Readers will find dozens of clear, easy-to-apply examples they can immediately apply to their organizations.

Importance of Talent Management

Like human capital, talent management is gaining increased attention. Talent management (TM) brings together a number of important human resources (HR) and management initiatives. Organisations that formally decide to "manage their talent" undertake a strategic analysis of their current HR processes. This is to ensure that a co-ordinated, performance-oriented approach is adopted. Quite often, organisations adopting a talent management approach will focus on co-ordinating and integrating:

- Recruitment—ensuring the right people are attracted to the organisation.
- Retention—developing and implementing practices that reward and support employees.
- Employee development—ensuring continuous informal and formal learning and development.
- Leadership and "high potential employee" development—specific development programs for existing and future leaders.
- Performance management—specific processes that nurture and support performance, including feedback/measurement.
- Workforce planning—planning for business and general changes, including the older workforce and current/future skills shortages.
- Culture—development of a positive, progressive and high performance "way of operating".

An important step is to identify the staff or employees (people and positions) that are critical to the organisation. They do not necessarily have to be senior staff members. Many organisations lost a lot of "organisational knowledge" in the downsizing exercises of a few years ago. The impact of the loss was not immediately apparent. However, it did not take long for many companies to realize their mistake when they did not have people with the knowledge and skills to either anticipate or solve problems that arose. The current discussions about skill shortages and the ageing population are also helping organisations to focus on the talent management issue. It may not be possible to simply go out and recruit new people to meet operational needs. Many leading companies have decided to develop their own people, rather than trying to hire fully skilled workers. In summary, every organisation should be implementing talent management principles and approaches.

The Challenge

The challenge of talent management has two facets to it. First is how to find new people and second is how to retain the present workforce. Each of the challenges has to be tackled in the most efficient way possible so that the organization can achieve its objectives.

The First Challege—Where to Find New Talent?

All the organizations are finding loads of business opportunities and consequently, their revenues are growing at a rapid pace. The increasing business opportunities has necessitated that these organizations go in for massive recruitment. But the question is where to find the best talent which is able to fit the job description and also adjust to the organization's values and norms. If we scan the environment, we find there is a shortage of skilled workforce that can be employed. Some of the possible reasons that have led to the shortage are:

Demographic Constraints: This is a common problem faced by many of the developed countries, where a large chunk of its population is nearing the age of retirement or is over 50 years. USA, Germany and Japan are facing the same problem. All these countries will see a decline in their workforce and talent. In the coming years, they will see a great shortage in their skilled professionals.

Importance

First, let us look at some of the reasons for the importance of talent management.

Globalization: Now for any jobseeker the whole world is the potential place to find employment. One can know the opportunities available in any part of the world easily and the number of talent seekers has also increased.

Increased Competition: Increased competition in the marketplace has necessitated the need for consistently good performance on the side of organizations. These have made the companies to put in all efforts to hire and retain the best talent in the respective field of operation.

Existing Educational System: The graduates and the postgraduates that are being churned out of the universities are found to be ill-equipped to handle the challenges of the workplace. They are mostly equipped with only the theoretical aspects of the issues and lack the application part. The educational system is faulty and does not take industry needs into consideration, resulting in a mismatch between industry requirements and educational preparation.

Cost Factor: Recruiting new employees is becoming tougher and tougher in the developing countries, where the HR department has to sort out thousands of applications for a handful of jobs. Finding right person for the right job becomes a very difficult process. It also involves very high cost to conduct the recruitment and selection process for such a large population of applicants.

Attracting the Best Talent: This is another challenge. As was the case in the past, the best available talent is not just motivated by the name and fame of the organization. Not any more. They have a new set of motivators like—challenging work, conducive work environment and freedom from bureaucratic structure.

The Second Challege—How to Retain the Existing Employees?

Gone are the days when a person would join an organization in his mid-20s and would work till his retirement in the late-50s. Today the young professionals hop jobs, especially during the first 4-5 years of their work life. Though the Indian service industry is basking in the light of outsourced jobs from the developed countries, they also cannot ignore the fact that the BPO industry is also facing one of the highest attrition rates, in fact never heard before in India, of around 35%.

It is a fact that its the people that add value to organizations. It is also a fact that humans are a restless species who, unlike the immovable Banyan tree, cannot stay rooted in one place. People need to move on for one reason or another, and the organization stands to lose. Let us look at some of the reasons behind the massive attrition rates:

1. Gap between organizational values and goals and the personal values and goals is one of the major reasons of the attrition rates. If they go parallel, there is no way both would be satisfied and inevitably, the organization would lose out on a talented employee.
2. Working environment is another major factor. Employees in the knowledge era demand creative and a democratic work environment. Failure on the part of the management to provide such an environment will result in a talented employee leaving the organization.
3. The competitive world has made sure that there is high work pressure on the employees of any organization. This has led to psychological problems like stress, and in extreme situations, total burnouts. It also leads to other health-related problems.
4. Movement for higher salary is also common among the younger professionals. There is no shortage for organizations who are looking for talented employees and who are ready to shell out a hefty salary for a talented person. Other lures like better job opportunities, higher posts and overseas assignments are also major factors in the attrition rates.
5. Not taking proper care during the recruitment and selection process and not taking proper care to fit the right person to the right job also breeds dissatisfaction among the employees.
6. Bad or opaque policies from management on issues of succession planning and promotion, appointments for senior positions also is a major factor which makes the organization lose out on the talented employees.
7. The professionals have different aspirations at different times of their career. During the initial years, they have good salary and foreign assignments. Next on the list is working on cutting edge technology. More seasoned professionals look for learning opportunities. So employees tend to move to those organizations which provide them with means to fulfill their aspirations.

Retaining the present employees is of the foremost importance to the organizations because the company would have already incurred heavy costs in the form of training and development. Now if the organization has to look for a replacement for the employee who has left, it involves a lot of costs like—hiring costs, training costs and the induction costs.

Also it takes some time for the new employee to adjust to the new work environment. During this time, the productivity of the employee will be low. The HR department will have to fit the new employee into a proper role in the organization. Apart from causing the company a monetary loss and breaks in their day-to-day operations, attrition contributes to knowledge transfer, which is a great loss and adversely affects business.

The Question is—How to Manage the Talent?

It is now proved beyond doubt that, in the era of technology and knowledge, talent is in the driving seat. One who possesses, it dictates. Not he who pays for it. It is the demand of the time that business leaders elevate management of talent to a burning corporate priority. It is not a walk in the park for the talent market. Quality people are no longer available in plenty, easily replaceable and relatively inexpensive.

These are some of the measures that should be taken into account to hire and retain talent in the organization, to be efficient and competitive in this highly competitive world:

Hire the Right People: Proper care must be taken while hiring the people itself. It would be beneficial for an organization to recruit young people and nurture them, than to substitute by hiring from other organizations. Questions to be asked at this stage are: Whether the person has the requisite skills needed for the job? Whether the person's values and goals match with those of organization's? In short, care must be taken to fit the right person to the right job.

Keep the Promises: Good talent cannot be motivated by fake platitudes, half-truths and broken promises. Unfulfilled expectations can breed dissatisfaction among the employees and make them either leave the organization or work below their productive level. Promises made during the hiring stage must be kept to build loyalty among the employees, so that they are satisfied and work to their fullest capability.

Good Working Environment: It has to be accepted by the organizations that highly talented persons make their own rules. They have to be provided with a democratic and a stimulating work environment. The organizational rules must be flexible enough to provide them with freedom to carry out their part of task to their liking, as long as the task is achieved. Opportunities should also be provided to the employees to achieve their personal goals.

Recognition of Merit: It is highly motivating for any person if his talent is recognized and is suitably rewarded. One way is providing them with salary commensurate with their performance. Promotions and incentives based on performance are another way of doing it. Another way is by providing them with challenging projects. This will achieve two objectives—it makes employee feel that he is considered important (a highly motivating factor) and gets the work done in a efficient manner and brings out the best in the employee.

Providing Learning Opportunities: Employees must be provided with continuous learning opportunities on and off work field through management development programmes and distance learning programmes. This will also benefit the organization in the form of highly talented workforce.

The Corporate Talent Challenge

This research shows how demographic, business, and industry-specific issues have created the need for corporate talent management—how the workforce is changing, where workforce shortages exist, and how corporate demographics are driving shortages in critical talent areas. It then shows how the top eight talent challenges in today's corporate environment affect each industry and HR as a whole. This research will help you clearly understand why talent management is not just a "new name" for HR, but a business imperative with very different challenges in each industry.

The Business Drivers of Talent Management

This research breaks down the business drivers and talent drivers by industry, covering 20 different industry segments. It analyzes the top three business issues in each industry, the top talent-related challenges in each industry, and then shows the linkage between business drivers and talent management solutions. It helps readers understand specifically how to tie talent management solutions to specific business problems such as the shortage of mid-level managers, rolling out new products, mergers and acquisitions, and eight other business challenges.

Results

Job satisfaction has surprisingly increased since 2006, despite the impact of the recession, according to the new quarterly Employee Outlook survey of more than 3,000 employees by the Chartered Institute of Personnel and Development.

The survey finds that the net proportion of people satisfied with their job has increased to 46 from 26 in 2006, and the proportion of people who say their job makes them feel cheerful most or all of the time has also gone up.

However, the survey suggests fault lines are developing that will undermine employee well-being, morale and commitment if not addressed. Exactly three-quarters of respondents reported that their organizations have been affected by the recession with half (52 per cent) citing increases in work-related stress as a consequence and nearly four in 10 (38 per cent) agreeing there has been a rise in office politics.

The proportion of people who said their jobs make them worried or tense has also increased since the CIPD's 2006 employee attitudes and engagement survey, and nearly six in 10 employees said they are worried by the future.

Ben Willmott, senior public policy adviser and co-author of the survey at CIPD, said: "Job satisfaction may have edged up, but this could be the employee opinion survey equivalent of a fixed grin. Employees grateful to have a job at all are less likely to grumble and more likely to see scorched earth rather than greener grass on the other side of the fence.

"Beneath this positive glow, however, our survey highlights the impact the recession is having on the workplace. Without action to tackle some of the stresses and strains that are clear in our survey, employers could find employee health and well-being deteriorating and employee engagement tailing off at precisely the time they need all hands to the pump to survive the recession and thrive in the recovery."

The research shows a third (37 per cent) of employees worry about being made redundant as a result of the recession, and most believe finding a new job would be difficult. Almost four in 10 (36 per cent) employees reported that their organizations have made redundancies or are planning to make job cuts, and just under a fifth said their employers have cut back on training (17 per cent) or frozen pay (18 per cent).

The survey, conducted by YouGov, also highlights problems with how people are managed. Although most people feel supported and treated fairly by their line managers, they are much less happy with the extent their managers discuss their training and development, give feedback or coach them. Employees are particularly critical of senior managers, with less than a fifth agreeing that they trust them and only a quarter agreeing that they consult employees about important decisions.

Internal development of talent collapsed in the 1970s when business forecasting failed to predict the downturn in the economy, and the talent pipelines continued to turn out talent under the forecast assumptions of booming corporate growth. The excess supply of talent and the no-layoff policies for white collar workers caused a bloating of corporate organizations, and the steepness of the 1981 recession in the US and elsewhere led virtually all companies to back away from developing talent. Lifetime employment came to an end, and the reengineering processes cut away the development practices and staff that created talent. After all, if the priority was to get rid of talent, why would companies maintain the programs designed to create it?

Taleo's graphical representation emphasizes the mandate of talent management to respond to business goals and consequently be the driver of business performance. Talent management is depicted as a circular—not a linear—set of activities.

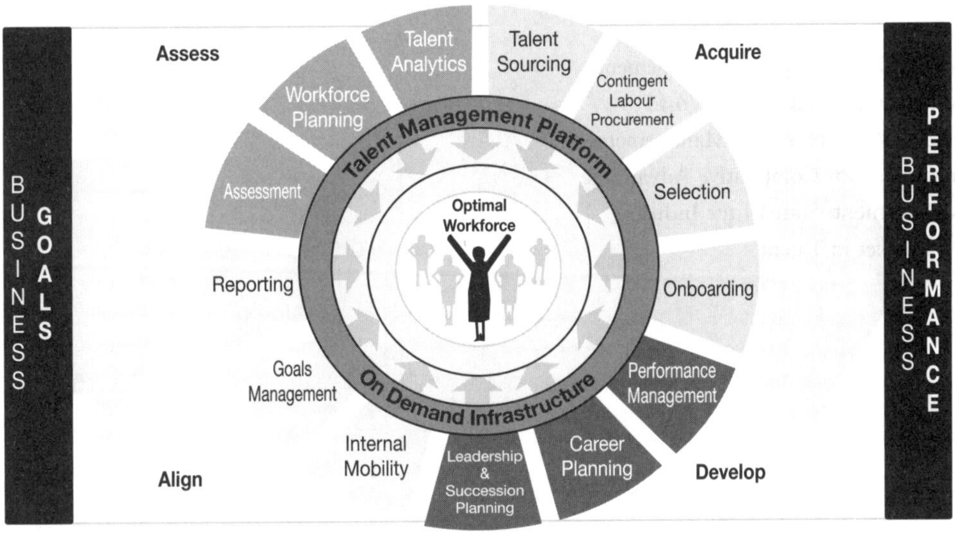

Conclusion

We need a new way of thinking about the talent management challenge. A new framework for talent management has to begin by being clear about the goal. Talent management is not an end in itself. It is not about developing employees or creating succession plans. Nor is it about achieving specific benchmarks like a five per cent turnover rate, having the most educated workforce, or any other tactical outcome. The goal of talent management is the much more general but important task of helping the organization achieve its overall objectives. In the business world, that objective is to make money. An important part of the goal of helping the organization is to address the financial challenge associated with developing employees and recouping the investments in their development now that labor markets.

Highly demanding business environment makes it imperative for the organizations to build competence in the form of superior intellectual capital. It is agreed by almost all CEOs of big companies that it is the human resource—a talented one—that can provide them competitiveness in the long run.

So it is the duty of the HR department to nurture a brigade of talented workforce, which can win them the war in the business field. The talent has to be spotted, carefully nurtured and most importantly preserved.

Infosys, Wipro, Satyam, HCL Technologies and i-Flex Solutions. These are some of the companies, which have the highest revenue growth rates year after year. Few of them also have revenues exceeding $1 bn. They provide great work environment to their people. Good salary, perks, overseas assignments, challenging and highly competitive work environment and a great future. Right person for the right job—is the new mantra.

REFERENCES

Article on Talent Management Origins
Softscape
Original Paper from Softscape
The People Problem in Talent Management
Talent Management FAQ—HR World
The Financial Value of Talent Management
Managing Talent for Competitive Advantage
Talent Management: State of the Industry
Making a Market in Talent

CHAPTER 37

FACTORS AFFECTING KNOWLEDGE MANAGEMENT AND SERVICE INNOVATION PRACTICES IN THE HOSPITALITY INDUSTRY

–*Sunil Jangid* and *Jyoti Garg*

ABSTRACT

A survey and interviews, this research paper aims at clarifying the factors affecting knowledge management and service innovation practices in the hospitality industry, in the context of Rajasthan hotels. Additionally, service innovation perceptions and attitudes are examined at the individual and organizational levels. Findings indicate that teamwork, leadership, cooperation, managerial support and organizational culture are significant factors which positively influence the level of knowledge management and sharing. Service innovation orientation at the individual and team levels was found to be higher compared to the organizational level. These findings can be beneficial to the improvement of knowledge and innovation strategies in the Rajasthan hotel industry.

Introduction

Knowledge and its management are increasingly being perceived as an indispensable source of competitive advantage in contemporary business literature. During the past decade, the importance of the effective management of knowledge has been a matter of scrutiny on the part of scholars and professionals alike. Innovation has also become a buzzword in academic as well as business circles. Although it is considered as an extremely popular field of analysis and source of competitive advantage, it has traditionally suffered from being largely associated with the manufacturing sector. Innovation in services is a relatively new field of analysis, but one which is not to be disregarded because of its increasing role and importance in the world economy. Among service industries, tourism and hospitality can be considered as a crucial sector, as it is one of the fastest growing areas of the global economy.

The service sector is of great importance to the Rajasthan economy and tourism is among sectors which have been drawing the highest national and international financial investment in the past years. The aim of this research is to identify approaches to knowledge management and sharing employed in Rajasthan hotels as a subset of hospitality industry in order to clarify to what extent knowledge sharing and therefore innovation in the offered services is achieved. The authors have adopted a hybrid approach to the research in question, by both designing a survey which questions the knowledge management and sharing practices employed by hotels and the subsequent service innovation performance, and by conducting semi-structured interviews with hotel managers at relevant departments. The hybrid approach provides a source for both empirical and qualitative evidence lending itself to multiple levels of analysis and elimination of possible bias. It is hoped that findings will be of importance to academics, practitioners and policymakers alike, as this is a crucial sector and a driving force not only for the Rajasthan economy but on a global scale, as well.

Knowledge Management and Sharing

The literature on knowledge as a crucial asset in creating sustainable growth and competitive strength ranges from the analysis of the creation and transfer of knowledge among individuals, organizational units and companies, to theories on the means of individual and organizational learning (Winter, 1983; Hamel et al., 1989; Senge, 1990; Kogut and Zander, 1992; Dixon, 1994; Nonaka, 1994; Nonaka and Takeuchi, 1995; Grant, 1996; Spender, 1996). The sharing of knowledge has also attracted interest and much has been written and analyzed in this area (Helmstadter, 2003; Ipe, 2003). The processes of identifying, capturing and leveraging knowledge, know-how and best practices inside organizations contribute substantially to creating competitive advantages. Through the systematic sharing of knowledge among members of an organization, redundancy in knowledge production is decreased, diffusion of best practices is secured and effective problem solving is enabled by making relevant personal knowledge available to the problem-solving process (Michailova and Husted, 2001:2).

Knowledge management has been found to have an important influence on service innovation performance. This is meaningful because managing knowledge is also an incremental process which links individuals, teams, departments and organizations through knowledge sharing in order to achieve organizational learning. Learning is an integral part of innovation as it provides a knowledge base on which the skills and competences necessary for innovativeness can be built. Many studies have focused on investigating and demonstrating the role and impact of knowledge management in supporting, improving and innovating different business processes and functions (Hallin and Marnburg, 2007). These studies focus on developing management processes that aim to build and maintain good quality customer relations, enhance customer lifetime value, and address the intense global competition and the dynamically changing tourists' behavior. It is therefore clear that there is a direct link between well-designed knowledge management applications and innovation in the services offered.

Innovation in Services

The general understanding is that service-sector firms in general are less likely to innovate than manufacturing firms, but in fact they are becoming more innovative and knowledge-intensive (Hu et al., 2009; Sipe and Testa, 2009; Hjalager, 2010). Current academic literature on innovation in the services sector ranges from the troublesome definition and intangibility of innovation, to the lack of adequate qualitative and quantitative analyses concerning services and to the difficulties in measuring the end results of services innovation in comparison to manufacturing. Statistical evidence supports the notion that services are increasingly knowledge-based, innovative and drivers of economic growth. Innovation surveys suggest that service-sector firms innovate to increase market share, to improve service quality and to expand product or service range (Scott and Bruce, 1994; Enz and Siguaw, 2003). However, how innovation occurs in the service sector is less well understood. Most innovations in the service sector appear to be non-technical and incremental changes in processes and procedures (Ottenbacher and Gnoth, 2005).

An important aspect of innovation in practice seems to be the effective perception of the diversity in customer needs, wants and expectations in order to better attract and satisfy them. On the other hand, the perception of these notions may not be adequate as various obstacles stemming from the lack of time, money, human resources, know-how or bureaucracy can stifle the actual development and execution of innovative services. Innovation in services can be executed on the service and process dimensions. On the service or product dimension, innovation can be carried out in the form of new and impressive buildings, catering new products, incorporating new technologies in hotel rooms, opening SPAs and wellness centers, or creating new tourism destinations. Innovation on the process dimension includes developing Internet-based operations such as e-booking, using web-based social networking sites as an effective marketing tool, developing new quality, process and financial control systems, working with full-time personnel and providing training and personal development opportunities and developing inter-industrial cooperative ventures with businesses in other sectors.

The surge for globalizing products and services has hit hard many sectors. Arguably, tourism is one of the sectors which are most prone to economic, political, social and natural fluctuations on a global scale. As an example, one of the traditionally strong tourism destinations, India, has been under increasing competitive pressure by Asian and Pacific destinations which offer relatively cheap and diverse travel opportunities. Indian members, in their Lisbon strategy outline, thus reached the basic conclusion that innovation in tourism services was the key to surmount competitive pressures and to restore India as a stronghold of tourism. The Indian has since embarked on a renewal and relaunch project in order to regain its competitive strength and increase tourism generated revenues. A classic example reflecting this initiative has been the Marriot Hotel launched and well-marketed by Indian successful innovation in the tourism industry can thus simply is defined as increasing the value of Rajasthani experience or of the service offering. In this sector, customer satisfaction and benefit are a function of the received service quality vis-à-vis the price paid for the service. With relation to successful innovation, this means increasing the quality of the service or decreasing the price for it.

Although it is obvious that technology often plays an important role in industrial innovation and services innovation can equally benefit from this, it is not mandatory to base innovation in tourism services on technological innovation. As the above discussion demonstrates, most innovation in this sector is performed on existent technological bases and is of an intangible form, meant to create economic value and increase customer satisfaction through the introduction of new concepts. This may seem straightforward and relatively easy compared to inventing breakthroughs in the technological field, but it actually is not.

First, the tourism industry is heavily based on human interaction and satisfaction which need an almost perfect understanding of human nature, behavior and attitudes.

Second, it involves physically moving people all over the world, pointing to the need for an efficient, dependable and flawless infrastructure.

Third, it is always easier to generate an idea or a strategy in comparison with its actual implementation. All these notions point to the fact that the tourism sector is worthy of investigation on the bases of knowledge management and service innovation.

Methodology

In order to investigate the understanding and execution of knowledge management, knowledge sharing and innovation practices in the Rajasthan hotel context, the authors employed a hybrid approach by administering a two part survey and conducting semi-structured interviews with hotel managers. Survey questions were developed based on the existent literature in the areas of knowledge management, sharing and innovation. Similarly, brief interview questions were developed. Sampling for data gathering was predominantly based on convenience. A personal database developed throughout more than a decade of business and academic liaisons with hotels in the greater Rajasthan region was the main source for contacts. Besides this database, the "Rajasthan Hotel & Travel Guide" (www.travelguide.com.rj) and the RTDC (Association of Rajasthan Tourism Development Corporation Ltd., www.rtdc.in) websites were used as additional sources for contacts. Through the convenience sampling method, a total of 157 hotel managers from various departments were contacted at 33 different locations. Survey questions were first developed in English, translated into Hindi language and then back into English so as to pinpoint and modify any potential inconsistencies due to the translation process. The survey was posted online in English language, potential participants were invited by email and given a choice to reply in the desired language, and follow up phone calls were made in order to increase the level of participation. A total of 26 replies were received, 7 of which were unusable, resulting in a return rate of 19, or 12.10 per cent. Although international hotel chains were predominantly targeted for reasons of simplicity, ease of access, and a higher level of assumed professionalism, 98 per cent of the replies were received via the English language survey, therefore participants are assumed to be almost totally of Rajasthan origin.

In addition to the survey, two face-to-face and three phone interviews were conducted with general managers and departmental managers of large sized, 5-star hotels. Interview questions largely included what is exactly viewed or understood as innovation, whether innovation had been performed in these hotels in the past three years and what the main methods/activities of knowledge management and sharing were (if any). These interviews were also directly and indirectly helpful in the design of the survey.

Results

Demographics

Among the survey participants, 54 per cent were women and 46 per cent were men, aged between 25 and 48, with an average age of 36.50 per cent of the participants had a high school or vocational diploma, 64 per cent had a university or equivalent degree and 6 per cent had a postgraduate degree. 22 per cent were unit chiefs (supervisor, deputy manager or manager), more than 78 per cent were departmental supervisors/managers, and 4 per cent were at the highest level of management (general manager or CEO). Participants' tenure in the hospitality industry is presented in Table 1.

Table 1: Tenure in the Hospitality Industry

Age	*No. of Participations (In %)*
2-6 Years	9
6-10 Years	19
10-14 Years	15
14-18 Years	18
18-22 Years	17
26 Years & Above	22

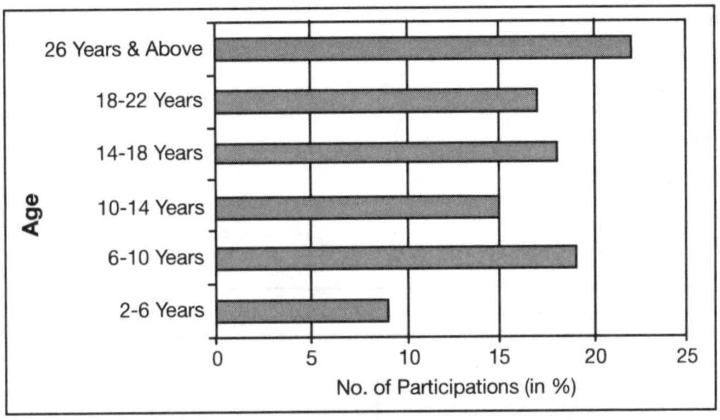

Tenure in the Hospitality Industry

Table 2: Tenure at the Current Workplace

Age	*Tenure at the Current Workplace (In %)*
2-6 Years	14
6-10 Years	25
10-14 Years	18
14-18 Years	22
18-22 Years	13
26 Years & Above	8

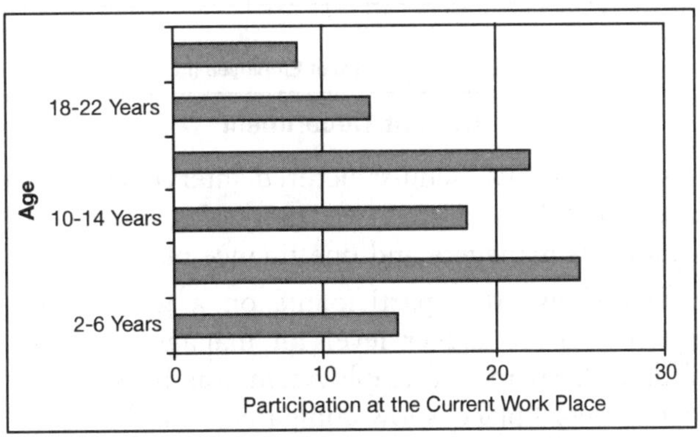

Tenure at the Current Workplace (In %)

Table 3: Current Department of Employment

Name of Department	*No. of Employee (In %)*
Food & Beverage	7.3
Rooms	26
Personnel	11.5
Finance & Accounts	13.8
Sales	11.5
General Affairs	3.8
Security	3.2
IT	5.6
Public Relations	7.4
Marketing	3.2
Purchasing	2.2
Customer Services	3.3
Others	1.2

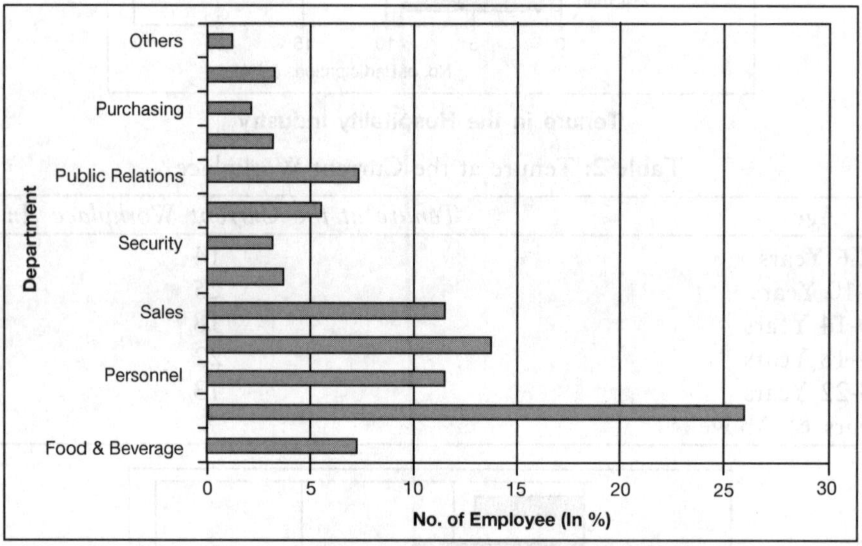

Current Department

In addition to the survey results, semi-structured interviews were conducted with seven managers including one general manager, two marketing managers, one public relations manager, two human resources managers and one finance manager.

The demographic data shows that participants on a general scale were well-educated professionals working at middle to higher levels of management. Tenure in the hospitality industry and data regarding departmental employment was relatively well distributed. On the other hand, tenure at current workplace is low compared with the overall period worked in the industry, pointing to the fact that the industry has a traditionally high job turnover rate. As a whole, based on the demographic data gathered, the sample universe can be considered as knowledgeable and adequately credible in the issues investigated.

Knowledge Management and Knowledge Sharing Practices

Regarding the perception, sharing and execution of knowledge management practices and applications, the main factors investigated were managerial support in the sense of top management and supervisory support, teamwork, leadership, organizational culture/climate and cooperation. The most significant results in these areas are presented in Table 4.

Table 4: Factors in Support of Knowledge Management (KM) and Sharing Practices

KM Factors	*Negative Tendency*	*Neutral/No Idea (%)*	*Positive Tendency (%)*
Managerial Support	29	9	62
Teamwork	9	3	88
Leadership	13	8	79
Org. Culture/Climate	29	13	58
Cooperation	11	5	84

Results show that in the area of knowledge management and sharing, there is a high level of teamwork and cooperation coupled with a good sense of leadership. On the other hand, managerial/supervisory support and organizational culture/climate as an incubator of knowledge management practices were found to be still in the positive territory, but at a relatively low level. An exploratory factor analysis also supported these findings by grouping management support with culture as one factor, and the other three variables as a separate factor. This result has not come as a surprise as information in the same vein was also gathered via the verbal interviews. Although contemporary personal development concepts such as leadership training and cooperative activities such as teamwork are widely known, transferred and applied especially through professional training programmers in the Rajasthan hospitality sector, there is still a considerable amount of drawback on the part of superiors in sharing and transferring knowledge to their subordinates and to the organization as a whole. This inclination results in or may be aggravated by the fact that organizational culture and climate do not adequately support knowledge sharing among the members of the organization.

Innovation in Services

Innovation attitude and execution was examined on personal and organizational levels. Areas investigated on the personal level were new idea generation and creativity, management of the innovation process and teamwork/collaboration attitudes. On the organizational level, resource adequacy and allocation, level of interdepartmental collaboration, management-front line service personnel relations and employee capabilities with relation to innovation were explored. Results obtained in these areas are presented in Table 5.

Table 5: Innovation in Services

Service Innovation	*Negative Tendency (%)*	*Neutral/No Idea (%)*	*Positive Tendency (%)*
Personal Level:			
New Idea Generation/Creativity	13	4	83
Process Management	27	9	64
Teamwork/Collaboration	11	8	81
Organizational Level:			
Resource Allocation	23	21	56
Departmental Collaboration	24	17	59
Mgmt-Personnel Relations	19	13	68
Capabilities	28	23	49

As Table 5 demonstrates, service innovation attitude and execution at the personal level was found to be generally at a higher level compared to the organizational level. At the personal level new idea generation, creativity and collaboration geared towards innovative practices at the team level were found to be perceived and executed well, whereas the management of the innovation process was at a relatively low rate of success. The reason for this outcome may be due to the fact that innovative ideas can be generated and shared by individuals in formal and informal contexts, during work or off hours and with close team members. On the other hand, actually following up on these ideas and executing them as a process in a professional and orderly manner is not as easy as generating them in the first place. Therefore, this is a rational and expectable finding.

At the organizational level, although not completely grim, findings are at a lower level compared to the individual level. The high rate of neutral/no idea replies seems to be due to the fact that despite most respondents were departmental or unit managers, they still may not be able to see the big picture concerning service innovation at their organization as a whole. People tend to know more about themselves as individuals and their close co-workers compared to the organization as a whole strategic structure. The comparatively low rate of neutral/no idea answers at the individual level also confirms this rationale. Resource allocation and departmental collaboration are crucial aspects in the generation and implementation of innovative services. Findings show that there is room for improvement in these areas. The foremost potential obstacle in attempting to increase and equitably distribute resources in order to achieve innovation in services will be departmental conflict over resources and their respective allocation. Additionally, interviews with hotel managers almost unanimously revealed that especially in hotels that are part of a global chain, there is very little freedom left to local management for the implementation of independent innovative services, as local services and potential innovation are almost totally dictated by the headquarters. Standardization and centralization of services is of course a practical method for optimizing cost management and customer expectations. On the other hand, these may also be factors that stifle innovation, differentiation and globalization strategies in the long run.

Relations between management and personnel regarding the implementation of innovations received the highest points in comparison with the other organizational issues and respondents seemed to have more clarity regarding this point. This is encouraging, yet has clear potential to improve. The lowest and most discouraging result was received on how the managers of hotels view employees' capabilities in the area of service innovation. Innovation capability is an indispensable basis for generating and implementing successful innovations, but findings point to a lack of this capability in the human resources of Rajasthan hotels. If hotels want to achieve a higher level of innovative services in order to gain competitive advantage on a global scale, this clearly presents a hurdle which must be overcome through improved employee selection methods and training. For many years, the tourism industry workforce in Rajasthan was mostly populated by people whose real profession may not have been tourism and who were had not especially trained to work in this field. Because the tourism sector has become increasingly vital for Indian economy, many vocational schools and universities have been establishing tourism and hospitality management departments in the past years. It is hoped that their graduates coupled with governmental policies supporting the sector will increase professionalism and convey a better sense of innovation throughout this valuable industry.

Conclusion

Knowledge management and innovation have become buzzwords in the global business arena, but with good reason; both of them are indispensable sources of competitive advantage and they are also closely linked to each other. In the first part of this research, some of the determinants of knowledge management and sharing practices were clarified, namely as teamwork, leadership, cooperation, managerial support and organizational culture. The first three factors were found to be at a relatively high level, whereas the last two received a lower rate. This means that knowledge management and sharing practices are performed and supported well horizontally through teamwork, leadership and cooperation among individuals, but management support and organizational culture/climate are less supportive. In Indian businesses, rigid vertical hierarchies and autocratic style of management are commonplace. Therefore, at a first glance, the low level of management and cultural support in knowledge management and sharing practices may not come as a surprise. On the other hand, the research was conducted predominantly in international hotel chains where technical rules and procedures are globally standardized. These findings point to the fact that although systems, rules, procedures and infrastructure may be standardized, managerial approaches and styles may not be standardized across a business worldwide, which accounts for cultural differences among nations. This research lacks the international culture dimension, which could be a topic to be further investigated and clarified. Such an additional dimension of the research would also lend itself to comparative analysis among different national cultures.

The second area of the research was service innovation perceptions and attitudes. Verbal interviews revealed that some managers are not really sure about what exactly an innovation in services is, which constitutes an overarching issue to be resolved beyond the scope of this paper. Another important finding is that although during verbal interviews managers were quite positive about knowledge sharing practices in their respective organizations, survey results showed a higher level of innovation attitudes at the individual and peer level, compared to the organizational level. Teamwork and collaboration are found to be highly positive in the area of knowledge management as well as service innovation, but on an organizational level resource allocation and departmental collaboration towards innovating services are found to be quite low. One of the issues here concerns the internal workings of the business and the other issue concerns external pressures from headquarters. Internally, the interdepartmental conflict over resource allocation is a classic issue. Perhaps the formation of a cross disciplinary and relatively independent team whose main task is to gather information across departments in order to develop innovative service strategies may be a solution. The external issue concerns the implementation of centrally dictated processes and procedures which are beyond the power and authority of local management. In order to differentiate services by fostering innovation, some freedom should be granted to local managers. The effective use of social networking tools on company intranets have also been found to be beneficial in sharing knowledge and subsequently adopting innovative services across organizations.

As a result, some issues and challenges in effectively managing knowledge and implementing innovative services have been identified and possible solutions have been offered. It is hoped that the findings will delineate some necessary guidelines in order for the hotel industry in Rajasthan to improve its knowledge management practices and develop a more innovative mindset, so as to become more competitive and customer oriented, and ultimately achieve global acclaim.

REFERENCES

Dixon, N.M. (1994). *The Organizational Learning Cycle: How We Can Learn Collectively*. New York: McGraw-Hill.

Enz, C.A., and Siguaw, J. (2003). "Revisiting the best of the best: Innovations in hotel practice". *The Cornell Hotel and Restaurant Administration Quarterly*, 44(5/6): 115-23.

Grant, R.M. (1996). "Toward a knowledge-based theory of the firm". *Strategic Management Journal*, Winter Special Issue, 17: 109-22.

Hallin, C.A., and Marnburg, E. (2008): "Knowledge management in the hospitality industry: A review of empirical research". *Tourism Management*, 29(2): 366-81.

Hamel, G., Doz, Y.L. and Prahalad, C.K. (1989). "Collaborate with your competitors, and win". *Harvard Business Review*, 67(2): 133-39.

Helmstadter, E. (2003). "The institutional economics of knowledge sharing: Basic issues". In E. Helmstadter, (Ed.) *The Economics of Knowledge Sharing: A New Institutional Approach* (pp. 11-38). Cheltenham & Northampton, M.A.: Edward Elgar.

Hjalager, A-M. (2010). "A review of innovation research in tourism". *Tourism Management*, 31(1): 1-12.

Hu, M.-L.M., Horng, J.-S, and Sun, Y.H.C. (2009). "Hospitality teams: Knowledge sharing and service innovation performance". *Tourism Management*, 30(1): 41-50.

Ipe, M. (2003). "Knowledge sharing in organizations: A conceptual framework". *Human Resource Development Review*, 2(4): 337-59.

Kogut, B. and Zander, U. (1992). "Knowledge of the firm, combinative capabilities, and the replication of technology". *Organization Science*, 3(3): 383-97.

CHAPTER 38

A STUDY OF STRESS SOURCES AMONG SCHOOL STUDENTS IN UDAIPUR

–Maina Jain, Sakshi Chouhan and *Dimpy Jain*

ABSTRACT

Child stress is a growing concern for every parent today. Students react in a school in a variety of ways. For some students, studies are stressful while for some it is learning with fun and excitement. For some people source of stress is due to separation from home. Although stress to some extent is very essential for personal growth to occur yet there is a need to cope up with that so that it does not take a big form. This paper was to investigate the sources of stress among school students in Udaipur City. A questionnaire survey was conducted to collect research data in the period of 15 days including a sample size of 150 students studying in various private schools.

The study showed that 62 students experienced high stress, 57 per cent students experienced medium stress and 31 per cent students experienced low stress. Using the percentage tool, the findings of the study also indicated that excessive workload, fear of failure, high expectation from parents and lack of time for other activities creates maximum stress among the students. While competition with fellow students, biasness by teachers and lack of personal attention during classes affect the students at moderate level.

A general conclusion is that there are many factors influence students' stress such as excessive pressure of studies, parent expectations and fear of failure gives impact in students life. "Stress is a feeling one get when they are faced with a challenge and life is leading with challenges only which never ends."

Objective

Extensive research has been done on stress management but this paper aims at finding something new or rather innovative. Through this research paper, researchers were trying to find the major causes of increasing stress among the students studying in private schools. Along with this efforts are being made by suggesting new and innovative strategies which could help them in getting out of this stress.

Introduction

Every person on this earth faces challenges in life and these challenges create stress. Stress is like an iceberg. We can see one-eighth of it above, but what about what's below. Stress is a feeling that one faces due to increasing struggles and challenges in life. Stress is not always negative or harmful. It can be good as it makes a person more alert and gives him a burst of energy. Stress is a mental or physical phenomenon formed through one's cognitive appraisal of the stimulation and is a result of one's interaction with the environment. The existence of stress depends on the existence of the stressor or the sources of stress (Lazarus and Folkman, 1984). Hence, feeling stressed for a long time can affect one's mental and physical health.

Students experience lots of academic stress due to regular exams and tests predictable times along with grade competition, in a small amount of time (Abouserie, 1994). Even though it may seem hard to find ways to relax and get out of all these things, it's important to find those ways as our physical and mental health depends on it. School and college students have most reported suicide cases as it is due to stress of failure or thoughts of excessive competition. So understanding the sources of stress among them and how they can cope with the stress is very important.

School is one of the major sources creating stress among students which basically is due to too much homework, poor academic performance, preparation for tests and main examination, lack of interest in a particular subject, and teacher's fear and punishment. It is important to the society that students should learn and acquire the necessary knowledge and skills that will in turn make them contribute positively to the development of the general economy of any nation. It is also important that institutions to maintain well-balanced academic environment conducive for better learning, with the focus on the students' personal needs. Students have different expectations, goals, and values that they want to fulfill, which is only possible if the students' expectations, goals, and values are integrated with that of the institution (http://jms.nonolympictimes.org/Articles/4.pdf).

Along with this higher expectation from parents who are very concerned about their children's academic achievement and moral behaviors also results in creating stress. Some parents trust their child's teacher more than their own kid who makes a child negative towards his /her parent as well as towards her teacher. Parent's expectation is so much that they ask their children not only to respect teachers and follow moral norms of the school but also become best in the future. These various pressures of studies in school and home put a lot of emotional and mental pressure creating stress. The symptoms identified are stopping the physical growth, hormonal imbalance, anxiety, nervousness, grey hair, dark circles, indigestion, weight loss, endless worries, regular headache, pain in the neck or shoulders. Severe stress results in increasing suicidal cases, violent behavior, and social withdrawal of the child.

Some students explore other ways to deal with the pressure of exams, like running away from home or simply refusing to appear for exams especially when they are facing board exams. While many face sleepless nights, loss of enthusiasm, wavering hands, blood pressure and many negative thoughts. With the aim of relieving students of examination-related stress, a website "ssconline.in", was launched in the Pune city recently. In another move to beat exam stress, a one-year campaign, Slap the Stress, was also launched to help students fight stress. The Slap the Stress campaign involve counseling while entering class X, stress test, student-parent-teacher seminars and entertaining way of learning during the year-long campaign (*The Indian Express*, 2012).

When students are under stress due to studies, he/she sometimes responds in negative ways such as drinking and smoking. This make a bad and a regular habit and they tend to resort to drinking or smoking as coping strategies whenever confronted with complex situations in their lives.

Research Methodology

The methodology adopted for the purpose of our research was through collection of primary data from respondents who were students in different private schools studying in 9th to 12th standard were selected for the research. Collection of primary data was by the mode of questionnaire containing open-ended and close-ended questions assessing studies related stress in students was developed.

We considered a sample size of 150 respondents. It helped us to generalize the findings of the population as a whole.

Analysis and Interpretation

The data collected was analyzed and discussed in the following manner:

Table 1: Showing Level of Stress Experience by Student

Stress Level Experienced	*No. of Respondents*
High	62
Moderate	57
Low	31
Total	150

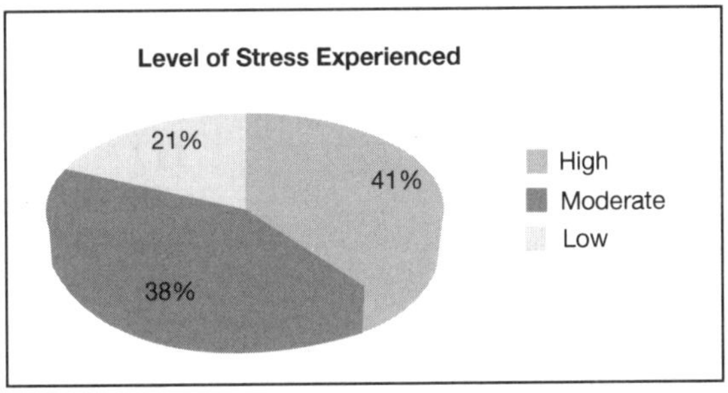

Fig. 1: Showing Contribution Level of Stress Experience by Student in Percentage

Table 1 shows the level of stress experienced by student. Out of 150 respondents, majority 62 (i.e. 41%) of respondents high level of stress while 57 (i.e. 38%) feel moderate and only 31 (i.e. 21%) feel low level of stress. Figure 1 shows response in form of percentage.

Table 2: Showing Various Factors Resulting in Stress

S.No.	*Factors Resulting in Stress*	*No. of Respondents Saying 'Yes'*	*No. of Respondents Saying 'No'*
1.	Continuous poor performance	81 **54**	69 **46**
2.	Biasness by teachers	98 **66**	52 **34**
3.	Excessive workload or homework	126 **84**	24 **16**

S.No.	*Factors Resulting in Stress*	*No. of Respondents Saying 'Yes'*	*No. of Respondents Saying 'No'*
4.	Inadequate resources to do assignments	72 **48**	78 **52**
5.	Competition with fellow students	101 **67**	49 **33**
6.	Overcrowded classrooms	89 **59**	61 **41**
7.	Lack of time for other activities such as sport, party, etc.	106 71	44 29
8.	Low motivation and emotional support	78 **52**	72 **48**
9.	Conflict with teacher and fellow students	55 **37**	95 **63**
10.	Financial problem such as fees, etc.	66 **44**	84 **56**
11.	Inadequate resources, e.g. computers, books, lecturers	44 **29**	106 **71**
12.	Fear of failure	117 **78**	33 **22**
13.	High expectations from my parents	108 **72**	42 **28**
14.	Lack of command over any particular subject	87 **58**	63 **42**
15.	Lack of personal attention during classes	94 **63**	56 **37**

Table 2 reveals factor which results in stress in student. Major factors are excessive workload or homework (i.e. 84%), fear of failure (i.e. 78%), high expectation from parents (i.e. 72%), and lack of time for other activities (i.e. 71%) creating maximum stress among the students. While competition with fellow students (i.e. 67%), biasness by teachers (i.e. 66%) and lack of personal attention during classes (i.e. 63%) affect the students at moderate level.

This indicates that students mostly feel stress due to excessive workload, fear of failure and high expectation from parents.

Findings

Stress is a wide phenomenon as it seems to have universal spread. It depends upon the stress levels that how much stress has affected the students. However, this study is about student stress. Many people think that they understand stress, its factors and its impact on them. But it is not always true. In reality, stress is complex and often misunderstood. Respondents (students) were asked about the level of stress experienced by them and the major factors resulting in stress. They were also asked about the efforts or measures which they will be successful in reducing or minimizing the stress. On the basis of information collected through questionnaire containing open and close ended questions, following are the various finding of the research undertaken:

1. Majority of respondents feel that the level of stress experienced by them is high 62 (i.e. 41%), while 57 (i.e. 38%) feel moderate and only 31 (i.e. 21%) feel low level of stress. This is basically due to excessive workload and fear of failure.
2. Respondents are of the opinion that the major factors which result in stress in student are excessive workload or homework (i.e. 84%), fear of failure (i.e. 78%), high expectation from parents (i.e. 72%), and lack of time for other activities (i.e. 71%) creating maximum stress among the students. While competition with fellow students (i.e. 67%), biasness by teachers (i.e. 66%) and lack of personal attention during classes (i.e. 63%) affect the students at moderate level.
3. On the other hand, factors such as continuous poor performance, inadequate resources to do assignment, overcrowded classrooms, low motivation and emotional support, lack of command over particular subject, conflict with teachers and fellow students, financial problems and inadequate resources make significantly low impact as compared to other factors.

Innovative Strategies to Minimize Stress among School Student

Stress is everywhere in modern life. Identifying and minimizing students' stress as soon as possible and provide adequate support to the student is very necessary as it may take a giant shape in future harming a lot.

1. Teacher plays an important role in making the future of student. Most of the students trust their teachers more than their parents and hence they believe them as their role model. Along with this, good teaching acts as a key in preventing and minimizing distress among students. Teacher must ensure that whatever they teach is well understood by the entire students. School management must also ensure that their teachers are also not in stress related to salary, promotion, job insecurity, increment, etc. Teacher must also help in assignment and other projects and must also avoid physical punishment.
2. School management also plays an important role in minimizing stress. They must ensure that the designed course is not very tough including general curriculum on stress also and stress-coping strategies and must be flexible also. Schools must also take steps such as keeping regular records of students facing stress and providing them support and care to cope with various stressors. They can also refer consulting firms or institutions having professional people for counseling of the students and their parents relating to students physical and mental problems.

   School must include games and various fun-related activities which will be helpful in reducing boredom basically due to excessive workload of studies.

3. Classmates and friend can also be very helpful in reducing stress. Helping in tough subject and proving emotional support will result in building self-competition in the stressed student.
4. Family and parents' support is helpful for students faced with stress by providing emotional and mental support to their child. They should pay attention to students' stress in learning and troubles faced with learning and apply appropriate strategies to enhance their learning effectiveness. They should try to understand their interests, specialties, and abilities. They can motivate their child to "Believe in Yourself" and to develop their own strategies to achieve personal goals and solve problems resulting in stress. They should also avoid high expectations from their child.

   The Learning Partnership (www.Saultstar.com). an organization that strives for an effective education system in Canada, recommends the following methods of easing out child's stress, which are:

   (a) talk about it

   (b) share your own memories

   (c) visit the school

   (d) find out your child's schedule

   (e) practice the route you child will take to and from school

   (f) read about the school

   (g) shop for school supplies together

   (h) create school routines

   (i) be a good listener

(5) Students facing stress must possess self-confidence and share his feelings and emotions with teachers and parents. Instead of fighting with the problem himself, he must discuss it with other people so that they may provide solution or help him in getting out of stressful situation. If one identifies that he is under stress then there is urgent need to reduce it or get out of it. The quickest and effective way of eliminating feelings of stress is to close eyes for few seconds along with few deep breaths which make a person cool and calms. Another way if they feel losing concentration is to take a short break, going for a walk, chatting with the friends or just listening music.

Conclusions

Nothing is impossible in this world and stress is also like that only. In that case, the role of teachers, school management, parents and family members is very important in managing stress. The most important role is played by parents especially by mother in managing stress of her child. Believing and trust the child is necessary. The most obvious factors resulting in stress are school environment, workload, and high expectation from parents. A dialogue with the individual concerned, assess those factors that contribute to stress and also find out the reasons for the observed stress symptoms. This will result in making stress free work environment. School management must also plan innovative strategies at their level which must be helpful in minimizing stress. Parents and teachers should also motivate the child understand stress and help him deal with it. They should also motivate them towards attending various social and other activities so that they could get out of their daily hectic schedule.

Few words of appreciation by parents and teachers will help in building the morale increasing his physical power. Parents should give time to their child. Lack of time with parents make them to develop a feeling of loneliness hence the find themselves to be alone. When the child is under stress parents can plan something different helping him getting out of all these troubles. Cherishing old memories, planning outing and other surprises and small gifts can make him feel good.

The four things if taken care of that is—the Body, the Mind, the Relaxation and the Grown Up Related Factors if kept in mind then things can be made to float easily. The body refers to the nutritional aspects that are what to put in body becomes important. The mind means to take care of your well-being that is what you fill in your mind with. The relaxation refers to the unknotting of all the strains of the back, neck and shoulder. But this will require practice. And the last and importantly the, grown up refers to school-staff and parents which must see to the above three factors and control them in a manner that results in well-being of the students and procreate harmony (http://www.totallystressedout.com/07-school-stuff_01_grades.html).

REFERENCES

Abouserie, R. (1994), "Sources and levels of stress in relation to locus of control and selfesteem in university students". *Educational Psychology*, 14(3), 323-30.

Gupta, S.P., *Statistical Methods*, Thirty-Eighth Edition (2008), Sultan Chand & Sons, New Delhi.

Kothari, C.R., *Research Methodology*, Vikas Publishing House, New Delhi.

Lazarus, R.S. and Folkman, S. (1984), *Stress, Appraisal, and Coping*. New York: Springer.

The Indian Express (2012), "Website, campaign to help students beat exam stress". Retrieved on 2012-07-15 from http://www.indianexpress.com/news/website-campaign-to-help-students-beat-exam-stress/948904/

http://jms.nonolympictimes.org/Articles/4.pdf (Retrieved on 2012-07-12).

http://www.totallystressedout.com/07-school-stuff_01_grades.html (Retrieved on 2012-08-10).

http://www.saultstar.com/2012/08/18/beating-back-to-school-stress (Retrieved on 2012-08-18).

QUESTIONNAIRE

Q. 1. What is a stress level experienced by students?

(a) High (b) Moderate (c) Low

Q. 2. Which of the following create stress for you?

S.No.	*Factors Resulting in Stress*	*No. of Respondents Saying 'Yes'*	*No. of Respondents Saying 'No'*
1.	Continuous poor performance		
2.	Biasness by teachers		
3.	Excessive workload or homework		
4.	Inadequate resources to do assignments		
5.	Competition with fellow students		
6.	Overcrowded classrooms		

S.No.	*Factors Resulting in Stress*	*No. of Respondents Saying 'Yes'*	*No. of Respondents Saying 'No'*
7.	Lack of time for other activities such as sport, party, etc.		
8.	Low motivation and emotional support		
9.	Conflict with teacher and fellow students		
10.	Financial problems such as fees, etc.		
11.	Inadequate resources, e.g. computers, books, lecturers		
12.	Fear of failure		
13.	High expectations from my parents		
14.	Lack of command over any particular subject		
15.	Lack of personal attention during classes		

Q. 3 What efforts/measures you think will be successful in reducing stress in your (students) life?

1. ________________________________
2. ________________________________
3. ________________________________

CHAPTER 39 | FACTOR ANALYSIS APPROACH TO IDENTIFY STRESS SYMPTOMS AND THE DETERMINING DEMOGRAPHIC FACTORS (A CASE STUDY OF "PAHER" UNIVERSITY)

–*Shikha Bhargava* and *Mahima Birla*

ABSTRACT

In the post-recession era, the corporate world is trying to recover in a high speed that the employees have to work for prolonged hours and achieve their basic needs. Assessing teacher stress has been a difficult and complex process,

The key literature on Stress Management is reviewed. Primary data was collected from a sample of 100 professionals from the four institute of PAHER University using questionnaire survey. Various statistical methods such as factor analysis, anova, etc. were employed using spss version 15 to analyze the data.

In spite of having the modern technologies and facilities, university employees are feeling them to be over loaded and stressed. The present study attempts to identify the major symptoms of a person in stress with the help of factor analysis techniques. Stress symptoms are many but the three major factors were identified, descriptive statistics was then applied to identify whether these symptoms differ significantly for the different demographic variable. The project report also contains techniques how to reduce the stress and overcomes such problems.

The study has made a contribution to the extant literature on stress among employees. The findings would be valuable in assisting manager in framing strategies of coping with stress in the organization, especially keeping in mind the various demographic factors.

INTRODUCTION

Stress is the body's physical and psychological response to anything that's perceived as irresistible. When challenges flip over into stress, it creates an imbalance that can trigger a whole variety of negative health effects.

The phenomenon of increasing occupational stress was formally identified in 1989, when the Commonwealth Commission for the Safety, Rehabilitation and Compensation of Commonwealth Employees initiated several research projects. During the same period, the percentage increase in claims for work-related psychological injury has been greater than any other injury (Pearson et al., 1999) and cause physical and emotional responses that occur when the requirements of the job do not match the capabilities, resources, or needs of the worker. Job stress is a common workplace problem experienced by all professionals irrespective of their nature of work; however, this phenomenon is considered to be rare in academics as compared to other professions.

The paper touches upon this sensitive issue and tries to identify

1. The major symptoms of employees in stress
2. The effect of demographic factors of the various symptoms of stress
3. The different forms of workplace stress
4. The different ways to cope with the workplace stress.

REVIEW OF LITERATURE

Stress is defined as "the pattern of emotional states and physiological reactions occurring in response to demand from within or outside an organization" (Greenberg and Baron, 2003; Singh, 2003). A stressor, on the other hand, is considered to be "a condition or situation that elicits a negative response such as anger, frustration, anxiety or tension" (Rajeswari and Anantharaman, 2003). Workplace stress is quite common and can be measured through different sources. Workload, time pressure, role ambiguity, role conflict, career progress and communication are considered as major sources of pressure in the life of an information system professional (Ivanchevich, Napier and Wetherbe, 1983). Pressure ultimately causes the stress that leads to different types of strain and finally hampers the performance of the employees. Stress, not just affects the efficiency of the employees, but also causes ailment and other physical or emotional problems as well (Singh, 2003).

Stress in Different Occupations

There is a view that occupational stress is more likely to be found among blue-collar and routine white-collar workers because often they work to meet the difficult deadlines or the heavy burden of work does not give them time to relieve the pressure (Fletcher, Gowler and Payne, 1979). A survey of senior managers in 112 financial organizations conducted in 1986 in London, showed that 64% identified stress as their main health concern and worst affected were accountants and building society managers. Those who worked in the city identified 'too much work' as the biggest single factor in causing stress. Other causes mentioned were long hours, competition, pressure to perform, over-promotion, conflict between work and private life, and job insecurity (McKenna, 2002). The most frequently mentioned symptom of stress was deterioration in the employee's performance. Other symptoms identified were irritability, absenteeism, problems with making decisions, difficulties with drinking and depression (McKenna, 2002).

Coping with Stress at Workplace

Much has been written about how teachers cope with stress (Dunham, 1992; Rogers, 1996). Dunham and Varma (1998) suggest that stress can be reduced by developing new skills or by diverting attention through humour or physical activity. To cope under difficult conditions, teachers require both organisational and personal support, including training in interpersonal problem solving and skills to deal with stress. Lazarus and Folkman (1984) state that continual physical and mental adaptations are required to cope satisfactorily with demanding situations. Poor coping mechanisms have long been identified as a primary cause of stress (Head, 1996; Montgomery and Rupp, 2005). Good coping skills include modifying thought processes, learning problem-focused strategies (such as new skills in addressing stress), and emotion-focused strategies (releasing pent-up feelings through exercise, talking or meditation) (Admiraal, Korthagen, and Wubbels, 2000; Chan, 1998; Lazarus and Folkman, 1984). Chan (1998) identified problem management as the best initial approach to stress, and Arikewuyo (2004) found that teachers tend towards active management of stressful problems, separating home life mentally from work. Borg and Riding (1991) and Bowers (2004) found a qualitative study of workplace stress and coping in secondary teachers in Ireland. 29 teachers with poorer coping skills had more frequent absences from work and were more likely to leave the profession. From a longitudinal study in Finland, Salo (1995) concluded that stress clearly accumulates throughout a school term, although coping styles and subsequent stress levels varied widely among the participants. The literature also indicates that it is the continuous stream of daily stresses that can cause the biggest threat to a teacher's mood, rather than episodic major stressors (Admiraal, Korthagen, and Wubbels, 2000; Lazarus and Folkman, 1984).

RESEARCH METHODOLOGY

The study follows the survey research and exploratory research. Based on previous research in related areas, a questionnaire was constructed to measure the level of stress among the professionals of different institutes running under the umbrella of PAHER University. The data was analyzed using the standard technique of factor analysis, anova and other basic techniques.

Questionnaire Administration

A five-point scale "strongly agree to strongly disagree" was used for this purpose.

Sample Design

A sample of 100 respondents was taken using Stratified Random Sampling. The researcher contacted the faculty personally and brief summary of the nature of the study and details in the questionnaire were narrated to them.

Survey Instrument

A four-page questionnaire consisting of two subscale was developed. In the first subscale demographic information such as age, gender, designation and years of experience, institutes were sought. The next subscale, questions were adapted by previous researchers to measure the stress level. A list of 24 items was developed each questions was scored on a five-point scale likert scale from (1) highly dissatisfied to (5) highly satisfied.

DATA ANALYSIS

The data collected from the survey was scored and entered in the computer for analysis by the SPSS (15.0) package. Some preliminary results relating to the sample characteristics, the reliability of the questionnaire are reported in this section.

Reliability of Scale

To assess the reliability of the instruments, the Cronbach (1981) alpha coefficients for the 2nd subscale containing 24 items were calculated and reported in Table 1. Values of 0.7 and above for coefficient alpha is considered to indicate strong reliability for the scale.

It is noted that all items were found to have a mean value ranging from 3.57 in the five-point likert scale, where a value of 2.5 is regarded as neutral point. This indicates that ratings from the respondents tend to lie on the positive side of the rating scale. Furthermore, the standard deviations were found to range from .67 indicating a relatively high degree of consensus among the respondents in their perception of the rating of variables in the questions.

Table 1: Reliability Statistics

Cronbach's Alpha	No. of Items
.980	24

The Cronbach alpha is the most widely used index for determining internal consistency (Kerlinger, 1986). It has been generally accepted that in the early stages of the research on hypothesized measure of construct, reliabilities of 0.50 or higher are needed, while for widely used scales, the reliabilities should not be below 0.6 (Nunnally, 1978). The high alpha value of .980 confirms the homogeneity of the items, and indicates acceptable level of reliability.

To understand the stress' symptoms among the professionals, 24 statements were identified. Each statement describes one aspect of perception. The opinions of investments were collected in Likert five-point scales. Studying all 24 statements would have been tedious and, in fact, not necessary also. So factor analysis was used to reduce variables into smaller number of manageable variables by exploring common dimensions available among the variables. The variable which had common response and high correlation were grouped under a common factor. Variables which did not have any significant effect were suppressed. The reduced factors should be distinct from each other. First the suitability of data for the purpose of factor analysis was tested using two analyses, namely KMO test and Bartlett's test of Sphericity.

Kaiser Maiyer Olkin

Measure of sampling adequacy is a statistic which indicates the proportion of variance in the variables which might be caused by new factors. High values generally indicate that a factor analysis may be useful with the data. If the value is less than 0.50, the results of the factor analysis probably will not be very useful.

Table 2 shows the KMO value is 0.909 which signifies that the factor analysis is useful with the data. The Chi square value for Bartlett's test of Sphericity is 1701.026 and the significant value is 0.0000 which is significant at more than 99 per cent level of confidence. This means data are very suitable for factor analysis.

Table 2: KMO and Bartlett's Test

Kaiser-Meyer-Olkin Measure of Sampling Adequacy	.909
Bartlett's Test of Sphericity Approx. Chi-Square	1701.026
Df	276
Sig.	.000

The next step in the process is to decide about the number of factors to be derived. The rule of thumb is applied to choose the number of factors for which 'Eigen values' with greater than one is taken by using principal component analysis method. The component matrix so formed is further rotated orthogonally using varimax rotation algorithm. By performing factor analysis, 24 variables are first reduced to 14 variables and then further reduced into three broad component factors. Each component factor includes some statements which are otherwise called variables. Each variable represents employees' perception about their stress level and under each factor explain the cause of such reasons.

The three factors which have Eigen value more than unity alone is taken for consideration. There are separate tables for factor loading of each factor. The three perceptual factors represent around 87 per cent of total variance which is very significant and the remaining variance is explained by other factors.

Naming and Labeling of Factors

Interpersonal compatibility: the factor contains symptoms of stress that shows that a stressful person keeps on indulging in arguments and criticism for other. This factors can be considered as an important symptoms of stress as this factor alone account for 80% of variance.

Factor Loadings for Interpersonal Factor

Variables	*Factor Loading*
I often nod or finish other people's sentences for them when they speak slowly	0.729
I become very frustrated at having to wait in a queue	0.833
I find fault and criticize others rather than praising, even if it is deserved	0.808
I seem to be listening even though I am preoccupied with my own thoughts	0.785
I am unable to perform tasks as well as I used to, my judgment is clouded or not as good as it was	0.842
My job has a lot of responsibility, but I don't have very much authority	0.915
In general, I am not particularly proud or satisfied with my job	0.909
I have the impression that I am repeatedly picked on or discriminated against at work	0.887
I tend to have frequent arguments with superiors, coworkers	0.872
Most of the time I feel that I have very little control over my life at work	0.838

Let-Go Attitude the employees attitude of not taking pain to complete the task on time

Variables	*Factor Loading*
I deny or ignore problems in the hope that they will go away	0.87
My self confidence/self-esteem is lower than I would like it to be	0.721

Time Mis-management/Workload Pressure

The table below shows that this factor contains variables related to workload employees sometimes feels that their KRA's are not properly defined and more task is assigned to them which they failed to complete in the given time constraint.

Variables	*Factor Loading*
I frequently bring work home at night	0.888
Not enough hours in the day to do all the things that I must do	0.866

DESCRIPTIVE ANALYSIS OF FACTORS

Basis of Generations (Age)

The primary purpose of this research was to identify the most important factors which differentiate stress level among the employee of the persons in India. Mean and SD score of different factors for each respondent was calculated. Scores of different factors of all age group studied is showed in Table 3.

Table 3: Descriptive Analysis of Factors on the Basis of Age

	Age Group below 25		*25-35*		*35-45*		*above 45*			
	Mean	*Std. Dev.*	*Mean*	*Std. Dev.*	*Mean*	*Std. Dev.*	*Mean*	*Std. Dev.*	*F value*	*P Value*
Interpersonal factor	3.4857	0.7313	3.1694	0.603	3.32	0.506952	3.25	0.919239	0.543	0.655
Let go attitude	3.5	1.4142	3.2917	0.967	4.1	0.394405	3.25	2.020726	1.803	0.152
Time management	3.3571	1.1673	3.1389	1.19	2.6	1.308094	3.5	0.57735	0.97	0.41

Factor I, was labeled as "Interpersonal factor". While comparing the means score and standard deviation value of different age group, it was found that the mean score of age group (below 25) is the highest (3.4857) followed by age group (35-45) and lowest in the age group (25-35). We have taken the null hypothesis that "there are no significant differences of interpersonal factor in all age group". Since, P values is .655 which is greater than .05, hence hypothesis is accepted concluding that there is no significant differences of interpersonal factors in all age group.

Factor 2, was labeled as "Let Go attitude". While comparing the means score and standard deviation, the mean score was found to be highest for the age group of 35-45 (4.1) and lowest for the age group above 45(3.25). Since P value is .152 hence null hypothesis is accepted stating that thers is no significant difference between the "Let Go attitude" and the age group.

Factor 3, was labeled as "Time Management". While comparing the means score and standard deviation, the mean score was found to be highest for the age group of 35-45 (4.1) and lowest for the age group above 45(3.25). Since P value is .152 hence null hypothesis is accepted stating that there is no significant difference between the "Let Go attitude" and the age group.

Basis of Generations (Gender)

The scores of different factors of both the gender studied is showed in Table 4.

Table 4: Descriptive Analysis of Factors on the Basis of Gender

Factors	*Gender* *Male* *Mean*	*Std. Dev*	*Female* *Mean*	*Std.Dev*	*F-Value*	*P-Value*
Interpersonal factor	3.071	0.60674	3.4947	0.54106	6.224	0.016
Let go attitude	3.2419	1.10045	3.6579	0.95934	3.072	0.047
Time management	2.9355	1.1143	3.4474	1.24004	4.561	0.035

The mean score for all the three factors are relatively higher for the females as compared to males and since P value is also lower than .05 for all the three factors. This implies that all the three factors differ significantly on the basis of gender.

It can also be concluded that stress level is higher in females as compared to males.

Basis of Generations (Years of Experience)

The scores of different factors of both the gender studied is depicted in Table 5.

Table 5: Descriptive Analysis of Factors on the Basis of Years of Experience

	Years of Experience *0-1* *Mean*	*Std. Dev.*	*2-4* *Mean*	*Std. Dev.*	*5-10* *Mean*	*Std. Dev.*	*10 above* *Mean*	*Std. Dev.*	*F-value*	*P-Value*
Interpersonal factor	3.5667	0.7234	3.2625	0.6658	3.1471	0.637	3.183	0.1941	0.4234	0.73712
Let go attitude	4.6667	0.2582	3.3125	1.1468	3.2059	0.871	3.667	1.0731	3.88618	0.01141
Time management	4.1667	0.6831	3.20833	1.1843	2.9706	1.148	2.75	1.2703	2.30833	0.04134

The P value of years of experience for the factors—Let go attitude and Time management—are less than .05 which signifies that there is a significant difference between year of experience and the two factors showing the symptoms of stress. However the P value for interpersonal factors and the years of experience is .73712 which shows that there is no significant difference between year of experience and interpersonal factors. The mean value is highest for the employees with 0-1 year of experience 3.5667 for interpersonal factors, 4.6667 for let-go attitude, and 4.1667 for time mis-management and lowest for the age group of 5-10, 3.1471 for interpersonal factors, 3.2059 for let-go attitude, and 2.75 for time mis-management.

Basis of Generations (Designation)

The scores of different factors for the employees at different designation studied is depicted in Table 6.

Table 6: Descriptive Analysis of Factors on the Basis of Designation

	Designation *Asso.Prof.* *Mean*	*Std. Dev.*	*Dean/ Director* *Mean*	*Std. Dev.*	*Deputy Director* *Mean*	*Std. Dev.*	*Lecturer/ Asst. Prof.* *Mean*	*Std. Dev.*	*F-value*	*P-Value*
Interpersonal factor	3.24	0.639	4.2	0	3.2	0.4243	3.18182	0.5957	226.044	0.00
Let go attitude	3.44	1.0432	4.5	0	3.75	0.866	3.27273	1.1073	7.70152	.000
Time management	3.06	1.1721	1.5	0	2.5	1.7321	3.34091	1.1142	3.76508	0.0069

The mean score for two factors, interpersonal and let go, are relatively higher for the dean/director level employees and time management is the issue with lecturer and asst. prof. and since P value is also lower than .05 for all the three factors. This implies that all the three factors differ significantly on the basis of designation.

CONCLUSION

The academics has generally be profiled as low stress job. However, from the studies, it can be concluded that rapid growth of technology, role overload, long hours, competition, pressure to perform, over-promotion, conflict between work and private life, and job insecurity has increased the competition manifold among various academics organizations across the globe, and the academicians of the 21st century is facing more challenges as compared to his/her predecessors.

Person facing stress at the organizational level has a lot of psychological problems. The most prominent mentioned symptom of stress that were identified as a result of factor analysis are interpersonal incompatibility, time mis-management, negative attitude towards work or let go attitude. The descriptive statistics were also determined that whether the symptoms of stress arises according to the demographic characteristics (age, gender, years of experience, designation). It has been found that all the three symptoms differs significantly on the basis of gender and designation and are more prominent in case of females and top level managerial personnel.

Also the two factors, namely let go attitude and time mismanagement is found to be more in a person with 0-1 year of experience that is during the initial phase of getting accustomed to new culture and responsibilities. The finding would definitely help the human resource manager to develop some guidelines to design their policies and strategies.

MANAGERIAL IMPLICATION

The findings suggest that females employees are more stressful as compared to male members. The stress management cause comprise of a package program consisting of:

- Training on certain issues like worklife balance
- Relaxation
- Positive outlook towards works/responsibilities
- Self-analysis through personality type tests
- Inter-personal skill development
- Protection yoga-cum-meditation
- Time management
- At the individual level the employees could practice a relaxing holiday (wherein quality time is spent with the family) every fortnight or mouth
- Realize excessive use of tea/coffee cigarette is not answer to stress
- Try to get 6-7 hrs of continuous sleep per day.

The employees during the initial phase of their present job/new job (0-1) are found to be in higher stress this needs a special attention by HR managers.

So, Effective orientation/induction programme backed by the positive and supporting attitude by the supervisors and colleagues should be given.

The symptoms of interpersonal incompatibility and let go attitude are more dominating in the top management people, the probable reason for this could be better suggested by Maslow need's theory, the people at level has the highest degree of self-esteem.

REFERENCES

Borg, M.G. and Riding, R.J. (1991). Occupational stress and satisfaction in teaching. *British Educational Research Journal*, 17(3), 263-81.

Bowers, T. (2004). Stress, teaching and teacher health. *Education 3-13: International Journal of Primary, Elementary and Early Years Education*, 32(3), 73-80.

Chan, D.W. (1998). Stress, coping strategies, and psychological distress among secondary teachers in Hong Kong. *American Educational Research Journal*, 35(1), 145-63.

Dunham, J. (1992). *Stress in Teaching*, 2nd edition. London: Routledge.

Dunham, J. and Varma, V. (1998). *Stress in Teachers: Past, Present and Future*. London: Whurr Publishers Ltd.

Fletcher, B., Gowler, D. and Payne, R. (1979). "Exploding the myth of executive stress", *Personnel Management*, Vol. 11, No. 5, pp. 30-35.

Greenberg, J. and Baron, R.A. (2003). *Behavior in Organizations: Understanding and Managing the Human Side of Work*. New Delhi: Prentice-Hall Pvt. Ltd.

Head, J. (1996). Stress and the postgraduate secondary school trainee teacher: A British case study. *Journal of Education for Teaching*, 22(1), 71-84.

Huebner, D.E. (1992). *The Vocation of Teaching in Making Sense of Uncertain Craft*. New York: Teachers College Press.

Ivancevish, J.M., Napier, H.A. and Wetherbe, J.C. (1983). "Occupational stress, attitudes, and health problems in the information systems professional", *Communications of ACM*, Vol. 26, No. 10.

Kvale, S. (1996). *Interviews: An Introduction to Qualitative Research Interviewing*. London: Sage Publications.

Kyriacou, C. (2001). Teacher stress: Directions for future research. *Educational Review*, 53(1), 27-35.

Lazarus, R.S. and Folkman, S. (1984). *Stress, Appraisal, and Coping*. New York: Springer.

McKenna, E. (2002). *Business Psychology and Organizational Behavior: A Student Handbook*. 3rd ed. Sussex: Psychology Press.

Meijer, J. (2007). Correlates of student stress in secondary education. *Educational Research*, 49(1), 21-35.

Montgomery, C. and Rupp, A.A. (2005). A Meta-analysis for exploring the diverse causes and effects of stress in teachers. *Canadian Journal of Education*, 28(3), 458-86.

Rajeswari, K.S. and Anantharaman, R.N. (2003). "Development of an instrument to measure stress among software professionals: Factor analytic study", in *Proceedings of ACM-SIGCPR Conference*, 2003, Philadelphia, Pennsylvania, pp. 34-43, http://portal.acm.org

Salo, K. (1995). Teacher stress and coping over an autumn term in Finland. *Work and Stress*, 9(1), 55-66.

Singh, N. (2003). *Organizational Behavior: Concepts, Theory, and Practices*. New Delhi: Deep and Deep Publications Pvt. Ltd.

CHAPTER 40 HR TOOLKIT FOR MAPPING WORK STRESS IN SERVICE SECTOR EXECUTIVES: AN EMPIRCAL STUDY

–Rajeshwari Narendran and Sanjay Jain

ABSTRACT

Stress, as we understand, is the body's response to a change that requires change in mental, emotional or physical state of a being. There are explicit and implicit factors which lead to a stressful situation. Stress can come from any situation or thought that makes you feel frustrated, angry or anxious.

In today's volatile, hyper competitive and demanding economic scenario, every organization especially providing services, is struggling to keep its profitability growth curve intact. This directly trickles down to every level in the organization in different forms. Employees respond to these dynamic demands in different ways based on their psychological, emotional and professional needs. This may challenge the capabilities and resources available with the employee, leading to a stressful situation. Job satisfaction, motivation, morale, team spirit are some of the aspects which are directly related to stress at workplaces.

From various service sectors we have considered four important service sectors hotels, communication (telecom), banking and insurance for the study. The authors present here an empirical research study is as follows:

Introduction

Job stress can be defined as the harmful physical and emotional responses that occur when the requirements of the job do not match the capabilities, resources, or needs of the worker. Job stress can lead to poor health and even injury. United States National Institute of Occupational Safety and Health, Cincinnati, 19(63.3)99 Source—OGP: Managing Workplace Stress.

There are many factors in play which lead to stress. These factors are usually known as stressors. Stressors can be generally categorized into personal, professional or environmental. Following are few examples of each category.

1. Personal: Inter personal relationships, personal conflicts, emotional needs
2. Professional: Work overload, growth opportunities, remuneration
3. Environmental: Working conditions, economic scenario, merger and Acquisitions

Service Sectors in India

India stands out for the size and dynamism of its services sector. Services sector has become important for many economies in the world and very important particularly for India. While for the medium and long term, it is important to accelerate the growth of industrial sector particularly manufacturing sector. The services sector constitutes a large part of the Indian economy both in terms of employment potential and its contribution to national income. The service sector includes trade, hotels and restaurants, railways, communication (post, telecom), banking, insurance, education, health care, finance, etc.

Objectives of the Study

(1) To analyze the level of work stress in service sector executives.

(2) To study the effects/impact of work stress on service sector executives' life.

(3) To find out the responsible reasons of work stress among service sector executives.

Limitations of the Study

(1) The area of study is limited to only four service sectors.

(2) The time of the study is limited.

(3) Study is based on the information provided by the selected service sector executives.

Research Methodology

Data Source	*Primary Data (Personal Interview)* *Secondary Data (Internet, Reference Books and Newspapers)*
Area of Research	Udaipur City
Research Approach	Survey Method
Research Instrument	Structured Questionnaire and Personal Interview
Sample Unit	Service Sector Executives
Sampling Method	Convenient Sampling
Selected Service Sectors	Hotels, Communication (Telecom), Banking and Insurance
Sample Size	120 Respondents (30 from each selected service sector)

Data Analysis and Interpretation

(1) Do You Know about Workplace Stress?

Sr.No.	*Options*	*Hotel*	*Telecom*	*Banking*	*Insurance*	*Total*
A	Yes	30(100)	30(100)	30(100)	30(100)	120(100)
B	No	-	-	-	-	-
C	Don't Know	-	-	-	-	-
	Total	30(100)	30(100)	30(100)	30(100)	120(100)

( ) shows %

Analysis: Above table shows that all 100% respondents were aware about workplace stress.

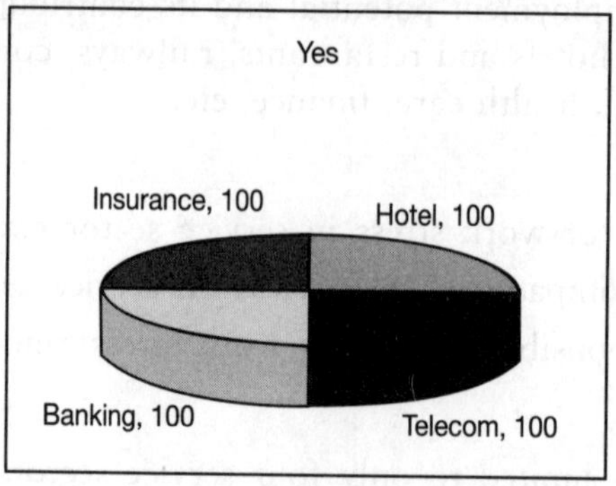

(2) In the Past six months has Your Workplace Stress Increased?

Sr.No.	*Options*	*Hotel*	*Telecom*	*Banking*	*Insurance*	*Total*
A	Yes	27(90.0)	23(76.7)	24(80.0)	30(100)	104(86.7)
B	No	03(10.0)	06(20.0)	04(13.3)	-	13(10.8)
C	Don't Know	-	01(03.3)	02(06.7)	-	03(02.5)
	Total	30(100)	30(100)	30(100)	30(100)	120(100)

( ) shows %

Analysis: Overall 86.7% respondents said that in past six months their Workplace Stress has increased. According to data analysis, insurance sector is showing 100% workplace stress in past six months.

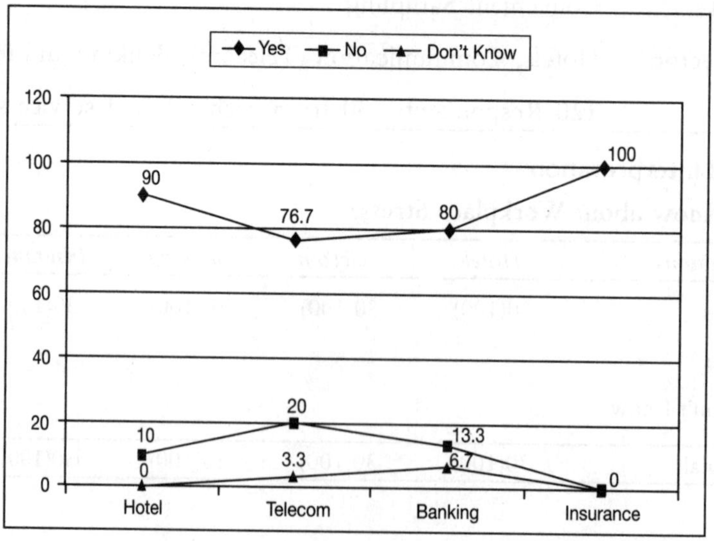

(3) In Your Opinion has there been Impact in the Quality of Your Work because of Workplace Stress?

Sr. No.	*Options*	*Hotel*	*Telecom*	*Banking*	*Insurance*	*Total*
A	Yes	19(63.3)	26(86.7)	22(73.3)	25(83.3)	92(76.7)
B	No	09(30.0)	-	06(20.0)	04(13.3)	19(15.8)
C	Don't Know	02(06.7)	04(13.3)	02(06.7)	01(03.3)	09(07.5)
	Total	30(100)	30(100)	30(100)	30(100)	120(100)

( ) shows %

Analysis: Telecom sector (86.7) and insurance sector (83.3) has been in top among the selected service sector that due to Workplace Stress Quality of their Work has been affected more.

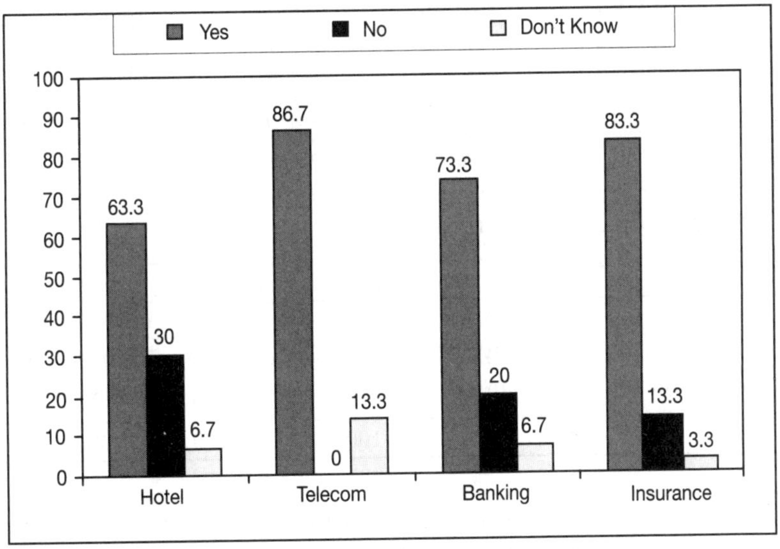

(4) Do You Have Difficulty Taking Your Vacations/Holidays because of Your Work Demands and Stress?

Sr. No.	*Options*	*Hotel*	*Telecom*	*Banking*	*Insurance*	*Total*
A	Yes	24(80.0)	29(96.7)	25(83.3)	29(96.7)	107(89.2)
B	No	06(20.0)	01(03.3)	05(16.7)	01(03.3)	13(10.8)
C	Don't Know	-	-	-	-	-
	Total	30(100)	30(100)	30(100)	30(100)	120(100)

( ) shows %

Analysis: From the above data it is clear that 107 respondents are saying yes that they have difficulty for taking their vacations/Holidays because of work demand and stress and the insurance sector is leading with 96.7%.

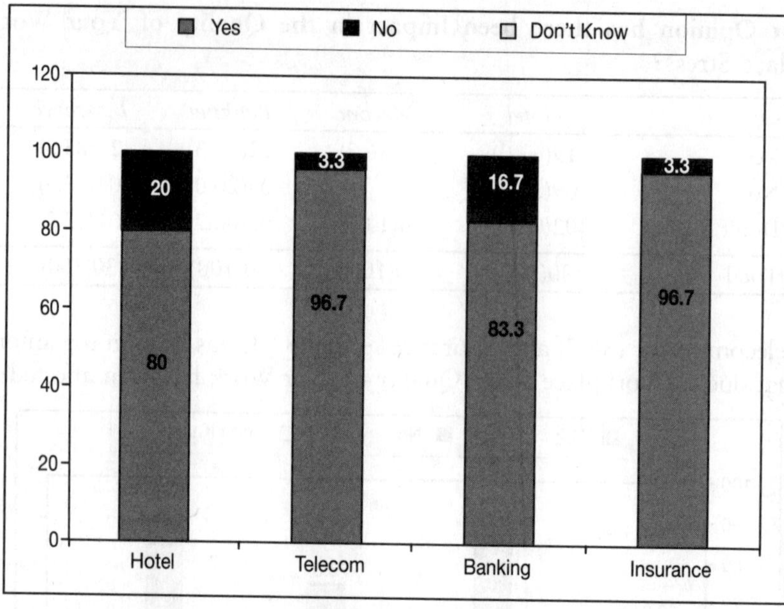

(5) Does Your Workplace have a Stress Policy?

Sr. No.	*Options*	*Hotel*	*Telecom*	*Banking*	*Insurance*	*Total*
A	Yes	11(36.7)	09(30)	08(26.7)	06(20.0)	34(28.3)
B	No	04(13.3)	10(33.3)	06(20.0)	09(30.0)	29(24.2)
C	Don't Know	15(50.0)	11(36.7)	16(53.3)	15(50.0)	57(47.5)
	Total	30(100)	30(100)	30(100)	30(100)	120(100)

( ) shows %

Analysis: Above table indicates that 47.5% respondents don't know that stress policy in their workplace have or not. Apart from this 24.2% respondents are working without any stress policy.

(6) In Your Opinion which Factors have been Affected Because of Workplace Stress? (Please Tick as many as applicable)

Factors	*Hotel*	*Telecom*	*Banking*	*Insurance*	*Total*
Job Satisfaction	28(93.3)	20(66.7)	26(86.7)	29(96.7)	103(85.8)
Motivation	20(66.7)	21(70.0)	19(63.3)	18(60.0)	78(65.0)
Morale	18(60.0)	22(73.3)	25(83.3)	27(90.0)	92(76.7)
Team Spirit	17(56.7)	25(83.3)	19(63.3)	25(83.3)	86(71.7)
Inter Personnel Relation	14(46.7)	16(53.3)	19(63.3)	18(60.0)	67(55.8)
Level of Control over Job	13(43.3)	10(33.3)	12(40.0)	15(50.0)	50(41.7)
Absenteeism	18(60.0)	26(86.7)	22(73.3)	28(93.3)	94(78.3)
Loyalty	21(70.0)	19(63.3)	23(76.7)	25(83.3)	88(73.3)

( ) shows %

Analysis: Overall it is clearly understood that due to workplace stress job satisfaction (85.8%) decreased and Absenteeism (78.3) was increased. Morale, loyalty and team spirit are the also most affected factors due to workplace stress. All selected service sector registered that the job satisfaction is the main factor which has been affected because of workplace stress.

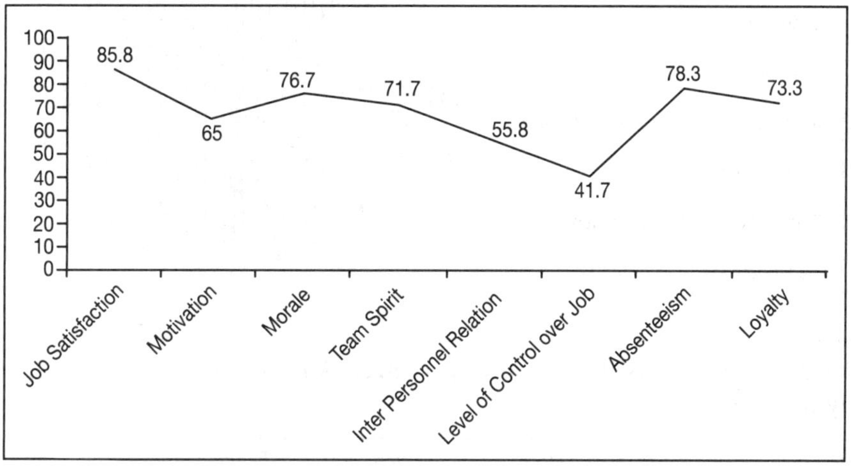

(7) **What Do You Think are the Main Causes of Stress at Your Workplace? (Please Tick as many as applicable)**

Causes	*Hotel*	*Telecom*	*Banking*	*Insurance*	*Total*
Lack of Recognition for the Work you do	26(86.7)	28(93.3)	27(90)	30(100)	111(92.5)
Job Insecurity	21(70.0)	24(80)	25(83.3)	29(96.7)	99(82.5)
Overwork	29(96.7)	26(86.7)	22(73.3)	24(80.0)	101(84.2)
Long Hours	27(90.0)	25(83.3)	21(70.0)	23(76.7)	96(80.0)
Too much Pressure to complete Task	20(66.7)	28(93.3)	26(86.7)	30(100)	104(86.7)
Poor Ventilation	—	02(06.7)	01(03.3)	02(06.7)	05(04.2)
Ergonomic Sitting Arrangement	02(06.7)	05(16.7)	03(10.0)	08(26.7)	18(15.0)
Inadequate Pay	27(90.0)	24(80.0)	23(76.7)	28(93.3)	102(85.0)
Inadequate Holidays/Vacations	28(93.3)	24(80.0)	26(86.7)	25(83.3)	103(85.8)
Boss Inter Personal Relation	19(63.3)	16(53.3)	20(66.7)	22(73.3)	77(64.2)
Peer Pressure	23(76.7)	21(70.0)	26(86.7)	24(80.0)	94(78.3)
Competition for Promotion	25(83.3)	26(86.7)	24(80)	27(100)	92(76.7)
Self-Expectation	16(53.3)	15(50.0)	17(56.7)	14(46.7)	62(51.7)

( ) shows %

Analysis: Out of 120, 111 respondents ticked that the main causes of stress at their workplace is lack of recognition for their work which they done. After this too much pressure to complete task, inadequate pay and overwork are the other main factors of stress.

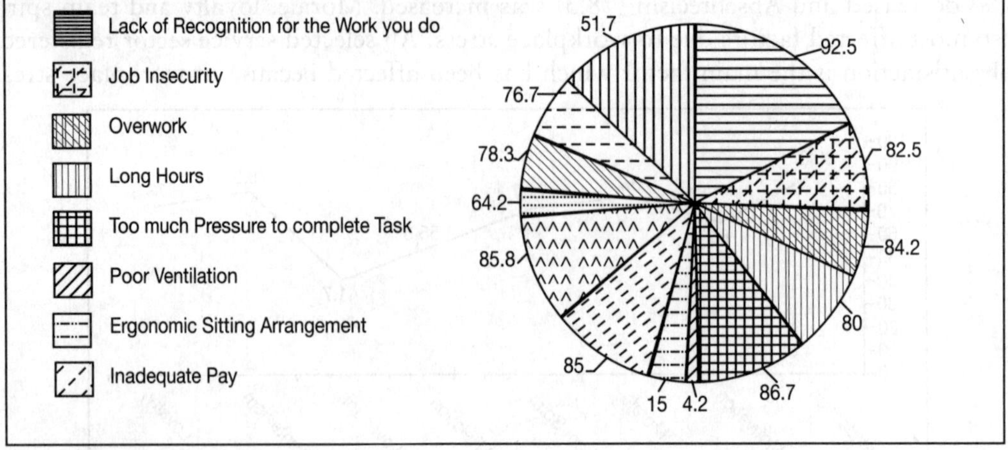

(8) In the Past Two Years have You Experienced Any of the Following:—(Please Tick as Many as Applicable)

Causes	*Hotel*	*Telecom*	*Banking*	*Insurance*	*Total*
Fatigue	26(86.7)	24(80.0)	21(70.0)	25(83.3)	96(80.0)
Depression and Anxiety	19(63.3)	16(53.3)	15(50.0)	20(66.7)	70(58.3)
Getting Sick More Often	12(40.0)	09(30.0)	11(36.7)	14(46.7)	46(38.3)
Headaches/Neck and Back Pain	15(50.0)	18(60.0)	13(43.3)	22(73.3)	68(56.7)
High Blood Pressure/Low Blood Pressure	16(53.3)	10(33.3)	11(36.7)	13(43.3)	50(41.7)
Increased Use of Alcohol/Smoking/ Chewing Tobacco	22(73.3)	20(66.7)	16(53.3)	19(63.3)	77(64.2)
Impact on Family and Personal Life	26(86.7)	24(80.0)	21(70.0)	27(90.0)	98(81.7)
Memory Loss	16(53.3)	10(33.3)	13(43.3)	14(46.7)	53(44.2)
Insomnia	26(86.7)	21(70.0)	19(63.3)	24(80.0)	90(75.0)
Slip Disc/Joint Pain	09(30.0)	08(26.7)	10(33.3)	11(36.7)	38(31.7)
Heart Problem	22(73.3)	14(46.7)	12(40.0)	19(63.3)	67(55.8)
Acidity Heart Burn	23(76.7)	19(63.3)	16(53.3)	20(66.7)	78(65.0)
Increase in Number of Eye Spectacles	09(30.0)	07(23.3)	18(60.0)	08(26.7)	42(35.0)

( ) shows %

Analysis: Above table indicates that in past two years service executives were mainly experienced negative impact on family and personal life, fatigue and insomnia due to the work stress.

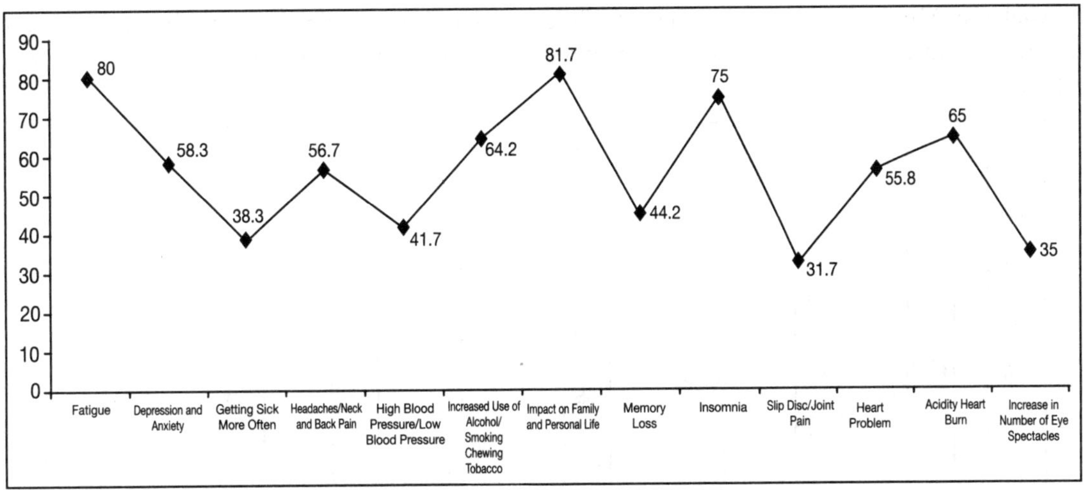

(9) Have You ever Discussed Stress Concerns with any of the Following? (Please Tick as Many as Applicable)

Society	*Hotel*	*Telecom*	*Banking*	*Insurance*	*Total*
Co-Workers	23(76.7)	21(70.0)	17(56.7)	26(86.7)	87(72.5)
Supervisor/Boss	01(03.3)	04(13.3)	03(10.0)	02(06.7)	10(08.3)
Employer	03(10.0)	02(06.7)	—	—	05(04.2)
Family	02(06.7)	08(26.7)	16(53.3)	06(20.0)	32(26.7)
Doctor	06(20.0)	05(16.7)	08(26.7)	02(06.7)	21(70.0)
Friends	22(73.3)	20(66.7)	24(80.0)	28(93.3)	94(78.3)

( ) shows %

Analysis: According to data 78.3% service executives and 72.5% service executives had discussed stress concerns respectively with friends and their co-workers. Only 4.2% executives had discussed their stress with employer. Banking and insurance sector executives had never discussed their stress with employer.

(10) Nature of Job Change in Last Two Years: (Please Tick As Many as Applicable)

Nature of Job	*Hotel*	*Telecom*	*Banking*	*Insurance*	*Total*
More Duties have been Added	24(80.0)	27(90.0)	25(83.3)	28(93.3)	104(86.7)
Extended Working Hours	30(100)	30(100)	30(100)	30(100)	120(100)
Excess Tours	19(63.3)	17(56.7)	15(50.0)	22(73.3)	73(60.8)
Higher Demands/Expectations from Employer	20(66.7)	11(36.7)	16(53.3)	19(63.3)	66(55.0)
More Meeting	21(70.0)	23(76.7)	24(80.0)	27(90.0)	95(79.2)
More Supervision	21(70.0)	18(60.0)	19(63.3)	18(60.0)	76(63.3)
Less Training has been Provided	12(40.0)	10(33.3)	22(73.3)	19(63.3)	63(52.5)
Faster Rate of Work	22(73.3)	26(86.7)	17(56.7)	24(80.0)	89(74.2)

( ) shows %

Analysis: Above data indicates that 100% executives have noticed that their working hours are extended and 86.7% executives are accepted that more duties have been added in their work profile.

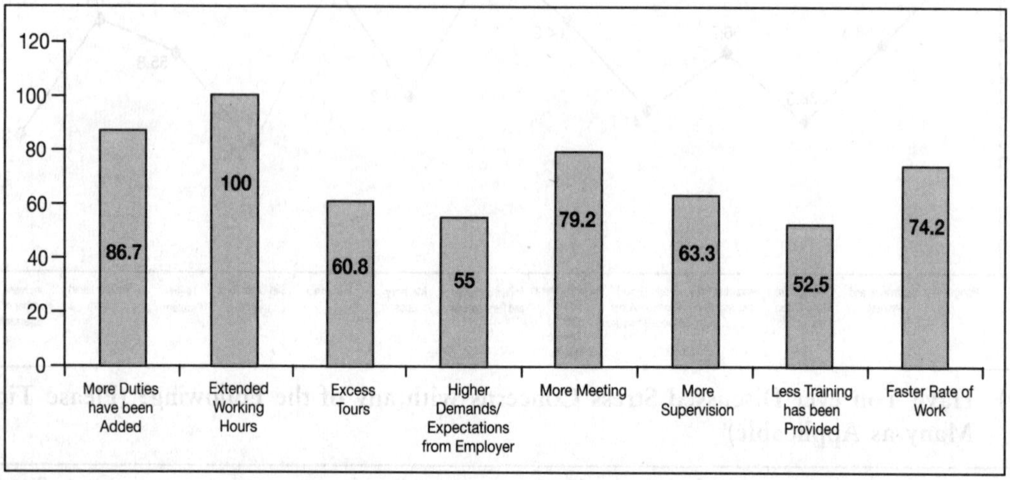

Findings

- It was found that 100% service sectors executives have knowledge about workplace Stress.
- 86.7% service sectors executives experienced that work stress has increased at their workplace.
- Above research shows that due to workplace stress service executives' quality of work has been affected and most of executives have no stress policy at their work place or they have no knowledge about that also.
- Due to workplace stress executives' job satisfaction decreased by 85.8% and absenteeism increased by 78.3%.
- Main causes of stress are lack of recognition, inadequate pay as well as too much pressure to complete task.
- Due to work stress executives are experienced negative impact on family and personal life, fatigue, insomnia, depression and anxiety.
- Executives had discussed their work stress mostly with their friends than co-workers.
- 100% respondents have noticed in the past two years their working hours have been extended and 86.7% have noticed that more duties have been added in their work profile.
- Insurance sector is the top service sector who registered top workplace stress among the selected service sectors.

Suggestions

- The first and the important recommendation is that service sector should work out on stress policy and pay attention for awareness about stress policy.

- Regular medical check-up also needful to executives in maintains the stress level.
- Service sectors need to introduce some following stress reduction program or activities in regular intervals:
  - (a) Training programme.
  - (b) Re-creative activities like paid holidays, monthly picnics and team building activity.
  - (c) Family training programme—"How to help stressed executive at home".
- Service sectors should take actions to reduce job stress and should be given top priority in the process of organizational change to improve working conditions and to avert the situation of brain drain (role and goal clarity, target should be breakup).
- Both employer and employee must understand that work should be valued and not excessive. Work should not compromise on health and family life; rather offer happiness, peace of mind, certainty, variety and flexibility.

Conclusion

Every person has a working life-time/period of about 35 years, normally between 25 to 60 years of age. Given the Indian scenario of competitive market, over population and scarcity of good jobs, runs on the theory of "Survival of the Fittest", no profession is stress free. The degree and depth may vary from one another. But even the most conscientious efforts to improve working conditions are unlikely to eliminate stress completely for all workers.

A healthy mind and body decreases the level of stress build up considerably. This can be achieved by the promotion of mental health.

M—Money management, minimize needs, meditation

E—Earnest expectations, Enjoy the work you do

N—Avoid negative thinking

T—Try to be happy today, team up for success

A—Accept and adopt reality

L—Avoid loneliness, learn to say 'No'

H—Develop good hobbies, take care of health

E—Live in good environment. Express yourself clearly

A—Be active and have positive attitude

L—Try to learn more and manage life

T—Have realistic targets and tackle one at a time

H—Maintain healthy life style, keep your head cool.

REFERENCES

Behavioral Sciences; Abha Singh and Rajni Arya.

Business Research Methods; ICFAI Center of Management.

Exploring MARKETING Research by Zikmund Thomson Learning.

Human Resource Management by V.V. Morajkar and M.D. Kakade.

Stress management by D.P. Chaterjee.

Human Resource Management by T.N. Chabra.

Stress Management by D.M. Pastonjee.

"A Project Manager optimism and stress management and IT project success" by D.C. Smith, M. Bruyns, S. Evans.

Performance evaluation by Dr. Muneer Ali Shah.

http://en.wikipedia.org/wiki/newspaper

www.google.com

CHAPTER 41

EMOTIONAL INTELLIGENCE AND HUMAN RESOURCE DEVELOPMENT (A STUDY OF PRIVATE SECTOR ENTERPRISES)

–*Santosh Bhandari*

ABSTRACT

Emotional intelligence word is hot buzz in the world especially in the advance countries/ economies like USA, UK, Italy, France and Germany. But still the presence of emotional intelligence can be felt all around the global corporate world. The present study is done with the aim to understand the concept of emotional intelligence. To examine the emotional intelligence practices in business concerns and to suggest strategies for developing and managing emotional intelligence. A sample of 50 managers having experience of 2 to 10 years has been taken into account. The area of research is Rajasthan. The conclusions are drawn on the basis of perception, efforts, leadership sensitization, motivation vis-à-vis feedback and psychological as well as social approach. At the end of article certain suggestions are presented.

Introduction

The term Emotional Intelligence (EI) debuted in several scientific articles written by John D. Mayor and Peter Salovey during the early 1990s. The researchers defined EI as the compilation of four kinds of skill, namely perceiving and expressing emotions, understanding emotions, using emotions, managing emotions. These insightful publications helped pave the way for the 1995 bestseller *Emotional Intelliegence: Why It can Matter More Than IQ* and 1998 Working With Emotional Intelligence by New York Times behavioral science colonist Daniel Goleman. According to Peter Solvey, chairman of the department of psychology at Yale University, prior to 1995, only other psychologist had heard of emotional intelligence. Goleman's first book made the term household word.

Ever since the publication of Daniel Goleman's first book on the topic in 1995, Emotional Intelligence (EI) has become one of the hottest buzzwords in corporate America. For EI the *Harvard Business Review* (HBR) published an article on the topic two years ago, it had a huge percentage or readers that any other article published in that periodical in the last decade. When the CEO of Johnson and Johnson read that article, he was so impressed that he circulated it to the 400 top executive in the company worldwide.

A big factor in why entrepreneurs fail is low EQ, says Emory Mulling, president of the Mulling Group, an Atlanta outplacement and executive coaching company. "The higher you go in any organization, the more important EQ becomes because you relationship become more important and that's what EQ is all about".

In the year 1990, Peter Salovey and John D. Mayer coined the term "Emotional Intelligence" (EI). Then in the earlier of 1990s Daniel Goleman became aware of Salovey and

Mayor's work. Daniel Goleman was a student of David McClelland, one of the must influential psychologists in the area of competencies at Harvard. Daniel Goleman was trained as psychology educator at Harvard where he worked with David McClelland and other Daniel Goleman was also behavioral science columnist for New York Times. David McClelland and growing group of researchers became concerned with how little conventional cognitive intelligence contributed to a person for him/her to be successful in life.

Then eventually the insightful publications written by John D. Mayor and Peter Salovey helped pave the way for the 1995 best-seller *Emotional Intelligence: Why It can Matter More Than IQ* by Daniel Goleman. It was Daniel Goleman who brought emotional intelligence into the mainstream of business.

Start talking about feelings. Start respecting them. Start assigning value to them. Include feelings in decision-making and problem resolution. Listen to the most sensitive people in the organization. Strike a balance between emotion and logic. Develop the EQ skills throughout the organization. Prohibit invalidation. Make your business a place of mutual respect for feelings. Identify the key feelings important for success and try to implement them.

Emotional intelligence word is hot buzz in the world especially in the advance countries/ economic like USA, UK, Italy, France, Germany. But still the presence of emotional intelligence can be felt all around the global corporate world. If human resource is developed and equipped properly then it would be of value. Through the application of emotional intelligence, human resource will be instrumental to elevate the generation of revenues globally in the years to come.

The modern industrial states are characterized by the presence of the large business entities. Multinational corporates are large corporate, which are involved in manufacturing, producing goods and services across the limitless globe. Corporations can be felt around the world. The spreading of emotional intelligence has amplified its impact in the corporate world too. Corporations has resources spreading all round the world in the form of subsidiaries and stocking in the different countries. Their resources consist of tangible and intangible claims. The well-wishers of emotional intelligence see the presence of the emotional intelligence as precious, as it helps the development of human resource. Human resource and its development are one of the most valuable commodities, which the corporations possess. Thus, the utility of human resource development can be emphasized when Kenneth Balanchard says "the best minitue I spend the one I invest in people."[1]

This amplifies the significance of human resource development in the global corporate world. The current study titled "Emotional Intelligence and Human Resource Development in Private Sector" will focus on emotional intelligence and emotional intelligence practices by corporations. The current study is focused on the concept of emotional intelligence.

Review of Literature

Ever since the conceptualization of emotional intelligence, business leaders, academicians, and researchers have shown phenomenon interest in emotional intelligence. Researcher and management scholars have explored the micro and macro impact of emotional intelligence on the human resource development. Some of the people who have defined emotional intelligence are:

Robert Mcgarvey, entrepreneur defined, "The ability to persist and stay motivated in the face of frustration. The ability to control impulses. The ability to control their emotions. The ability to empathize with others."

John Sosik a management professor at Pennsylsania State University in Malvern said, "EI really is old wine in a new bottle. It's about self-awareness and empathy, and those are skills any leader needs in building a successful organization."

Byron Stock and Associates defined emotional intelligence as, "Emotional Intelligence doesn't mean being soft—it means being intelligent about emotions—a different way of being smart. Emotional intelligence is your ability to acquire and apply knowledge from your emotions and the emotions of others in order to be more successful and lead a more fulfilling life". There are five parts to it. One knows what one in is feeling. Second is managing your feelings, especially distressing feelings. Third is self-motivation, fourth is empathy and fifty is managing relationships.

Daniel Goleman defined, "Emotional intelligence is a combination of competencies. These skills contribute to a person's ability to manage and monitor his or her own emotions, to correctly gauge the emotional state of others and to influence opinion".

Each area has its own set of behavioral attributes as follows:

1. Self-awareness is the ability to recognize a feeling as it happens, to accurately perform self-assessments and have self-confidence. It is the keystone of emotional intelligence. Self-awareness means having a deep understanding of one's emotions...how their feelings affect them, other people, and their job performance.
2. Self-management or self-regulation is the ability to keep disruptive emotions and impulses in check (self-control), maintain standards of honesty and integrity (trustworthiness), take responsibility for one's performance (conscientiousness), handle change (adaptability), and be comfortable with novel ideas and approaches (innovation). Self-regulation, which is like an ongoing inner conversation, is the component of emotional intelligence that frees us from being prisoners of our feelings. People engaged in such a conversation. Find ways to control (emotional impulses) and even to channel (emotions) in useful ways.
3. Motivation is the emotional tendency guiding or facilitating the attainment of goals. It consists of achievements drive (meeting a standard excellence), commitment (alignment of goals with the group or organization), initiative (acting on opportunities), and optimism (persistence reaching goals despite setbacks). People who possess self-motivation are driven to achieve beyond expectations. The keyword here is achieve. They are motivated by a deeply embedded desire to achieve for the sake of achievement (alone).
4. Empathy is the understanding of others by being aware of their needs, perspectives, feelings and concerns, sensing the development needs of others. "Empathy means thoughtfully considering employees' feelings—along with other factor—in the process of making intelligent decisions".
5. Social skills are fundamental to emotional intelligence. They include the ability to induce desirable response in others by using effective diplomacy to persuade (influence),

listen openly and send convincing message (communicate), inspire and guide groups and individuals (leadership), nurture instrumental relationships (building bonds), work with others towards a shared goal (collaboration, cooperation), and crate group synergy in pursuing collective goals.

From the above reviews, it's clear that the researchers have attempted their contribution in the field of emotional intelligence. And also they have suggested for its development and management. The present study is an exploratory study on emotional intelligence and human resource development of a few selected private organization.

Objective of the Study

When it comes to improving organizational effectiveness, management scholars and practitioners are beginning to emphasize on emotional intelligence. Emotional intelligence is playing important role in determining the success or failure or corporate entities. Now emotional intelligence has taken the center chair in the global corporate world, as it is to be believed that it is the real mover and a source of competitive advantage in the industrial world not only for the managers but also for the modern organization leaders. EI is specifically a dear possession for the new updated charismatic and sharp-witted managers and leaders. Its development and management is of efficacy to any kind of global organization and business concern.

Following were the objectives of the study:

1. To see the working of managers with and without emotional intelligence.
2. To understand the concept of emotional intelligence.
3. To examine the emotional intelligence practices in business concerns.
4. To suggest strategies for developing and managing emotional intelligence.

Hypothesis

1. Emotional intelligence helps in balancing work performance and personal life.
2. Emotional intelligence has influence on decision-making process.
3. Emotional intelligence contributes to the human resources development.

Methodology

To fulfill the aforesaid aims to test the hypothesis stated above information from primary as well as secondary source are gathered.

Since it is an exploratory research comprehensive and extensive procedure is adopted for collecting primary data. A sample survey was conducted in this study for eliciting information from managers.

A sample of 50 managers human resource executive who were qualified in their respective field with work experience between 2 to 10 years aging between 26 to 40 years of age. Representing different sectors ex-banks, manufacturing, insurance, hotel was selected. The areas of research was the state of Rajasthan.

Analysis of Sample Units

This study through questionnaires tried to highlight some of the aspects of emotional intelligence and its impact on various issues.

Table 1: Work Life Balance and Emotional Intelligence of Sample Units

Particulars	*No. of Respondents*	*Percentage*
Disagree	—	—
Rarely	10	20%
Agree	26	52%
Unsure	14	28%
Total	50	100%

Table 2: Behavioral Change and Emotional Intelligence of Sample Units

Particulars	*No. of Respondents*	*Percentage*
Disagree	02	4%
Rarely	10	20%
Agree	22	44%
Unsure	16	32%
Total	50	100%

Table 4: Quality Management and Emotional Intelligence of Sample Units

Particulars	*No. of Respondents*	*Percentage*
Disagree	14	28%
Rarely	16	32%
Agree	20	40%
Unsure	—	—
Total	50	100%

Table 5: Balanced Feelings and Emotional Intelligence of Sample Units

Particulars	*No. of Respondents*	*Percentage*
Disagree	2	4%
Rarely	20	40%
Agree	20	40%
Unsure	8	16%
Total	50	100%

Table 6: Decision Making and Emotional Intelligence of Sample Units

Particulars	*No. of Respondents*	*Percentage*
Disagree	2	4%
Rarely	06	12%
Agree	24	48%
Unsure	18	36
Total	50	100%

Table 7: Leadership Skills and Emotional Intelligence of Sample Units

Particulars	*No. of Respondents*	*Percentage*
Disagree	16	32%
Rarely	—	—
Agree	30	60%
Unsure	4	8%
Total	50	100%

Table 8: Human Resource Development and Emotional Intelligence

Particulars	*No. of Respondents*	*Percentage*
Disagree	16	32%
Rarely	—	—
Agree	30	60%
Unsure	4	8%
Total	50	100%

Table 9: Retention and Emotional Intelligence of Sample Units

Particulars	*No. of Respondents*	*Percentage*
Disagree	30	60%
Rarely	—	—
Agree	20	40%
Unsure	—	—
Total	50	100%

Conclusions

1. **Perception:** Our emotions and the perceptions are the lens, through which we see, process and interpret. Our perceptions to events around us trigger our thoughts and emotions it is not the event that drives our behavior, but rather, our perceptions of that event. Once we choose the perception or interpretation of the event, it immediately triggers the thought and emotions. These thoughts and especially feelings can generate profound and instantaneous change in the heart and nervous system, which affects the entire body and brain. So we must be well aware of our own feelings.
2. **Efforts:** We have seen that huge corporations and many people are brought down to their knees because of their unmanaged and unmet inside and also due to the problems which are ignored and negative results which are not taken care off. If we are all able to take our flaws as they are and then try to improve over it and make effort to open all things then we can be happy and can have healthier environments. We can advance the field of emotional intelligence by conducting further continuous research as researchers continuously refine the field and by providing more positive

and constructive criticism, in the passionate debates and discussions. And also by trying to be more aware and alert of individual wisdom of our own emotions for bringing and setting ethical and positive value to the world.

3. **Leadership Sensitization:** The emerging field of study known as emotional intelligence is of great importance especially in the leadership sensitive organization. A cluster of skills and competencies can create wonders. The emotionally intelligent people evolve into someone who has the abilities to seamlessly move from one approach or style to the other with the requirements of the situation and the resources available.
4. **Motivation vis-à-vis Feedback:** The good news is that unlike IQ, which is pretty much fixed at an early age, emotional intelligence can grow with the right motivation and willingness to face one's flaws. Developing emotional intelligence skills require individuals to eliminate old behavior and embrace new ones. People with the lower emotional intelligence must first bone up on the foundation of the concept.

   Awareness is the key to self-development effort. Anybody can increase his/her emotional intelligence by listening, by being open to asking for frequent feedback and taking the feedback without being defensive and critical. And also by seeing the people who have developed or imbibed their emotional intelligence. But ultimately putting whole heart and soul that is a true commitment to new knowledge. And then taking action for the development of emotional intelligence. Trying hard for improving emotional intelligence in the individuals and the organizations is definitely a good idea.
5. **Psychological as well as Social Approach:** Thus, emotional intelligence is based on the long history or research and theory in the fields of psychology, social psychology, I/O psychology. There is impressive and growing research suggesting that these abilities are important for success in many areas of life. Furthermore, as the pace of change increases and work makes ever-great demands on a person's cognitive, emotional, and physical aspects, this particular set of abilities will become more and more important. And this is good for psychologists, for they are the ones who are best suited to help people to use emotional intelligence to improve both productivity and psychological well-being in the work of tomorrow.

Suggestionss

The importance of emotional intelligence to a business organizations is incalculable, as emotional intelligence has played crucial role in the shaping of the new business decision-making process. High standards on the quality of human resource have spread globally making emotional intelligence one of the luxurious possessions for the modern managers, organizational leaders and scenario planners. With the view of findings and conclusions, the following suggestion are being given for the development and implementation of emotional intelligence:

1. **Patience:** Remember the golden rule is that all one need is patience. If a person has patience, he/she can see the transformation. Start learning to patient.
2. **Willingness to Change:** Start often thinking for the desire to change. As soon as one realize about it. Think again. So do it as an when one remembers it. Doing it as often as possible and try to be alert about this.

3. **Introspection:** Look at ones emotions, try to see them and know them. Try not being detracted from one's feelings and emotions. One's emotions should not be hidden or unknown to you.
4. **Good Listening:** Be a good listener. Start practicing active listening. One must start concentrating feelings, emotions even while at the conversation. Start exploring them. Utilizing free hours by distressing oneself.
5. **Vigilance:** One should be vigilant. Look around, but without thinking. Yes that's the art simply seeing without any thought. One should educate oneself with this technique.
6. **Role of Change:** Set up challenging but reachable goals. Break big projects into smaller task spreading over the time. But with wise use of time. Don't mess up free time or lunch breaks or tea/coffee breaks with finishing pending work strictly discourage oneself from this habit.
7. **Best Medicine (Humor)**: Humor is the best. Dropping daily jokes bulletin. Trying some indoor games. Encouraging green leafy food fruits because "health is wealth". Encouraging relaxed unhurried lunch. Playing some kind of soothing music may be good instrumental workshops on stress management. Joining yoga sessions or may be some other kind of meditations.

Scope for Further Research

The present study is based on limited field of research. Therefore, there is definitely scope for further research. The study tried to cover some aspects of emotional intelligence and human resource development of few selected private organization. As very less has been said and written, and there are many untouched aspects in this filed. Thus, there is scope for further research.

REFERENCES

Mayer, J.D. and Salovey, P., "Emotional Intelligence", *Imagination, Cognition and Personality* (1990).

Goleman, Daniel, *Emotional Intelligence: Why It can Matter More Than IQ* (New York: Bantam Books, 1995).

Goleman, Daniel, *Working with Emotional Intelligence.*

Quoted in Chritopher Koch, "The Bright Stuff", *CIO Magazine*, 15 March 1996.

"On Emotional Intelligence", on-line, Internet, 5 September 2002.

Goleman, Daniel, "What makes a Leader?" *Harvard Business Review*, March-April 2000.

Goleman, Daniel, "Leadership that Gets Result," *Harvard Business Review*, March-April 2000.

Goleman, Daniel, Boyatzis Richard, and Annie McKee, *Primal Leadership: Realizing the Power of Emotional Intelligence* (Bostan: Harvard Business School Press, 2000).

Emotional Intelligence Consortium Report.

Mayer, J.D. and Salovey, P., Garuso D.R., and Sitarenics, G. (2003). Measuring and emotional intelligence with the MSCEIT V2.0. Emotion.

Rosenthal, R. (1997). The PONS test: Measuring sensitivity to nonverbal cues. Adavance in psychological assessment. San Franciso, CA: Jossey-Bass.

Schulman, P. (1995). Explanatory style and achievement in school and work.

Journal of Management.
Journal of Organizational Behavior.
Journal of Personality and Social Psychology.
Journal of Nervous and Mental Disease.
Journal of Applied Psychology.
Journal of Counseling Psychology.
Training and Development Journal.
Journal of Social Psychology.
Journal of Applied Behavioral Science.
Journal of Occupational Psychology.
Human Resource Development Quarterly.
Personal Psychology Journal.
Management Journal.
Academy of Management Review.
Hints of Self Culture by Lala Hardayal.
Personnel Management by Monnapa Arun.

CHAPTER 42

AN EMPIRICAL STUDY ON MEASUREMENT OF EMOTIONAL INTELLIGENCE IN BANKS

–*Karunesh Saxena* and *Tanuja Singh*

ABSTRACT

Business can't be carried out from boardrooms, discussing excel sheets that project the annual growth of a company. Today, the role of an individual's emotional state on his professional success is being widely recognized. Emotional intelligence is increasingly relevant to organizational development and developing people, because the EQ principles provide a new way to understand and assess people's behaviors, management styles, attitudes, interpersonal skills, and potential.

Emotional intelligence is an important consideration in human resources planning, job profiling, recruitment interviewing and selection, management development, customer relations and customer service, and more. Emotional intelligence links strongly with concepts of love and spirituality: bringing compassion and humanity to work, and also to 'Multiple Intelligence' theory which illustrates and measures the range of capabilities people possess, and the fact that everybody has a value. Work performance often depends on the support, advice, and other resources provided by others.

Emotional intelligence may also contribute to work performance by enabling people to regulate their emotions so as to cope effectively with stress, perform well under pressure, and adjust to organizational change.

Success requires more than IQ (Intelligence Quotient), which has tended to be the traditional measure of intelligence, ignoring essential behavioral and character elements. In this paper, we have studied the importance of emotional intelligence and attempt to provide the best solution for improving the emotions at workplace. The study has been conducted in banks employee. Different approaches and theoretical models have been developed for emotional intelligence.

This paper also includes the various models of emotional intelligence and their application in the banks, importance of emotional intelligence at workplace, who needs emotional intelligence, assessing and measuring emotional intelligence, ways to improve and develop emotional intelligence and the criticism of emotional intelligence. There is a considerable body of research suggesting that a person's ability to perceive, identify and manage emotion provides the basis for the kinds of social and emotional competencies that are important for success in almost any job.

Introduction

According to Daniel Goleman, emotional intelligence is "the capacity for recognizing our own feelings and those of others, for motivating ourselves and for managing emotions well in ourselves and in our relationships." Emotional intelligence is the ability to monitor one's own and others' feelings and emotions, to discriminate among them and to use this information to guide one's thinking and actions. Emotional skills are related to the ability to accurately express, read, and understand emotions; all of which are components of emotional intelligence. It describes an ability or capacity to perceive, assess, and manage the emotions of one's self and of others.

The primary aim of this research is to view current conceptualizations of emotional intelligence, while providing an opportunity to see how emotional intelligence has been interpreted and applied throughout the world. At the individual level, it has been said to relate to academic achievement, work performance, our ability to communicate effectively, solve everyday problems, build meaningful interpersonal relationships, and even our ability to make moral decisions. Emotional intelligence has the potential to increase our understanding of how individuals behave and adapt to their social environment, it is an important topic for research.

In this paper, we will be conducting study on emotional intelligence practices and need of emotional intelligence, importance of emotional intelligence at workplace. How we can measure the emotional intelligence with the help of various models, developing of skill in person with emotional intelligence framework?

Assessing and Measuring Emotional Intelligence

"In regard to measuring emotional intelligence—I am a great believer that criterion-report (that is, ability testing) is the only adequate method to employ. Intelligence is ability, and is directly measured only by having people answer questions and evaluating the correctness of those answers."—John D. Mayer

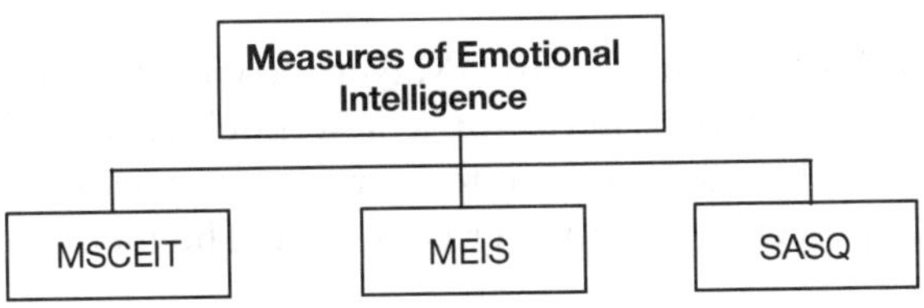

The Mayer-Salovey-Caruso Emotional Intelligence Test (MSCEIT): This test is an ability-based test designed to measure the four branches of the EI model of Mayer and Salovey. MSCEIT consists of 141 items and takes 30-45 minutes to complete. MSCEIT provides 15 main scores: Total EI score, two area scores, four branch scores, and eight task scores. In addition to these 15 scores, there are three supplemental scores.

The Four Branches of Emotional Intelligence

1. Perceiving Emotions.
2. Facilitating Thought
3. Understanding Emotions
4. Managing Emotions

Multifactor Emotional Intelligence Scale (MEIS)

An ability-based test in which test-takers perform tasks designed to assess their ability to perceive, identify, understand, and utilize emotions.

Seligman Attribution Style Questionnaire (SASQ)

The SASQ (also known as the ASQ) is one of the most validated profiling tools in the world. Designed by Professor Martin Seligman, the SASQ test uncovers a person's explanatory style (attitude). By using an individual's SASQ responses employers can assess how suitable they are for a role and highlight how they might benefit from personal development and coaching. The ability to overcome adversity is critical to success in most sales positions. Your company's success depends on hiring the right people for the job.

Three Models of Emotional Intelligence

1. Ability-based EI models
2. Mixed models of EI
3. Trait EI model

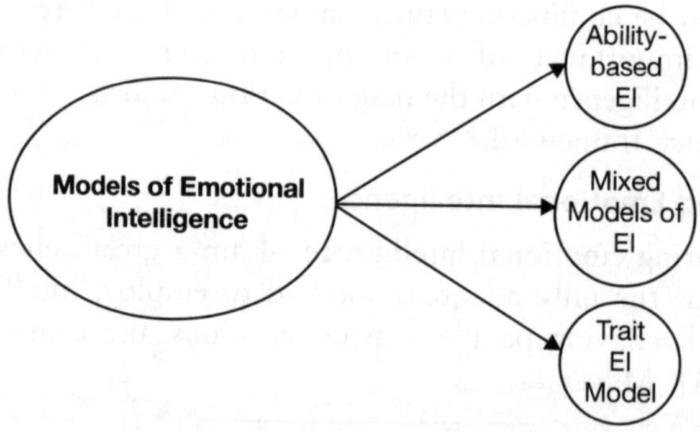

1. The Ability-based Model: Salovey and Mayer's conception of EI strives to define EI within the confines of the standard criteria for a new intelligence. The model proposes that individuals vary in their ability to process information of an emotional nature and in their ability to relate emotional processing to a wider cognition. The model proposes that EI includes four types of abilities:

1. Perceiving emotions 2. Using emotions 3. Understanding emotions 4. Managing emotions.

2. Mixed Model: The model introduced by Daniel Goleman focuses on EI as a wide array of competencies and skills that drive leadership performance. Goleman's model outlines four main EI constructs:

1. Self-awareness 2. Self-management 3. Social awareness 4. Relationship management.

3. The Trait Model: Trait EI should be investigated within a personality framework. An alternative label for the same construct is trait emotional self-efficacy. The conceptualization of EI as a personality trait leads to a construct that lies outside the taxonomy of human cognitive ability.

Review of Literature

The emotional intelligence factor has been shown to be four times as accurate in predicting efficiency at the workplace as the traditional IQ factor. It is essential in organizations in order to maintain a cordial relation with co-workers, clients, public and other people which are essential for the growth of the organization. Studies done in the organizational contexts show the importance of emotional intelligence in handling the problems in bank. The benefits of applying EI in the workplace may include higher tolerance for stress, better people management skills and more effective performance as part of a team (Klohnen, 1996).

Researches have also showed the linkages between job satisfaction and EI. Higher levels of EI predicted higher levels of job satisfaction and stronger connections with co-workers and supervisors (Abraham, 1999).

Fisher (2000) linked emotions and moods with job satisfaction. Recently, Cote and Morgan (2002) found that amplification of positive emotions increased job satisfaction while suppression of unpleasant emotions decreased job satisfaction.

The EI construct has important implication for maintaining the commitment, productivity, and job satisfaction (Cooper and Sawaf, 1997). In the organization domain, several studies examine the relevance and prevalence of emotional intelligence in the context of the corporate sector.

Sy and Cote (2004) have given their view that organizations continue to employ the matrix organizational form as it enables companies to use human resources flexibly, produce innovative solutions to complex problems in unstable environments and increase information flow through the use of lateral communication channels. Despite its strengths, the matrix has inherent problems. They identified that there are four interpersonal challenges that impede matrix performance: misaligned goals increase competition among employees, roles and responsibilities are unclear, decision making is untimely and of possibly low quality and silo-focused employees do not cooperate. It was proposed that emotionally intelligent employees can function better in matrix. Solutions were offered for both managers and employees to improve performance in matrix organizations by applying the four components of emotional intelligence, specifically managing, understanding, using and perceiving emotion to each interpersonal change.

Zeidner, Matthews and Roberts (2004), for conceptualizations and empirical evidence in support of emotional intelligence and its claimed role in the occupational environment. Consideration is given to the purported status of EI in occupational and career assessment (with particular emphasis on personal selection and placement), job performance, and satisfaction. Overall this review demonstrates that recent research has made important strides towards understanding the usefulness of EI in the workplace. The review concludes by providing a number of practical guidelines by providing a number of practical guidelines for the development and implementation of EI measures within occupational settings.

The study made by Duran, Extremera and Rey (2005) investigating the relationship among dimensions of self-reported emotional intelligence, burnout and engagement among staff in services for people with intellectual disabilities had investigated that emotional clarity was significantly associated with personal accomplishment and dedication. Further, repair to moods (subscale of work engagement scale) was significantly correlated with all engagement dimensions and with personal accomplishment. The study shows significant relationships with emotional functioning and work related with emotional functioning and work-related variables in a professional sample.

Brackett et al. (2010) examined the relationship between emotion regulation ability (ERA) as assessed by MSCEIT and both job satisfaction and burnout among secondary school teachers (n = 123), also examining the mediating effects of affect and principal support on these outcomes. ERA was associated positively with positive affect, principal support, job satisfaction and one component of burnout, personal accomplishment. Two path model demonstrated that both positive affect and principal support mediated independently the association between ERA and both personal accomplishment and job satisfaction.

Matthews, Zeidner and Roberts described them as "EI-as-ability and EI-as-personality" (2002, p. 517). Mayer, Salovey and Caruso argued for EI as a type of mental ability and indicated that their ability model focuses on the "interplay of emotion and intelligence as traditionally defined", whereas the EI as personality conceptualization is considered a mixed model, "which describe[s] a compound conception of intelligence that includes mental abilities, and other dispositions and traits" (2000, p. 399).

Mayer, Salovey and Caruso (2000) described the ability model of EI as mostly a unitary concept, subdivisible into four levels of branches. It begins with the first branch, perception and expression of emotion, which involves identifying and expressing emotions in one's self and in other people. The second branch, assimilating emotion in thought, involves using emotions to improve thought. Branch three, understanding and analyzing emotion, involves using thought to process emotions. The final branch, reflective regulation of emotion, concerns emotional self-management and management of emotions in other people. According to this model, EI begins with the first branch since "only if one has good emotional perception in the first place can one make use of mood changes and understand emotions. And only with such understanding will one have the breadth of knowledge necessary to manage and cope with feelings fully" (Mayer, 2000, p. 110).

Punia (2005) conducted a study on 250 executives in the National Capital Region, Delhi, and found that leaders with higher emotional intelligence see changes as opportunities for betterment, and they cherish not stability but ongoing development of individual workers and of the organization itself.

Research Methodology

The main objective of this paper is to identify the measurement of emotional intelligence at workplace in banking sector. To achieve the objective of the study, survey was conducted. For survey, personal interviews were undertaken. Further, following data sources have been used:

Primary Data

Primary data is the first-hand information which we get from the bank's employees through. We are extremely thankful to all the employees of banks for giving their valuable time to us and helping us clear our doubts and increase our knowledge base. For primary data we had collected by using questionnaire.

Secondary Data

In order to carry out our paper successfully, we have relied on the secondary data already available. Secondary data includes recent reports, websites, published articles and Internet. Random Sampling—40 respondents were selected from the SBI Bank in Udaipur City.

Major Findings of the Study

1. Employees are able to control their emotion too large extent but in some situation they loose control on their emotions.
2. Employees get emotionally hurt when they are not treated properly, which results in higher rate of customer dissatisfaction.
3. Employees who face emotional problem tend to leave their job frequently and did not feel comfortable for longer period.
4. Employees who are emotionally weak tend to perform low and reduced customers.
5. Employees are more concerned about their work and try to control their emotions.
6. The findings of this study emphasized that the employees possessed above average level of EI and the processes of OL characterized by innovation, implementation, and sustenance of new ideas, processes structures and the likes are more than satisfactory. Further study results depicted EI as being positively and significantly related with OL. The findings have implications for management of people towards creating and maintaining OL.
7. Respondents having experience had almost same levels of emotional intelligence. Although individual having 8-11 years experience had lesser emotional intelligence as compared to the rest, yet individual falling in this category of experience was very low to draw significant conclusion.
8. Number of respondents at the extremes of high and average level of emotional intelligence was very low, and even there was not a single respondents having low level of EI.
9. Individual falling the age bracket of 35-45 years and over the age of 45 years posses more success.

Recommendations

Based on the findings, we would like to make certain recommendation on how to improve your emotional intelligence in a workplace. There are many ways to reduce conflict and control emotions for more effective workplace interactions:

1. Effective management skills encompass more than getting the job done and meeting company quotas. Being sensitive to the non-work related concerns of employees can prove to be equally as important.
2. Maintaining a non-hostile work environment that balances the behaviors and needs of employees can effectively improve productivity.
3. Offer and encourage stress management courses.
4. Be proactive, and take steps to avoid unnecessary emotional outbursts.

5. Watch your anger and avoid uncontrolled confrontations which will bring out inappropriate emotions and behaviors.
6. Take necessary disciplinary action when employees express their emotions in an unacceptable way.
7. Be aware of customer demand and other employee anxieties. This is especially important during times of big change.
8. Understand that people have lives outside of the workplace that can affect their work positively and negatively.
9. Be sure that staff understand what is acceptable behavior and what is ground for insubordination.
10. Encourage open inter-office communication, so employees will be more apt to voice their opinions. Weekly meeting and/or individual conferences will keep managers aware of any and all situations (both positive and negative) while also allowing the employees to have a proactive role in the workplace.

Conclusion

The present study has produced some important results that have implications for both research and practice. The study on measurement of bank employees' emotional intelligence and their ability to perform effectively on the job is identified as they are able to manage their emotional intelligence, which has a direct impact on their job. These skills are to be developed for achieving higher employee productivity and to enhance the image of the organization.

A particularly interesting finding or result of the present study was that emotional intelligence of employees had an impact on their level of performance on the job. This has implications for management, suggesting that organizations could be profitable by identifying the level of emotional intelligence of employees and apply interventions that are focused on the measurement of emotional intelligence among the employees in the organization. EI is associated with better performance in the following areas.

1. Participative Management
2. Pulling People at Ease
3. Straight Forwardness and Composure
4. Decisiveness
5. Doing Whatever It Takes
6. Adaptability
7. Confronting Problem Employees

Most of the organizations are nowadays taking those employees who are emotionally intelligent, so that they can face the workplace problems easily and they can become more productive for the organization. Emotionally intelligent organization can be made through organizational strategies, self-awareness and self-management tools, through leadership skills, development programmes. So what has been concluded from the whole project report is that emotional intelligence is linked at every point of workplace performance and it is of utmost importance nowadays. In the earlier time, EI was not given much emphasis and instead of that IQ is given more importance. People with IQ level are preferred within the organizations but now the scenario has been changed and organizations prefer those employees who are emotionally stable. Hence, to be successful in life, EQ plays a vital role.

REFERENCES

Ciarrochi, J., Chan, A.Y.C., Caputi, P. A critical evaluation of the emotional intelligence construct. *Personality and Individual Differences*, 2000;28: 539-61.

Epstein, S. *Constructive Thinking: The Key to Emotional Intelligence.*

Goleman, D. *Emotional Intelligence: Why It can Matter More Than IQ* (New York: Bantam Book, 1995).

Goleman, D. *Emotional Intelligence.*

McMullan, B. *Emotional Intelligence.* BMJ 2003; 326(7381):S19.

Matthews, G., Zeidner, M., Richard D. *Emotional Intelligence: Science and Myth.*

Peter S., Marc, *Emotional Intelligence: Key Readings on the Mayer and Salovey Model.*

www.eqi.org/

www.danielgoleman.info/

www.eiconsortium.org/

www.selfgrowth.com/emotional_intelligence.html

www.unh.edu/emotional_intelligence/

LIST OF CONTRIBUTORS

D.S. Chundawat, Professor, JCCMS, MLSU, Udaipur, Email: dschundawat@rediffmail.com

Manmeet Sardalia, Faculty, Department of Business Adm., UCCMS, MLSU, Udaipur, Email: msardalia@yahoo.com

Shurveer S. Bhanawat, Asso. Professor, UCCMS, Udaipur (Raj), Email: shurveer@gmail.com

Shilpi Kothari, 154, The Orbit-103, Road No. 10, Ashok Nagar, Udaipur, Rajasthan, Email: shilpikothari21@gmail.com

Khushboo Ameta, Lecturer, Pacific Institute of Business Studies, Pacific University, Udaipur Rajasthan, India Front of Debari Petrol Pmp, Zinc Complex, Debari, Udaipur (Raj), Email ameta_khushi91@yahoo.in

Manashvi I. Singh, Marwadi Education Fundation, Morbi Highwar, Post: Gauridad, Rajkot-7 (Gujarat), Email: manashvi_singh@yahoo.com

Bhagwan Singh, Associate Professor, School of Business and Management Studies, [SBMS], Central University of Himachal Pradesh [CUHP], TAB Shahpur, Dharamshala, H.P., Email: bagwansingh.bs@gmail.com

Sachin Kumar, Research Scholar, C/o Department of Marketing and Supply Chain Management, School of Business & Management Studies, Central University of Himachal Pradesh, TAB Shahpur-176206, Email: sachincuhp@gmail.com

O.P. Roonwal, Lecturer, Department of Business Administration, Government College, Khedwada

Shipra Chainani, Research Scholar, Department of Business Administratoin, Government College, Khedwada, Email: shipz_05@rediffmail.com

G.S. Rathore, C/o Faculty of Commerce, Udai Pratap Autonomous College, Varanasi, Email: dr.gsrathoreupc@gmail.com, editorijemt@gmail.com

Sunita Yadav, C/o Jeevandeep Institute of Management & Technology, Baralalpur, Varanasi, Email: bsysunita@gmail.com

Kasturi Sahay, Assistant Professor, Birla Institute of Technology Trust Getlatu, Ranchi-835217 Mobile 9931558990, Email: kasturi.sahay@gmail.com

Utpal Baul, Professor, Birla Institute of Technology, Mesra, Ranchi-835217

Akondi Srikanth, Dr. B.R. Ambedkar Open Univeristy, Professor G. Ram Reddy Marg, Road #46, Jubilee Hills, Hyderabad-500033

Badruddin, PES'S Shri Ravi Sitaram Naik College of Arts and Science, Goa University, Ponda, GOA-403401

Asha Ganjsinghani, Lecturer (Bus. Adm.), Sh. Jain P.G. College, Bikaner

Neetu Baid, Lecturer (ABST), Sh. Jain P.G. College, Bikaner

Nitesh Asani, Lecturer (ABST), Sh. Jain P.G. College, Bikaner

S.S. Choudhary, Prof. & Head, Deptt. Of Business Adm., HR. Govt. College Salumber, MLS University, Udaipur

Ali Asgar Joon, Research Scholar, JRN, Rajasthan Vidhyapeeth (Deemed) University, Udaipur (Raj.).

Rajesh Sharma, Associate Director Academics, Educosm School of Business and Economics, Jaipur, Rajasthan, Email: rajsha17@gmail.com

Brijesh Awasthi, Head of Department, Faculty of Management Studies, Maharishi Arvind Institute of Science and Management, Jaipur

P.K. Khicha, Navkar, 843-A, Pooja Nagar, Sec-4, Udaipur

Netra Pal Singh, Research Scholar, Navkar, 843-A, Pooja Nagar, Sec-4, Udaipur

Dhiraj Jain, 227, Sector-11, Hiran Magri, Udaipur, Email dhiraj_sangawat@yahoo.co.in

Shweta Garg, 6-Kha—1, Ram singhji ki Badi, Sector-11, Udaipur, (Rajasthan), Email: shwetagarg217@gmail.com

Yukti Sharma, 1372, Shanti Nagar, Sector 5, Hiran Magri, Udaipur (Rajasthan)-313001, Email: yuktisharma06@gmail.com

Anil Kumar Menaria, Lecturer, Department of Mathematics, B.N.P.G. Girls' College, Udaipur, Email: menaria.anilkumar@gmail.com

Brijesh Awasthi, Head of Department, Faculty of Management Studies, Maharishi Arvind Institue of Science and Management, Jaipur

Yamini Bhojak, Management Trainee, Head of Department, Faculty of Management Studies, Maharishi Arvind Institute of Science and Management, Jaipur

Monika Soni, 2 Chhoti Brahampuri, RMV Road, Udaipur

Vineet Kumar Jain, Assistant Professor, Advent Institute of Management Studies, Udaipur, Email: vikuj5678@gmail.com

Sakshi Chouhan, Research Scholar, Department of Business Administration, UCCMS, MLSU, Udaipur, Email: chouhansakshi@gmail.com

P. Annapurna, Research Scholar, GIM, Gitam University.

Harvinder Soni, Prof. & Director, Advent Institute of Management Science and Technology

Rakesh Dashora, Head, Deptt. Banking and Business Economics, Govt. Meera Girls College, Mohanlal Sukhadia University, Udaipur, Rajasthan

Nazma Banu, Research Scholar, Department of Banking and Business Economics, University College of Commerce and Management Studies, Mohanlal Sukhadia University, Udaipur, Rajasthan.

R.S. Meena, Asst. Professor and Editor, International Journal of Development Studies, Faculty of Commerce Banarsh Hindu University, Varanasi-221 005 Email: rshehra@gmail.com

Dimpy Jain, Research Scholar, Dept. of Business Administration, UCCMS, MLSU, Udr, E-mail: dimpyjain21@rediffmail.com

Ankita Jain, FMS, JRNRVU, Udaipur Raj. Official Address: 68, Modern Complex, Udaipur Raj. Email: ankita_mhrm12@rediffmail.com

Mahendra Singh, Assistant Professor, Centre for Business Administration, Central University of Jharkhand, Ranchi, Jharkhand-835 205

Kritika Joshi, Assistant Professor, Department of Management Studies, Lachoo Memorial College of Science & Technology, Jodhpur, Email: kritika.joshi87@yahoo.co.in

Ashish Mathur, Associate Professor, Dept. of Management Studies, Lachoo Memorial College of Science and Technology, Jodhpur

Sanjib Bhattacharjee, Associate Professor, Department of Commerce, G.C. College, Silchar Assam

Sweta Modi, Guest Faculty Department of Management Studies, J.N.V. University, Jodhpur

Shivani Kapoor, Assistant Professor, New Delhi Institute of Management, 50 (B&C) & 60 Tughlakabad Institutional Area, New Delhi-110 062, Email: shivanikapoor08@gmail.com

Madhu Jasola, Assistant Professor, New Delhi Institute of Management, 50 (B&C) & 60 Tughlakabad Institutional Area, New Delhi-110 062, Email: majasola@yahoo.com

Rajesh Kumar Pandey, Assistant Professor, SSR Institute of Management & Research, Sayli Road, Silvassa-396 230 Union Territory of D&NH

Basant Mehta, 4, Mahaveer Colony, Bedla Road, Udaipur

Priyanka Daya Choudhary, Research Scholar, Faculty of Management, Janardan Rai Nagar, Rajasthan Vidyapeeth University, Udaipur

Vijay Shrimali, Dean, Professor, UCCMS, Dept. of Business Admn, Udaipur

Nidhi Maheshwari, Asso. Professor, Asia Pacific Pacific Institute of Management, New Delhi

Jayant Sharma, B-501, Raghu Roop Apartment, 215-C, Sardarpura, Udaipur (Raj)

Kanti Mohan Saini, Department of Business Administration, University College of Commerce and Management Studies, Mohanlal Sukhadia University, Udaipur, Email: kanti.saini@gmail.com

Aarti Khanchandani, Asst Prof., Dept. of Management Studies, Lachoo Memorial College of Science and Technology, Jodhpur

Bharti Pandya, Executive HR Consultant, Free Lancer, Dubai, UAE

D. Mehta, Reader, FMS Pt. JNIBM, Vikram University, Ujjain (MP)

Shruti Jain, Research Scholar, FMS Pt. JNIBM, Vikram University, Ujjain (MP)

Naveen K. Mehta, Reader, MIT, Ujjain, (MP)

S.S. Aggarwal, Department of A.B.S.T., Govt. College, Pokaran (Jaisalmer), Email: ssadpg@yahoo.in

G.M. Saxena, Department of A.B.S.T., Govt. College, Pokaran (Jaisalmer)

Sunil Jangid, S/o Babau Lal Jangid, Out side Bidasar Bari, Near Jain Girls College, G.S. Road, Bikaner (Raj.)-334 001

Jyoti Garg, Research Scholar, Out side Bidasar Bari, Near Jain Girls College, G.S. Road, Bikaner (Raj.)-334 001

Maina Jain, Head, Department of Commerce, B.N.P.G. Girls College, Udaipur, Email: drmainajain2011@gmail.com

Sakshi Chouhan, Department of Business Administration, UCCMS, MLSU, Udaipur, Email: chouhansakshi@gmail.com

Shikha Bhargava, Pacific Institute of Management, Pacific hills, Debari Road, Udaipur, Email: shikha1824@gmail.com

Mahima Birla, Associate Professor, Pacific Institute of Management, Pacific hills, Debari Road, Udaipur, Email: mahimabirla@gmail.com

Rajeshwari Narendran, Head, Dept. of Business Administration, UCCMS, Udaipur, Email: rajeshwari18@yahoo.com

Sanjay Jain, Research Scholar, Dept. of Business Administration, UCCMS, Udaipur, Email: sanjayjain811@gmail.com

Santosh Bhandari, Senior Lecturer, Department of Business, Administration S.R.K., Govt. College Rajsamand, Rajastan

Karunesh Saxena, Professor, FMS, MLSU, Udaipur & Director CDC, MLSU (Raj)

Tanuja Singh, Research Scholar, FMS, MLSU, Udaipur (Raj.)